REALIZING AWAKENED CONSCIOUSNESS

RICHARD P. BOYLE

REALIZING AWAKENED CONSCIOUSNESS

INTERVIEWS WITH
BUDDHIST TEACHERS
AND A NEW PERSPECTIVE
ON THE MIND

 COLUMBIA UNIVERSITY PRESS   NEW YORK

Columbia University Press
Publishers Since 1893
New York   Chichester, West Sussex
cup.columbia.edu

Library of Congress Cataloging-in-Publication Data
Boyle, Richard P., interviewer, author.
Realizing awakened consciousness : interviews with Buddhist teachers and a new
    perspective on the mind / Richard P. Boyle.
    pages   cm
Includes bibliographical references and index.
ISBN 978-0-231-17074-1 (cloth : alk. paper) — ISBN 978-0-231-17075-8 (pbk. : alk. paper) —
    ISBN 978-0-231-53923-4 (electronic)
1. Enlightenment (Buddhism) 2. Buddhists—Interviews. I. Title.
BQ4398.B68   2015
294.3'442—dc23
                                2014029753

Columbia University Press books are printed on permanent and durable acid-free paper.
This book is printed on paper with recycled content.
Printed in the United States of America

c 10 9 8 7 6 5 4 3 2 1
p 10 9 8 7 6 5 4 3 2 1

COVER DESIGN: Archie Ferguson

Contents

Preface

When I was a young sociology professor some forty years ago, a colleague mentioned one morning that a Japanese Zen master was teaching in downtown Los Angeles. One thing led to another, and a few months later I found myself in a weeklong Zen retreat at a former Boy Scout camp high on Mount Baldy. Four or five days into the silent retreat, as I walked out of the meditation hall into daylight, I suddenly felt the faintest kind of pop, like a soap buddle bursting, and all of my perceptual senses opened to a clarity and vividness I had never experienced before. It was a bit like when your ears pop and you can hear everything more clearly, but this experience was more vivid. It only lasted a short while, and nothing but the remarkable clarity of perception occurred. But it seemed like something very important had happened to me, that I had come a step closer to experiencing reality face to face. Not only was the experience delicious, it also seemed to prove what I had always suspected—there was something beyond the world where I had thus far spent my life.

That's the way my path started. Buddhism holds that, if properly followed, the path leads to awakening, to a qualitatively different and truer way of experiencing reality, so now I had no choice but to follow that path, as best I could, wherever it went. It turned out to be a tricky path and didn't always go as advertised. Following it required not only dedication and effort but also discernment and a fair amount of luck. I tried living in the monastery on Mount Baldy (that didn't work well), living in the mountains of northern New Mexico (that worked pretty well), and then (as much from financial necessity as choice) settling in Albuquerque to work as a research sociologist and continue my Buddhist practice on my own.

Life was good, but years went by without much apparent progress. By the time I retired I had pretty much accepted that awakening wasn't going to happen to me. The question then was, Is there anyone else out there who has experienced awakening and would be willing to talk about it in a relatively straightforward, conversational way?, not using Zen-speak or the other forms of Buddhist jargon that have always been opaque to me. Then I would at least know that some people not too different from me had first-hand acquaintance with this thing called awakening.

As a social scientist, I had spent my life researching questions not very different from this one, so with the free time that retirement afforded I worked out a strategy for finding awakened Westerners (if any existed), rather like Diogenes with his lamp, searching for an honest person. I put together a list of Buddhist teachers who seemed especially likely to have experienced awakening and asked if I could interview them for a book. I said I wanted them to tell me about the path they had followed, and also about where it had led them. To my pleased surprise, eleven of the nineteen teachers I contacted agreed to be interviewed, and the transcribed texts of those interviews make up the heart of this book, chapters 1 through 11. All of the teachers described at least some level of experience with awakening, which certainly exceeded my expectations.

Now I had an answer to my question about whether awakening ever really happens in the modern world. But these teachers not only told me about their experiences but also somehow managed to catalyze within me an awakening experience of my own. I realize very keenly how suspicious that must sound, how counter to the conventional perspective of the objective scientist, but what happens happens, and in this case it can't be deleted or ignored. My experience of the world just became dramatically different.

A wonderful advantage was gained from this—what the teachers found difficult to tell me in words, they were able to communicate by bringing me in to share their experience. If only that form of communication was available for all people to share! But the advantage of knowing more was countered by the daunting challenge of trying to find words of my own to think about and express what awakening consists of.

Everyone who experiences awakening must find their own way to talk about it. My way is that of a person trained as a social scientist, lugging around a huge bag of what Lévi-Strauss would call "intellectual bricolage" that I've accumulated along the way. The first, and formative, intellectual influence was the sociological version of social psychology called symbolic interactionism, which began with the philosopher George Herbert

Mead and developed, most importantly for this book, into Peter Berger and Thomas Luckmann's magnificent Social Construction of Reality. As I worked to develop a framework for talking about awakening, the ideas I had collected from psychology, anthropology, and linguistics all began to fit into that symbolic interactionist framework. Finding the right way to incorporate them took some time, but once the basic pieces were in place the rest seemed to fall together neatly and effortlessly. For someone who has long labored at the arduous work of theory construction, the last few months were amazing, like fitting the last pieces into a Rubik's cube. It was like something that happened, not something I did, other than being in the right place at the right time, with the right teachers and the right accumulation of bricolage passed on to me by giants.

Physicists sometimes say about their theories that if it is beautiful, it is probably true. More than anything, this book aims to take what has been known for a very long time and develop a new way of talking about it. That language will doubtless jar the ears of some people. My hope is that it provides a way to express that ancient knowledge that will be helpful for people living in the modern world.

Acknowledgments

Conceiving a project like this and getting it launched is delicate and tricky; support is especially crucial and deeply appreciated. My special thanks go to Paula England, who has through the years kept me in touch with her path of training and learning with Shinzen Young. When I described to her, by e-mail, the plan I was hatching to ask Buddhist teachers to tell me their path stories, she went to work, telling Shinzen about it and also recommending the project to two other teachers with whom she had studied, Gil Fronsdal and Shaila Catherine. Very few sociologists are also long-term, sincere Buddhist practitioners; her help and support was special.

My friend, the writer and Zen monk Zenshin Michael Haederle, was also critical at the beginning and in moving this project into the interview phase. We talked over preliminary thoughts and began shaping the central ideas that informed the interview design. He played an active role in selecting teachers to invite, and participated, sitting in my dining room, in the interview with Ken McLeod. When chapters 12 and 13 were in rough draft, he went over them with editing and interpretive suggestions.

An important little nudge came when I met Shinzen Young at the 100th birthday celebration for Joshu Sasaki and told him about what was going on in my head at the time. He liked the idea, and when he later officially launched the project by giving the first interview, I had a precedent in hand to give the project some legitimacy.

Two boosts came much earlier. I wrote an article back in 1985 relating my experiences with Zen to the teachings of George Herbert Mead, and sent the paper to my old friend Norm Denzin, a leading figure in symbolic interactionism. I only asked for comments, but he liked it enough to publish it in an annual series he edited. The second boost was similar. I had written a manuscript in 1982 in which I pulled quotes from the written records of selected Zen, Sufi, and Christian mystical teachers. After finishing it I had a strong (and correct) feeling that I didn't know what I was talking about. But my old friend Leonard John Pinto (another Buddhist sociologist, but with a strain of Catholicism thrown in) read it and urged me to send it to an academic press. I'm glad I didn't take his advice, but I have remembered his encouragement these many years.

The third, and last, Buddhist sociologist I know of, David Preston, gave important comments and suggestions through several phases of the writing. Thank you, David.

From here on, there are two main, more or less discrete roots to review. The first is in science, especially sociology and most especially symbolic interactionism. My introduction came in an undergraduate course with the late Aubrey Wendling, who also sent me on to graduate work at the University of Washington with Robert E. L. Faris, S. Frank Miyamoto, and my dissertation advisor, Otto Larsen. While teaching at UCLA I was privileged to enjoy stimulating interaction with Ralph Turner, Mef Seeman, and Harold Garfinkel. And especially, although I have never met them in person, my deepest thanks to Peter Berger and Thomas Luckmann for writing what was one of the maybe six most important books of the twentieth century, *The Social Construction of Reality*.

Turning to sociologists not primarily known as symbolic interactionists, I owe so much to my year of postdoctoral study with Harrison White, for what I learned about both mathematical sociology and being a responsible but widely searching scientist. From Warren TenHouten, my friend and colleague at UCLA, I learned about neurosociolinguistics and the implications of right-left hemisphere functions for social behavior. And finally, Charlie Kaplan, a pure spirit of living inquiry, has supplied wonderful touches of positive energy through the years.

Outside of sociology, my cognitive psychologist friend, Peder Johnson, not only helped with my questions and provided a bit of education in that field but also let me use his lab to carry out some priming experiments during an earlier stage when I was looking for a way to do research on semiawakened consciousness. Also at the University of New Mexico during the 1980s, the linguist Vera John-Steiner helped me with her subject and gave me support during the early phases of my work on awakening, and Richard Coughlin of the Sociology Department collaborated on research on worldviews.

The only neuroscientist I know in person is Jim Austin, and his work is featured throughout the book. But the published research on meditation has provided information that helped structure my more cognitive work. Special thanks also go to Julie Brefczynski-Lewis for taking the time to reply to my inquiry about aspects of her work.

I want to thank my colleagues and students at the Institute for Social Research, University of New Mexico, for providing a supportive and stimulating environment during the years when my research centered on evaluating early childhood programs. The same is true for the dedicated people involved in the programs I was evaluating, especially Andy Hsi and Bebeanne Bouchard, UNM Pediatrics. From them and others throughout the nation who are working to help poor children and their families I learned about approaches in practical psychology that apply to all people. Among the many in this group, I want to single out Victor Bernstein for the insights he opened up for me.

The second major root of this project was nurtured by people who in one way or another are Buddhists, or at least fellow travelers. My thanks to Gary Snyder for his reply to something I sent him many years ago, in which he commented on the (unworkable) research ideas I was hatching at the time and gave some advice about Zen teachers.

And then there was my formal training. I feel indebted to the late Joshu Sasaki for the ten years I spent with him. He opened doors, showed me there was a world full of wonder there to learn about, and started me on the practice and path that has continued since. Sandy Stewart was the head monk when I started, and I also learned from him. Since then, so many wonderful friends have come into my life through Rinzai-ji Zen centers that I can only mention a few. The Bodhi Manda Zen Center in Jemez Springs, New Mexico, was my sangha for many years, and my friendships from those years are still treasured (one, whom I met in the hot springs, I later married). My thanks to Seiju Bob Mammoser and Hosen Christianne Ranger for running Bodhi at the time and for marrying us. Sue York and Chris Worth have been through so much because of the Sasaki scandal, and I thank them for their contribution to my understanding of its impacts. Just during the past year I have benefited from talks with David Rubin and Brian Lesage, both Buddhist teachers and former Sasaki monks.

Finally, enormous thanks go to the teachers whose interviews are reported here, for their absolutely critical contributions to the book and the help and stimulation they gave outside of the interviews. Three anonymous reviewers went over earlier drafts carefully and provided important and helpful comments. The book draws heavily (in fact depends) on the work of several scientists whom I thank collectively. They receive enough attention in the book to make their contributions evident. And of course, thanks to Jim Austin, who has firm roots in both science and Buddhism. I especially appreciate his telephone calls, checking up on me and giving support.

I suppose my editor at Columbia University Press, Wendy Lochner, was just doing her job when she responded to the first draft by saying she would like to hear more about some things I said in the closing chapter. It took me another two years to say more, and that chapter grew into four (chapters 14–17). But it was what I wanted to do anyway, and I feel privileged to have had the opportunity and encouragement.

My thanks also to Lynda Miller for technical help with computer programs and the photographs.

And of course, at the end of the acknowledgments comes the author's wife, Anne Cooper. She has more than earned that place of honor: she transcribed many of the interviews; read, advised on, and edited drafts as I finished them; took care of the photographs and contributed artistic suggestions; and made me promise not to gush about anything else.

REALIZING AWAKENED CONSCIOUSNESS

Introduction

Legend has it that soon after his enlightenment, Siddhartha Gautama was asked what made him different from other people. He replied, "I am awake," so they gave him the title "Buddha," meaning "one who is awake." Now in Western culture enlightenment has a different meaning, having to do with rational inquiry. Immanuel Kant wrote "What Is Enlightenment?" as a proclamation that the age of enlightenment was open to everyone (or at least, to all those ready to cast off their "self-imposed immaturity" and use their "native intelligence" to begin thinking for themselves). Both kinds of enlightenment refer to natural capacities native to everyone, which if developed and used allow us to see the world more clearly and without distortion. This book is about awakening, but as an intellectual undertaking it proceeds fully in the tradition of rational inquiry. In fact, the two can work together, and chapter 16 examines how this symbiosis is operating in the modern world. One thing at a time, however, and to avoid confusion I will stick with "awakening" and leave "enlightenment" for the other path toward truth.

It was trying to understand awakening, and hopefully experience it directly, that started me on the project that became this book. I had spent almost forty years looking for an answer in the traditional Buddhist manner, first studying with an accredited teacher and then continuing with a sincere practice on my own. Life was good, those many years, except that I still had no answer to the question I had been pursuing. There comes a time, in many undertakings, when progress seems blocked and it might be better to try something else. So I began to think that if I couldn't answer the question on the basis of personal experience, perhaps I should look for people who might know more about it and ask them what they had learned.

As a research sociologist, I thought interviewing would be the appropriate way to proceed. I wanted to maximize the likelihood that the people interviewed had themselves experienced awakening (although I was not sure at the time if such an experience was really possible). How does one go about finding an awakened person, especially given that many of them begin by denying that they have awakened? Because I had no idea what awakening really meant, and because there is no accrediting agency to certify levels of attainment (nothing equivalent to, say, the National Academy of Sciences), I decided to look for Buddhist teachers who were well known, had excellent reputations, had published or been interviewed extensively, and whose writings especially intrigued me. I tried to get representatives of the three major Buddhist traditions (Zen, Tibetan, and Theravada/vipassana) with good proportions of men and women.

I wanted interviewees who would be willing to talk about details of the path they had followed and about where it had led them, in their own words rather than by relying on Buddhist jargon. I stayed with Buddhists from Western nations in order to make communication simpler and minimize differences in cultural background. Consequently, the teachers interviewed here all come from North America, Europe, and Australia.

This procedure produced a list of nineteen Buddhist teachers, eleven of whom agreed to be interviewed. Only two teachers with predominately Tibetan training accepted my invitation, and both had rejected at least some of their Tibetan roots. Due to a much higher response rate among men than among women, I ended up interviewing eight men and only three women. Although this was a less representative group than I had hoped for, I was overjoyed by the quality and candidness of the interviews these eleven teachers provided.

All of the teachers described at least some level of experience with awakening. So by the time I had completed the first few interviews I already had an answer to my first question: Does awakening ever really happen in the modern (Western) world? Yes, it does!

The Interviews

The interviews were conducted between March 2009 and April 2010, all of them in person except the one with Shinzen Young, which was done by phone. At the start of the interview I asked each teacher to tell me about their path in Buddhism—how they got started, where it had led, and what their life was like now. Often that was the only structuring necessary, but at times I probed slightly to clarify what they had just said. The interviews lasted from one and one half to two hours, and were recorded, transcribed, and edited. The final edited version was then sent to each interviewee for corrections or additional comments, but no substantive changes were made. The final texts of the eleven interviews make up the heart of this book, chapters 1 through 11.

Here are biosketches of the teachers:

Shinzen Young grew up in West Los Angeles as Steve Young. He began his path intellectually, studying Asian languages at UCLA and then researching Buddhism in graduate school at the University of Wisconsin. In 1969 he went to Japan to do his Ph.D. dissertation on the Shingon School, which is derived from eighth-century Vajrayana Buddhism. While there he began both Zen and Shingon practice, learning to meditate while counting his breaths and then proceeding to some very brutal Japanese retreats. The discipline and pain worked for him; he learned that if he stayed focused, the discomfort wouldn't bother him so much. After doing this for one hundred days in a row during a particularly intense retreat, he had mastered the ability to keep his mind quiet, concentrate, and stay attentive. On returning to the United States, he maintained this practice on his own for several years until his first awakening experience occurred. This is an almost prototypical example of what in chapter 13 will be called the "no separation" property of awakening, and is especially interesting because rather than gradually fading out, as these experiences typically do, it permanently changed a basic perspective of his consciousness.

Later on, he began serving as a translator for Joshu Sasaki Roshi in the Rinzai Zen tradition. However, he continued to explore other traditions of Buddhism, and studied with several vipassana teachers from various parts of Southeast Asia, including S. N. Goenka (with whom Stephen Batchelor also studied). Shinzen incorporated vipassana teachings and practices into his methods and philosophy of teaching, but has remained independent of any single lineage or school of Buddhism. He refers to his approach as basic mindfulness. He now lives in Burlington, Vermont, but travels extensively to lead retreats and consult on scientific studies dealing with mindfulness.

In 2012, the basic mindfulness system was utilized in fMRI studies at Harvard Medical School. Researchers used four of its techniques to help answer a fundamental question concerning what neuroscientists call the default mode network. Several of the system's science-friendly features contributed to stunningly clear and credible results.

Shinzen is the author of *The Science of Enlightenment* (2005), *Break Through Pain* (2010), and numerous YouTube videos and articles (www .basicmindfulness.com).

He characterizes himself this way: "My life integrates many disparate worlds: I'm a Jewish guy who got turned on to science by a Jesuit priest. I teach the expansion-contraction paradigm of Japanese Zen mounted within the noting technique of Burmese vipassana, equipped with universal ethical guidelines derived from early Indian Buddhism." He also says, "My life's passion lies in exploring what may arise from the cross-fertilization of the best of the East with the best of the West."

John Tarrant was born in rural Tasmania, Australia, in 1948, but when I interviewed him he was living among the vineyards of Sonoma County, California. In between working as a fisherman and then as a political activist studying and working with aborigines, he earned a dual degree in human sciences and English literature from the Australian National University. Throughout, however, two themes guided him toward Buddhism: first, childhood experiences of being "one with things . . . [where] you and the trees and the people are not different," and second, the poetic sensitivity that continues to find expression in his writing. From early on, he was fascinated with Chinese poems and with the classical koans that he discovered in books. He studied briefly with two Tibetan teachers in Australia, then with the Korean Zen master Seung Sahn Sunim in New York, and finally with Robert Aitkin Roshi in the Harada-Yasutani tradition of Japanese Zen, from whom he received Dharma transmission.

During a *sesshin* with Seung Sahn in a borrowed martial arts dojo on Long Island, he had an important early experience: "I was sitting there, and the Korean pads were really thin and my knees were hurting and it was November and it was cold, and I realized, *This is great*. . . . Everything started to open up for me. It was perfect now. . . . All that stuff that happens when you're meditating." That sounds a bit like Shinzen Young's description in its austerity and discipline, but neither Shinzen nor Tarrant is committed to that kind of approach. Tarrant also talks about the "warmth and the loving quality" that he found, of "the fundamental vastness . . . and kindness of the universe."

Today, Tarrant directs the Pacific Zen Institute in Santa Rosa, California, and continues to be a rich and creative source of both prose and poetry. His books include *The Light Inside the Dark: Zen, Soul, and the Spiritual Life* (1999) and *Bring Me the Rhinoceros* (2008).

Ken McLeod was born in 1948 in Canada. He developed a strong interest in religion while in high school but felt frustrated by the books available for him to read. In his third year at the University of Waterloo he began looking into Buddhism, but in those days there were few books on the subject available in English. After graduation and marriage, he passed up a fellowship to do graduate work in mathematics in England and started bicycling east across Europe with his wife. In India they found Kalu Rinpoche and began studying Tibetan Buddhism with him, an immersion that became a total commitment and lasted more than twenty years. During this time Ken did two intense three-year retreats, translated for the rinpoche, and helped set up several Buddhist centers in Canada and the United States.

By 1989, however, McLeod felt increasing doubt and dissatisfaction with Tibetan Buddhism, and after Kalu Rinpoche passed away, he let go his ties to its institutions. Free to explore new approaches, he pioneered a successful new career as a meditation consultant and author. He also developed a consulting practice, coaching senior executives in leadership and communication skills. About this time he admitted to himself that he had long suffered from serious depression and sought help from psychologists, friends, and a diet that better suited a chronic digestive problem. Then, in 2008, something that he read led to what he calls his "road to Damascus" experience. This involved a complete release from ideas, Buddhist and others, and also from much of the depression and physical discomfort he had experienced. It was the start of new spiritual understanding as well, including the experience discussed in chapter 13 as an example of "not knowing," of experiencing consciousness as coarising with action and perception in each new moment.

McLeod is known especially for his pragmatic, innovative approach to the path toward awakening. He founded his organization, Unfettered Mind, in 1990 in Los Angeles, where he has lived for over twenty years. Currently he is quietly wandering the globe, exploring and reflecting, and occasionally teaching. His writings include *Wake up to Your Life: Discovering the Buddhist Path of Attention* (2001), *An Arrow to the Heart* (2007), and *Reflections on Silver River* (2013), as well a steady flow of articles and translations in Buddhist magazines.

Ajahn Amaro was born Jeremy Horner in Kent, England, in 1956, and went through the English primary and boarding school system, which he calls his first raw experience of *dukkha*, suffering. This may or may not have led him to begin wondering, at the age of ten or eleven, What is God?, What is real?, and How can you be free?. Since he knew of no way to find answers, he went to the University of London and completed honors degrees in psychology and physiology. There he was able to connect, outside of the university, with the author and lecturer Trevor Ravenscroft and with the circle of people who had gathered around him. Getting to know and talk with them gave him confidence that others shared his questions and that there were ways to seek answers. So after graduation he bought a one-way ticket to Asia, and wandered around for a few months until he found a monastery in northeast Thailand that followed the Thai Forest tradition and the teachings of the late Ajahn Chah. This felt right to him, and he has remained a monk in that tradition and organization to this day—the only one of the eleven teachers interviewed here who has continuously followed a traditional monastic life.

After two years in Thailand, Amaro returned to England, where one of Ajahn Chah's most senior students, Ajahn Sumedho (originally from Seattle) had established a monastery and teaching center. These were years when Amaro made great advances along his path. Although he says he never had a "Shazam!" experience, he reports progressing gradually but steadily to greater understanding and a deeper awareness of what life is really about. He also worked hard, in ways that he describes in detail, on overcoming some of his bad habits (like worrying, or taking himself too seriously). Whereas he describes himself at university as a partying carouser, he came across in the interview as witty and wise, but still fun-loving.

At the time of the interview Ajahn Amaro was coabbot of Abhayagiri Buddhist Monastery near Redwood City, California. In 2010 he returned to England to succeed Ajahn Sumedho as abbot at Amaravati Monastery.

Martine Batchelor was born in France in 1953. She was initially attracted to political activism rather than spiritual concerns, but when she read a collection of the Buddha's talks that someone had given her, she was struck by the message that before you try to change others, it might be a good idea to try to change yourself. After some time in England exploring Asian gurus and their writings (none of whom impressed her very much), she decided she needed to encounter Buddhism firsthand. So she saved some money and traveled overland, through Nepal and Thailand, ending up in Korea. There she found her teacher, the Zen master Kusan Sunim, and became a Jogye Zen nun. Ten years of meditation and study with Sunim provided the foundation for the continued spiritual development that she tells about in her interview. She also met Stephen Batchelor when he came to Korea to study with Sunim, and in 1985 they left monastic life, got married, and moved to England. Since then she has been writing, teaching, and leading meditation groups in Europe and the United States, while living in a small town near Bordeaux. She is the author of *Women in Korean Zen* (2007) and *The Spirit of the Buddha* (2010).

Shaila Catherine grew up in a suburb of San Francisco, California. While in high school in 1980 she heard about meditation from a friend and immediately wanted to learn more. So she took a class, sat diligently, and continued meditating and attending silent retreats through college. In 1990 she finished graduate work and traveled to India. Her first stop was Bodh Gaya, the place of the Buddha's enlightenment, where she attended a three-week retreat led by Christopher Titmuss, a Dharma teacher from the United Kingdom. Soon after this retreat, she met the Hindu teacher H.W.L. Poonja. Through a dialogue process, Poonjaji opened her mind to what might be described as a direct experience of emptiness. For several years she lived primarily with Poonjaji in Lucknow, India, and traveled periodically to Thailand to practice meditation in forest monasteries, to Nepal where she received teachings from Tibetan lamas, and to retreats led by Western Insight Meditation teachers elsewhere in India and the West. In 1996, Titmuss invited Shaila to teach. She then spent a year studying Buddhism in England, and returned to her home in the United States by 1998.

Shaila has an enduring appreciation for silent meditation and has accumulated more than eight years of silent retreat experience. In 2003, she devoted a ten-month retreat to the development of deep states of absorptive concentration, known as *jhāna*, and their application to insight. She authored *Focused and Fearless: A Meditator's Guide to States of Deep Joy, Calm, and Clarity* (Wisdom, 2008) to encourage the development of *jhāna* as a basis for liberating insight.

Since 2006, Shaila's practice of concentration and insight has been guided by the Burmese meditation master Venerable Pa-Auk Sayadaw. He teaches a systematic approach that prepares the mind with strong concentration and carefully analyzes mind and matter before progressing through a traditional scheme of sixteen knowledges that culminate in the liberating realization of *nibbāna*. She wrote *Wisdom Wide and Deep: A Practical Handbook for Mastering* Jhāna *and* Vipassanā (2011) to help make this traditional approach to meditation accessible to Western practitioners.

Shaila teaches meditation internationally, and is the founder and principal teacher for Insight Meditation South Bay, a Buddhist meditation center in Silicon Valley (imsb.org).

Gil Fronsdal was born in Norway in 1954, and grew up in Los Angeles, Switzerland, and Italy. He has lived in the San Francisco Bay area much of his adult life. With an interest in ecology, living simply, and improving the natural environment, he first majored in environmental studies and then graduated from college with a degree in agronomy. His lifelong interest in Buddhist practice began during the two years he dropped out of school in the middle of college. Hitchhiking around the United States, he stayed in various communes, where he was introduced to Shunryu Suzuki's book *Zen Mind, Beginner's Mind* and Chogyam Trungpa's *Cutting Through Spiritual Materialism*. This brought him to the San Francisco Zen Center. He stayed with that organization for ten years, practicing at its three centers: Green Gulch Farm, Tassajara monastery, and the main temple in San Francisco. He found the Zen practice quite beneficial and inspiring.

When San Francisco Zen Center had a leadership crisis in 1983, he accepted an invitation to go to Japan. As with several other teachers interviewed for this book, regulations required that he leave the country in order to apply for a new visa. The visa never arrived, but while waiting in Bangkok he became involved with vipassana training. He liked the long, intensive retreats, including an eight-month retreat in Burma during which he experienced a deeper and more intense meditation experience. On returning to the United States, he went to a three-month vipassana retreat at the Insight Meditation Society in Barre, Massachusetts. Here the process of deepening the practice continued. Two years later Jack Kornfield invited Fronsdal to participate in a four-year vipassana teacher-training program held in Spirit Rock, California.

By 1990 Gil found himself on a "dual-track" Buddhist path. In addition to the vipassana training with Kornfield, he had continued his Zen training and eventually received Dharma transmission as a Zen teacher through Mel Weitsman in the Shunryu Suzuki lineage. At the same time he was doing academic work that culminated in a Ph.D. in Buddhist studies at Stanford. In 1990 he also began leading a small meditation group near Stanford. That sitting group grew into the Insight Meditation Center of Redwood City, California, which he presently directs.

Gil was married in 1992 and has two children. He says that monastic life was easy for him, but that marriage and a family pushed, stretched, challenged, and inspired him in ways that were as transforming as any other aspect of his Buddhist practice.

Fronsdal is the author of *The Issue at Hand: Essays on Buddhist Mindfulness Practice* (2008), *A Monastery Within: Tales from the Buddhist Path* (2010), *Unhindered: A Mindful Path Through the Five Hindrances* (2013), and *The Dhammapada* (2006), a translation of a Buddhist classic.

Stephen Batchelor was born in Britain in 1953, where he grew up immersed in the counterculture of the 1960s. At age eighteen he hitchhiked east through Europe and beyond. When the going got tough in Iran, his traveling companion mentioned Buddha's remark that "Life is suffering." This intrigued and disturbed him so much that when he reached India he went straight to Dharamsala, the capital-in-exile of the Dalai Lama. There he began studying Buddhist philosophy and doctrine with Geshe Dhargyey. He continued for two years and was ordained as a monk. But he also participated in vipassana retreats under S. N. Goenka (with whom Shinzen Young also studied), where he learned mindfulness meditation. This proved to be a fruitful combination—during the next three years he had several important insight experiences. There was a problem, however: what he was studying in the Buddhist texts did not seem to link up with what he was learning from the insight experiences. There was an "acute disjunction."

Stephen found some help with this problem in the writings of Dharmakirti, a seventh-century Buddhist philosopher, whom he studied when in 1975 he followed his Tibetan teacher, Geshe Rabten, to a monastery near Geneva, Switzerland. Dharmakirti held that the function of meditation and spiritual study was to learn to experience and live in the world as it really is. Stephen has been guided by that teaching ever since, first through two years studying Zen Buddhism in Korea and then, after meeting his future wife, Martine, at that monastery, at Sharpham North Community in Devon, England, and in life as an independent author and teacher.

Since 1985 Batchelor's path has focused on applying what he learned from fourteen years of Tibetan and Zen Buddhist training, and from the awakening he experienced, to everyday life in the world. In his most recent book, *Confession of a Buddhist Atheist* (2010), he concentrates on how Gautama lived his life after his awakening, studying all written records of his teachings and activities, and also paying attention to the political and social environment in which the Buddha had to live and the people (like King Pasenadi) with whom he had to deal for the (then unnamed) movement that had started around him to survive. A second way Batchelor resolved the disjunction between Buddhist teaching and his personal experience was to reject any parts of Buddhism that set up beliefs and ask followers to accept them. He has written, lectured, and debated extensively on the subject. With Martine, Stephen currently lives in a small town near Bordeaux.

Pat Enkyo O'Hara was born in 1942 and grew up in San Diego, where she graduated from the same high school I had attended several years earlier. The 1950s in Southern California were "rebel without a cause" years for many young people, and like the beatniks she identified with, Enkyo began reading what books on Zen she could find. For twenty years, while pursuing a Ph.D. in media ecology and becoming a professor at New York University, she read books on Buddhism and tried, occasionally, to sit on her own. Finally she started formal Zen study, at Zen Mountain Monastery near New York City, with John Daido Loori Roshi. She says it took her that long to submit to direction and be part of a group, but that when she did the discipline and social support provided just what she needed.

Four or five years later the AIDS epidemic hit New York, and Enkyo plunged into working with dying men. This changed the focus of her practice completely, from improving her life to expressing compassion and helping others. Along with this flow of empathy came an increasingly frequent experience of one of the characteristics of awakening described in chapter 13—a "dropping of the distance between me and the other."

Enkyo's formal Zen training continued in the 1990s as she began studying with Loori Roshi's teacher Taizan Maezumi Roshi, in the Harada-Yasutani lineage, and continued her work with koans. She found Maezumi to be both inspiring and an excellent teacher, and has kind and insightful things to say about this otherwise controversial man and about his contribution to her development. She was ordained by Maezumi in 1995. After his death, she received Dharma transmission in 2004 from another of his students, Bernie Glassman. She had known Glassman for some time, and worked with him in New York on the Greyston Bakery project and other social action efforts for which he is well known (see Glassman's interview, chapter 10).

Enkyo is currently abbot of the Village Zendo in Greenwich Village, which began in 1985 with one or two people coming to meditate with her in her apartment. The group grew larger and larger, until she had to retire from her position at NYU and find a way to rent space in Lower Manhattan. Over the years, she and her students have built the Village Zendo into a large, vibrant, and socially active community.

Bernie Glassman was born in 1939 and grew up in Brooklyn. Initially his interests were in technology and engineering, although he does remember doing research, at age twelve, on the question, Is there a God? by reading what some classical thinkers had to say on the topic. Then in college he was assigned *The World's Religions* by Huston Smith, which included one page on Zen. But that one page was enough to set Glassman to reading everything he could find about Zen Buddhism.

When he graduated, in 1960, and moved to Los Angeles to work as an aeronautical engineer at McDonnell-Douglas, he began doing *zazen* on his own. In 1962 he found a Japanese Buddhist temple in downtown Los Angeles, where he began meditating and met Maezumi Roshi, then a young monk, who a few years later started a center of his own and became Glassman's teacher (initially Bernie was his only student). During that time Glassman also earned a Ph.D. in applied mathematics from UCLA. But what he really wanted to do was to have "the classical awakening experiences."

He had his first in 1970, an experience of oneness. Then in 1976 he had two deeper experiences, which he describes as states in which all attachments "to any of your conditionings" disappear. After that he felt no need for more experiences and changed his direction radically, from working on spiritual development in the traditional context of a Zen center to working in the world with all the different kinds of people who live in it.

Glassman received Dharma transmission in 1976, moved back to New York, began teaching at the Zen Center of New York, and wondered what to do about the hunger and suffering he saw around him. He felt that the Buddhist approach should not be thought of as "good people helping poor people" but as an opportunity to be shaped and informed by the people with whom one is working. In 1982 he and others opened Greyston Bakery in Yonkers, New York, an effort to help alleviate homelessness in that neighborhood by providing a job to anyone, regardless of background, and using the profits for wide-ranging community development projects. But he also understood that helping others can be a practice, in the classical Buddhist sense: a way practitioners can realize the oneness of life by opening up to the immediate presence of human diversity. In line with this, in the mid-1980s he began leading retreats not in the Zen Center but on the streets of slums, where the participants lived with the homeless as the homeless. These were highly successful and have been continued by his students around the world. Following this idea of retreats in environments that confront participants with realities that challenge their attachments to what they have always taken for granted, Glassman and his students have also held a long series of retreats in Auschwitz.

In 1996 Glassman founded the Zen Peacemaker Circle, which among other activities is currently working to develop "Zen houses." These are located in troubled neighborhoods, where Buddhists will both practice meditation and minister to the needs of the people around them. His writings include *Bearing Witness: A Zen Master's Lessons in Making Peace* (1999) and *Infinite Circle: Teachings in Zen* (2003).

Joseph Goldstein, born in 1944, grew up in the Catskill Mountains of upstate New York. He studied philosophy at Columbia University, where in a class on Eastern religion and philosophy, one theme in the *Bhagavad Gita* unexpectedly awakened in him a new possibility for living in the world: "act without attachment to the fruit of the action." Although at the time, this idea was just a small seed of understanding, it contributed to a sense of search and inquiry. After graduating in 1965, Joseph volunteered for the Peace Corps and was sent to Thailand, where he started going to a Buddhist temple that offered courses for foreigners. There he was introduced to Buddhist meditation, and although he had the usual beginning difficulties, it gave him a glimpse of how the Buddhist path could provide a way to explore the mind.

After his stint in the Peace Corps, Goldstein realized that he wanted to practice meditation more intensively. He traveled to India and met his first teacher, Anagarika Munindra, who had just returned to Bodh Gaya after nine years of study and practice in Burma. Since then, Joseph has continued to study and practice vipassana or insight meditation. More recently, he has also practiced with some renowned Tibetan teachers. To describe where this path has led him, Joseph likes to use a framework taught by the twelfth-century Korean Zen master Chinul: "sudden awakening/gradual cultivation." Insights and openings occur suddenly; then they must be gradually cultivated in all aspects of one's life.

On returning to the United States in 1974, Goldstein, along with two other young Americans who had been studying Buddhism in South Asia—Sharon Salzberg and Jack Kornfield—founded the Insight Meditation Society in Barre, Massachusetts. IMS has grown and expanded steadily, helping to meet a strong interest in vipassana Buddhist practice in the United States. Shaila Catherine (chapter 6) and Gil Fronsdal (chapter 7) both studied at the Barre IMS and presently lead their own meditation centers in California.

Joseph continues to lecture and lead retreats, and has authored a number of important books, including *Insight Meditation: The Practice of Freedom* (2003), *One Dharma: The Emerging Western Buddhism* (2003), and *Mindfulness: A Practical Guide to Awakening* (2013).

Serendipity

A funny thing happened toward the end of the interviewing. Once you start a research project, especially one as exploratory as this, you can never be sure where it will take you. While doing their best to tell me about their experiences with awakening, the teachers also somehow managed to catalyze within me an awakening experience of my own. This was wonderful for me personally, of course, and it helped me tremendously in understanding what they said in their interviews. At the same time, "having an inner personal experience" doesn't fit accepted research formats, because the trade-off for deeper understanding is subjective bias. This is a warning to readers: what I have to say from here on is unavoidably colored by that experience.

As evidence that scientists can have awakening experiences too, the appendix presents an interview with James Austin, neurologist and medical school professor. Austin has studied and practiced Zen for some years, and he tells a path story similar to those of the teachers. His awakening came early one morning on the outside platform of a London subway station. The properties of the experience are quite similar to those described by the teachers but, in my reading anyway, show even more of the objective attention to detailed description that should be expected of a scientist.

Analysis

Taken all together, the interviews provide strong support for the argument that the human species possesses—has within its physical being—the capacity for a mode of conscious awareness that is qualitatively different from our ordinary form of consciousness. After I had gathered this evidence, the next task was to focus that argument more clearly through qualitative analysis of the interview texts. In chapters 12 and 13 I try to identify shared patterns and common themes running through the eleven interviews.

Chapter 12, "Developing Capacities Necessary for Awakening," examines the paths the teachers followed, paying particular attention to the practices they engaged in and the teachings that provided them with guidance and inspiration. All of the teachers devoted many, many hours to meditation. Although the specific forms and techniques varied, they didn't seem to consider the technical details as important as what they learned along the way. In particular, the interviews mentioned three distinct capacities that must be developed and strengthened: control of attention (necessary for quieting the mind), detaching from or letting go of conditionings, and nurturing the growth of compassion. Whether nurturing compassion is a necessary or merely a desirable development is not resolved in this chapter, and starts a thread to be followed in chapter 13. The details of the path stories thus describe the way different practices and teachings were used to facilitate development of these three capacities.

In chapter 13, "Properties of Awakening Experiences," all segments of the interviews that seem to refer to experiences of awakening, or awakened awareness, are pulled out for more careful analysis and sorted into groups on the basis of similarity. A considerable amount of interpretation was sometimes required to do this, but there are two checks on the process. One is that the phrases and my interpretations of them are laid out explicitly, with page identifications so that the quotes can be located in the interview chapters in their full context. The second check is that a preliminary draft of this chapter was sent to each interviewee so that they could see and comment on my interpretation of their quotes. Their responses are included following my analysis.

The final sorting of interpreted quotes produced three clusters that describe three distinct ways awakened awareness is different from ordinary awareness. A conceptual definition was given to each cluster based on its distinctive properties:

1. No separation from one's environment. Awakened awareness is generated from a perspective in which the environment is a whole system in which we participate as one more or less equal part, not from the usual perspective of the self as central focus and protagonist operating at some remove from others around it.

2. No emotional attachments to the self or to social reality. We can observe what is going on in the world and act appropriately, but emotional connections with the scripts that normally govern this activity have been unplugged, and we watch the flow of awareness with freedom and equanimity.

3. Awareness coarises with action, freely, as an interdependent process. What we become aware of and what we find ourselves doing in each moment emerge together spontaneously as we interact with our environment.

Although understanding each of these properties conceptually is not the same as experiencing awakening, the definitions provide a way of relating awakened consciousness to ordinary consciousness.

While chapter 13 attempts to sum up the positive aspects of awakened consciousness, it would be misleading not to also mention negative aspects. Western Buddhism has repeatedly been rocked by scandals in which some presumably awakened teacher has indulged in sex, alcohol, or drugs in ways that not only were self-destructive but also caused suffering to other people. Sexual abuse of students has been widely, and infamously, reported in recent years, particularly by teachers in Japanese Zen traditions. Hurting other people requires an absence of compassion, so chapter 13 ends by concluding that it is possible to have awakened consciousness without possessing compassion.

Theoretical Integration

Chapter 14, "Evolution of Ordinary and Awakened Consciousness," approaches awakening from a different direction. The properties of awakened consciousness derived in chapter 13 are, intellectually, neither complicated nor esoteric. Why, then, do almost all humans in the world today spend their lives blinkered by ordinary consciousness? This chapter says it is no accident, but rather a natural twist in a long process of evolution. While the evolution of consciousness began with one-celled organisms, the important story begins with vertebrates and has four parts. First, some species of mammals and birds became more and more clever, including those closest to our line (apes and australopithecines). Second, some early hominid species, perhaps *Homo erectus*, began to use that improved cognitive capacity to develop their communication systems into protolanguages that allowed communication about objects and events not present in immediate perceptual experience.

Third, as protolanguages progressed into the "true" languages of *Homo sapiens*, something else completely new developed. As our species began using language to link perceptual experience with words and symbols, and then went on to talk and think about things that happened in the past, things that might or might not happen in the future, or abstractions with no basis in perceptual experience at all, we began to have at our command a symbolically represented world existing parallel to the perceptually represented world of animals. This is usually called "culture," or at a finer-grained level, "social reality." Social realities are built by humans talking with each other, and infants born into a group begin learning its social reality at the same time that they learn language.[1] This version of reality becomes internalized so deeply that it becomes virtually unquestionable, so that as adults we experience life through a layer of social reality placed on top of perceptual reality. The word "carapace" has been used to describe the way social reality creates a shell within which we live and through which we experience the world around us. I sometimes think of my personal symbolic representation of the world as an exoskeleton.

The fourth part of the evolutionary story took place at the biological level. As language and the elaboration of social reality proceeded and became the basis for social life and social institutions, the hominid brain both grew in size and differentiated into specialized areas and systems capable of processing all the information and computations necessary for living in social reality. When the brain interprets perceptual experience by filtering it through symbolic systems representing social and personal reality (and in the process forces perceptual reality to fit into the structures of social reality), we have ordinary consciousness.

To understand awakened consciousness, we have to begin by going back to some hypothetical time before language and social reality began to be invented, and then try to imagine what it would be like to live solely in perceptual reality. The suggestion of chapter 14 is that the core of awakened consciousness is like this early, purely perceptual mode. Our brains are larger than those of animals, of course, and we have language and the symbolic representations that it makes possible. These are incredible resources but also set two traps: reification of social reality and construction of the social self. As long as we think social reality is real and the self-construct is us, and care as enormously as we do about how that self is doing as it wanders around in that reality, we are trapped in ordinary consciousness.

As soon as we began to talk, as children, we began constructing the social self as a proxy version of ourselves, just as we began constructing our own version of the rest of social reality. Following this theme, chapter 15, "The Awakened Baby?" looks at what developmental psychology has to say about the transformation of human babies into adults. The starting point is that babies have yet to acquire language, and so they have no social self, no concern about social reality, and no apparent sense of separation from the world around them—all properties of awakened consciousness. Furthermore, the loss of these properties and the development of ordinary consciousness in children seems to parallel or follow slightly after corresponding stages in the development of language. So there are some intriguing connections. While they don't prove that ontogeny recapitulates phylogeny, they deserve further investigation.

The story of human consciousness continues in chapter 16, "The Human Condition and How We Got Into It," by examining the final stages leading to the dominance of ordinary consciousness. Here the question turns from why most humans today live their lives within ordinary consciousness to the consequences of modern ordinary consciousness for subjective experience and for behavior. Although we think of our species as the crown jewel of evolution, many people admit that life in ordinary consciousness has not turned out to be all that great. Chapter 16 therefore looks at how human societies and individuals have tried, historically and today, to live with what the Buddha called *dukkha*. *Dukkha* is usually translated as "suffering" or "dissatisfaction"; it means that life in ordinary consciousness is inherently unsatisfying and anxiety-provoking. In modern terminology, the human condition is life within the shell of ordinary consciousness. Our species has always had to deal with this condition, and the kinds of remedies with which we have tried to prevent or relieve its symptoms make quite a list.

The first strategy, the one recommended and taught by the Buddha and discussed at great length in this book, is to awaken, that is, to transcend ordinary consciousness. A second strategy is more or less in line with this. It involves following the Buddha's advice about how to prepare for awakening, whether or not it actually takes place. For people living in modern postindustrial societies, this is the rationale for meditating, for trying to live mindfully in perceptual reality and follow a moral path based on wisdom. This solution is also evident in preliterate societies, where attention to perceptual reality is typically part of the culture and way of life. Chapter 17 therefore begins by examining a prototypical preliterate society, the Pirahãs of the Brazilian Amazon. They are of special interest because according to the linguist Daniel Everett, their language and culture seem almost intentionally designed to focus attention on immediate experience.[2] When day-to-day Pirahã life is compared in detail with the practices that chapter 12 says are basic to the Buddhist path, there is a very close resemblance. And if we then compare what Everett says about Pirahã personality traits with the properties of awakened consciousness described in 13, the Pirahãs come out looking very much like awakened Buddhists. So the implication is that a whole society can keep alive and healthy the capacities needed to enjoy awakened consciousness by structuring their culture and lifestyle in ways that promote activities and attitudes similar to those of Buddhism. Like almost all humans, Pirahãs have a social reality that they accept as true, but their emphasis on mindful attention to perceptual reality seems to provide enough balance to keep the *dukkha* of ordinary consciousness at minimal levels.

A third strategy for living with *dukkha* goes in a different direction. It probably dates back to the evolution of specialized brain systems for language and ordinary consciousness, which became part of our genetic heritage. This strategy involves two tactics: first, construct as a special component of social reality a set of beliefs that explains why things happen in life the way they do. Life will still include some physical suffering, but we don't have to feel anxious or afraid because we know that whatever happens makes sense as part of some larger plan. Second, support and reinforce those beliefs with the strong consensus of a cohesive social group. The ontological basis for social reality is the shared belief by a social group that it is real and cannot be questioned. This strategy has worked fairly well throughout human history. In today's world, however, shared trust in social reality has been challenged and disrupted by forces that have developed within social reality itself.

For an analysis of these forces at work that is remarkably consistent with Gautama's original *dukkha* theory, chapter 16 turns to Anthony Giddens's *Modernity and Self-Identity*. Lord Giddens begins with the most distinctive feature of modern society, its extreme dynamism, producing not only rapid social change but also rapid acceleration in the rate at which change is taking place. Social reality no longer provides satisfactory explanations for what is happening. As a consequence, its taken-for-granted nature, "the main emotional support of a defensive carapace or protective cocoon which all normal individuals carry around with them as the means whereby they are able to get on with the affairs of day-to-day life,"[3] is increasingly called into question and made to feel less and less solid. When social reality is disrupted, people experience higher levels of *dukkha*, which Giddens calls ontological insecurity: "On the other side of what might appear to be quite trivial aspects of day-to-day action and discourse, chaos lurks. And this chaos is not just disorganization, but the loss of a sense of the very reality of things and of other persons."[4]

Giddens applies his version of the *dukkha* model by first asking what has caused this extreme dynamism of modern society. He identifies as a primary culprit the fact that we no longer protect the sanctity of our social reality but actually encourage people to question it. That is, questioning social reality and the nature of the self—a tradition that has existed in the West at least since ancient Greece—now has actually become institutionalized, built into our social reality and given positive value. This is a remarkable and unprecedented occurrence—a social reality that is continuously questioning itself. A major consequence of the blooming of ordinary consciousness, therefore, has been not only social change caused by science, technology, and improvements in the material quality of life but also an unrelenting intellectual attack on the beliefs people had previously taken for granted. And one consequence, of course, has been increased *dukkha*; unsurprisingly, we find more energy being put into attempts to reduce or resolve the problems it causes.

Three kinds of response to *dukkha* are strongly alive today and play an important role in shaping modern life. One response has been to reassert traditional social reality, in particular traditional religious belief systems that provide people with answers and group support. Data on the growth of fundamentalist churches and on the popularity of science denial as a way to reject ideas that do not fit traditional beliefs document this.[5] The second response has been to embrace skeptical inquiry and learn to tolerate, even enjoy, the existential ambiguity it engenders. This shows up in the steadily increasing numbers of "religiously unaffiliated" people in the United States today. The third response, and the subject of this book, tries to move away from the dominance of ordinary consciousness by practicing some form of meditation or following something like the Buddhist path. The number of people responding this way has also been growing.

Chapter 17 pulls the most important ideas laid out in the previous chapters together into two conceptual models, one for each mode of consciousness. Aside from providing a concise summary, these models are meant to help researchers formulate hypotheses and design methods for investigating them, so that the study of awakened consciousness can proceed energetically in company with the more established traditions of scientific research. Because to ask, as this book does, What is awakening? is not to float an esoteric question somewhere out beyond the realm of practical and intellectual discourse. It is at least possible that the future of the planet depends on finding an answer and applying it.

By displacing perceptual reality with symbolic representations based heavily on social reality, ordinary consciousness opens wonderful possibilities for creative achievement but also dooms us to live with a reflected, refracted, and edited view of the world. We live according to the Thomas theorem: "If men define situations as real, they are real in their consequences."[6] If we believe that something is true, we may act in ways that are crazy or murderous as a result—and humans have shown themselves capable of believing an incredible variety of things and acting accordingly. When those traditional beliefs are threatened, as they are today, efforts to reassert them can be strong and sometimes violent, causing the "culture wars" and political conflicts manifest in the United States today. Finding ways to live in health, peace, and happiness with our own invention, language, is the crucial challenge we may finally have to face.

1
Interview with Shinzen Young

Shinzen Young is the author of The Science of Enlightenment *and* Meditation: A Beginner's Guide. *I interviewed him by phone at his home in Burlington, Vermont, on April 18, 2009, although we had met in person previously.*

BOYLE: What I'd like you to do here is tell about how you got started in Buddhism and where your path led from there.

SHINZEN: I will try to restrict my account to what might be called the effects of the practice. Before undertaking the practice, I studied it. I was originally an academician, studying Buddhism at UCLA and acquiring a solid intellectual background. I went to Japan toward the end of 1969, in order to study Shingon Buddhism, which is a Japanese form of Vajrayana, with the intention of writing a Ph.D. dissertation on that school of Buddhism.

When I got there, though, they wouldn't teach me anything. They said, "Well, you have to become a monk and actually practice these things." I wanted to study at Mount Koya, which is the headquarters of the Shingon school, but they put me off, saying, "No, you can't get in here, you have to go elsewhere." I was just waiting around and studying texts. There are something like a hundred temples on Mount Koya, but I wanted to get into this particular one. I wanted to study Shingon because very few Westerners had studied that school at all deeply. In any event, while I was waiting around I met one of the professors at the local university who had a Zen sitting group. This guy, although he himself was a Shingon monk, had done Zen and had a weekly *zazen* group. He said, "Well, if you're going to do Shingon practice you have to learn how to sit." Although I had a depth of intellectual information about

Buddhism, I had very little understanding of what it really was. I just had information, a lot of it. So I didn't understand the connection between learning how to sit and doing the tantric rituals that are, of course, forms of meditation. I didn't quite realize that. Learning how to sit didn't compute, but he said I could come to his *zazen* group every week and he would teach me. So I went to the group, and he gave me breath-counting meditation. That was the beginning of my practice. The first thing I discovered was how untenable my body and mind were. There was a lot of physical discomfort associated with the sitting and a lot of monkey mind. That early experience, especially toward the end of a sit, definitely hurt. My thoughts were really chaotic, and it was extremely difficult to concentrate.

I continued to do breath counting—a pretty standard Zen way to start people. Then at some point I started to notice toward the end of the sit that the voice in my head, although still there, was not as loud, not screaming as loud. My breath was slowing down spontaneously. The discomfort was still there but not as noticeable. So I went to him and said, "My sitting is becoming interesting." He said, "Interesting in what way?" I described it, and he said, "Oh, you're starting to go into *samadhi*," in the generic sense of *samadhi*, meaning concentration, a concentrated state. It was a light concentrative state. But he said, "That's good. Now you have to stay in that state all the time. That's your job. Try to get into that state all the time."

Eventually they let me into the temple I wanted to be in, but they wouldn't teach me anything. I was just waiting around and doing shit work, *samu*—to me, seemingly meaningless physical tasks. They said, "Those simple tasks are simple in order to make it easy for you to be in a *samadhi* state while you do them." I was sort of like, "Duh. I never would have figured that out." They said, "That's the idea. While you do the simple tasks, go into *samadhi*, and then you'll be able to do it in more complex tasks, all the time." So I continued sitting. Sometimes it was more focused, sometimes less focused. But being in *samadhi*, tasting that highly concentrated state, then became a goal. I decided, *Okay, that's good. That's what I want to do.* It's a free, legal, and interesting high. I tried to do it during tasks, including more complex tasks, and it became sort of fun. It was like a challenge—how complex a task could I do and still taste a little bit of *samadhi* as I did it?

So I had discovered an altered state, and now I had something that was like a little secret and I could do it all the time. Then my Zen teacher sent me to my first *sesshin*. That was horribly painful, excruciating. It was in southern Japan, it was summer, and it was hot. There were mosquitoes. They were breaking sticks on people. My whole body was shaking. By the end of the *sesshin* I was coming apart at the seams, emotionally. Literally, in the last ten minutes of the last sit of the seven days, I thought I was going to start bawling. I started to scream in my head, *You're not a baby, don't cry. You're not a baby, don't cry.* Then I dropped into a really deep *samadhi.* The pain drove me, and then the pain broke up into this flowing energy. My mind stopped, pretty much. I could have stayed there forever—it seemed that way, at least. Not that the pain didn't bother me, but it broke up into a flow of energy that was pleasant. The talking in my head pretty much turned off, and it was like, *Whoa, this is a very altered state.* That showed me what could happen and involved several high points, or watersheds.

The first watershed was the spontaneous slowing down of the breath, and the fact that although the voice was still there, it was more distant. The next watershed was, "*Okay, that's samadhi. You can get into it counting your breath. Now do it in daily life. Build it through a sequence of more progressive challenges, starting with raking the sand and wiping the floor, etc.*" So that was the second watershed: *I can do this while I'm moving around.* The third watershed was, *Oh my god, pain can dissolve into energy.* That was a real eye-opener, like, *Whoa, who would have ever thought that is possible?*

Eventually the monks at the Shingon temple said they would train me, in the Shingon way. That involves a hundred days of isolation, in the winter. You do tantric rituals three times a day, and, "Oh, by the way, we do it the old-fashioned way here, which means that before each one of those tantric rituals you have to take off all your clothes, fill this bucket from this frozen cistern with ice water, and pour the ice water over your naked body." It was winter, right? They started me off at the winter solstice. The towel that I would attempt to dry myself with would freeze in my hands. The water became ice as soon as it hit the wooden floor. There I am, barefoot on ice, trying to dry myself with a frozen towel.

I had noticed during this ordeal that if I stayed in *samadhi*, in a concentrated state, it was not exactly pleasant, but manageable. But if my attention was scattered, if I was in a lot of thought, it was hellacious. On the third day of this hundred-day commitment, looking at ninety-seven more days, I had an epiphany: *Okay, there are three forks in this road. I'm either going to spend ninety-seven days in abject misery, or I'm going to give up and go back to the States in black disgrace, or I'm going to stay in some sort of* samadhi *state for the next ninety-seven days.* I didn't like the first two alternatives, so the third is what I tried to do.

Of course, there's *samadhi* and then there's absolute *samadhi.* This was nowhere near absolute *samadhi.* In retrospect it was a light concentration state, but it was still tasteable. It's what Mike Csíkszentmihályi, a major figure in positive psychology, calls a "flow" state. It's like "in the zone," all right? It's conscious awareness. You're concentrated, and the concentration is intrinsically rewarding. By the time the hundred days were over, the *samadhi* at some level was permanent. I was always aware of being in that state, all the time, 24/7. That was a watershed. It wasn't deep, but it was there.

BOYLE: You didn't hear the voice in your mind? It was not there as permanently? How would you describe its presence?

SHINZEN: I'd say it was still there. I mean, it's still there now. But I could taste *samadhi*. The voice was not screaming in my head in such a way that I identified with it. The *samadhi* was more like the taste of my body. The breath slows down and there's a taste that goes with it, in the body. If we take *samadhi* to be a continuum from light concentration to full-blown physiological trance, then I was somewhere on the light end. But it had become permanently tasteable in my being. That was cool, that was a watershed. Then I just worked to deepen it, deepen it, deepen it.

Eventually I came back to the United States. Because of being in this highly concentrated state, I noticed that things looked very different, coming back to the United States this time. I'd been to Japan once before as an exchange student before I practiced meditation, and when I came back I had this horrible reverse cultural shock. I mean horrible. I didn't want to be in the United States, I hated it. I wanted only to be in Japan. I was twenty-one and really depressed to be back in the States after one year away. This time I spent three years in Japan, in Buddhist temples, and when I came back I had no reverse culture shock. I was completely happy.

I realized that what I learned in three years of being in a monastery in Japan was not just how to be comfortable in a monastery. I learned how to be comfortable anywhere. That was amazing, actually. After returning to the States, my preoccupation for years was to go deeper and deeper into this state of tranquility, which I equated with turning off or getting rid of thought and, broadly, getting rid of self. If I had a thought or a sense of self, then I considered myself a failure. The good news was that I had tasted *samadhi* and had this thing I could cultivate. The bad news was that, without realizing it, I was suppressing the sense of self. Buddha said that there is no self, and in trying to progress toward that state I had developed an aversion to thought in general, and "I-am-ness" specifically. If being enlightened means that you don't have an experience of self, then when I had an experience of self I took it to mean that I wasn't making progress in my practice. That caused an attitude of seeing *samadhi* as a suppression of thought, or an absence of thought, and more broadly, as an absence of a sense of I-am-ness. You know how golfers can be pretty good golfers, but they develop a quirk that messes up their game? I saw it in a movie about golfers. They get one bad habit and it's really hard to get rid of it. I had developed that same kind of bad habit in my practice.

But my original teacher, the one who got me to sit, the Zen professor, gave me a koan when I left Japan: "Who am I?" He said, "This *samadhi* stuff is great, but you have to go beyond *samadhi*. You have to get *satori*, enlightenment. That's a whole other thing." He said, "Work on the koan, 'Who am I?'" "Well, how do I work on that koan?" "Just turn consciousness back on itself." That was the instruction. So I was trying to suppress my thoughts and get into *samadhi*, but I was also trying to work on "Who am I?" and asking, "Where does thought come from, where does consciousness come from?" I did that for a few years, and things were pretty good, because I had this little edge on life.

Then, probably sometime in the mid-'70s, I was reading and getting stoned all day, and I was alone. I had been staying with my parents, but they were away, so I had the place to myself. I had been alone all day, and I realized, *Oh, I haven't done any sitting today.* I was actually stoned on marijuana, but I thought, *It's getting late, I should probably do my sitting.* So I put down the *zafu* and sat, and the instant I sat down, the koan was there: "Who am I?" Then suddenly there was no boundary to me at all. I was so shocked I actually got up. And there was still no boundary to me. I was walking around, looking at things, and there was no border between me and anything else. But I still had thoughts. Some sort of negative thought came up, and the walls started to laugh at me for having a negative thought. Of course that's a projection, but there was a kind of intimacy between inside and outside. That was just emblematic of what was going on. I thought, *Oh my god, this doesn't have anything to do with whether I'm concentrated or not concentrated. There is just no boundary separating me and what is around me.*

I thought, *This is too good to be true. This isn't going to last.* Then I turned on the TV and I was watching cartoons or something, but it was still there. It was getting late and I thought, *I'm going to wake up tomorrow and it's going to be just a pleasant memory.* But when I woke up the next day it was still there! It didn't go away, and it never went away. It was like the classic sudden *kensho* experience. I was just walking around in this magic world of oneness. I walked around the block a whole week, enjoying this experience. I knew that the tradition is that when you've had an experience like this, you're supposed to go to see a roshi or someone who knows. The only roshi I knew was Maezumi Roshi, the L.A. Zen Center guy. I didn't know him well, but I did know him. I called him up and said, "Something has happened with my practice and I'd like to discuss it with someone who is competent."

I didn't know him that well, but he was a Zen master. I half expected him to say, "You're full of shit, kid, get out of here." I knew I'd had a significant experience, no one was going to convince me otherwise, but I didn't know how he was going to respond. I just wanted to run it by someone. And it was total affirmation, like, "Yep, that's it." He said, "It's just the beginning. This is just the first crack, you're going to have to open it wider, wider, wider. But it's what we mean by first *kensho* experience, and you did good. Don't stop there. Just keep going and going."

So I did. I was practicing on my own and exploring what I had learned. A couple more years went by—I'm not good on the chronology. Then the boyfriend of an ex-semigirlfriend of mine who was living at what was then called Cimarron Zen Center called me. They needed an interpreter for Sasaki Roshi during a *teisho*, and they didn't have one. He knew that I spoke Japanese, so he asked me if I would be willing to be the interpreter. I said yes. That was the first time I encountered Sasaki Roshi. I interpreted for him, and even though I'd had these experiences and had done all my Ph.D. work in Buddhist studies except for the dissertation, I couldn't understand what he was talking about at all. It didn't sound like anything I had ever heard in any other teaching—father and mother, expansion-contraction, you know, positive and negative and zero. It was like, *What is this guy talking about?* I mechanically translated what he said from Japanese into English, but I didn't get it.

I continued to translate for him, but I didn't do *sesshins* with him. After a number of years it started to make sense to me. I realized, *Oh, he's just radically innovative. This is standard enlightenment, but from a very subtle and deep and advanced perspective, with a very creative, innovative paradigm.* I also realized that I still needed a teacher. I never became his *deshi*, his student, officially. He dangled the hook. He wanted me to become one of his monks. I wanted to keep my independence, and he was very kind in that regard. He's let me essentially graze on his Dharma for twenty-five years, without having to commit to being an official student. Which is pretty amazing, actually.

So now I had a roshi, the real thing. That altered my practice in two significant ways. One is that I realized the error in suppressing the sense of self. What you have to do is allow the self to arise and pass away. Sasaki talks about that. He talks about no self and self, constantly—they're both natural—and where the self comes from, etc. He disabused me of that bad habit I had had, of trying to suppress thoughts specifically and self in general. That was a real paradigm shift. I started to love the realizing of the personal self, rather than subtly be averse to it.

Then I started to internalize his paradigm for how consciousness works. To wit: there is zero, but zero is inherently unstable, therefore it polarizes into expansion and contraction. But expansion only knows how to expand and contraction only knows how to contract. Therefore, in the push and pull between them they vibrate space into existence, which is then further vibrated by expansion and contraction until that space is nurtured into a feeling, thinking self, which either realizes, "Oh, I was born in the cleft in between Father and Mother, and I know exactly what to do, which is to give everything I got from Father back to Father and everything I got from Mother back to Mother. I will disappear. I will become Father and Mother. There will be no separation, therefore, between Father and Mother, and they will come back again to zero." Or, the self that does not realize that fixates on itself and suffers, and believes, "I am a thing." That's his essential paradigm, and I began to actually experience it. That became the way that I formulated the practice for myself.

Meanwhile, I had been living in a place called the International Buddhist Meditation Center. It was [led by] Dr. Thich Thien-An, who was a Vietnamese Buddhist monk. It was right down the street from Zen Center of Los Angeles and somewhat north from Cimarron, but still in the Buddhist ghetto in downtown L.A. It was international—they had representatives from all the Buddhist traditions. By this time I was one of the more experienced meditators there, and I was morphing into the role of teacher. People were coming to me for instruction in meditation. I was starting to run classes and so forth. Initially I did Zen. I had people count their breaths, I whacked them with the *keisaku*, maybe even gave them koans (I can't remember). We were chanting the Heart Sutra fast in Japanese, eating with chopsticks, Japanese Zen-style stuff.

There were Vajrayana people there, doing Deity Yoga, with which I was familiar because that was my original ordination, although it wasn't what I was mostly practicing. But there were also vipassana teachers, people teaching mindfulness practices from Southeast Asia. I noticed that they attracted a lot more people than were coming to my East Asian Zen sittings, and they seemed to be getting quick results with people. I started to look into mindfulness, or vipassana practice, and two things struck me. First, of the three major practice traditions—Zen, Tibetan Vajrayana practice, and vipassana or mindfulness—Zen and Vajrayana are highly modified for a specific cultural niche, East Asia in the former case and Indo-Tibetan medieval shamanic culture in the latter. They're culturally specific, whereas vipassana is much less culture-bound. It's a more primitive form—primitive in the sense of early. It's an early form of practice, close to what the Buddha taught and less modified for a specific cultural milieu. Of course it's somewhat modified for South and Southeast Asia, but it's pretty easy to extract vipassana from its cultural background. You don't have to eat with chopsticks or chant fast in Japanese to do the vipassana practice. You can eat with a knife and fork. You don't even have to chant; the scriptures are in English. It's easier to adapt to this tradition.

The other thing that struck me is that vipassana is very systematic. Zen is very intuitive. I by that time had a pretty good background in math and science, and I am drawn to things that are systematic and structured and algorithmic. I thought, *I should look into this*, which led to studying with teachers from various parts of Southeast Asia and South Asia. The upshot is that I took a technique that is called "noting," which is part of one of the Burmese lineages of vipassana practice, the Mahasi lineage, and figured out a way to use it to bring people to the experience of expansion-contraction and zero, rather than using koans. So I've taken Sasaki Roshi's expansion-contraction paradigm, and I've mounted it in the noting technique associated with Theravada Buddhism, and I emphasize a strong ethical paradigm, also based on the Theravada tradition. That's what I now teach. The other thing I discovered was that if you interactively coach a person in real time, they are much more likely to get the practice and understand it and internalize it than if you do things the more traditional way, which is: "Here's the cushion, here's the posture, here's the technique, now go off and do it and we'll talk in a few days." Instead of doing that, I started to sit down with people and micro-interactively guide them and modify the guidance based on what they were experiencing. I'm trying to guide them toward seeing that the nature of consciousness is expanding-contracting space.

In terms of my personal experience there is at least one other watershed. So far I've described *samadhi*, and I described what might be called wisdom. But we haven't talked about behavior change. Objective changes in observable behavior are a hugely important part of this practice. So in terms of how this has influenced my external behavior, I would say that there are probably three areas, the third of which I'm still working on, still struggling with. The first behavior change is that I used to not like to be around people—I would avoid people. As I stated, after having those early experiences of being in *samadhi*, I found that I could be around people. I didn't avoid people anymore, I became a more social being. So that was one change of behavior.

A second change in behavior is that I used a lot of drugs, even after my first *kensho* experience. But then I went to a Goenka retreat, which is in the U Ba Khin lineage of Burmese tradition, where you sweep through the body. As I was sweeping through the body for ten days, I noticed some very slight discomfort in my chest. I didn't really pay that much attention to it, I just noticed it once or twice. At the retreat, the thought occurred to me that it must be the result of all that marijuana smoke I had put in myself. But it was no big deal, I didn't say, "Oh my god, that's awful," or whatever; it was just a little sensation I was aware of. *Oh, there's a little congestion there, it must be the smoke.* On the day I returned from the retreat I didn't seem to have any inclination to smoke marijuana.

Then another day passed, and I thought, *I don't want to do it.* Then about a week passed, and I realized I wasn't going to use drugs anymore. I just didn't want to anymore. It wasn't on again, off again, on the wagon, off the wagon. It wasn't even a conscious decision. It just happened. And I thought, *Holy shit, this stuff really works.* Some part of my body, the part that was enjoying getting high, talked to another part of my body, the part that was being traumatized, and they decided on their own, without me knowing, that we weren't going to do this anymore. It was like plastic surgery had been done on my psyche and my soul, without my even knowing about it. That was an effortless, permanent behavior change. I'd had a ten-year run with marijuana, which just stopped dead. That was a behavior change.

But the behavior issue I'm still struggling with, the one I actually went to a psychiatrist about, for eighteen months—not that long ago—is that I'd always been a perennial procrastinator. It sounds funny, but actually it has messed up my life. It's serious. I could go into the gory details. Let's just put it this way: every one of my peers has written several significant books. But I haven't, and my perennial procrastination is the reason. It interferes with my ability to help people. It's getting better, but I needed external support— a combination of the practice plus the psychiatrist—for behavior modification. I came to realize that the procrastination is driven by five sensory phenomena. If I can keep track of them and penetrate them with mindfulness, with concentration, clarity, and equanimity, then I can change the behavior. But if I lose track of them then I become subject to the avoidance behavior.

I call them the five Rs—this was an insight that allowed me to begin to change the behavior that had been in my life for so long. They are all words or phrases that end in R. Like the three Rs are reading, writing and 'rithmetic, well, this is the five Rs. It's not alliterative, it's rhyme—they all end in R. The first one is "fear," by which I mean the body sensation of fear. The second is "cheer," by which I mean the joy/interest flavor in my body. The third is "tear," a sudden hint of sadness around my eyes and face. Those are the three bodily flavors. Fear and tear are the sensations I avoid if I procrastinate. Cheer, or interest, is the reward that I get if I procrastinate. I can surf the Internet or go to the library and have a great time. So fear, tear, and cheer are emotional flavors in my body that seem to control my behavior, unless I can detect and have equanimity with them, in which case they don't.

Then there's a physical sensation, a nonemotional sensation, of poor coordination that arises in my body. If I try to change a behavior, I lose my balance a little bit. I'm wobbly. I'm disoriented (physically, not intellectually or emotionally). I call that "can't steer." I've talked about this in public, and other people who have tried behavior change have come to me and said, yes, they get the same thing. You don't know whether to turn right or turn left. Your body is poorly coordinated. My hypothesis is that it's related to the cerebellum, which not only affects balance but also seems to be where behavior patterns are stored. That's just a crazy conjecture, but anyway, in the emotional body there's fear, tear, and cheer, which is an internal reward-and-punishment system that controls the robot. On the physical level in the body there's this "can't steer" disorientation—can't quite control my body kind of thing.

Then in the mind there is the fifth R, which is "blear." When I resist the procrastination and try to do "the right thing," I often get confused and stupid, and can't think straight. So I discovered that there are these five sensory phenomena, three in the emotional body, one in the physical body, and one in the mind: fear, tear, cheer, can't steer, and blear. They seem to be able to control me, the robot, unless I can keep them distinct in awareness and have equanimity with them—all five simultaneously! If I can simultaneously detect and sensorily accept all five at once, then they no longer control me and I can overcome my tendency to procrastination. But if I lose track of even one or can't sensorily accept even one, then they control me like a robot and I give in to my lifelong habit of procrastination. So that's my model for behavior change; it has allowed me to actually get better. But I still need the external support. That's why I believe, as many modern Western teachers do, that sometimes formal practice alone may not be enough. Some people may need a behaviorally oriented accountability and support structure in the form of a counselor, a sponsor, or a therapist. And that brings us to the end of the story. I think that covers all the high points of my last forty-five years—at least with regard to practice breakthroughs.

BOYLE: Has your *samadhi* changed, deepened, over the last twenty years?

SHINZEN: Oh yes, the *samadhi* continues to get deeper and deeper. But now the *samadhi* is sort of indistinguishable from the wisdom. I use a different model now. If we take *samadhi* to mean concentration, I now use a model where I look upon the mindfulness as having three dimensions: concentration, sensory clarity, and equanimity. If I have enough concentration, sensory clarity, and equanimity, then my experience is the flow of expansion/contraction and zero. When I don't, then my experience is that of a fixated self encapsulated in rigid time and space. So I would say that there is absolute *samadhi*—that's zero. Absolute *samadhi*, zero, doesn't last very long, but I'm aware of it hundreds, probably thousands of times during the day. And each time, I'm aware that myself and the surrounding scene are born from and return to it. In between those moments of absolute *samadhi*, I'm aware of relative *samadhi*, which just means enjoying a concentrated state.

BOYLE: And the *kensho*, where you no longer feel the distinction between your self and everything around you, that informs the *samadhi*?

SHINZEN: Yes, they all inform one another.

BOYLE: That's been the way you live, for some while now? It's not something you work on, like you work on the procrastination. It's something that is there.

SHINZEN: The oneness? The no-boundary thing?

BOYLE: The no-boundary and the *samadhi* thing, that cluster, that way of being.

SHINZEN: Yes, that's there whether I like it or not. I don't want it at times.

BOYLE: That's what I mean. It has become a permanent state. You don't get up in the morning and sit and say, "I want to get back into this."

SHINZEN: When I say "no boundaries"—you know, my concentration wavers, like anybody else's. The difference is that I don't care how concentrated I am. It makes no difference to me whatsoever. Well, to be honest, I probably have a little preference for the concentrated state, but in the end, that's just a state of attention. But the "no boundary" thing—that never goes away. It can't go away—because the boundary was never there to begin with. Something that was never there isn't going to come back. [Laughs]

2
Interview with John Tarrant

John Tarrant now directs the Pacific Zen Institute, which is devoted to teaching koans in new and accessible ways. His writings include Bring Me the Rhinoceros: And Other Zen Koans That Will Save Your Life; The Light Inside the Dark: Zen, Soul, and the Spiritual Life; *and* Zenosaurus: An Online Course in Koans. *The interview took place at his home near Santa Rosa, California on May 11, 2009. Anne Cooper participated.*

BOYLE: When I began this project, I thought the mental activity would interfere with, maybe overwhelm, my *samadhi* practice. But as things have turned out, I've been learning so much that actually contributes to my practice. I'm not just getting a path story; I'm actually being affected by it, learning from it. So I approach the interviews prepared to learn on more than one level.

TARRANT: Well, what you're touching on there fits one of my theories about how the Dharma grows in our culture. It grows through conversations. It doesn't only grow by doing martial arts-style practice, where you just deeply concentrate. That's fine and good and dandy, but the Dharma is also held socially. Human beings are social creatures, and even something as introverted as this practice is held by collaborative groups of people. One of my models would be, maybe, the old Tibetan universities, but also the early European universities like the University of Paris, or Milan, where people would come together and start gradually trying to talk about reality with very poor tools, and then experimenting with methods, empirically. In Buddhism in general, and in Zen, I think there is always that intent to be empirical and then see what you have discovered and try to talk about it.

One of the primary things that is probably pretty clear from my writing is that there is both the long arc of a practice that saturates you and stains you, that dyes you through in various ways, but also the slice through time and space now, in which everybody has the capacity for deep understanding at this moment, not in some future time when they have done years of practice and held their mouths the right way. As you talk to people your own practice changes, would be one of the principles that I'm trying to work with. In the mission statement for our organization I put, "Conversation." This covers meditation, koans, conversation, inquiry, and the arts—the way I see it, these are all interacting ways to cover the same core things.

COOPER: Could you talk a bit about the role of koans in your personal practice?

TARRANT: Well, autobiography is just another form of fiction, so I can tell this in different ways, according to how I remember it. But that question about koans is a good way to go in. I was drawn to Zen through the Chinese and Japanese poets—particularly the Chinese poets. When I came across koans, they were dazzling to me. I was in Australia, and the only meditation training available at that time was . . . there wasn't any, actually. Hatha yoga was happening, and there was an intellectual backwash from the British interest in primitive Buddhism.

So I read a few things. There wasn't any Zen. Eventually a few Tibetan teachers came through, and I studied with them. But koans were interesting to me, so I started working with koans, myself. I had to invent the wheel, and I made all the mistakes you make, but I'm not sure that was a bad thing, although it was slow. I just knew that I didn't have any guidance. I also knew from my understanding of how art works, from poetry, that it seemed like the Chinese masters were saying that guidance wasn't necessarily going to help anyway. So why not have a whack at it?

I started working with particular koans, mainly the koans in the Japanese Rinzai line. There were particular koans that were traditionally given to someone as a first koan, called Dharmakaya koans—introductory koans, like, "Q: Does a dog have buddha nature? A: No!" would be a classic one, and "The sound of one hand." I don't know whether I got anywhere or not from doing that. I think I did. I had a fairly intense life in the outer world—I was a professional fisherman, and then later on I was a lobbyist for aboriginal land rights and things like that. This practice felt like a way to have a kind of steadiness inside everything else I was doing. So I was very interested in meditation in action.

BOYLE: So were you doing sitting meditation?

TARRANT: Yeah, yeah, I sat every day. But I was very aware that it wasn't about sitting or standing. I think of sitting meditation now as a sort of emblematic moment, or paradigmatic moment, in which you get to fully experience what it is to be alive, to get the full presence of foreground and background in being human. Maybe it's a little easier to notice that when you sit, but it's not intrinsic to sitting or not sitting. At the moment I'm quite interested in people who have clear meditation-in-action experiences, like surgeons. . . .

So yes, I got in through the poets, and koan study, because koan work seemed to be making the sort of nonlinear moves that made sense to me. I'd studied Western philosophy with some intensity and burned myself out on it, really. It felt like an incredible amount of brilliance. And either I wasn't understanding it correctly, which was possible, or the brilliance just made my experience of life thinner rather than richer. First I thought, *Maybe there's something wrong with me*, which was quite likely, but the more I went to koan work, then it was the other way—the richer my experience and my life became. So I said, "Oh, I'll go that way." That's how I got into it. I was working in politics, this funny world that was happening at that time. I was interested in aboriginal land rights. At the same time I was going back to university to try to complete a degree, at the National University of Australia. So I was lobbying, and intermittently appearing at the university, and meditating. I did a lot of aikido at that time too. It was somewhat interesting. But the meditation became more interesting, ultimately. I was more interested in the aikido as a transformation of mind practice than as a martial art. I was interested in what it did to my mind.

COOPER: You were college age at this time?

TARRANT: No, my biography, which is not so relevant to this, is that I accidentally graduated from high school a year early, and didn't know what to do. It hadn't occurred to me, so I immediately enrolled in the nearest university, which was the University of Tasmania, just to get out of high school. Then it was Vietnam and the draft, and I sort of had this dread about all that. I grew up in a culture where all the young men go off to fight. I wanted to be able to do that, but I kept investigating Vietnam and finding out I just couldn't bring myself to do it. I was hoping I could find this was a good war, but it was not. I thought, *Oh no.* So I got kind of pissed off with Vietnam, and I opposed the draft. I dropped out of college. In a way that was interesting—it put my life on a completely different course from what I would have been expected to be—an attorney or doctor, I don't know. I also realized that I didn't want to spend the rest of my life on the fishing fleets or things like that. I must have been about twenty-five, twenty-six then.

BOYLE: You went to South Asia then?

TARRANT: No, no, I never went to Asia. I made a couple of strategic decisions about what I wouldn't do. Everybody in Australia in those days went to London. I didn't want to do that, I wanted to go to America. Michael Ondaatje said a great thing when he came from Sri Lanka to London, and then from London to North America. He said that in London he could have been a good poet, but he couldn't really have been a good novelist. When he came to North America he was able to think things he couldn't think in Britain. It wasn't that he was aware that he couldn't. It was just that the chaos and the openness in the United States actually makes for intellectual possibilities, he felt.

And it might be true that if you come out of a rather disciplined, British colonial education system and then get opened out, maybe the two things together will fit well. Anyway, it was clear to me that I wanted to come to the United States. I didn't want to go to Japan. Also, as far as studying Zen, I had understood from working and studying with aborigines and then meeting the Tibetans—I really understood that people so much want to teach you their culture. They can't sort out what's culture and what's transformation of mind and spirituality. They can't tell the difference because it's them, the way I can't tell the difference between what those things are in me. I just knew that I'd be a really bad fit with Japanese teachers. I knew that I didn't want to spend three years sweeping a temple. Not because I was too good for that, but I'd done so much of that. I'd worked in the mines. I judged that it would not have been an initiating experience for me; it would have bored me.

Also, Australian culture is extremely collaborative. "Collaborative" isn't quite right, but extremely allergic to hierarchy. It wasn't because I had a big authority problem so much, but the ways I learned would not be helped by having people telling me what to do in the Confucian sense. I wanted a different kind of guidance. I wanted a vessel in which I could learn, rather than to have somebody saying, "You need to sweep the garden, that's how you learn." I'm not sure I was right, but that's what I believed at the time. So I ended up coming to the United States instead of Japan.

The first koans I did with Seung Sahn, the Korean teacher. I had one of those deep experiences with him. He used to have these funny little places all over the East Coast. I just went and sat a few short days of *sesshin* with him, somewhere on Long Island. Michael Katz, the book agent, who is one of my close friends, had exactly the same experience with Seung Sahn. You'd walk into an interview with him. He'd ask your name, and then he'd say, "Who are you really?" something like that. Then he'd start hitting you with a stick, but he'd hit you in slow motion so you knew exactly how long you had to answer. You either liked or hated that method. I loved it. So immediately I started yelling at him. Something just started coming out of me. I had a real experience of the critical kindness of meditation. I started to be able to answer koans.

That was where everything started to break open and shift for me. Some-body had gotten a martial arts dojo on Long Island. This wasn't that long ago, like the late '70s. There were photos of people kicking and hitting, chopping boards with their hands and things like that. It was really funny. It was a gray, concrete brick place, with a washing machine. And the guy whose martial arts dojo it was, who lent it to Seung Sahn, did not meditate. His wife wasn't that thrilled about it. She'd walk through with young kids to run the washing machine, which was in the basement. It was sweet, and chaotic. I was sitting there, and the Korean pads were really thin and my knees were hurting and it was November and it was cold, and I realized, *This is great.* And everything started to open up for me. It was perfect now.

I realized that I understood the koans he was asking me. He suggested I travel with him, but I thought—again, I thought he was a great teacher—but I actually wanted to learn the system. I had already connected with Robert Aitken, on the way over. I thought Robert Aitken wasn't interested in Zen in the way I was, in the possibilities of transformation. He was more of a scholar. But he had kept meticulous notes from his teachers, and so I wanted to find out about the classical spine of the tradition handed down in the Japanese line. I'm not sure if this was a good decision, but it was the one I made.

Seung Sahn wasn't at all interested in that. He was making his own koans, which was great, and he had had a big awakening. He was trying to jump people into his awakening all the time. It was like what I do, actually. That was interesting, and good, but I wanted something else. When I really wanted to understand English poetry, I learned Anglo-Saxon. I wanted to do something like that, something that wasn't directly relevant—men-tally I just work that way. I want to learn: here's what Hakuin said about it and here's what Koun Yamada said—that sort of thing. Aitken had all this in his notes. He was struggling along in a fairly humble way, admitting he didn't understand koans very well. But he was well read. I felt I could understood what the koan masters were on about, but I thought if koans were to survive in our culture, I wanted to know that level of the oral tradition. It was like getting little sponge dinosaurs and putting them in the water and having them expand.

There's a typical thing that's not in most narratives—the tension between mentors and students. In the classical Japanese or Chinese narratives, the Confucian system is always present. The actuality in America is that mentors and students are always wrestling in universities and Zen centers and other places of learning. Students are always talking with teachers as co-explorers, because that's how our culture does things. It's not Confucian. I hate to say Oedipus, but there's an intrinsic conflict in mentoring in our culture. There's an intrinsic instability about leadership. We admire the leader and then we try to assassinate him, and things like that. So that would be part of it too.

My first training was with some lovely Tibetan teachers who very much had the guru model. I liked them a lot; I liked a guy called Lama Yeshe— he's famous. He had a sidekick who was the bad cop in the deal, Zopa Rinpoche. He's still alive. Lama Yeshe everybody adored. He was a very easy person to connect with and so on. But the Tibetan system was that you identify with your teacher so much that you get out of all your trips that way. I think that's easier to do with a teacher who is of another culture and therefore intrinsically unknown to you in a fundamental way. But I just knew I didn't want to go that Tibetan route, learning Tibetan culture, learning the language and deference forms, and all that. And it would have been the same with the Japanese.

So I went to study with Aitken. I was the first person to finish koan study with Aitken, and so there was a certain amount of feeling around with the tradition he'd received from his primary teacher, Koun Yamada. And Yamada used to supervise Aitken's people. Yamada was one of that generation who'd had a painful experience during the war in Japan and tried to resolve his existential issues through very deep meditation and having an awakening experience. I liked him a lot. He was the first person who told me I should teach. Something I tried to ignore at the time.

COOPER: Can you talk a little bit about awakening experiences through koans, and your own personal experiences?

TARRANT: Well, two things happened. One was, I had had experiences as a child in which I was one with things. "One with" is a poor way to put it, but, you know, where you get the figure-ground reversal: what you thought was foreground is not so important and what seemed like background comes forward. You and the trees and the people are not different. I had had that sort of experience as a child, and having asked people, I think that's not uncommon. And that's one of my interests, to record that kind of experience. Then I realized that I wasn't in touch with that anymore, that I was outside of life in some way. I realized that the problem was that I had too many thoughts, and I was believing my thoughts too much—that my thoughts were running me.

At first I just tried to get rid of the thoughts, regardless of content, and then later on I realized there was an issue of the content of thoughts. When people ask, What's the place of emotions in Buddhism?, that issue comes up. How much should you be sad when someone dies? So that is the sort of question Buddhists start asking themselves. At first I realized that the thoughts were just there, even if they were stopping me from experiencing things, because my mind was too full. And then later on I realized, *Oh, it's the identification with the thoughts, not just the thought that's there.* We think we are our thoughts. We define our consciousness by what we are thinking, and think it's us.

At first, anyway, I had the idea of getting rid of my thoughts. I played sports when I was a kid, and I knew about those moments when you don't have thoughts, when you're free, you're moving, in the Tao. And I also had a mystical experience of realizing that I was just part of the universe, the same as the universe. I think what happens is that you just start noticing it. Things like, *Oh, there's not a problem.* You're just walking around, meditating or doing anything. Everything just feels right.

You get these little moments of reality, moments of clarity. At first I thought, *Oh, I've got to grab that.* And then I realized that didn't work. Grabbing fills your mind with the grasping, so you don't have the moment of clarity anymore. That's pretty standard stuff. Everybody's noticed that one. With Seung Sahn, I remember sitting there meditating and it was boring and interminable, in this cold place. There was no romance, no ancient museum, no *Masterpiece Theatre* of Asia, the way temples attract young people. But suddenly it was perfect. I'm looking at concrete blocks all day. I'd rather be looking at trees. But it was great. I had that freedom, there wasn't a problem. *Everything I need is here now.*

That's putting more of an "I" into it than there was. It's just the perfection. I think the Sanskrit word is "Tathagata," which I relate to the "thusness" of things, the thusness of one's own being. Just the completeness of form itself. And with that I realized immediately that the koan was linked to this part of things. Later on I developed the understanding that even if you're not thinking about the koan, if you've taken on a great koan, then whatever is happening to you is somehow in the field of that koan. I thought that was a rule of thumb. You think your interaction with a highway patrolman is not to do with your koan, but it is. That was a much later thing, after I started teaching and observing people. People would come in and say, "Oh, you know, I'm not having anything to do with my koan." I'd say, "Well, what's happening?" They'd say, "Well, I'm just really happy all the time, but I'm just not doing my koan." Or, "My whole life is falling apart." "Well, what koan are you working on?" "Oh, the one about the cart where the wheels and the axles fall off the cart." That's what emptiness is, a disassembly of the structures that aren't working for you. They fall off.

Then, after Seung Sahn, I was with Bob Aitken. His system was different from Seung Sahn's system. There are various classical koan lines. Some are like Seung Sahn, which was more forceful, and others are careful and scholarly: "This person said this, another person said that." Aitken came down through that line.

His koan questions were interesting to me, so I thought I would just hang out with them. I noticed the standard phenomena, such as most people get. I felt like, *Oh, I'm right there, I'm at the gate, I need to step through.* Then that thought, *need to step through*, moved me away. Or, *It's like I'm on top of a cliff, I need to jump off.* Then I couldn't. And I realized I was afraid. And as soon as I noticed that I was afraid, I wasn't.

Aitken's teacher, Koun Yamada, came out of the Harada-Yasutani line. He had originally been in the Rinzai line. Then he was with Harada and had his big awakening experience there. Yamada definitely had a concentration on the big *kensho* model, and was pushing that. Then I realized that it wasn't an accurate model to the extent that it was linear. I was for having a big experience, but it wasn't a linear process for me. I was in a very, very deep place in a retreat once and my mind got incredibly busy. In previous retreats I had found that to be a problem, but this time I just found it funny. That's when everything stopped, and I woke up and could see through the koans. I started just laughing. Then everything seemed filled with light, and all the people seemed wonderful. That went on—the laughter went on for about six months or so. So then I just knew that I could answer any koan questions.

I realized I hadn't known why the questions had been set up. But I felt very grateful to the people who originated these koans that had been handed down to us. Even poorly handed down, they were a gift. Even if you just read them in a book, or if you heard them from someone who didn't understand them but trusted them and was willing to work with you, then sooner or later they might capture you. That was what essentially happened with me. So I was tremendously grateful for that. And then after that I had various experiences from time to time. "Last week I didn't understand it as well, but this week is great." But really we are just falling into what's here, all the time.

BOYLE: You referred one time to what you might call your major awakening. Was it incremental like that, or could you . . . ?

TARRANT: Well, I remember looking at lightning when I was really young, and then as a teenager I remembered it, and I thought, *I wonder why I remember that?* Then I thought, *Oh, that's in a way how I've always experienced reality, as sort of a flash that shifts.* So in some fundamental way, that's why I like the systems that show you things changing in jumps, rather than a slow progression. As a child I had various experiences like that. I suppose that with Seung Sahn I felt like I got the *prajna.* And then with Aitken, I got some other things.

I think having a lot of questions, a curriculum, allows you to embody what you have discovered. I found that useful. If you're interested in transforming your mind, then you have to use a pedagogy. My story about that was that we could be more hip about pedagogy—about how there are individual differences. Having become a teacher and having watched people come from other systems, and having seen the results of those systems, I think that the sort of "beat yourself to death through the koan" model, which was one of the Japanese koan systems that Harada definitely pushed, is not very effective. I mean, there were a few people who discovered how to hack the system, as I did. But most Westerners take that system as rejecting their experience, over and over again, as telling them, "You're doing it wrong." I don't think that's how the Japanese take it. The Japanese say, "You're lazy," "You're not trying hard," to each other. Then they feel, *Oh, he loves me, he cares about me.* Whereas Westerners think, *Oh, I'm doing it wrong.* They get caught identifying with that thought.

I realized it was more valuable to get hints from teachers and then try things for myself. The teachers essentially were coaches, and I had to make the meditation my own, work out all that was going on with me. It was like the process of discovery in writing poetry or fiction. I found this approach freeing, and connected to the depths. If you notice something when you're at depth, then it's a strange and interesting thing. And what you're noticing is reality. Anything that comes up, whether it's the moon or a feeling or a thought or a person, is reality, perceived without walls in the mind.

BOYLE: To pick up a thread there, something that was particularly resonant with me in your writings had to do with relaxing. Because after all these years, I just six months to a year ago had an experience where I suddenly relaxed so dramatically that it was like dropping down to a sub-basement. I was so much more grounded than ever before, and underneath the reality that was swirling around up above, and the key to that was to just be in a more deeply relaxed state than I'd ever experienced before. I didn't care about making things happen. I'd been such a doer. What you said about relaxing was tremendously helpful for me. Can you follow that thread back? When were you first aware that relaxing was a key thing?

TARRANT: Well, let's do a dialogue about that, because it's happening now, it's here in the room. And if it's here in the room, then it's not necessarily located in one of us, it's just what it is to be human. So then the idea that *Oh, I'm a separate person who's doing these clever techniques to get to a certain goal* becomes funny. One of the clues for me was something one of the old, old teachers said. I think it was Hsiang-yen, you know, the hang-from-the-branch-by-your-teeth guy. He had a big awakening experience. He couldn't understand his koan, and he'd given it up to be strictly a gardener. Then a stone hit the bamboo and went *tock*. He said, "Oh, one *tock* and I've forgotten all I knew." Then he came back and he was studying with Guishan and Yangshan, who wasn't convinced. Yangshan said, "Well, you've got something there, but I don't know." And Hsiangyen said, "Well, if you don't believe me, ask the newest person who just stepped into the meditation hall." And that convinced Yangshan.

And I thought, *Oh, that's true, isn't it?* The dog has buddha nature. Everybody really has it, and they don't have it at some abstract time, in the future. It's not a potential to actually have it. It's here in the room now. At first I thought it was a matter of, Oh, how much do you want to notice that? In another way, it's What do you call noticing? It's really here. Everything you're doing is an expression of the flowers of emptiness. So it's happening now, and it can't not be happening.

So then the striving. . . . It's also happening when we're striving. There's a great koan about that. It says, "People go to wild places to search for their true nature. Where is your true nature?" Even when you're out there striving, where is it? Obviously it's right there with you. We don't quite look— I suppose I'd say we don't quite look under our feet, so we're looking out there, when it's here. Meditation is a little sample of not looking at, not chasing it out there.

BOYLE: So this was becoming clear to you from the beginning?

TARRANT: I think of the moment when I just kept trying to get my mind to be perfectly still and clear and spacious. I felt I was going along pretty well, in the right way. And my mind went *bang*—emotions, thoughts, stories, advertising jingles, popular songs. It was an incredible flood, and I realized it wasn't a matter of a linear manipulation. If you can become one with the universe, you've got to stop trying to manipulate the universe. You just can't do those things that you once thought worked. You know, I told you about facing those concrete walls at Seung Sahn's, and realizing, *Oh, there's nothing wrong with this.* But then there were other moments when I thought, *Oh, I've got to jump off the cliff in meditation, I've got to go deeper.* That assumes that you're not there, that you're not really deep. To think that is to miss your depth.

BOYLE: You mean not to not try, but just be in a place where things begin happening?

TARRANT: Yeah, yeah, I think of that thing in the *Rhinoceros* book I wrote about my mom. My mom was good at being her. It was easy for me to get cubist with my mother. She had a talent for producing that in people, disassembling their adjustment to the situation. And then I realized that I didn't have to manipulate her, or manipulate my own mind either. It was just a matter of taking what I had already discovered to an area where it hadn't necessarily occurred to me to go before.

So the way I'm seeing it, the koan is always there with you. You may just not have noticed that it is. So it's a matter of meeting the koan. Naturally then, you're just going to be more relaxed. You're going to think, *Oh, whatever it is, it's going on. This person's furious with me, or this person wants this from me, or this person*—whatever it is. Or, *I want this from me.* I think one of the big things in Zen is stopping the manipulation of others, trying to impress them or trying to get them to be or feel a certain way. And also then to stop trying to manipulate oneself to feel a certain way, to think a certain way, to be a certain way, or turn into a certain kind of animal.

BOYLE: One final thing I wanted to ask was—this is what people like me wonder about people like you, or other established, long-run teachers. . . .

TARRANT: Established long-run teachers are just, like, all different. It's very hard to assess somebody else's enlightenment, and it's not very interesting to do. Being an established long-term teacher and two dollars will get you stamps. It's like, it's not an interesting thing to walk around with a jacket on. So maybe it's not interesting to walk around with a jacket on that says, "I'm not an established long-term teacher," and think, "I'm not a teacher, I'm not enlightened, I'm not at that level." I mean that's a dull jacket.

BOYLE: What is life like for you now compared with before you left Australia?

TARRANT: Well, I had so much going on in my mind then. The simplest way to put it is, I was caught. I would have moments of freedom, and huge amounts of nonfreedom. One easy way to describe "being present" is in terms of the interior decoration model. It's like you're in prison when you're trying to just paint the walls, rather than kick them down. Even if you're trying to kick down the walls, you're still in prison. When you're free, you can't find any walls. One way to explain what being in prison is like is believing things. It's living according to a map instead of according to what is continually forming and coming. So I think I spend a lot less time living from my maps.

BOYLE: But you do find yourself living from your maps occasionally?

TARRANT: Well, that's an interesting question. Maybe you could help answer that, collaboratively, because it's the sort of thing that we talk about. I have a group of people who work on koans. We think about these things. I think that stories, narrative fictions, just form themselves. Suddenly they're there. And then you notice, *Oh, I'm expecting this person to meet my friend.* Or, *I'm expecting . . .* I had a narrative going when my nephew [who was visiting Tarrant at the time of the interview] left the house, which said that there would be nobody in the house—but now there are two people in the house [Boyle and Cooper], because I hadn't looked at my calendar. I had forgotten because I had just gotten off a plane. And that's fine. So it's not a matter of whether there's a story structure, it's whether you stick to the story when it becomes a problem. Even that's not a problem, but it can feel like a problem. Like, *Oh, this is totally different from what I thought the map was.* Is it empirical, can you just dance with the music that's playing rather than with the music you thought would be playing? I think it's like that.

BOYLE: But that's what it's like for you? For me, dealing with the map and then being present is an ongoing effort. It's not something that I just . . .

TARRANT: I think that partly it's a matter of just observing. Any moment of freedom is all of freedom, right? So if you have a moment of freedom and you really observe it closely, you find that you are not unfree anywhere in it. So what's the difference between you and Buddha at that moment? Well, it's hard to find. That you're thinking about the hamburger and Buddha was thinking about the mayo, or something. So there's no real difference. Then any moment of unfreedom is just another way of not relaxing, not letting go of the story. You were impatient, or you just thought that plans shouldn't have been laid, or something like that. And either we find what we are thinking uninteresting and let go of it—big deal—or we're prepared to suffer in the service of it. In the second case we have a whole story about *This is a bad place, I want to get to somewhere else. I want to get there on time. I want to get some sleep to do the radio interview the next morning.*

It's more fun to think, *Oh, fortunately the plane's late.* That gets into darker stuff, like *Fortunately I've got cancer.* I mean, not darker, but more intense stuff, and I like the way that koans don't flinch from the hard bits. A person I know just died. That's it too, what we came here for, the life we wanted. You have to relax into that too. If somebody's dying, they probably don't want somebody panicking. They probably want somebody who is just accompanying them, with nothing to do. Relaxation's the only sane response. But it also applies to oneself. If something's happening that you're having a hard time with, then if you relax into that, you might not remember that it is hard. The people who invented the koan system did do difficult situations. They didn't pretend they weren't difficult. There wasn't that primeval Buddhist fantasy of wandering around the forests of India picking fruit. It was more like, "No, you've got to deal with the whole fact of burning cities." Especially when we're still dealing with this in the world today, stopping the generals from going to war, and so on. So there's some way we've got to be at ease in the middle of it, because it's not going to slow down, settle down. The world is always going to be on fire. We've somehow got to be at ease with it. That way, I think, when we're relaxed, we're much more likely to make sane decisions.

It's also not just a matter of being indifferent. The Tibetans have a notion in which there's the narrow vehicle, the fundamental vehicle, which is guarding the mind and doing right, which you find in the vipassana tradition. Then you have the Mahayana, which has more of a sense of participation and doing things for others and participation in the world. You're not trying to get away from the world because others are there and need assistance. The fundamental goal of the Theravada tradition is cessation—there's nothing appearing. The Mahayana goal is more one of awakening to participation. If someone's hungry, we want to feed them—a natural human thing to do. Then the Tibetans have their next step up. They call it the Vajrayana, the Indestructible Way, the tantra, the level above. The level at which one realizes more deeply not just the emptiness of things but the fundamental way in which one *is* things. Things like your hand, the tree, or you, something like that. One realizes that even the delusion itself is true nature, buddha nature. Some of my Tibetan friends say, "Oh, what you guys are doing is Vajrayana Zen." They mean that in Zen, the koans would be the equivalent of the Vajrayana.

The big thing I didn't say, I suppose, that I should say, is I actually wanted clarity, but I found there was a warmth and a heart quality in the koan tradition. Koan traditions often attract young men who have a martial temperament. So you have yelling and breaking sticks over other people's backs and things like that. You find that in the tradition, and sometimes in temples today. But the thing I found was just the warmth and the loving quality of my experience of the universe. We're not here for very long, and it's beautiful. And maybe we can look after each other. "After each other" may be putting it too strongly, but maybe we can be generous with each other, enjoy each other. There's a fundamental vastness and eternity about that experience of the kindness of the universe. It's not just a personal feeling, though I have nothing against personal feeling.

But you know, it's hard to teach, because everybody's got to discover it. The things you say might lead people in the wrong direction. People hear you say, "Sit still," and everybody then breaks their knees. Or you say, "Try to keep your mind quiet," and their minds are busy keeping themselves quiet. Or you say, "Relax," and people start trying to do it. It's tricky to coach. That's why I do think conversations are important. I hold my koan seminars as conversations.

I will say one more thing. There is a classical spine to the koan work. In the Rinzai line, for example, the best answers were passed down. This was taken in the Western tradition to mean there is a right answer to a koan. I didn't experience it that way. I experienced an elegance—perhaps in the way mathematicians talk about beauty. It's really just another human system, although an intelligent one that I've certainly committed a great deal of my life to. Particularly if someone looks like they're going to be a teacher, I try to get people to experience the classical possibility in the koan. Hakuin, and people who followed him, worked out responses to koans. They said, "Well, this is probably the best one for this koan." They wanted the student to get this, you know. There's a big point here that the student might get with this koan. I'll say, "You have to embody a koan. When you're responding to a koan, it's got to be somehow physically present to you."

I've met a lot of people who just hit their head against their koan and were actually saying they had a very interesting engagement and their lives were transforming, but they were not necessarily seeing it quite like Hakuin did. It's a little like best practices in medicine. Best practices change. Nobody uses leeches very much anymore. In fact, now people use antibiotics a lot less, if they can. Then I realized that another parallel process started to happen, in which the koan would grip somebody's life. This has a vast effect that is much different from some answer that they'd given in the interview room. I think that would be the big division in koan work now. If you just want the Hakuin answers, people can sort of get to them after a while—like Sudoku. It may be a bit of a shift to get to them, but it's not always a big change. Letting yourself be exposed to a big koan, you take the ride, letting the koan have you, and letting life shock and surprise you. You truly meet the possibilities in life. While someone's doing that, their answers to traditional questions may seem incoherent and might actually be incoherent. But they might be in the right place. I've tried to really open out the koan work, so that there's the possibility of changing your life, now, in the koan.

So when I have a koan seminar, people talk about a koan. They nibble away. The Japanese system is tight and secret, perhaps because it's an island culture. We're not. I've found that just learning the classical spine comes easily, because it's not very hard. People used to go for years and have a tiny little awakening. Then they worked and worked to get it bigger. Now people can have an awakening much more quickly. What do you call an awakening? It's just a matter of, can you step into reality? That's why I found koans worth staying with, just as a good poem, a good piece of music might change your life today.

Rhino was written as a sort of calling card for what koan work might become in our culture. It can change the moves you make in your life because the koan teaches you to trust the moves you make. The koan stories, the traditional classical stories, are just like ours. They're full of, "Somebody did something for a while, gave up, then it came and got her."

That would be another process we're in now. All the metaphors were male (well, not all of them, but 98 percent of the metaphors were male), and that's gone. "You must 'penetrate' the koan," and things like that. What if you just *receive* the koan? We know there are enlightened women, but their history is not as well known.

3
Interview with Ken McLeod

Ken McLeod's most recent book is Reflections on Silver River. *The interview took place at my home in Albuquerque, New Mexico, on August 15, 2009. Zenshin Michael Haederle participated.*

BOYLE: Can you tell us how you got started with Buddhism?

MCLEOD: I was at university in the 1960s in Canada. Early on in high school I had a definite interest in trying to find some depth in Christianity, and read things like [John A. T. Robinson's] *Honest to God*, a bit of Paul Tillich, and a few others—Whitehead, for example—but it didn't really lead me anywhere. Then at university—the University of Waterloo—I dropped all of that. Around the third year I began to look into Buddhism and other Eastern religions a bit, but it was very difficult to find much stuff in those days. I did happen across D. T. Suzuki's *Essays in Mahayana Buddhism* and Zen. I think I may have come across [Philip Kapleau's] *Three Pillars of Zen*—I'm not sure.

I was engaged to be married, and I was fairly active in the New Left, there in Waterloo. I received a scholarship to do a Ph.D. in mathematics, in England. My fiancée said (and I should have taken this as a warning sign), "While you're getting your Ph.D., do you mind if I cycle around the continent?" I thought that was kind of a cool idea, so I ended up trashing the scholarship. One thing led to another, and we ended up in Tehran, where I had hepatitis A. We thought, *What the hell are we doing?* We decided we would go to India and learn something about meditation and then find our way back to Canada. Someone gave us the name of a Buddhist mission outside Delhi, and when we got there a Dutch nun, a Buddhist nun, gave us the name of Kalu Rinpoche in the West Bengal-Darjeeling area. So we went to see Kalu Rinpoche. We'd done a little bit of reading on the way, but we didn't know very much about Tibetan Buddhism. Somehow we were sufficiently impressed with Rinpoche's presence that we stayed, and just became progressively more involved. I learned Tibetan. That was 1970.

HAEDERLE: What was it like when you first encountered Kalu Rinpoche?

MCLEOD: Well, he had a monastery a few miles outside of Darjeeling, outside a small town called Sonada. He had an afternoon class for Westerners. Westerners rented places around, and practiced and showed up for teaching. That's what we did. I think that what Rinpoche said then basically sums it up. He said, "Now you've taken refuge, I'm your father. Now learn Tibetan." That's totally congruent with the family model of Indo-Tibetan Buddhism. He becomes your spiritual father, you move into a spiritual family, you move out of your birth family, and that's it.

BOYLE: So the first important period was when you met Kalu Rinpoche and stayed there for nine months, learning Tibetan and studying with him. What about him made you want to immerse your life in this? Why would you take refuge?

MCLEOD: It made sense. I mean, I didn't have any mystical experiences or a feeling that I had encountered my teacher from a previous lifetime, or anything like that. There was nothing magical, mystical, or mysterious. Clearly I was looking for some kind of meaning, and this presented a path. There were things you could do. There was a whole technology, a set of practices, a lot of stuff you could learn in a way that Christianity didn't offer. Protestant Christianity didn't present things in that way. So we started learning stuff, and doing the practices. And I was hopeless, completely.

BOYLE: Did he speak English?

MCLEOD: No. There was a translator there who knew more Tibetan than I did at that point. By the end of nine months I was just beginning to be able to converse. I didn't take any formal training in Tibetan. It was all out of dictionaries, old grammar books that had sat in Calcutta warehouses getting eaten by worms, things like that.

BOYLE: Were you comfortable during this time, as opposed to the stories some people tell about going into a Japanese monastery and being almost tortured?

MCLEOD: There was no test of your devotion or intention, or anything like that. The first meeting I had with Rinpoche, he said, "Are you here as a tourist or are you interested in Buddhism?" I said, "I'm interested in Buddhism," and that was that.

BOYLE: But you spent a great amount of time in meditation?

MCLEOD: Heavens no. When I first started I literally could not sit for more than a minute. The reason for that only became clear to me many, many years later. Then I learned of a practice where you did prostrations called *ngöndro*, and that sounded like something I might be able to do. *Ngöndro* means "groundwork." It's a set of four practices that prepare you for other forms of meditation, mahamudra in particular. You go for refuge, doing a full prostration for every refuge prayer, 100,000 times. Then you do a purification practice, reciting a mantra 100,000 times while you imagine being purified by a deity. Then 100,000 offerings of the universe to all the buddhas of the three times. And finally, 100,000 prayers to your guru or teacher while you cultivate intense devotion. I think I was the first of Rinpoche's students to actually do the prostration practice, *ngöndro*.

BOYLE: You began doing that during this nine-month period?

MCLEOD: Yes, both my wife and I finished all four sections of the *ngöndro* during those nine months. Full prostrations. I've done them four more times since then. But there were lots of things we didn't know about practice. My wife said at one point, "I didn't know you were meant to be focusing on the purification of your body, I thought you just said the words of the mantra."

BOYLE: And you had conversations with Rinpoche during that time?

MCLEOD: Yes, but they were just conversations.

HAEDERLE: What was he like?

MCLEOD: Kalu Rinpoche never raised his voice above a whisper. Ever. He was a very patient person, explained things quite clearly. He stressed very fundamental aspects, so anytime a new Westerner showed up we'd all go back and start at the beginning, *again*. We heard that basic talk any number of times. He taught very traditionally, the Tibetan cosmology and so forth. I realized later that he took us through a good part of one of the standard texts in the Kagyu tradition, which is the Jewel Ornament of Liberation. He was very open, in that he taught Westerners quite willingly, not like a lot of Tibetan teachers at that time. And he took them seriously as students.

BOYLE: In spite of the repetition, you had a sense that this was going somewhere?

MCLEOD: Yes. In the Tibetan tradition one of the pervasive frameworks is a thing called *lamrim*, which means graded path, or series of steps on the path. There is a whole genre of texts, which are *lamrim* or graded path texts. It is probably the primary pedagogical framework used in all the

Tibetan traditions. You start with basic teachings on human birth, death, and impermanence; *samsara*; the six realms [of existence]; and progress to things like the four immeasurables—loving-kindness, compassion, joy, and equanimity—then the meditations of taking and sending and compassion, up to the six perfections, *bodhichitta*. All of those things. That can be done very concisely or it can be done in great depth. From there you might be introduced to other aspects of practice. Rinpoche encouraged people to practice a Vajrayana meditation in which you identified with being the embodiment of awakened compassion, the six-syllable mantra, *Om mani padme hum*. This was very close to Rinpoche's heart.

BOYLE: You covered this, or at least got a taste of it, during that nine-month period?

MCLEOD: Oh yes. Ingrid and I did all four sections of *ngöndro* and the Chenrezig practice. We were introduced to some other meditations too, but those were the principal ones. Then a year later Rinpoche did his first North American tour. He said he was going to the West, and would I be able to assist with that? I didn't have any money, so I wasn't sure what I could do to assist him. But my parents wrote a letter, which allowed him to get a visa to Canada. Then my wife and I took a huge amount of stuff to Delhi, which was sent through diplomatic courier to Canada. He traveled separately and visited a number of countries, principally France, where he also had a lot of students. Then he showed up in America and said he was coming to my parents' farm—which was a hobby farm, not a real working farm. Rinpoche stayed there for about five weeks, and people gradually came and invited him to other places. Things unfolded from there, and that is when I became his interpreter, because there wasn't anybody else. The people who were meant to be translating completely fell through, so I ended up becoming his translator.

HAEDERLE: You had mastered enough Tibetan at that point?

MCLEOD: "Mastered" is a very generous term. Strange things happen when there are thirty people in a room who know absolutely no Tibetan, one person who knows no English, and you're meant to know both. After a while, you do.

BOYLE: At the end of that five-week period?

MCLEOD: We visited centers in Toronto and Montreal, and then moved out to Vancouver. He stayed a couple of months in Vancouver, where he established a center. He asked me to stay in Vancouver and look after the *lama* [Tibetan Buddhist teacher] whom he left there. For the next two years I translated a lot of teachings and helped develop the center. Rinpoche came back in 1974 for a second North American tour, and this time I toured with him everywhere that he went, as his translator. That was about six months or so, I guess.

A few years later, in 1976, Rinpoche announced that he was going to set up a three-year retreat for Westerners, in France. So a group of us in Vancouver started to earn some money in order to do the retreat. Being completely unskilled, I got a teaching assistantship at UBC, to get my M.A. in mathematics, while my wife and I became foster parents. So we had a household full of kids for a year. Other people worked in an iron mine, in the Queen Charlotte Islands, where they earned their money to go to the retreat.

HAEDERLE: Can you say something about what three-year retreats entail?

MCLEOD: A three-year retreat is a form of training in the Kagyu and Nyingma traditions, principally. The time is really three years and three fortnights, because according to the *Kalachakra Tantra*, that is the time when if you take a certain number of breaths and you are completely in attention for all of those breaths, then you are done. But it's an intensive form of training, and was revitalized in the nineteenth century by Jamgön Kongtrül the Great. Kalu Rinpoche had been the retreat master in Tibet, and then had set up a three-year retreat in Bhutan when he was asked by the royal family to do that. When he took over the monastery in Sonada, that is the first thing he did.

HAEDERLE: How does one pass a day in a three-year retreat?

MCLEOD: In Kalu Rinpoche's three-year retreats you were trained in both the Karma Kagyu tradition and the Shangpa Kagyu tradition, the Shangpa Kagyu being a small but very potent line of transmission that goes back to the twelfth century. And that's what we did in the three-year retreat—we had transmissions of two complete traditions. A typical day went like this: you get up at four, meditate until seven, and meet for morning ritual. Then you have breakfast, meditate from nine to noon, have lunch, then meditate again from then to three-thirty or four o'clock. Later on in the retreat we did a yoga session, but we didn't do that at the beginning. Then there's evening ritual, then dinner, which is usually just a light soup or something, then mediation from seven until nine. After that there were several more practices you did until you went to sleep, around ten or so. Then up again at four.

BOYLE: So somewhere during that time you made the transition from doing the prostrations to sitting meditation?

MCLEOD: I'm terrible at sitting meditation. I mean, I persevered at this. It's what made me extremely sick in the three-year retreat. I have a colon problem; I should never have tried to do normal meditation posture. I got very, very ill. Other people sit easily, but it has never come easily to me. If I'd been in any other tradition I probably would have dropped out of Buddhism, because I just couldn't sit still.

BOYLE: The theme I want to pursue here is this: you had choices all the way along. You did the three-year retreat, but you could have gone off in a different direction. All of us have done lots of different things that were fun for a while, or involved us for a while, but we ended up going on to something else. What kept you on this path? Were there doubts in your mind? Something kept you going on this.

MCLEOD: Suzuki Roshi said in *Crooked Cucumber* that he was too stupid to leave. He just stayed. He didn't realize it was an abusive situation, he just stayed, and something came out of that. For me, there were a few critical points. First, it made sense. There was a system in effect, and a pretty rational presentation of Buddhist teaching, which you could really get your teeth into, and it didn't involve—at least I didn't think it involved—believing in something that was problematic. But I do recall people back then saying, "Gee, Ken, you have incredible faith." I couldn't relate to their comments at all, because it never felt like faith to me. Now I know what faith feels like, because one of the practices—*ngöndro* practices, particularly guru yoga—is all about faith. I practiced that, and practiced it quite deeply, and through that I came to know how powerful faith is as a tool for really opening to insight and direct experience. But when people said, "You must have tremendous faith," it didn't have that association for me. I wasn't really clear what they were referring to. The best I can say is, it felt right. We were being exposed to teachings. When Rinpoche said he was going to do a three-year retreat for Westerners, we had heard about all these teachings, but we never expected to actually be able to learn them. So it was like, "Oh, we can really learn everything here? And develop that level of depth of practice?" That sounded like an extraordinary opportunity. So there was never any question. Other people thought it would be a good idea, but then they ran into all kinds of obstacles. As one person famously put it, "Wanting to do this three-year retreat isn't enough." Which I thought was very well said. But I didn't feel like it was any kind of special quality in me, at all.

HAEDERLE: Was Kalu Rinpoche there for most of the time?

MCLEOD: For the three-year retreat? No. He gave all the empowerments before we went into the three-year retreat. He visited the retreat, over the three-year period, two, three times? He left one of his lamas who had done a three-year retreat as our retreat director. So he gave the instruction, and everything like that. When it was over Kalu Rinpoche came to the ceremonies, to bring us out of the three-year retreat. And then we went on to the next one, which I was also part of.

HAEDERLE: Did you have any contact with the outside world during this time?

MCLEOD: Very little. Men and women were housed in separate retreats. But we could send notes back and forth. We never left the compound at all. It was enclosed, and it was sealed. The only people who came in were visiting teachers and our retreat director. Our cook lived inside, and he went back and forth, and occasionally a doctor visited. And that was that.

HAEDERLE: And what happened?

MCLEOD: Nothing. We just practiced all the time, and learned, and studied.

HAEDERLE: And what happened to you?

MCLEOD: Well, I got sick on the first retreat, really quite ill—the colon problem. I didn't know it was a colon problem, it was just a big, big obstacle. That made following the retreat schedule very difficult. I couldn't sleep sitting up, which is one of the things that we do in the three-year retreat. Other people didn't have any problem with that. They just learned to sleep sitting up. Our retreat director, I think, had not laid down to sleep for thirty years.

BOYLE: What advantages is that supposed to confer?

MCLEOD: Lighter, more restful sleep; clearer mind. So many things happened. Probably the most significant was that Rinpoche had scheduled two months for meditation on compassion, called taking and sending, *tonglen*—Mahayana mind training. Independently I decided to do it in the traditional way, which was to do a proper grounding in loving-kindness and compassion. So I spent the first month doing loving-kindness for two weeks and then compassion. Those were very powerful for me. They made a huge difference. Doing compassion meditation that way is basically like taking a knife to your heart and cutting it open. It's pretty intense.

I didn't know I had changed, but I got a report back from my wife: "They're saying it's much easier to live with you now, Ken." I mean, there were various internal problems in those retreats, as you can well imagine. We had seven people trying to sort out how they were going to manage themselves. But that period of time made a big difference, and was one of the reasons I've always put a great deal of emphasis with my students on the four immeasurables [loving-kindness, compassion, sympathetic joy, and equanimity].

We did a lot of *yidam* practice, which is tough stuff, a lot of elaborate visualization, a lot of mantras, and that made me really sick. One of the things that happens when you are doing long-term retreats is that any energy imbalances that you have in your system come out as illness. And I had a lot. Then we went through the more advanced practices: six yogas of Niguma, six yogas of Naropa, six yogas of Sukhasiddhi. Three complete transmissions, which is unusual. I had a fair number of experiences there, but because of my problems I could never stabilize anything. Other people did, I think, in the retreat. But by the end of the retreat I realized that there was tremendous power in these methods, and I thought that I had only scratched the surface.

At the end of the first three-year retreat it was clear that everybody was going to be sent to a center to teach. The only way that I saw of avoiding that was to do a second three-year retreat, which I did—my wife and I both did. I really didn't want to be sent to a center, and I was given permission to do a second retreat. Much to my parents' consternation—but they came around.

BOYLE: So you were not yourself motivated to become a teacher?

MCLEOD: No. I've always thought that in Buddhism, and probably in other arenas, one of the qualifications of being a teacher is that you don't want to teach.

So we did the second three-year retreat, which went extremely smoothly for my wife, and was one of the darkest periods of my life for me. The physical problem got worse, and I went into what I now know to be a state of quite deep depression. It was pretty black for two years or so. I didn't know what it was, I didn't have any diagnosis at that time. I wouldn't have a diagnosis until maybe fifteen or twenty years later. It was just really, really hard. When I finished I was very weak physically and emotionally. Rinpoche apparently told my wife that I was so ill that I shouldn't do any more three-year retreats. He never told me that. So we made our way back to Canada, in 1983.

BOYLE: But again, you'd never considered going off to another life?

MCLEOD: No. I very nearly exited from the second three-year retreat, but that was right at the beginning. There were eleven people in the second retreat rather than seven, and there was much discord. Several of the new people just shouldn't have been in the retreat—they didn't have sufficient stability, etc. I was really angry about that. So I considered for a month or so exiting from the retreat, but then I realized that to do so would probably set some kind of precedent that would be really problematic historically.

It's amazing how these things work. I decided to stay for the sake of the tradition. That was my decision, and once I had made that decision I just continued on.

By this point I really wanted to have deep experience. Even though, as I say to my students, I had reached a point in the second three-year retreat where my body said to me, "Ken, you can go and get enlightened if you wish, I'm not coming." I didn't know how to relate to that at all. Being a good WASP, I didn't know how to relate to those kinds of things.

BOYLE: You said you had a number of briefer experiences, which didn't boost your practice or get integrated into your practice. They were more like appetizers?

MCLEOD: It's more that they showed what was possible. In other words, I knew that the practices worked, and I knew that I knew how to do them, but my health issues wouldn't let me do them. That meant that after the three-year retreat I went into a very difficult period where I was extremely prone to depression. I also felt, once Rinpoche had sent me to Los Angeles, that I was now condemned to teaching people practices that they would be able to do and I would never be able to do. So the bitterness I felt about that was challenging, shall we say.

Many years later I came across a poem by Stephen Crane:

In the desert
I saw a creature, naked, bestial,
who, squatting upon the ground,
Held his heart in his hands,
And ate of it.
I said, "Is it good, friend?"
"It is bitter—bitter," he answered;
"But I like it
Because it is bitter,
And because it is my heart."

I could really relate to that!

After that we went back to Canada and had our lives nicely settled there, doing adult education, teaching in community colleges. Then Rinpoche sent me to Los Angeles. My wife didn't go. That's when I started teaching.

HAEDERLE: So this is about the mid-'80s, in Los Angeles?

MCLEOD: Yes. I set up a center, working from scratch, but I didn't ever enjoy it. I made a lot of innovations, got a lot of people upset about stuff.

Separated from my wife. Well, to be honest, I got involved with somebody else and then separated from my wife, which I'm not terribly proud about, but that's how things go. I had resigned myself to this as what the rest of my life was going to be. I was in my late thirties at this point. I was slowly recovering physical strength. I wasn't depressed all the time, but very subject to it.

HAEDERLE: Had you ever ordained?

MCLEOD: No. I had ordained as a layperson, but I'd never taken monk's vows. During the retreat we were ordained as laypeople, but I've never regarded myself as a monk.

HAEDERLE: So I guess this is a critical question. If your life was in such a bleak place, as a result of this practice, then go back to square one. Practice is supposed to be liberation from suffering. How is it that you found yourself in this puzzle?

MCLEOD: One can conjecture all sorts of things here. I have a much better understanding of my own psychology now than I did then. The retreat experience showed me that the practices worked, the teachings were true. That meant the problem was me, which is not a conclusion I would come to today, but certainly the conclusion I came to then. The other thing is that by this point I was very heavily steeped in the Tibetan tradition. I could only see things from the perspective of the Tibetan tradition, and in terms of that system I didn't have any choice.

Here is where Los Angeles was a corrupting influence. People would say to me:

"Well, why are you here, Ken?"

"Because Kalu Rinpoche sent me."

"Well, why did you obey Kalu Rinpoche?"

"Because that's just what you do in the Tibetan tradition, you do what your guru says."

"So you chose to come here."

"No I didn't, Kalu Rinpoche sent me."

That was the way the logic worked for me. It took six or eight months at least, with people who had become trusted advisors pushing, before I finally made the cognitive leap: I had chosen to accept this as a system.

That's a very powerful shift, because now everything comes into question. And more and more stuff came into question as that rattled around inside me. I had accepted the Tibetan system of doing things. There were a lot of things that I had never questioned, because they're never questioned in the Tibetan tradition.

Even so, I still did things my own way, and I found a significant tension, a consistent tension between what Kalu Rinpoche expected me to do in L.A. and what I felt was appropriate. That tension was summarized when I was translating for Kalu Rinpoche when he was teaching a retreat in Southern California, at Big Bear Lake. What Rinpoche said was this, which was entertaining to everybody except little me:

> When Ken came to Los Angeles he was very skillful. He taught people to meditate on their breath, and they felt good about doing that. So lots of people became interested in meditation and he built up the center and now we have this retreat with everybody here. This is good, he was very skillful. Well, maybe he was skillful. Maybe he was just afraid to tell the truth. I'm not afraid to tell the truth.

Then he went on about the hell realms, and karma and stuff. Everybody was laughing uproariously while I was translating. That was basically Rinpoche's perspective on it. He didn't like it. I went to see Rinpoche in 1988 because I realized this was probably the last time I would see him. He was getting progressively weaker—he was eighty-nine at this point. So I went to see him with the very specific purpose of thanking him for everything that I had received, but also to tell him what I was going to do. So rather than stumble through this with my soft voice, which Rinpoche at that point had great difficulty hearing, I had his secretary translate for me. I explained that virtually everything I knew about the Dharma I had learned from him, and that I had received all of these transmissions and empowerments and I thanked him for that, and that I'd done a lot of work helping to develop the centers in Vancouver and L.A. and various other places. Then I said that in the future I wasn't going to do any more work on the centers, because it wasn't something I was particularly good at. But what I would do was take a phrase that Rinpoche used all the time, that the purpose of the Dharma is to benefit the mind. I said, "This you have said many times, I have taken this to heart, and I will undertake for the rest of my life to teach the Dharma to help people's minds."

Of course, Rinpoche turned around and had a meeting with all of my students and talked with them for an hour and a half about why centers were important. So obviously he wasn't happy about it at all. But I didn't give him much room for argument. I wanted to make it clear, since this was our last meeting, that while I was grateful, this was the direction in which I was going to go. I felt very clean about that, and that was important.

But earlier, Rinpoche had asked all of his senior students, particularly those who knew Tibetan, to come to India to start on a translation project, so I participated in that. I closed the center at that point, because with me away there was no income, and went to India. We translated about eight hours a day, but the rest of the time was our own. I spent a lot of time thinking about what I was going to do when I went back to Los Angeles. That is when the idea of becoming a meditation consultant arose. One of the things that I had found problematic was that people would study, or practice meditation, and they would wrestle with a problem for three to six months and get all bent out of shape, when it could have been taken care of in a three-minute conversation. I wanted to have a format in which I was getting actual information about people's practice. So I became a meditation consultant. Well, I fumbled around with that when I came back, but after about two years I had a private practice. I had enough clients that I could rent an office. That became the basis of Unfettered Mind. And I never looked back.

So for a while I was doing both of those things, carrying on the center, even though it was only on paper now, and doing stuff for Unfettered Mind. I didn't start Unfettered Mind until after Rinpoche died, in 1989. But after a couple of years, about 1992, I let go of all formal connection with Tibetan traditions, completely. But I also had no position in any institution.

BOYLE: So, you were in L.A., you were depressed sometimes and had the remnants of physical weakness and illness. Had you changed your position for sitting and doing meditation?

MCLEOD: Not for a very long time. I couldn't sit for more than a half hour at a time, and I avoided ceremonies like the plague, because they just made me sick. I tried to do a Zen *sesshin*, and I got very sick after three days. It wasn't until the mid-'90s that I finally gave up and started sitting in a chair.

BOYLE: Did you use other activities as meditation, like taking walks?

MCLEOD: No, depression immobilizes you, so you do very little. After a year or so I realized that one of the people who started studying with me in Los Angeles knew a hell of a lot more than he was letting on, and he started to teach me tai chi. Very gradually, that had a beneficial effect. I worked a little bit with Iyengar yoga with a good teacher, but it wasn't a good form of discipline for me. She pushed me straight into the trauma in my system, and it was like stepping into a black hole of pure fear. I said, "No, I don't think so." I mean, that was not very pleasant.

Tai chi was more congruent with me. My relationship with this person moved from me being the teacher and him being the student to having a student-teacher relationship that went both ways. And we discovered that both of us were stuck in our spiritual practices, and we discovered that each of us had the keys to unlock the other. So over a twelve-year period, we met almost weekly, exchanging our technologies. His background was in Gurdjieff and martial arts, and mine was in Tibetan Buddhism. That was a very rich relationship, and he continues to be a good friend even though he has moved away. A lot of the stuff in *Wake up to Your Life* has come out of that interaction, and that way of approaching things. So that was a gem that happened in L.A., the last kind of thing you'd expect. But it was very important.

Haederle: You said it took seventeen years before you were able to identify your depression for what it was?

McLeod: It became clear that during the early years in Vancouver, 1973–74, I had the same problem. I didn't do anything for a year except read science fiction. And do *ngöndro*. That was it, because I was depressed. In the early '90s a psychiatrist and professor of psychiatry at UC Irvine, a guy called Roger Walsh, went out of his way to help me and create some opportunities. Very kind of him. He made an offhand comment to me, saying, "Ken, have you ever considered depression?" I just dismissed it. But in 1997 things were getting intense. I knew of a therapist who specialized in depression, so I went to see him for EMDR [Eye Movement Desensitization and Reprocessing] work, and it was completely ineffective. The first session I had with him, he said, "If this doesn't produce anything within five or six sessions then it is very unlikely to," and by the fifth or sixth session it was clearly not working. But he spent an extra twenty minutes with me, and I recall that kindness.

When things continued to deteriorate I went back to see him, and worked with him for several years. He was never very effective with the depression, but together with the work that I was doing in tai chi and a number of other things, there was gradual improvement. Oh yes—the reason I went to see him was that I called Roger and said, "I want to talk with you about depression." He said, "I'm so glad you called, Ken. I've been waiting five years to have this conversation." We had a forty-five minute diagnostic conversation, and he said, "You've got double depression: dysthymia and clinical depression." That's when I started working with this therapist. By this time I was long separated from my second wife. I was teaching and doing various things, but I was often just crawling during the day. One of the problems here is that the dynamics of depression and the dynamics of meditation are similar. If you practice meditation it's very easy to become depressed, if you're subject to it. That's something I learned. There's a great deal of inertia in me, which in all honesty I can really only attribute to the depression. I'm not one of those people who goes out and explores things and tries to fix them. The depression doesn't move me in that direction.

Eventually the therapist that I was working with reached out to an extremely good practitioner of EMDR who had basically retired, and twisted his arm for me. That turned out to be a very fruitful thing. I'm not immobilized the way I used to be, at all. I've learned slowly, over time, that a very large amount of it was diet-related. That's why I don't eat high-fiber food, because it activates the colon the wrong way.

There's a strong relation between the colon and depression—it's just like that. If I get the wrong foods, I go down really fast. I've stopped being polite. Now I say, "No, it just isn't good for me." The first time I was ever able to actually do any kind of retreat, since the three-year retreats, was in 2003 when I did a retreat at Tara Mandala. For that I had complete control over what I did. I could lie down, sit, anything I wanted. That turned out to be a very deep retreat. It made a lot of difference, in a lot of different ways. It simplified a whole bunch of stuff. I was very happy about it. I said, "Oh, that's interesting."

In 2006 I started a series of retreats at the Mandala Center in Des Moines, New Mexico. The first was a dzogchen retreat, a three-week retreat. I'd never taught a retreat that long. Then the next year I taught a ten-day retreat on illusory body, because I felt an obligation to pass on some of the stuff that I'd received. I taught a lot of the stuff that I'd never touched, advanced Vajrayana, illusory body, illusory form. That went very well, since it's intimately connected with compassion. The second year I decided that I would teach clear light and dream, because that would complete the transmission of those practices and I felt an obligation to do that. It was an excruciatingly painful teaching experience for me, partly because the diet wasn't good, so I was subject to depression, and partly because it took me right back to the three-year retreat and all the pain I had experienced there. It was pretty horrible, but I got through it. My students were actually quite upset to see how much difficulty I was having. That was hard for them.

Then last year, 2008, I did two ten-day retreats, the first one on *maha-mudra* and the second on dzogchen. In between, something shifted in me, which has created a huge number of problems. But I found a couple of other people who shared the problems, which makes me feel better, and I can trace it to the exact thing that started it. It's a line in a book by a person who was a relatively obscure professor of philosophy and economics at the London School of Economics, a guy called John Gray. He had written a number of books, but one called *Straw Dogs* had come out in Britain in around 2000. I was reading it at that time, in 2008. Now I'm on my third time through it. It is an extraordinary attack on liberal humanism. It's a very effective attack, quite deep. It has this line in it: "Philosophers claim that they are seeking truth, when actually they are seeking peace." I'd read the line before, but something shifted. It was my light on the road to Damascus.

BOYLE: This was only last year?

MCLEOD: Last year. At that point I now saw Buddhism as any other religion, riddled with assumptions and beliefs. It was just like, *Oh, it's full of bullshit like everything else. Oh, shit, what can I do now?* There was a real problem. I almost stopped teaching completely. I got through the second retreat, I'm not sure quite how, because students were there to learn something.

But I came back. I mean, my mind was very clear most of the time. Very still, very quiet. Something very deep physically had let go, so there was a whole level of discomfort that wasn't there anymore. I'd had to stop drinking alcohol, because my body couldn't tolerate it, but I found that I could have a sip of wine now and then, which I like. Now I can drink a glass of wine with a meal and have no ill effects. So there was change in the physical, the emotional, the spiritual levels, right across the board. Meditation has become much easier; in fact, I don't even worry about it now. I mean, I practice every day, although some days my mind is quieter than others.

Out of this experience came the philosophy, very deeply held: there is no enemy. That's taken absolutely. I had no idea what I was doing. My students, with whom I talked about this, laughed. They said, "What's the big deal, Ken? This is what you've always taught us." "I did?" I finally got it right at one of my teacher-student trainings. One of my senior students said, "I don't see what the big deal is, Ken. Here you've just said, 'We cannot know what this experience we call life is, yet we have to navigate it.' I don't see how that's different from the two truths: emptiness and apparent reality." When he said that I laughed, and said, "You're right." But it was now totally different as an internal experience. All this business about timeless awareness I now respond to by saying, "Just because you can experience timeless awareness doesn't mean there is a timeless awareness."

BOYLE: I felt when I read the lines in *An Arrow to the Heart,* which was written before your road to Damascus experience, that they opened some things up for me.

MCLEOD: That is exactly what it was intended to do.

BOYLE: But now you are telling me that you hadn't actually experienced some of it yet.

MCLEOD: No, I mean I had come to some things, but what happened last year was on a whole different level.

BOYLE: You managed to write that whole book feeling depressed and in a much more limited state?

MCLEOD: Well, I could communicate it to people, but I didn't experience it, which has a lot to do with the depression and being shut down. It was there in me, I just didn't have any connection with it. Which is interesting.

HAEDERLE: Something about that line that you quoted from the philosopher John Gray. This idea of seeing Buddhism as any other religion sounds as though it somehow took out the foundations beneath a kind of faith structure.

MCLEOD: No, I'd say more of a belief structure. John 16:32: "Know ye the truth, and the truth shall make you free." This is complete bullshit. I realized—and you get this all in Tibetan Buddhism, Mahayana Buddhism more than Theravadan—if you know the truth, then you will be free. It's all this "wisdom is the path," and it's completely wrong, it's highly problematic. I realized that I had operated under the assumption that if I could know how things were, then I would be free of suffering. It's not true.

If one makes a distinction between factual reality and practical reality, Buddhism initially was practical reality. Somewhere along the way I knew this, because my tag line for Unfettered Mind is "Pragmatic Buddhism." Something in me sensed that a long time ago. There is a quote from Miyamoto Musashi, which I adapted because he was talking about martial arts, but it is absolutely my attitude toward Buddhism, to the effect that, "Many people feel when studying martial arts (or Buddhism) that what you learn will not be useful in the world. The true way of the Buddha is that what you learn gives you the skills that are useful in the world, and should be taught and practiced in a way that can be used in any situation." So it is a completely pragmatic approach, and I just realized, *This is what I do.*

But, yes, something shifted in me, so I didn't know where the walls were. I had no reference. One of my students in Santa Fe is a very smart business consultant. I was talking with her and described what had happened, and I said, half-joking, "I've got a marketing problem now." She looked at me and said, "You've got a *big* marketing problem." She got it immediately. So what are you going to do with it?

HAEDERLE: Do you think that in your body you were holding a kind of cognitive dissonance around all of this?

MCLEOD: I wouldn't say I'm free of it yet. A piece has fallen away. I wouldn't say all of it has. Not even close. I think it's much deeper than cognitive dissonance. Something, obviously. But all of this stuff is encoded in the body, and many approaches to Buddhism don't recognize that, or try to override the body, or whatever. I tell people, "You've got to go through the body." Then I continually drive them back to their body experience. It's quite different from the way they do it in the vipassana tradition. I know many people who practice the vipassana tradition, and they're not in touch with what's going on in their body. They really aren't. They've got a whole different schema, and it's just as problematic.

I was talking to the head of a very large company, and he said, "Ken, what's life like for you these days?" "Well, imagine that you're walking over the Grand Canyon." He said, "Walking into the Grand Canyon?" "No, *over* the Grand Canyon." Now, it's not the Wile E. Coyote thing, where if you look down you start to fall. You're not sure what's up, what's down, what's forward, what's back. That's what life is for me today.

It's settled down a bit. But I had a nice talk with John Tarrant, and he seemed to relate to it very straightforwardly. Yesterday I got in touch with Stephen Batchelor, whom I've known for some time. He has, through his own route, come to very similar conclusions. There is a small group of us.

BOYLE: But you exist. It's amazing to me.

MCLEOD: It's very interesting, because Stephen approaches it differently from the way I do. From his point of view, this is what Buddha was really talking about, and everything else is an accretion. So when he talks to other people, they look at him and say, "You know, you're not really Buddhist," and his internal response is, *Well, actually, I feel like I'm really following the Buddha's path more closely, while you're stuck in some beliefs.* My point of view is, *Well, I don't know, maybe this is what Buddha was doing.* Stephen has the scholastic knowledge, which he has researched very deeply. But I know I don't have the beliefs that many other people do—in fact, 90 percent of what they are talking about is bullshit. So I don't belong there.

HAEDERLE: I was thinking about your interaction with your student in Santa Fe. You talk openly about this with your students?

MCLEOD: Not with all of them, but with students who are closer to me, senior students. It's been upsetting for them. They are, like, I've really pulled the rug out from under their feet. One of them has been very good after a year of being absolutely furious and upset with me. I just kept hammering,

hammering her, on her attachment to an ideal. When she finally started to let go, she said, "Oh." Any form of idealism is problematic. So that was a big piece of her practice. I just kept pulling the rug out until she finally said, "Okay, I'm tired of falling down. No more ideals."

Other students have had problems as well. I've always been pretty transparent, which is one of the things that has distinguished me from a lot of teachers. I had an interesting experience once during teacher training. I had everybody, for this particular session, bring a mask, a physical mask, because I wanted them to explore teaching with a mask and teaching without a mask. I had them see what it was like to interact with someone who was wearing a mask, and to be wearing a mask yourself, and all the different combinations. Then, as two of these people were interacting, the person who was in the teacher role and didn't have his mask on was just fumbling. He couldn't get it. I said, "Put your mask on." He immediately began to teach absolutely correctly. So masks are not bad or good, they're just different ways of relating to this role. I did not learn any of that from the Tibetan tradition. I wasn't taught it, I learned it. There are pros and cons to wearing a mask. In the Zen tradition you always teach behind the mask. In most of the formal traditions you are mostly teaching behind the mask. It's effective; it's just different. But generally I'm not wearing a mask when I teach, and that is one of the things that distinguishes me from a lot of teachers.

4
Interview with Ajahn Amaro

Ajahn Amaro is abbot of Amaravati Buddhist Monastery in southeast England, and the author of Rain on the Nile *and other writings. We talked on November 9, 2009, in Redwood Valley, California.*

BOYLE: A path story begins with when and how you first became interested in Buddhism. Can you tell about that?

AMARO: I should start the story when I was ten or eleven. That was the age when I first began asking myself spiritual questions. I grew up in England. My parents weren't churchgoing people—like most English people, they were nominal Church of England types. The schools began every day with a Christian service. So Christianity was in the air, but it never made any sense to me. It never appealed to me. I had various questions for teachers, or the chaplain, but the answers never made any sense. They just didn't appeal or didn't strike any notes. Whatever these people were talking about, I felt they didn't really understand; it was all nonsense. I didn't start thinking seriously until about the age when I went from a fairly idyllic primary school environment to boarding school. I was a day pupil, but the brutalities of the English boarding school system were startling. The kind of thing you see in movies, and some of it's true. Obviously I had suffered before, but that was really my first raw experience of *dukkha*. Like, *This is really painful.* That was really when I began to question: *What is real? What is good?* And also, particularly, to ask myself, *How can you be free, as a human being?* I was born in 1956, so by the age of ten or eleven it was all happening, those questions were in the air. I started asking myself, *What is God? What is that referring to?* I really tried to figure it out on my own: *God seems to be the most important thing there is, yet no one around here seems to really understand* what *that is.* It certainly didn't seem to be there in church. It was more than anything a sense of, *I really want to figure this out and understand it.* But being English, there are some things we talk about with friends, and at school, and with family, and some things we don't talk about. The kind of rough-and-tumble gang of friends wasn't where you said, "Let's sit down and talk about the nature of God," or "What do you think is ultimately real?" It wasn't in the air. So it was very much a thing that I just looked at for myself. It was very much just me, looking out the window at the stars and trying to figure out how the universe works, how everything is put together.

That was carrying on in the background until I got to about fifteen, sixteen. By that time there was more of a possibility that other people around me would be interested in that kind of area, heavy philosophy, ultimate reality, psychedelics. That domain started to be something you could talk about with your friends, in the middle of long rambling chat sessions. But even though I had a sense of spirituality—by that time spirituality was the most important thing to me—I had no idea how to really access it, or how to embody that kind of truth. The inklings I had were there in different kinds of experiences, but I also felt, *What's the point, what does this all mean?* I had a sense that there is an ultimate reality, some kind of ordering principle for the universe that you could touch, or that you could intuit here and there, but how could you really know that on an ongoing basis? It was there, in the background, and it became more and more something that I was interested in. Obviously there were other things I could do with my life—you know, go to university, study this or that, or go wander around in India. But the thing that was most interesting to me was, whatever it was that I did, I wanted it to be some kind of doorway to understanding this internal reality. The most interesting thing to me, and the most meaningful thing, was this sense of inner spiritual reality. The external activity that led to that was circumstantial, and not so crucial.

I didn't have a particular draw to any religious system or spiritual training. Nothing really sparked my interest. I was a partygoer, so most of those kinds of experiences were through all-night boozing and dancing, the teenage party realm—more a Dionysian approach to spirituality, which was all around at that time. When I left home and went to university, I studied physiology and psychology. I had majored in sciences in high school, physics, chemistry, and math, and in England what you take during the last two years of high school determines what you can study in university. By the time I was lined up to go to university I realized that the thing I was really interested in, like religion, ancient history, and philosophy, I didn't have the qualifications for. They were all arts subjects. I didn't know Joseph Campbell at that time, but it was exactly his field that was the kind of thing I was most interested in, the interplay of mythology, ancient history, religion, and psychology. When I was growing up as a kid, most of what I read was mythology and fairy tales. So I thought, *What kind of degree course can I do that gets close to that?* Since I had to enroll in the science faculty, psychology and physiology were the closest I could find. I went to London University, and while I was there I came across a teacher out of the Rudolf Steiner tradition who was giving lectures. He wasn't connected to the university, just a freelance teacher, and I started going to his talks. His name was Trevor Ravenscroft. He wrote a well-known book called *The Spear of Destiny*. He was the one who triggered not just an interest, but more a confidence in the spiritual dimension of life. His lectures covered a huge range of different things, not just Steiner's teachings but also a lot about history and different kinds of spiritual practices. Going to his talks and then spending time with him and the people in his group made it clear that spirituality was the only thing that was really interesting to me.

I had many career possibilities. My interests were in arts and literature and such, my skills were in science, and I had family opportunities in the business world. There were all kinds of things I could do—people would say, "You can do this, or this, or this. . . ." But it was through going to those talks, and spending time with the people in that group, that it sunk in that there was actually only one thing that I really wanted to do. But it didn't have a form; I just knew that what I was interested in was spiritual development. How I would go about doing that was not clear. Whether I did that through being a scientist or a poet, or living in a commune and growing carrots, writing the great novel, that didn't really matter, wasn't significant. It was more some way to arrive at that kind of understanding. Because it became clear, as I read more widely, that the people I really resonated with were the enlightened mystics. People out of the Sufi tradition, or the Hindu tradition, or from China. So when I read things by, say, Sri Ramana Maharshi, or Sufi teachings, or Chuang Tzu, I found the words would just jump off the page. It became clear to me that whatever it took to get to be where these guys were speaking from, I would do it.

BOYLE: And they often had an account of what they had done in order to get to where they were.

AMARO: Exactly. Then once I had finished my studies at the university and gotten a degree, I needed to somehow pitch myself into this process and get some sort of spiritual training; I couldn't just stay there drinking retsina. That's what led to me to go to Thailand. I had no particular interest in European spirituality, so I decided to go to Asia and immerse myself in whatever kind of spirituality I found there. I hadn't even read any Buddhist books—Buddhism hadn't made it into the picture yet. I'd had a brief contact—a friend at university had taken me along to hear some teachings of a Tibetan master, in London, in 1976. His Holiness Dudjom Rinpoche was giving teachings. Sogyal Rinpoche was translating. That was all very good, but it didn't really click, it was nothing really exciting. It was not until I actually went to Asia, and I was in that environment, that I met Buddhism in a more direct, all-encompassing way. That was in 1977.

I wrapped up everything I had in Britain, so that I had no obligations there. I went on a one-way ticket to Asia. But after traveling for a few months, around Indonesia, Malaysia, and Thailand, I found I was spending my time hanging out with the same white middle-class educated bunch of stoners that I'd been living with in England, and I thought, *This is ridiculous. Here I am making my journey to the East and it's just like life in a pub in England. The temperature's a bit different and the backdrop has changed, but otherwise it's just the same old, same old.* So I cut away from the tourist, Western traveler scene, and went off to what I heard was the most remote and unvisited part of Thailand, the northeast, where I had heard no tourists ever went. It was boring—there were no beaches or mountains or anything of that nature. I really went there because it was away from that scene, and because I'd heard that very few people spoke any English. But I had also heard that the people in that region of Thailand were incredibly friendly and welcoming. So I thought, *Great!* I had one address, of some people who worked at a refugee camp. That's what took me to Ubon Province. The people who I'd been told to contact were away that weekend, but the folks who were there let me stay the night. Then the next day I thought, *Well, I'd better move on, because I'm not really that welcome here. It was nice of them to put me up for the night, but I need to move.*

It was at the refugee camp that I heard about Ajahn Chah's branch monastery, where some Western monks lived. This was about ten miles outside of the town of Ubon. Some of the people at the refugee camp had met some of Ajahn Chah's foreign students just a week before, at Christmas. There were so few foreigners in the province that they had taken Christmas presents to the monastery, so they had a fresh memory of having visited there, and they said, "Oh, there are these Western monks there, maybe you'd be interested in visiting them." And I thought, *Well, monasteries—I'm not too sure about that, too many rules.* So the first sense I had was a bit forbidding. Then I thought, *It might be interesting. I could see what they are up to, maybe learn a bit about Buddhism.* Thailand was a Buddhist country, but I knew nothing about Buddhism. I'd come here to immerse myself in Asian spirituality, so I should maybe take the opportunity to do this. I made my way to the monastery, and that was my first contact with Ajahn Chah's teaching and his methods of training. I was more of a hippie anarchist type, so I didn't like rules and institutions and suchlike. On an intellectual level I objected to organized religion; I was thinking of Asian spirituality more in terms of Carlos Castaneda's "Don Juan", the sorcerer's apprentice, freewheeling yogis under a tree, that kind of thing.

But then coming into this monastery, I met the Western monks and the villagers who were around, and they just seemed to be so incredibly sane, and uncomplicated and friendly. There was this very powerful magnetic attraction to the way of life, even though intellectually I objected to rules and institutions. On the gut level, what I met there was such a perfect fit. These people were practicing meditation, they lived a simple life, they were all incredibly honest. They had stopped doing all the things I wanted to stop doing, like drinking and smoking, and suchlike. They were doing all the things I wanted to be doing, like practicing meditation and living close to the earth. Everyone lived in little huts in the forest and followed a very simple, natural daily routine. So I thought, *Well, I don't know anything about Buddhism, but these people seem to know what they're doing.* I could see the result—very clear-eyed, sane, level-headed, good-hearted people, both the Westerners and the locals.

In the Buddhist tradition there is a daily interaction between the world outside the monastery and the monastery itself. The monastery serves as something like a communal center. People relate to it as a sort of community hall, as a place to get advice about their problems, a place to have as a spiritual sanctuary—a cross between being a marriage guidance and counseling service, a visit to the park, and going to church. All of those things. It's very much a part of the social sphere of the village, even though the forest monasteries are outside of the village. There's a strong connection—it serves a positive and clear role within village life. Every morning the villagers would come in with us and spend time helping out. They couldn't speak any English, but you could see the way they functioned and the way they related to the monks. There was this very natural, calm, good-hearted, comfortable way that they lived and communicated. So something on a very deep level said, *Whatever it is that these people are doing, you need some.* That was what caught my interest. That was the main thing. I thought, *I deliberately came to this place on a one-way ticket, so maybe I should stick around.* That was January of 1978.

As I said earlier, ever since I was a kid I'd had these concerns about freedom and truth. A big conundrum for me was how human beings can be free. We're always bound by various things, like having to follow the rules of your parents, the rules of the school, the rules of society and the judiciary and the police force. We're bound by social conventions, the force of gravity, by not having enough money to buy everything that we might want to have. Everywhere you look you see these limitations. Yet you didn't have to be very imaginative to see that even the very rich, like people who are millionaires, you could see that they are bound by all sorts of restrictions. My godfather was a millionaire, but he was not a particularly happy man. He lived in a stately home, and he had a lot of difficulties in his life. It doesn't come down to simple things like having more cash or evading the law. So there was this question, how can we really be free? It was really because of coming across those teachings from different spiritual masters that I got the sense that these people knew what freedom was. These were free people. How did they do that? It was clear that it was some kind of internal change that we make as human beings. That was the only thing that could make us free, because it wasn't a matter of being a political leader, or being rich. It wasn't just a matter of deciding, "I'm going to be a free person, I'm not going to worry about what people think of me. I'm just going to do whatever I like." You could decide that as much as you wanted to, but it wouldn't work. A decision, or an intention, is not enough.

It was also really clear to me that the whole question of freedom was connected with desire, because that seemed to be where the two clashed. If you could gratify your desires, you were free; if you couldn't gratify them, you weren't free. That seemed to be the equation. Up until then I'd never really questioned the nature of desire. I want this, I want that, and therefore I should have it. I'm either gratified because I get it or disappointed because it's not enough. Or I don't get it and I'm frustrated. But it always seemed to me that freedom and desire had this intimate connection with each other, and that somehow I wasn't getting the equation right. Like one of those math problems where you're trying to solve an integral equation and it's just not working. One of those annoying calculus problems: *There's a solution here, but I'm just not getting it.*

After I decided to stay at the monastery, the abbot chatted with me and got me settled and oriented, acquainted with the routine. Then after a little while, coming up to the evening of the next day, I thought, *Wait a minute, I don't know what we're supposed to be doing with this meditation period. Everyone's sitting here with their eyes closed, and I don't have a clue what to do.* So I asked a novice, who was an Australian guy, "How do you do this meditation? What is it that everyone's doing?" So he explained the basics of mindfulness of breathing, and also the Four Noble Truths and the relationship between desire and suffering, which I'd never heard of before. He's the one who introduced me to that. He said, "Basically, Buddha said, 'Life is suffering.'" I said, "No, that's not right; I'm fine, I'm not suffering." "Well, you may not think you are, but you are." I was big on denial in those days.

Anyway, he explained how the mind comes up with different things that we want, and that it's because of getting caught up in our desires that we create suffering. This was complete news to me, I hadn't heard it phrased that way. Then he explained how what happens is that the mind says, "I want something, I've got to have something." But desire is a liar, because the fact is you don't really need it. So he explained that as we buy into different forms of desire, in doing so we create the causes of *dukkha*, dissatisfaction. *That doesn't sound right*, I thought, but he carried on: "If you learn to watch desire, see it come and see it go, then that's the way to not create the causes of suffering. That's the basic engine of insight and liberation, seeing that desire arise and pass away and realizing that you don't have to be swept up in it." I had never come across that idea in my life. Also, prior to this, I'd always been a very optimistic person, but during the previous few weeks I'd started having my first experiences of deep existential dread, feeling that maybe I was just an air-headed optimist, a *luftmensch*. Maybe I was pathetically bound to positive ideas, while there was actually no possibility of freedom, no liberation, no enlightenment. Maybe all of this was just a stupid joke, and we are condemned to exist miserably, minimizing the pain as much as we can, and wait until it is all over. I had been having inklings of this sort of existential dread coming on. It was deeply disquietening: *I don't want to think that; that is not true; I really don't want that to be true.* But there was this suspicion brewing that it was, and that, if I was going to be realistic, I would have to give up on the idea that any kind of liberation or freedom was really possible. That was priming me for coming into the ease of meditation.

After this novice, Peter Hazel, had explained this, I thought, *The next time we have meditation I'll give it a try and see whether it works, see what he's talking about.* The next period of meditation was in the evening. There's no supper in Theravadan monasteries, just one meal a day, in the morning, then nothing until the next day. There we are, sitting meditating in the evening, and I start to get hungry, and I think, *Hmm. I'd really like some pineapple. Now, this is a desire. What was it that Peter was talking about? "When a desire arises you can just watch it."* But I really want some pineapple. But he said, "*If you just wait, and watch that desire, then you'll see that it passes away.*" So I stayed there for a while, and then I tried to go back to my breath and was following my breathing, and then my mind got caught up with something else. Then I suddenly realized, *Oh, I've forgotten about the pineapple.* What hit me was that, *Ah, I didn't get the pineapple, and* nothing is missing. That was a huge "Aha!" experience. That was it. Something clicked. *I didn't get the pineapple and nothing is missing. He was right.* Somehow the implications of that all clicked, almost audibly, saying, *That's it! All you've got to do is stay with this and it will be the way out.* I don't know why it was so obvious, why everything clicked into place, but it was right there. So I didn't leave.

Obviously my mind was not totally peaceful then—I was twenty-one years old, highly confused, overeducated—but I stayed on. I went through the various stages of novice ordination and then became a monk the next year. But I still had a lot of confusion. My mind was incredibly busy, and the idea that my mind would ever stop thinking and become still was inconceivable. But the key piece was that I knew the way toward freedom. Something on a deep level knew that it was totally possible. It would be a long journey to make, but it was doable.

The more I heard about Buddha's teachings, the more I realized that not only had somebody been there before, but there was an enormously comprehensive and thoroughly worked-out system of knowledge and understanding. He had worked it out infinitely better than I had ever done. And there was a whole support system to help you carry it out. There were people who showed up every day and put food in your bowl, and were enthusiastically cheering you on, in order for you to be able to carry this out. So I thought, *This is great.*

It's a very common experience. It's not like you're discovering anything that's radically new. It's more like what you learn is giving a shape to things that you'd already intuited, that you already understood in some vague way, shape, or form, a framework that helps you put that all together. It's more like rediscovering something that you'd already somehow encountered or sensed, but you'd never had a name for it. Certainly for many of the people I know, their experience of meeting up with Buddhism could be characterized as, "This is what I'd always thought, but I didn't know that is what

it is called." Particularly the nontheistic side of it—it is a completely dedicated spiritual practice, but it is not based around a god figure. The Buddha
Dharma was a perfectly formed spiritual philosophy but with no ultimate
being as a creator, ordainer, decider, and director. I felt a profound sense of,
Ahhh—that's great. It wasn't that I was an atheist, not that kind of anti-God
type, but that ultimate reality as some kind of superethereal being never
fit. But I didn't know what did. So, coming across the Buddha's teaching, a
completely nontheistic expression, was a profound cause of faith arising.
Faith that you can have a totally committed spiritual path and no super-
being who is "out there" in the model. There are all kinds of deities in the
Buddhist cosmos, but they are simply other entities, like human beings or
animals. The idea of the godhead as a sort of superperson is not there. That
gave me a lot of faith, and interest.

BOYLE: So you had the pineapple desire vanishing, which was an important clue that something was happening. Then the system and the social
part were comfortable, and you fit in there and felt compatible, and you
stayed in Thailand in that monastery. Was there a progress through that, in
the sense of a deepening of insight?

AMARO: Not so much while I was in Thailand. I was in Thailand only
for two years. Then just before the two years were completed, my father
had a heart attack. I had been thinking of coming back to England anyway,
just to see family. But the heart attack precipitated my leaving Thailand and
returning to England. Ajahn Sumedho had just started up a new monastery
in England. I hadn't met him, but people had talked about him a lot because
he was Ajahn Chah's first Western student. After the initial inspiration, and
with a sense of tremendous faith, the first year I was in Thailand was a hon-
eymoon period, just delightful. But in terms of insight, nothing particular took shape then. In fact, it seemed that things got harder and harder,
largely because of the sense of how much needed to be done. I realized,
Gee, this really is quite a steep mountain. Whew, this is really a lot of work. I
think it also had to do with the fact that there really wasn't much in the way
of instruction. The monk who was the abbot of the branch monastery for
Westerners didn't do a lot of one-to-one teaching. He was an American, a
Vietnam vet; he was much more of a practical guy and he didn't do a lot of
explaining Dharma or giving meditation instruction. After I took full ordination as a monk I was pretty much on my own, without much guidance.
That was one of the reasons things got harder and harder.

When I went to England, however, Ajahn Sumedho had just opened
up this new monastery near the south coast, Chithurst Monastery, and he

was giving two or three Dharma talks a day. He's a brilliant expositor of the teachings and an excellent meditation guide, and being around him, all the bells started going off. He had studied with Ajahn Chah for ten years. He's a gifted explainer, and a profound embodiment of the teaching as well. He used excellent examples and he was good at presenting the teaching.

Most of the insight that I experienced was from studying with him, and the community as it was forming in England. I got there the end of 1979, so it was from 1980 onward. That was a rich and powerful time in my spiritual life. I was a junior monk, so I didn't have any responsibilities. I didn't have to do any teaching, I was very much in the student role. My meditation developed a lot more clarity and focus during those years. Before that I had a lot of energy and a lot of faith, but I didn't really have the tools to direct it in good ways. Being there in that situation, I could channel that energy and guide that in more skillful ways. I had a lot of positive meditation experiences during those years.

One of the things that was really interesting, which was not so much an accomplishment as an embarrassment, was recognizing how, in the effort to practice meditation in the pursuit of spiritual excellence, your mind can get focused on yourself. You can have this overarching idea that what you are doing is for the sake of all human beings, but it can get channeled into "me and my enlightenment program." That was something that really became apparent during those years. I had good meditation experiences, but then I got more and more focused on, *Yeah, this is really great, I'm going to make the big breakthrough here.* Then it suddenly struck me that this self-centered perspective or motivation had snuck up, and it was suddenly all about me and the thrill of achieving. Having grown up through a competitive academic system, through sports and suchlike, I suddenly realized that the spiritual endeavor had become me trying to outplay everybody else. I saw how those noble spiritual aspirations were getting co-opted by the competitive urge, of me wanting to be the best, trying to be the *most* committed, the *most* wise, the *most* competent, the *best* meditator who sits longest.

I think Ajahn Sumedho was trying to point out what I was doing, because I was always trying to be the best at everything. He actually gave me a medal one day, but I didn't get the clue. It was interesting, because eventually I realized that even one's good intentions and noble efforts, like spending hours and hours a day meditating or being incredibly helpful and unselfish, can get co-opted by the acquisitive, competitive self. That was really a helpful thing, to see how that self-centered, ego-inflated quality can take over spiritual practice. I hadn't really recognized it, so it was important to see.

Another kind of insight happened during an all-night meditation that was held every week, on the lunar quarters. We would usually finish the night formally at four a.m., with the morning chanting. Then people would either leave to get some rest or stay on sitting until dawn. On one of those nights I remember, I sat up all through the night and was sitting there as the dawn came. What happened was the recognition that the mind was free of any kind of obstruction, that all of the classical hindrances were absent. Thus there was no desire, there was no aversion, there was no restlessness, there was no doubt, there was no dullness. The mind was just clear and bright. There was mindfulness, there was energy; it was tranquil and peaceful and bright. There was a clear sense of how beautiful the mind is, and how utterly simple, how completely ordinary, how beautiful it is when not cluttered with obstructions. It wasn't as though I came to a *Shazam!* experience, with trumpets from the clouds or anything. In a sense it was a profound experience of normality, but in that it was incredibly sweet and delightful. I recognized that this is what the mind is like. There was no sense of "me"; it wasn't a male mind or a female mind, or a monastic mind or a lay mind, or an English mind. There was a sense of, *This is what the mind feels like when it's free of encumbrances. Incredibly normal and pleasant—an incredibly delightful ordinariness.*

What those experiences do is give you a benchmark with which to measure all the "busy with this" or "pained by that" or "flattered by this" or "worried about that" times. It's not a conscious memory; rather, there's an unconscious baseline that is remembered. You're not remembering now how to ride a bicycle, but you can get on a bike and you can do it. Baselines make a lot of difference. Even though that experience isn't there all the time, there's a recognition that, *Oh, this is what the mind is like in its natural state*—completely ordinary.

After four years at Chithurst Monastery, I did a long walk (our tradition is a wandering order) 830 miles up to the north of England, in Northumberland. I lived in that little monastery for a couple of years. It was a much smaller community, about five people. Chithurst Monastery was much larger and busier—about twenty-five people lived there, and a lot of construction was going on. The monastery in the north was a much smaller group. In the wintertime it was cold and snowy. The retreat period in January and February would be incredibly quiet.

On one retreat I was doing sitting meditation in the stone cottage on the top of a hill in Northumberland and walking meditation outside in the snow. It was a contained, quiet situation, really excellent for meditation. My mind had always been very chattery, but after six or seven years of meditation it was getting quieter, and during the winters there I noticed that it was getting much easier for my mind to be still. Whereas before I'd always experienced meditation as a wrestling match, where you're trying to get your mind to quiet down, to be reasonably steady and stable, it became easier to just stop thinking. I would decide, *Okay, let's just stop thinking,* and my thoughts would stop. Because of that, and my mind being quiet and thought-free, I began to notice, *This is the mind without thinking.* And then a sense of, *This is pretty boring.* Rather than being joyful or having a bright quality, there was this sense of, *Okay, my mind's not thinking—big deal.* There was a strange, pervasive, bland quality.

That was mysterious. It wasn't like one of those experiences I had had at Chithurst, where my mind was bright and joyful. It was quiet, but there was more of a deadness, a sterility. This was strange. It was so quiet; there wasn't a lot to stimulate the mind, not a lot of thinking going on. I began to wonder: *It doesn't seem like there's anything wrong. The mind's concentrated, there's no aversion, there's no lust, there's no doubt—all the hindrances are gone, but how come this is so bland? This is like wet cardboard. Is this supposed to be nirvana? How could you build a world religion around this? Either Buddha was the greatest con man that ever lived, or I'm getting something wrong here.* Day after day it was the same; day after day it was like this.

I thought, *This is really strange.* I couldn't figure out what was wrong. It seemed like all of the conditions that were supposed to indicate that the mind was free of greed, hatred, delusion, and hindrances were in place, but yet there was this ho-hum, bland feeling. So I thought, *Maybe I need more joy, get some light in here.* I started trying to do loving-kindness practices, to crank up the joy factor. But that seemed like smearing pink paint over everything. It didn't work at all. I was really puzzled by this. I was assuming that there was something missing: *There's no brightness, there's no vivacity, no joy there. It's not alive. Why is this?*

Then one day it dawned on me: *Maybe it's not that something is missing, maybe there's something here that's getting in the way.* There was a plugged-up feeling. I thought, *What's here that could be getting in the way?* I went through the usual list: there was no aversion, no greed, no fear or lust. So what could be here that could be clogging everything up? Then I suddenly realized: I *am. It's* me; me *the meditator,* me *the one who's doing it,* me *the one who's the experiencer, the doer.* That was another major light bulb. Because as soon as I had that thought, it was clear that it was the truth. It was like when you get the clue in a crossword puzzle and suddenly, *That's it!* Even if you haven't spelled out the anagram, you know that's the one.

So then I thought *That's really interesting, because definitely that's what's here. It's "me-ness."* It's *I*, this is *I* being, *I* feeling. I remembered a practice Ajahn Sumedho had taught, years before, using the question, Who am I? When he taught that, back in the early 1980s, I noticed that it was a very good way of stopping the thinking mind. It would leave the mind very bright and clear. It immediately occurred to me that maybe I could use that question, Who am I? or What am I? as a way of pinning down the sense of self. And at the same time, listen to the inner sound, what's called the *nada* sound, the ringing silence of the mind. So I thought, *Well, let's try that.* I started using that inquiry practice, focusing the mind and then asking that question: Who am I? Who's meditating? Who's asking this question? Who does this moment belong to?

What happened was that as soon as I started to bring attention back onto the subject in that way, like turning the camera around onto the photographer, there was an immediate transformation. Whereas before, I felt like I was in this little gray box, in this little cottage on a hill in Northumberland, as soon as I used this practice to help the sense of self to fall away, as soon as I asked that question: Who's the owner of this, who's the meditator?, under that scrutiny the sense of self couldn't hold up. Like, if all the lights are on, a conjurer can't do his trick, because people can see how the moves are done. What happened with me was that the walls of the little gray box just fell open. It was like suddenly being in a field of flowers and warm sunlight. *Oh, this is different. It's a whole different atmosphere.*

I'd had that experience early on, about how the inflated sense of self and ambition and competition can take over, but I'd never realized how insidious, pervasive an effect this more subtle kind of self, this "me, the doer" can have. I got really interested in using that as a focus for meditation, looking at that feeling of self, using these practices to notice whenever a feeling of self arose. Then I would steer the quality of wisdom to dissolve it. That was a big moment, seeing that, because its influence had been invisible, like gravity—I didn't even notice it was there. It was only when the mind had quieted down, after six or seven years of meditation, that there was enough stability in the system to be able to see what was going on.

That was a very helpful insight. It wasn't like I would never get lustful or greedy or irritated again. Rather, it was simply that I'd seen something I'd

never seen before. I'd had no idea of the effect of the sense of self, that clinging to the "I, me, mine" feeling. I'd never had a sense of how that worked
and what the effect of it was. Seeing that was a really important moment,
and also seeing the power of using the right kind of wise reflection, investigation. *Dharmavicaya* [investigation of the truth, especially about self] is
another word used to describe the process of investigating feelings of self
and then through the investigation, through the application of an analytical
tool, helping those attachments to break up.

BOYLE: Did the walls stay down, or did you do this again every day for a
long time?

AMARO: Well, they didn't stay down. However, there are many times in
meditation where, once you've seen the trick, you can't un-see it. You can
get distracted, but you still know how the trick works. Even if you get carried away and caught up with other things, you know what's going on. It's
like any other kind of learning—if you learned French thirty years ago, you
can't remember all the vocabulary today, but it's still there.

After a couple of years in Northumberland, I was invited to go to Amaravati, which had just opened in 1984. Ajahn Sumedho had acquired an old
school in Hertfordshire, just north of London, and that became a retreat
center, teaching venue, and training monastery for both nuns and monks.
It was a big place, and I had some administrative skills, so I was invited
to go and help out there. I was delighted to spend some time with Ajahn
Sumedho again. I spent ten years at Amaravati, from 1985 to 1995, helping
out, doing a certain amount of both teaching and administration.

BOYLE: You were busy, as opposed to the quiet winter snows of Northumberland.

AMARO: Yes, it was the other end of the spectrum.

BOYLE: That's always been hard for me. I mean, my practice just goes on
hold when I have big projects under way. What was your experience?

AMARO: Good. I'm a gregarious person. I enjoyed it—one of the few
who really did. It was a residential community of about fifty people. When
we had retreats, another forty-five people would be there.

BOYLE: You were able to keep your meditation going well, including that
falling down of the walls where you became aware of the self and the not-self?

AMARO: Well, somewhat. There was so much going on during the
course of a day. There wasn't a conflict, but it was a different environment,
so it required the use of different resources. Maybe something of that same
kind of insight into not-self, but there it was brought into action by having
to deal with having five meetings a day, and going off to different teaching

engagements, and being available for anyone and everyone who had any kind of problem or question.

BOYLE: So you brought new resources to bear. Could you say something about what those resources were?

AMARO: It had a lot to do with not making a problem out of anything. Amaravati had been a decrepit school. Its administrators knew seven years before they actually sold it that they were going to close it, so they did no maintenance on the school buildings for seven years. Twenty-two buildings, 55,000 square feet, so it was an incredible amount of physical work just to get the place in shape. Then there were 50 people to bring together in a new monastic community. There were any number of things to contend with. My practice centered around adaptability and being ready to be open to whatever the day brought.

At the beginning of each day, during the morning sitting, I would deliberately set the intention: *Okay, here we are, sitting in the quiet of the hall in the early morning. After the bell rings, at the end of the sitting, the* bardo *of the world will begin. Don't believe in anything that happens between the bell at the end of the morning sitting and when you're back in your room alone, sitting at the end of the day.* I would very consciously bracket the whole of the day, create a framework for it. *The real life at Amaravati is silence, solitude, stillness; all the rest is just the phantasmagoria of the day. Don't fight against it. Do it, follow it through and relate to it sincerely, but remember that it's the* bardo *of the day.*

BOYLE: In your book *Small Boat, Great Mountain*, you quote a teaching of the Buddha: "Wherever there is something that is intended, something that is acted upon or something that lies dormant, then that becomes the basis for consciousness to land, and where consciousness lands, that then is the cause for confusion, attachment, becoming, and rebirth." That struck a real chord with me, because it's a problem for me. For you, bracketing is what works.

AMARO: Well, that was my way of establishing that attitude—don't make a place for any of it to land. In Britain there are a number of freewheeling "gentlemen of the road" who like to wander and stay in Christian monasteries around the country. We got on that circuit for a while. These guys didn't really like the Buddhist discipline, the fact that everyone in the monastery has to follow the same rules. The idea of no supper didn't go down so well. Anyway, there was a time when one of these wanderers was staying at Amaravati. He was an eccentric character, quite intelligent and outspoken, but also quite intuitive. I was really struck by something he said one day. In that era there was a big courtyard in the center of the monastery. I was walking across this courtyard from the monks' *vihara* over to the main hall while this fellow was passing by. He looked at me and said, "What are you doing, walking around like you don't exist?" I was just walking across the courtyard, but at that moment, I had the sense of being very contained and was just observing, feeling the body walk; I was not on my way to the next thing, but was just being there. And somehow this guy had seemingly picked up on the very thing that I was working to do. It really made me chuckle, that this flakey gentleman of the road had seen that, somehow, and given voice to his impression—"What are you doing, walking around like you don't exist?" I wasn't walking in slow motion or anything. To the casual observer it was just Ajahn Amaro walking across the courtyard. I'm not making any claims about that, but it was curious that somebody picked up on that unentangled attitude and expressed it the way he did. It always stuck in my mind that not giving the events of the day a place to land can also be discernible from the outside.

Some insights during those years were not based on profound states of meditation. Every morning after meditation and the chores period we would have breakfast, and Ajahn Sumedho would often give a daily teaching. There would also be notices read and different exchanges. The whole community was gathered; everyone was there and everyone was paying attention. I noticed that in those kinds of situations, if I made some sort of witty remark or said something that could pass as profound or interesting, and everyone laughed or made approving noises, I would feel an enormous flush of delight. But alternatively, if I said something that fell flat or was stupid, and everything went quiet while everyone looked at the carpet, then I would feel a breaking-into-a-million-pieces feeling. This was deeply distressing. I thought, *Look at this, isn't it interesting—if it goes one way, the world is perfect and you're happy. If it goes the other way, it's the end of everything, it's broken into a million pieces.*

So I began to reflect on how much my mind was conditioned around "approval" being good and "rejection" being bad. I began to see, more and more, that I had a strong psychological habit of seeking approval and wanting to be liked, while dreading being rejected or disliked. That was interesting—a very strong piece of conditioning. It's really a powerful force. I started to look at and examine that, and use this same kind of investigation, or reflection, to explore it: Who's afraid? Who's afraid of being rejected, who's afraid of failing?.

That exploration led to an even more interesting area, where I suddenly realized that my basic response to life was to worry: if it exists, worry about it. Again, this was so pervasive and so deeply rooted that I had never noticed it. By this time I'd been in robes for ten years or so. I saw that if something existed, my first response was to worry. I took responsibility for it, I made it my problem, and I worried about it. It was so normal that I'd never even realized it.

It's also interesting that the feeling of self was more visible than the feeling of anxiety. This was a peculiar realization. Perhaps it's because anxiety is buried more deeply in the reptile brain. The "I" feeling is more out in the superego, near the cortex area, but fear is deep tissue, reptile brain material: "Threat. Protect." So I decided to look at that. A kind of practice Ajahn Sumedho had taught, but which I'd never really made much of, involved using the physical body as a reference point for emotion. He would often talk about anxiety or worry being a knot of tension in the solar plexus. Now I'd heard him say this, and I'd paid attention to it during guided meditations, but I'd never made much of it. But I got so interested in the anxiety reaction, which could be triggered by anything, like sitting in a traffic jam waiting to get to the airport. You know, *Are we going to make it, are we going to make it?* Or whether it was just, *What's the right time to end the meeting? Have I eaten too much food today?* Whatever it was, I could see that my first reaction was to fret: if it exists, fret. What I started to do was to make that feeling of anxiety a deliberate meditation object. At the beginning of the day, I would set an intention that whenever the mind went toward anxiety, I should take note of that, bring the attention into the body, and see where it was felt. Let the mind rest on that feeling and see if I could let go of it.

So I started out with that intention, every day. Because things were so busy at Amaravati that it was always easy to be swept up in the content of events. This was a really interesting period of my meditation, and I worked specifically on that area for two or three years. It was a pervasive and deeply rooted habit, incredibly strong. It wasn't just a quick, *Oh, look at that,* then *ding,* off it goes. It was a really, really deeply rooted habit. I noticed whatever I was worrying about: whether so-and-so was unhappy with what was going on in a meeting, or whether I was going to get to an appointment, or whether I'd written a letter in a good way and people would like it. Then I'd say, "Oh, there's anxiety. I've just written this letter and now there's this thought: *Oh, I hope she likes it and she's happy. Oh dear, what will happen if she doesn't like it?*" I would deliberately notice that feeling and take the attention *off* the object, withdrawing attention from the letter or the person and bringing it into the body. And sure enough, every time, there would be this knot of tension in the belly. I would consciously notice that feeling and then let the power of attention, of awareness itself, be the relaxing agent. It's not as if I thought, *Oh, this is a thing that shouldn't be here, I've got to get rid of it.* More just seeing how uncomfortable the feeling is and letting the intuition sink in that, *Gee, this is really uncomfortable, why am I doing this to myself?*, letting the relaxation come as a natural letting go, rather than, *I should let go, because this is the right thing to do.* You see the difference?

BOYLE: Yes! It's striking to me that this is something that you observed, and then you arrived at an intellectual analysis that led you to follow Ajahn Sumedho's teaching on how to deal with anxiety.

AMARO: Well, it's also very much the style of our teacher, Ajahn Chah. He used reflective thought and investigation a lot. If you read his teachings, if you look at that collection made by Wisdom Publications called *Food for the Heart*, over and over again he'll describe this process of working on some particular issue or looking at some kind of trait, and it's almost like he's having a conversation with himself. He describes his trains of thought, or how he looked at things. So it's very much in that style. I guess that's why I was drawn to him as a teacher. He functions in a way that I feel compatible with.

To continue the piece about anxiety—I would go to that feeling and let the mind stay with it until the tightness in the gut had relaxed. The last part of it is to go back to the object—back to the letter you were looking at, the person you were having a conversation with, the traffic jam you were stuck in—to look at it again. Suddenly it's a different traffic jam. It's lost its shimmer of threat: *Oh, it's just these cars sitting in the road. If it means us not getting to the airport, that's not such a terrible thing. Here we are, and the cars aren't moving. Either we'll catch the plane or we won't.* Then we see how different those two worlds are, the world seen through the eyes of fear and through the eyes of no fear. By seeing the difference between them, we let that be an informing influence. *How does this feel? Oh—very different.*

I explicitly worked on that for two or three years. I made that the centerpiece of my practice until the habit had shifted. That's how long it took to shift, two or three years. I don't continue it now because I don't need to. I find I don't relate to the world in that way. If I compare how my mind operates now with how it did twenty or twenty-five years ago, it's very different. Anxiety was such a pervasive habit. Even if there isn't a feeling of self, the habit of attachment is the cause of fear. It's a protective instinct. The instinct is still based on primal reactions to predators, like saber-toothed tigers, or contention with the tribe across the valley. Now my mind doesn't get worried in the same way. That was one of the most striking features of the Amaravati years.

BOYLE: Then after Amaravati you came here, to Redwood Valley.

AMARO: I spent the first rains retreat here in California in 1995. It was before this monastery opened, it was in a different place somewhat north of here. Three other monks and I spent the rains retreat here in 1995.

BOYLE: And you had to do the same thing all over again, physically— you had to build a new monastery.

AMARO: Yes, we had to do construction. But we don't have a tenth of the number of meetings. It's a smaller community, and we take on a lot fewer duties. Amaravati is only twenty-five miles from London. It was deliberately set up to be accessible by a large number of people. It was set up to be a teaching center, so it's a magnet attracting all sorts of people. Here at Abhayagiri Monastery, we're two and a half hours from San Francisco. We're not a retreat center. We don't hold big public events here. It's a different complex of qualities, much simpler. We've done a lot of construction, but putting up buildings is much less complicated than living in a community of fifty people. We also delegate responsibility, so it's not as though my co-abbot, Ajahn Pasanno, and I have to decide everything. We're a very egalitarian outfit in terms of decision making and job sharing.

BOYLE: Could you say something about what's been happening with your spiritual life since then? Further development, baselines, anything along those lines?

AMARO: Well, it's a bit of a stretch because, as you've probably already guessed, we don't think in those terms very often. However, there have been some noticeable benchmarks. Probably the most striking is the way of handling responsibility. Maybe it's an extension of the nonanxiety. As human beings we can get very attached to outcomes, wanting things to go well, not wanting things to go badly. In years gone by, when things went right I would tend to say, "This is great! Things have really gone well. This is marvelous!" Or, "Oh no, this wonderful thing has led to this big problem. Dang, how did that happen? Gee, never saw that coming." You get enough of those cycles, and you learn. When some absolutely appalling, dreadful thing happens, rather than thinking, *What are we going to do?! This is awful, everything is falling apart,* I would think, *Well, this will probably bring something very beneficial with it. We don't know what that might be, but don't get upset, because now that X has fallen apart we have an opportunity to do Y.* Now I tend to see that things always contain their opposites, that it's never a matter of looking at the superficial characteristics of success or failure, at whether things are going well or going badly. This was not exactly an "Aha!" event but more a broadening of view.

There is also the aspect of the way I now tend to relate to people. If people are happy and inspired by me now, I don't think, *Oh great! She's inspired, this is wonderful!* And similarly, if someone's depressed, and looking harrowed, haggard, I don't think, *Oh, what am I going to do? I've got to make sure so-and-so is all right.* Rather there is a sense of allowing more space for the world to be the way it is, not getting caught up in other people's happiness and unhappiness. It's not as though I don't care, it's not indifference, but more like an accommodation to the way the world is.

BOYLE: You're saying that there was no single sudden enlightenment experience, but a series of small ones. And then a lot of working on yourself in ways where you've identified a problem and the things that are available to help work on it, and you stay with that.

AMARO: Yes, I have never had any kind of *Shazam!* moment where suddenly everything was permanently different. In our tradition our teacher never made much of that kind of thing. He tended to play down such experiences. Teachers tend to attract people of similar natures, and groups of all kinds tend to have an in-house language. If the teacher has had a big *Shazam!* experience and chooses to talk about it often, then that tends to be what happens in the student. Our teacher tended to not make a big thing about that—even though he had the reputation of being an *arahant* [enlightened person] and certainly had a few *Shazam!*-like experiences himself. On these the most you could coax out of him was, "Well, that was a significant moment." But he wouldn't really go into any kind of detail. So that has been the house style.

BOYLE: I think that to some extent that is the style in Buddhism. I have to, to some extent, draw people out on this, get them to admit that it's not all just a continuation of ordinary experience, that at some point ordinary consciousness has changed.

AMARO: Right. So for people in our community, the most you'll get out of those who have had great experiences is something like, "It's different now."

5
Interview with
Martine Batchelor

Martine Batchelor is the author of Women in Korean Zen *(2007) and* The Spirit of the Buddha *(2010). She gives talks and conducts retreats throughout Europe and North America. She gave this interview during a visit to San Francisco, on November 10, 2010.*

BOYLE: The first question, concerning your path story, is how you got started. As I recall, you read the *Dhammapada* at eighteen, and that's what got you interested in Buddhism.

MARTINE BATCHELOR: Well, yes and no, because what happened was that from a very young age, eleven, I was socially and politically conscious. I was active in politics, along with some other people I knew. Then I met a group of musicians, and one of them was interested in meditation. He had this book, the *Dhammapada*, and reading the *Dhammapada* made me think differently. What the Buddha was basically saying, as I understood it then, was that before you try to change others, maybe you should try to change yourself. I thought it was a good point because I could see that I was very idealistic. That was 1972 or 1973, toward the end of the hippie movement. I was influenced by the freaks movement where everybody was supposed to love everybody. The beginning of my journey happened when I realized that there were things I couldn't just think away. I could not think jealousy away or self-centeredness away. I could aspire to the loftiest ideals, but that had no effect at all on changing my behavior or my thought. That's when what the Buddha said resonated. I thought, *Oh yes, he's got a point. I am experiencing what he's talking about, and maybe before going into politics I should practice meditation. Then there might be a possibility of some transformation.*

BOYLE: So you were sensitive to those things, and you responded to the message that came along. But it was four years later that you went to Korea?

M. BATCHELOR: Yes, because first I had to find a way to get there. I left home and did not go to university. I went to live in England, and in England I met all kinds of people who all did different things. That was between 1972 and 1975, and things started to happen, one could say, spiritually. The Karmapa, the former Karmapa, passed through with the Black Hat ceremony. The Rajneesh people were doing Rajneesh things. I tried different things, like one evening I would go to a Sufi evening, then for a week I'd try the Rajneesh method. But I could see that these things were not really resonating with me. I don't know if my experience with the Karmapa resonated very much. So I decided to travel. I decided to go east, and I worked to get a little money. I met Kalu Rinpoche in the south of France, but again that did not appeal to me. There was something that did not grab me, that did not appeal to me. What really appealed to me was China and Zen. So I planned to go to Taiwan.

When I left, I traveled overland and found myself in Nepal. It was a beautiful bus journey, an amazing bus journey from Pokhara to Katmandu, and the whole time I was thinking about money. Then I realized that you can be in the most beautiful place, but if you don't do anything with your mind, it doesn't make a difference. This is when I decided to investigate meditation seriously. I went to Thailand and spent a few days in a temple. However, being a feminist, I felt women were treated like second-class citizens there, and that did not appeal to me. I wanted to go to Taiwan but I couldn't get a visa, so I decided to go to Japan. I was flying on Korean Airlines, and they put "Korea" on my plane ticket by mistake. I met a Korean monk and he said, "Oh yeah, lots of meditation in Korea." I thought, *I can go there for a month. I have just barely enough money to do that.* Then I'd go to Japan to find work. So I went to Korea, and I stayed there. It was the best mistake Korean Airlines ever made.

BOYLE: Your book gives an account of what happened from the time you arrived in Korea until Zen Master Kusan died. You say that it took you a while to learn what meditation really was. But as time went on, your meditation deepened and you were better able to keep your mind clear. At one point you talk about something that happened during a retreat:

My domestic responsibility for the duration of the retreat was to clean the communal bathroom. I would do this chore at four o'clock every afternoon.

At the same time, though, another nun would appear and proceed to wash herself before performing an afternoon ceremony at which she had to officiate. This went on for several weeks and I began to feel extremely resentful. Then one day I went down at four o'clock, and it suddenly didn't matter any more that she was there washing herself. It was my time to clean and her time to wash. How wonderful it felt to be free of resentment! Although a small incident, it was somehow very meaningful to me. It showed that meditation worked quietly. Without my intentionally forcing any changes, it dissolved the grasping and attachments that gave rise to the irritation.[1]

Remember that experience?

M. BATCHELOR: Yes, sure. I had gone to the nunnery, and I was meditating on the question, What is this? I was not consciously thinking, *I should do this, I should do that.* Every day at four o'clock I was upset when she came into the bathroom I was cleaning, but this did not disturb my meditation. When I left the bathroom I went back to doing my meditation and forgot about being upset. What I found interesting was that after two weeks I suddenly did not feel upset when she came into the bathroom. There was no resentment, there was just a kind of warm, how to say it, equanimity. Then I understood what to me is the most important thing about meditation—the de-grasping effect. Cultivating concentration and inquiry dissolves the grasping. But it is a subtle effect. I call it the "*phht*" effect, the fact that by just doing meditation, something is released. So then when you are again in contact with a certain situation, you don't grasp at it anymore. That's why I am not so focused on "big bang" meditation experiences. I think that's why when people do a retreat, say a seven-day retreat, they generally report that it continues to work for the next three months. Because there has been a kind of releasing, and that releasing stays active until they get very busy and everything comes up again. I encourage them to continue not so much with the sitting, the formal sitting, but to continue with the awareness. I would say the effect can last a little longer that way.

BOYLE: That is an important theme. What I am interested in is how a little insight experience like this feeds into your development, and what you learned from it.

M. BATCHELOR: When I was in Korea I was not thinking much about these things. I was just doing the job, the job being to meditate. That's what I did. Because, you see, in Korea you are in the Zen tradition, the Rinzai Zen/Linchi Chan/Ganhwa Seon tradition. In this tradition there is a great emphasis on awakening, on the big bang experience. Any of the things that

I describe in the book are just ordinary stuff in terms of that Zen tradition, in terms of the criteria that were there around me. My experience really was just with what was happening. I did not reflect on it particularly. It was only after I left the monastery and became a teacher, when I was talking about these experiences that I had had, that they began to make sense. Not in terms of a big bang experience, but in terms of what I call de-grasping. That is why I include them in my talks, because to me they are more important.

Even before the bathroom experience there was another experience, which really showed me how it worked. For the first time, I was sitting in meditation for the full three-month period completely on my own. All the other people had gone to other places, and so I was sitting in meditation by myself. It was a little difficult, because as I was sitting the meditation did not seem to work, and since it did not seem to be working, I thought that maybe I should be doing something more useful. So I got up from my cushion and went to do something that seemed more useful, which was to read a Zen book. I got the book, and I sat down and tried to read it and I couldn't read it. That's when I realized that although I had the feeling that the meditation was not working, actually it *was* working. My mind had gone to a place that was relatively calm, even if it did not look that way. It was a very small insight that showed me that a little de-grasping had occurred. I could not get interested in the book because I was in a different state, a kind of equanimous state. I was not in the doing state, I was more in the being state. That's when I thought, *Ah, although it doesn't look like it is working, actually it is*. That was the first time when I realized, *Oh yeah, this works differently from what is emphasized in general*.

BOYLE: That's why I'm doing these interviews. Because that's what I felt, that things were not happening the way I read about them. It's so easy to overlook things that actually are very important because they seem so normal and undramatic.

M. BATCHELOR: Yes. To go back to the debate about sudden versus gradual, I think we've emphasized the sudden when actually the sudden and gradual together makes more sense. Yes, you have a little experience, but it works at both levels: you have a kind of sudden letting go, a sudden thing that happens, and then you have two things, the gradual *drip, drip* effect of what you are doing in your daily life but also the effect of doing the meditation.

BOYLE: Have we finished covering your time in Korea?

M. BATCHELOR: When I was in Korea I had, in a way, different insights. But I only realized later that they were insights, not at the time they happened. It was only after I was teaching that I started to look at my experience in Korea in a different way. When I was in Korea I was just doing the job, which was to meditate. It was only after I started teaching that I began to understand what I had been doing.

BOYLE: Can you think of other things that happened in Korea?

M. BATCHELOR: Yes. Many of these small insights convinced me of this de-grasping effect. I think what we experience in meditation is not a way of getting into another reality or something behind the veil of illusion. Everything that we experience, whether it be a mystical experience, insight, meditative experience, whatever, is de-grasping. I don't think it matters too much what you do, if you do Zen practice, or Tibetan practice, or vipassana practice. Generally de-grasping will happen in some way. It's like, we feel differently in comparison to how we feel when we are grasping.

De-grasping happens in different ways. One important experience happened after I had been six month or eight months in Korea, while I was sitting in meditation. I was asking my koan, What is this?, and suddenly I saw that I was totally self-centered. That was the first time I saw that, ever. Up to that moment I thought I was the greatest, most compassionate person in the world. And then I saw very clearly that all my thoughts, feelings, and sensations were about me. That was really important to me. But it did not awe me; I just saw it.

BOYLE: Did you have an understanding of that, an insight into that at the intellectual level?

M. BATCHELOR: No. I just saw it so clearly at that moment. It was the clearest thing I've ever seen. Then I saw also that the other four people in the meditation room were exactly the same. I thought it was funny. After that, the job was to diminish the self-centeredness. But when you have an insight and you see something you have not seen before, it doesn't mean that the insight remains the same, because the "bang" effect is not there anymore. The insight becomes part of the way you see things, part of the concentration and inquiry of meditation.

By coming back again and again to the breath or to the koan, what happens is that you don't feed your conditioned mental habits so much. You diminish their power by not going on with them, by not identifying so much with them. You come back to the meditation, and it becomes more quiet and spacious. You come back to the functioning of the pattern, you are not going for any eradication of the pattern. For example, planning— you come back to planning, to making a plan, but you don't obsess about it. That leads you to quietness, openness, and spaciousness. Then you are doing vipassana, which is a matter of looking deeply into impermanence or asking a question. We have a tendency to feel that things are permanent, which can get us into difficulties. By looking deeply, we will experience impermanence. We will become more aware of impermanence, and this will help us to become clearer. You develop a creative awareness, and then through that creative awareness you can see what goes on differently. So that, I would conclude, is the way meditation works.

BOYLE: That's a wonderful statement. But this was all so gradual.

M. BATCHELOR: When I was in Korea I was just sitting in meditation. But because I was in the Rinzai tradition, I was waiting for something special to happen. The big bang experience.

BOYLE: And it didn't come.

M. BATCHELOR: Yes, of course, nothing. I was not too interested in it either, but that was the framework, that was what I was supposed to experience. I did not experience the big bang, but I was still doing what mattered to me, which was to develop wisdom and compassion. I was going on my little way while everybody was talking about awakening and so on.

BOYLE: When you had that experience of realizing that you were self-centered, that wasn't just an intellectual insight. For me, sometimes it's so subtle. It's like a soap bubble popping, and everything is a tiny bit clearer. But it's not gradual—the soap bubble breaks and everything is a little bit different, suddenly just a little bit different.

M. BATCHELOR: It's sudden because you see something suddenly. It's always been there, but it's only now you see it, so the sudden aspect is that you see it, and it lasts two minutes, five minutes, and then it becomes a memory. It becomes a memory, and then what you have to do is a gradual process in order to really organically live it. By seeing that you are so self-centered, you can start to work on being more other-centered, in a conscious way.

BOYLE: But in the Korean tradition you were instructed to always be working on that one koan.

M. BATCHELOR: Yes.

BOYLE: For example, when I interviewed Ajahn Amaro, he talked about things like this. When he realized that something was a problem with him, then in his tradition there was a method to use that applied to that particular problem. Whereas in the Korean tradition . . .

M. BATCHELOR: No, no. You don't have specific methods. To me, the way it works in the Korean Zen tradition is that you just cultivate insight in the Korean way, and then over time you have a de-grasping. But you are training in ethics, meditation, and wisdom, all three, when you work. This is made very clear in Korea. Every two weeks you recite the bodhisattva precepts, the fifty-eight bodhisattva precepts, and you are supposed to live according to them. You are in a certain environment, a very communal environment. Then you have to apply the methodology in a living environment. That's what I did for ten years. It was a living environment, which helps for transformation.

BOYLE: That's good, that's what I wanted to clarify. Because it is so important, I think, for any student who is working on their practice.

One other thing that I am curious about is that Stephen [see chapter 8] never comes in here. But you met him in Korea?

M. BATCHELOR: Yes, I met him in Korea. He came when I was six years into my stay in Korea. He arrived and I told him to change his clothes at the airport, because he was not wearing the proper clothes. Then I had to teach him the ropes, how to live in Korea, because he had been a Tibetan monk. We got to know each other just as we were going along. But there was nothing special.

BOYLE: Was Stephen the reason that you left Korea?

M. BATCHELOR: No, the reason I left was because Master Kusan had died. When he died, it was like the sun had gone out. It was only after he died that I realized how important he had been. It was really like a hole, a big hole. Things were not the same. The next master who came along was not the same; that's when the possibility of leaving arose.

BOYLE: Stephen left at the same time and you both disrobed, got married, and moved to England?

M. BATCHELOR: Yes.

BOYLE: What did you do in England?

M. BATCHELOR: I was a house cleaner. I did that for ten years. We moved to a community, and that was great training.

BOYLE: What kind of community was it?

M. BATCHELOR: It was an alternative Buddhist community. It was very consensual. We lived there for six years, and that was where I learned a lot about actually applying the training. It was really good.

BOYLE: Were you teaching?

M. BATCHELOR: No, I only started to teach after I had been in England for four years. But to live in the community, to live with other Western people in a nonhierarchical model, was a great training. Not easy every day, but I practiced a lot there, I really worked. What I had done for ten years in Korea, I really applied for the next six years. I had several insights, experiences, when I was there. Community life is a very tough environment for a Westerner; it was like a pressure cooker for us. When it's hierarchical it's difficult, but easier; but when it's democratic and alternative, it's more intense. It is really an intensive training. It's much more intensive than sitting in meditation. So it was really good, I learned a lot there. Then I started to teach, and then through the teaching too I learned a lot and had more experiences.

BOYLE: Can you think of one or two or three examples of things that happened during that time?

M. BATCHELOR: The first thing was for me to see. I had been a nun for ten years, and then I got married to Stephen and we went back and for six months I felt I was eighteen years old. I had the emotional life of an eighteen-year-old, and that was sobering. I saw that when you are a monk or a nun you don't have to deal with any of that stuff. That was really eye-opening, and then after six months I decided, *You've been training for ten years, now you need to start to use it, really apply it.* Then things began to change in my practice. One thing I realized was that I was grasping at Korea geographically. A year and a half in, or two years in, I was in this beautiful Devon manor house, a huge estate by a river. It was one of the most beautiful landscapes in England, and suddenly I was walking one afternoon, it was sunny, and I was walking back from town toward the house and I stopped and I looked about, and I thought, *This is beautiful, this is beautiful for what it is.* Because up to that moment I had been thinking, *It ain't bad, but it's not like Korea.* That's when I realized I had been grasping at Korea, and because I was grasping at Korea I could not see the beauty of Devon. That moment I thought, *Ah, now I am in Devon.* I just saw it at that moment.

I had one of my major insights there. From way, way back I had the habit that if somebody hurt me, I would sulk, and I would do it for a long time. I was very bad about that. I would not look at the person, I would not talk to the person, I just cut off. Then one day this happened. Somebody had said something hurtful to me the night before, and in the morning when I arrived in the kitchen she was there. I could see the pattern arise, the pattern of shutting her off. I could see myself going toward it, but the creative awareness said, "Do something else." Then there was this incredible fear, and that's when I realized why change is hard, because it's easier to live with the pain of the known than the threat of the unknown. It was the power of the creative awareness, which made me think, *Let's try something different this one time.* So I turned to her, I smiled, and it was so easy. I thought,

Why did I not do this before? Then I never sulked and cut people off again, because I realized that it was painful, not only for myself but for the other person. In that moment there was compassion as I realized, *You can't behave that way, your cutting off and ignoring is so painful for the other person. It is so painful for yourself too.* From that time on I did not do it.

BOYLE: That was quite a long time ago, soon after you went to England.

M. BATCHELOR: This experience was maybe, I would say three years in.

Once I had what I would call a mystical experience in Korea, but it was in the oddest of situations. It happened when I was visiting a Catholic nun. It was amazing. She was in a hermitage—you know, they don't go out into the world. She was the one in charge of visitors. We talked for two or three hours, and the whole time we were talking there was an amazing light in the room. I thought, *This is weird, but why not, I need not do anything with it.* I thought, *Ah, this is interesting. Anything can happen.*

I had another experience that was kind of mystical. It happened while I was in London, about fifteen years ago. I was teaching Zen to a group in London, and as I was teaching them and also sitting with them at the time, suddenly I had this very, very strong experience of everybody having buddha nature. Very strong, and it was not just an idea. It was kind of an amazing feeling. After it was over I could see that I had a choice of going into the experience more or leaving it alone. Being the pragmatic person I am, I thought, *No, no it would not be a good idea to go down that way.*

BOYLE: This happened while you were in the retreat?

M. BATCHELOR: No, during a daylong sitting. It happened while I was teaching and sitting, and I thought, *If I want to continue to teach, it might not be a good idea to go into this kind of exciting and exhilarating experience. I don't want to talk about the experience, because it did not make any difference to me.* So I let it disappear. The only thing that was interesting was more on a scientific level—how did it feel to experience something like that? That's what I got out of it. I thought, *Hmm, that is interesting, I can see why people could get excited about this.* But I thought it was a bit too exciting, so I did not push it through. It was interesting to have it, just in terms of seeing what people experience. That's generally not what I experience; I am more interested in the de-grasping aspect.

BOYLE: But you could see buddha nature in these people at that moment?

M. BATCHELOR: Yes, sure. It was like any sudden moment, you can interpret it in many different ways. That's the way I interpreted it. It could have been interpreted differently by somebody else. What was interesting was the joy, the warmth, and the exhilaration. I could see how people could be enthusiastic about these experiences, because it is very elating. You feel something very different. But personally I thought, *Umm, that's a bit over the top*.

BOYLE: Oh really? How do you feel about it now?

M. BATCHELOR: The same as I felt then. It was interesting insofar as it made me possibly experience what somebody else might experience in that way and get very excited about. It was just what it was.

BOYLE: Well, that's true. I find it fascinating, so I am exploring it a bit. Could you say that you were better able to see these people the way they really were?

M. BATCHELOR: No, I am not saying that. I don't use this kind of language. No, it was the way it appeared. It was a perception. What you were saying right then is not my kind of language. No, it was more a feeling. I felt a total certitude in that moment, like what I call an organic certitude, that everybody had buddha nature from my point of view. But so what? You know, this could just be my interpretation, because if you are a Christian with the same experience, you might say God is everywhere, or somebody else would see something else. I had a feeling that then, in that moment, got interpreted through my Buddhist framework.

Personally what I am interested in, though I think it would be difficult to do, is to see how much what you experience and what you perceive is influenced by your framework. If you have a Christian framework, do you have a Christian experience? If you have a Zen framework, do you have a Zen experience? If you have a Theravada framework, do you have a Theravada experience, necessarily? Also, does the kind of meditation you do impact on what you experience?

BOYLE: That is what I was going to ask. Does meditation in general help you get past the framework that is conditioning the experience, whether you are Buddhist or Sufi or Catholic?

M. BATCHELOR: Personally, I don't think so. I would be surprised if it did, because you always see through your senses. You are asking if there is an experience that is beyond the senses. But if you have an experience that is beyond the senses, your senses are not going to get it.

BOYLE: But most of the time what we perceive or what we see—I am talking psychology now—is filtered through and rearranged by the existing structures of the mind, so that what you think you are seeing may be quite different.

M. BATCHELOR: I think when you do meditation you can dissolve what I would call the negative aspect of that. It is the exaggeration and proliferation that goes. I don't think the functioning of perception goes away, so that you have a tabula rasa experience before any functioning is operating.

BOYLE: Could you continue looking at your life during those times? If you think of something that stands out, I would love to hear about it.

M. BATCHELOR: To me the point of meditation is that we develop the power of the creative awareness. The more we meditate, the more power the creative awareness will develop, in many different ways, alongside the three trainings of ethics, meditation, and wisdom. In a way you develop more and more ethics, you develop more and more meditation, you develop more and more wisdom. They all feed each other. So yes, you can have small insights or big insights in terms of your relationship to others and in terms of the way you are. But I think also what you develop more and more is what I call stability and openness. You develop a strength within yourself that allows you to be with your feelings in a different way. You can experience your feelings, but within you there is a place that is stronger than that, and so you can have upsetting feelings and not be necessarily taken over by them.

I try to practice all the time, not just on the cushion but in daily life. I see things in this way, then in that way, and there is de-grasping in this way and that way. You may realize that there are some conditions that make it easy to be a good Buddhist, a good meditator, and other conditions that will make it more difficult. After I was in the community for a while, I realized that if I was tired I would become irritable, so then instead of going ahead and being irritated with somebody, I went to rest. Just different things like this; you start to see more clearly, not only your condition but also in the conditions of others. So again I would say it's not just, like, insight into yourself. I think it's more about how you are present to others, how you listen to them, how you respond to others, respond to situations. I think one has to be careful not to focus too much on insight, because this is very inner stuff. Personally I would say if you really develop meditation, then it makes a difference not only to your inner landscape but also to the way you are with other people.

One last learning experience, then, again having to do with seeing something differently and acting differently. This was when I was still a nun and I went back home because my father was very ill. I saw him dying, I saw his last breath. What was interesting is that up to that point I had believed in impermanence, but as in, "Oh, it's impermanent, the vase is broken, who cares, it's not mine, it's impermanent." If you want you can use the idea of impermanence in a fatalistic, easy way. But when I saw my father die, when I saw his last breath, then I experienced impermanence. What was interesting is that at that moment there was this incredible compassion for everything that was alive. It made me look at people in a very different way, instead of saying, "Oh, that person did this or that person is like that." It made me really see the fragility of each human being, whose life rests upon a single breath. That was one of Master Kusan's teachings, that our life rests upon a single breath. Then I really saw it, and to me what was interesting in that experience was that compassion arose, and from that compassion arose a different way to look at the self and others. A different attitude arose, which I cultivated, and this made me look at people in a more compassionate way.

BOYLE: That's beautiful. I am glad you added that.

M. BATCHELOR: The way I teach is not very formal; I always talk about different things from my own experience. If you look at my other book, *Let Go: A Buddhist Guide to Breaking Habits,* in there you have quite a few descriptions of this kind of thing. You have many more experiences there.

6
Interview with
Shaila Catherine

Shaila Catherine is the author of Focused and Fearless: A Meditator's Guide to States of Deep Joy, Calm, and Clarity *and* Wisdom Wide and Deep: A Practical Handbook for Mastering Jhāna and Vipassanā. *We talked at her home south of San Francisco, on November 10, 2009.*

BOYLE: What I'd like to do here is start with when you first became interested in Buddhism and follow that on through to your life today.

CATHERINE: I can give you a background sketch. I started meditating when I was seventeen years old and still in high school. I just loved it right from the start.

BOYLE: Were there other people in your high school doing it?

CATHERINE: No, no.

BOYLE: How did you hear about it, how did you learn that there was such a thing as meditation?

CATHERINE: When I heard a friend mention that his mother meditated, I immediately wanted to learn. So I took a class; it wasn't a Buddhist form of practice, but I meditated diligently every day for a few years. In college, when I was twenty or twenty-one years of age, I met someone who had attended a silent retreat, and it perked my interest. I found out the details and attended my first Buddhist silent retreat. As soon as I experienced the retreat format and some depth of meditative experience, I knew this was exactly what I was looking for. It presented a way to explore the mind. I kept attending more retreats, and then traveled to Asia after graduate school. That was in 1990. First I attended a three-week insight meditation retreat led by Christopher Titmuss that is held in Bodh Gaya, India, every January.

Bodh Gaya is near the pilgrimage site that commemorates the location of the Buddha's enlightenment.

After the Bodh Gaya retreat I traveled by train to Lucknow with a few friends and met a Hindu teacher by the name of H.W.L. Poonja (we affectionately called him Papaji). Poonjaji doesn't teach meditation; his approach involved dialogue and a mind-to-mind process. I spent the remainder of my four months' journey with Poonjaji. I came back briefly to the United States to take care of personal business, and then returned on a one-way ticket, intending to stay with him as long as possible. I lived in his home for a number of years, served the *satsang* and the people who came to receive teachings, and periodically visited Bodh Gaya, Dharamsala, Thailand, and Nepal to practice Buddhist meditation. For several years I alternated between living with Poonjaji and meditating in monasteries. Being in the environment of an extraordinary guru was intense; it was a time of my life that overflowed with spiritual experiences, but it was also burdened by the dynamics of spiritual community. The anonymity and seclusion of the monastic interludes were a welcome respite.

Although I spent a few years practicing in Buddhist monasteries and was dedicated to the meditation, I didn't shave my head or ordain. Additionally, I received teachings from a few Tibetan dzogchen masters in Nepal, and studied Buddhism for a year in England, until I returned to the United States in December 1997 and began teaching insight meditation. With the desire to intensify my practice, I sat a ten-month silent retreat at the Forest Refuge in Barre, Massachusetts (2003–2004), and cultivated *jhāna* as a basis for insight.

Jhāna refers to deeply absorbed states of concentration that sharpen attention and make the mind unified, steady, pliant, and capable of practicing intensive forms of insight meditation. To reflect on that ten-month retreat experience, I started writing. It developed into a guide to the cultivation of concentration in daily life as well as the deep states of *jhāna*, and was published as *Focused and Fearless* (Wisdom, 2008). Now I practice methods preserved in the Theravada tradition; my current teacher is the Venerable Pa-Auk Sayadaw of Burma.

BOYLE: Can you say something about the ways your understanding and practice deepened during the studies you've described? I don't want to concentrate too much on experiences, but it seems natural to me that they are an important part of development.

CATHERINE: Experiences do occur, but they must have an effect to be significant. I am suspicious of spiritual experiences. I've rarely found it helpful to speak about my own experiences. And I've found that most people are a little too impressed by their own experiences. Often I am approached by students who believe that they have had a significant, liberating, or enlightenment experience. Usually, however, these are nothing more than signs that concentration is developing. I would not want to talk about "spiritual experiences" extracted from a basic understanding of the nature of things and the results of mental purification. Every new discovery, every time we realize something beyond what is conventionally known, could be interpreted as a kind of insight. But what insights are liberating? What makes an insight or an experience significant?

In the Buddhist tradition, insight is primarily oriented toward seeing the impermanent, unsatisfactory, and empty or not-self characteristics of things. These insights have the potency to free the mind from misperception, ignorance, and grasping. Almost any insight into impermanence, unsatisfactoriness, and not-self has the potential to be transformative if we go beyond a superficial reflection on these characteristics. Few meditators, however, sustain the perception of impermanence long enough to dissolve habitual attachments.

I don't think that we should seek insights in meditation. Instead, we can clean up the mind. We can concentrate it if it's distracted; we can purify it if there is a problem with our actions; we can strengthen it with wholesome intentions and abandon unwholesome ones. There are a lot of things we can do to develop the mind and see phenomena clearly. We can develop wisdom by understanding perception, causal relationships, and material and mental processes. There really are many things that we can explore in order to see things clearly.

When we see things clearly, we realize that we can't grasp and hold anything. This recognition automatically brings disenchantment, dispassion, and not-clinging. The effect of a significant experience is that it frees the mind from attachment. Many superficial experiences are just reduced to a memory of something that happened a long time ago. If the mind wasn't actually purified in the process, I wouldn't consider it much of a spiritual experience.

BOYLE: That is the way things happened when I was starting a long time ago, that is all they were. But the phrase I would pick up here is that you acquire understanding about ordinary mind, and grasping. That creates the possibility of the deathless.

CATHERINE: If I perceive my experience in a way that is affected by clinging, then I am bound, caught, and suffer. If I see the way that this mind-body process works, and I recognize that it is nothing but momentary events that are arising and perishing, empty of any fixed place to take hold, then by recognizing emptiness, the mind may extract itself from conditioned patterns of grasping. Just because someone is not clinging, however, does not imply that they have realized the deathless. We may be calm, equanimous, and let things unfold, but until we have gone beyond the conditioned formations of all mental and material processes, we have not realized liberation.

The *Visuddhimagga*, a great fifth-century Theravada text, presents sixteen stages of insight that culminate in four stages of enlightenment. The progression begins when the meditator sees the arising and passing of material and mental phenomena very clearly. When the momentariness of all mental and material phenomena is vividly known, the mind may recognize the danger in it; become disenchanted, dispassionate; and the mind will turn away from conditioned phenomena to realize the deathless element—*nibbāna*. This experience has the quality of a vast, profound, all-pervasive, and unshakable peacefulness. This experience of peace has an immediate and enduring effect: the weakening or eradication of the ten fetters that defile the mind. It also seems to bring a striking quality of equanimity and internal balance to life. Enlightenment experiences are not defined by a temporary sensation, pleasant feeling, perceptual distortion, contact with a famous guru, or acquired knowledge; the experience is defined by a transformation of mind that eliminates the impurities of greed, hate, and delusion. The experience of *nibbāna* serves a function; if it doesn't do its job, then I don't consider it a significant experience.

The first stage of enlightenment eradicates the belief in an existing self or soul, attachment to rites and rituals, and doubt regarding the efficacy of the path. The second stage of enlightenment weakens the fetters of sensual desire and all forms of aversion. The third stage of enlightenment eradicates greed and hate. And the fourth stage, which is synonymous with complete enlightenment, occurs with the eradication of five more fetters: 1) attachment to the pleasure associated with fine material *jhāna*; 2) attachment to the immaterial attainments; 3) the conceit "I am"; 4) restlessness; and 5) ignorance. It's not possible to "be enlightened" and still have anger, greed, selfishness, or egotism overtake the mind, whether the spiritual experience occurred spontaneously, through defined meditative stages, or through the blessings of a guru. Experiences of worth will weaken and eventually eliminate the defilements.

BOYLE: You've mentioned different types of meditation that you've practiced. Could you elaborate on these a bit?

CATHERINE: In the 1980s I practiced a style of vipassana meditation that used mental noting. I had many personal insights that were sometimes associated with an emotional response such as tears of joy. These insights clarified my aspirations and infused my relatively disciplined practice with inspiration. Sometimes the experiences brought stillness so deep that nothing other than a profound sense of peace would pervade my perception of things. I usually noticed the benefits of meditation in how I engaged with my activities at school, at work, and with family. There was a distinct increase in equanimity, generosity, kindness, and patience, along with a decrease in the tendency to become irritated and distracted. These personal improvements and insights into my personality and tendencies, insights about who I am and how I operated in the world, were important to me at that age. They inspired trust in the path of meditation and the power of mindfulness, purified the mind, and oriented my life toward reducing greed, anger, and delusion. In the first few years of my meditation practice the emotional quality associated with experience was attractive—I thought, *Good, something is actually happening here.* But fascination with an emotional residue is an immature response to insight.

Many kinds of understanding develop through meditation: what is important and what isn't important, how the mind works and how it doesn't, how things come together and how they come apart, what things are and what they are not. Meditation gives us the opportunity to look into the mind and allow a deep settling and a profound investigation to occur. As concentration builds, we naturally start to understand the workings of the mind. The concentrated mind inclines toward something peaceful, it inclines toward something pure, and a meditator can explore that trajectory until it realizes the vast and unmistakable peace of *nibbāna.*

But I don't want to give you the impression that the only significant insights relate to *nibbāna.* I felt the suffering that comes from remorse, agitation, and distraction, and concluded many retreats with a strong commitment to cultivate the basic practices of virtue and renunciation. These general and personal insights transformed the choices that I made, how I used my mind, and how I lived. They had the effect of bringing my worldly actions into alignment with my spiritual aspirations. Although important to my personal growth and spiritual development, they are not what the Buddhist path points to as liberating insight.

Other, more impersonal insights tended to occur after the interest in those personal insights settled. I would just sit watching the mind in the simplest and barest way; I was observing the breath, body, sounds, and perceptions arise and perish. It became obvious that there was no self to be found in the mind-body process. Everything I could observe was just a momentary process that arose and passed away. There was nothing that I could call "me," "I," or "mine." That's the sort of impersonal insight that transforms deep tendencies of mind. In meditation, we examine the mind, and no matter how carefully we look, we just don't find anything that is stable enough to be called "I," "me," or "mine." Toward the end of the 1980s, that kind of impersonal insight would be happening regularly, in daily life as much as formal meditation.

BOYLE: But what happened during your time with H.W.L. Poonja didn't involve meditation so much?

CATHERINE: When I met Poonjaji in 1990, he asked me one question: "What do you want?" I had already been meditating for about a decade, and mindfulness practice had dissolved most other interests, so my commitment to awakening was very strong. I really only wanted to realize the truth of things, so I answered by saying that I wanted the experience of emptiness. In that moment I honestly couldn't think of anything else to want. Poonja did not work through a meditation practice. He engaged the disciple in a mind-to-mind inquiry process. I'm not sure what he did, actually, but by talking with a person he could bring the mind to an experience beyond concepts, and he could hold it there.

BOYLE: Really, through conversation? That's amazing.

CATHERINE: Yeah, it was quite amazing. Over the years that I lived with him, I saw him work with hundreds of people and open their minds to an experience of profound clarity and peace. One person might describe it as peace; another person might describe it as love or bliss; somebody else might describe it as just quietness, or an unbounded, unfixed, nondimensional, timeless quality of awareness. The experience has no limits on it and no position that one could take in it, through it, or in relationship to it. It is beyond the relation of self and other, beyond the concept that "I am having an experience" or "I had an experience." It is timeless—beyond the framework of past, future, or present.

Even though experiences are difficult to describe, they inspire us to incline our interests toward that which is most subtle and true. It is that inclination of mind that keeps us developing so that we don't become lazy and rest content with the memory, *Oh, that was a great experience.* For some people the experience lasted only an hour or two; for some people it lasted weeks or months; for some people it changed after they returned to their homes in the West; for some people the shift in consciousness lasted for years. And for some people it was a complete and enduring transformation that ended the habitual positioning of self in the process of perception.

Poonjaji had a unique and powerful way of working. He quickly settled my mind into a perception of the emptiness of all things while talking with me in his living room in Lucknow that first week in February, 1990. It felt like an altered perception that lasted for many years. My mind was light and clear, and it functioned well in the world, both when I was in Asia and also back at home in California, but nothing seemed to have any solidity or density. For example, I recognized a table, a car, and a cabbage, and would use them appropriately, but I did not perceive them as having any solidity. Everything appeared as just concepts representing dynamic processes or changing things. I knew what my social responsibilities, commitments, and duties included, and I performed family and work tasks effectively. I could function well, because the concepts were clear, but each moment of seeing, hearing, feeling, and tasting was known right in the moment of contact, as ephemeral and completely devoid of any reference to me. It was a surprisingly different way of being in the world. I felt light, buoyant, and unperturbed by any event, whether I was bargaining in an Indian bazaar, cleaning closets after my father's death, driving to work, cooking *dahl*, or sitting at the feet of my guru. I told Papaji that it felt as though he had stolen the subject away from the object in my mind, and had never given it back.

After some years, the "I" formation started to occur again. and perceptions began to appear dense. The blissful and buoyant quality of awareness diminished, and I perceived things more concretely. Self-concepts now arise, but I just don't believe them. My mind has seen things from another perspective long enough that it can't believe anything is solid, fixed, or self-existing. There was a definite shift in the way I understood phenomena. It is lovely to have an experience of the empty and selfless nature of things—this reduces the tendency to give rise to the deluded view of self in the future. Then, when "I" formations later creep into experience, it is easy to let go of them.

I usually visited India on a six-month visa. When my visa expired I would leave India and go to a monastery in Thailand, a meditation retreat in Europe or the United States, or visit my family in California, and then return to India as soon as possible. It's amazing how politics affects your spiritual life; my time with Poonja was determined by the six-month visa to India, and my time in the Thai monasteries was determined by the two-month visas for Thailand, with an occasional one-month extension.

BOYLE: I've picked up several stories like that from other teachers I interviewed. Getting visas or taking care of bureaucratic or business details changed the course of their path. They ended up going to a place they hadn't expected to go, and it was just wonderful.

CATHERINE: Yes, yes. It is interesting how our lives, choices, and experiences are affected by many mundane factors.

BOYLE: What I am learning about vipassana is that it seems to have ways of addressing specific issues and problems or doing special things. I assume that there are also guidelines that go with *jhāna* practice to help you along the way.

CATHERINE: I appreciate the technology of meditation taught in the Buddhist tradition. There is a methodical, systematic, "how to" approach that is not dependent on the presence of a guru. By learning the system, you learn how to work with your mind. In the *jhāna* practice, you learn how to skillfully hold the object of attention. You concentrate on a selected object, and so you must know that object clearly. You might, for instance, take the breath as the object; or a color, body part, element, space, consciousness; or a wish for the happiness of a certain person; and then concentrate the mind by focusing on that object. Forty objects are used for concentration practice in the Theravada tradition.

I was introduced to the concentration practices called *jhāna* in 2001, but I didn't become skilled in these states until a long retreat in 2003. Since 2006 I have been studying with Venerable Pa-Auk Sayadaw, who has taught me the forty concentration subjects and precise methods for applying the concentrated mind to insight.

BOYLE: So you go to Burma?

CATHERINE: No, he travels all over the world; I have only practiced with him in the United States. The really important part of the training for me has been to apply the concentrated mind to discern the ultrasubtle, non-conceptual, irreducible realities of material and mental formations. I might concentrate the mind by using any of the meditation subjects—breath; loving-kindness; the colors black, yellow, or white; or perhaps the wind or water element. These seem to be my current favorites. Whatever object I choose, I single-pointedly focus my attention on it until I dwell in a series of absorptions. When I emerge from the absorption, my mind is pure, balanced, quick, and pliant; it is capable of perceiving subtle formations easily and clearly. Although *jhānas* have many pleasant features and are considered altered states of consciousness, I have never considered them to be spiritual experiences. I consider them merely tools for making the mind capable of seeing reality as it actually is, rather than how we conventionally conceive it to be. A concentrated mind is stable enough to directly experience the impermanence of the object, and also the impermanence of the meditating consciousness.

We can discern not just that this is a table—table is a concept—but we can discern its subtle and specific characteristics, which may include hardness, roughness, heaviness, heat, or pressure. A meditator can apply the concentrated mind to examine all types of materiality and mentality to see that they are just momentary processes. If we look at the table at the level of concept, we might think that it can last or believe we can possess it. But when we discern its subtle constituent elements and functions, we see that what we call "table" is made up of impermanent, unsatisfactory, and not-self components, and that the perception of a table is known through an interaction of causally related mental and material events. For example, there must be consciousness, perception, contact with an object, attention to it, feeling of it, etc. A concentrated mind is stable enough to analyze these nonconceptual mental and material elements in the most refined detail.

The traditional meditation techniques presented in the *Visuddhimagga* cultivate skills for exploring the nuances of perception and subtleties of the mind. When we look at an aspect of something, for example its color, we can look not only at the color but also at the interrelated material aspects that support the color. We can look at the mind and the associated mental factors that function together to discern the color. When we look carefully, we know that the color changes. But it is not just the color that is impermanent; we see that all the material and mental processes are impermanent. The detailed nature of these traditional vipassana techniques encourages a comprehensive investigation of phenomena that expands the insight into impermanence. Seeing everything—material and mental; near and far; past, present, and future—arising and perishing over and over again brought my mind to experience a profound dispassion toward all mind-body experiences. It had a sense at first of just finally being fed up with phenomena and seeking rest. The mind was thoroughly disenchanted, and yet utterly free from aversion. This strange combination of equanimity, concentration, and clarity facilitates a breakthrough that releases attachment and takes the mind beyond concepts.

BOYLE: First, thank you, it's something I know nothing about.

CATHERINE: This approach to meditative discernment can appear to be a rather technical endeavor, but it offers us a method to cultivate concentration and wisdom as the foundation for release.

BOYLE: Now that you have laid down for me a description of the outside of *jhāna* practice, what I would ask you to do, as I have done with other people, is describe how *your* mind, rather than minds in general, learned these things by doing this practice. What did you experience subjectively, on the inside, as you were going through these practices?

CATHERINE: Subjectively it's very much the same. It is amazing how the lived experience is virtually identical to what is written in the texts, extraordinarily identical.

Some students enjoy expressing their experiences; they tell me immediately when some sort of insight or realization has occurred. Other students are quieter, cautious, and may never talk about their experiences. I don't think that one way is right and the other way is wrong. Living with Poonjaji, I witnessed many ways of being with profound spiritual experiences. Some people would cry out in joy, laugh, shed tears, write poetry, or sing songs; other people would sit in silence, or get up to serve in the kitchen. No particular expressive mode is a reliable indicator of the depth of spiritual transformation. Often powerful experiences are never expressed in words. But something changes, and that can be recognized—the complexion of the face, brightness of the eyes, shifts in attitude or disposition, expressions of generosity, joy, equanimity, selfless service, and ease of letting go may accompany spiritual experience. It varies from person to person.

BOYLE: Yes, that sounds right.

CATHERINE: I rarely reported my profoundest experiences to a teacher. Most often significant experience left me feeling quiet, silent, and grateful, but with no reason to speak. I had no questions to ask, since the insights resolved my doubts. I did not need approval or confirmation from a teacher because the experience was so clear. I just felt peaceful and happy, but with no pull to talk about the events. In fact, the personal and specific events that were bound by time and place felt hollow, and too irrelevant to mention. It may be useful to talk about the experiences only to those few people with whom greater clarity or further instruction can emerge through dialogue. Usually, I only reported experiences when I was directly asked. And only a few teachers ever asked. Those who could read the signs understood the progression and already knew what had likely happened. A few words were enough to indicate what I experienced. I think experiences should be honored and valued, but silence can honor experience.

No words can adequately describe a subjective experience that is beyond concept. Whether it is through an immediate and intuitive experience that happens with a guru or a systematic and methodical meditative technique that develops through sequential stages, once the mind turns to the death-less element, it goes beyond concepts. No concept will touch it, and any attempt to describe it can at best only point toward it.

BOYLE: For me, an experience doesn't stay permanently, but on the other hand it is certainly something to work with. That is what surprises me—it isn't something that has vanished, I can get back to it at a later time.

CATHERINE: It's interesting to consider how you might repeat, mature, or stabilize an experience. Consciousness always has an object; it needs an object to function. Through meditative training, we have learned to be mindful of the object of attention and hold that object wisely. Then, when the mind releases its entrancement with material and mental perceptions to take *nibbāna* as the object, we recognize that this is different; it is not a per-sonal experience. We can later analyze the state and stabilize the knowledge of it. Once we've had an experience of *nibbāna* and reviewed that liberation of mind, we learn to dwell with *nibbāna* as the object of consciousness and permit the realization to mature. Although the peacefulness and bliss of an enlightenment experience, which Theravadan Buddhists call the Path and Fruition Attainments, are exquisite, the trajectory of the mind is strongly inclined toward purity and will, after resting for a while with the bliss of *nibbāna*, seek to dissolve the remaining fetters and defilements.

BOYLE: This is something you are still working with, and I've just begun working with it. Incidentally, what this means for me is, when sitting down to meditate, there are certain things that I do to get my mind back into the right kind of place. Then I'll see what happens after that. But I have those things that I can do now that I sort of learned along the way.

CATHERINE: Yes, you learn the path.

BOYLE: This is very exciting and wonderful. It has been an amazing year. But you are studying this, you have not completed your studies. I don't know how to phrase this—the deathless, *nibbāna*, how is it with you now?

CATHERINE: (Laughs) What a question! I hope I won't stop practicing and studying until greed, hate, and delusion are totally eradicated. That is a tall order.

BOYLE: It is. My bad habits include getting too excited. That is my prob-lem with equanimity. I just get too intense and excited, so relaxing is the big task. In addition to the long list of other defilements.

CATHERINE: The potential for clarity and peace is quite awesome. It is important that we don't become satisfied with either minor or major attain-ments. I am suspicious of people who say that they have completed the path. Someone who has completed the path could never again manifest greed, hate, or delusion in any form whatsoever, not even in the subtle forms of impatience, indulgence in meditative pleasures, or pride. I am confident that this is possible, but I am certainly not there. My path continues. I have much to develop, much to learn, and much to still abandon.

BOYLE: What's so wonderful with the people whom I have been able to interview is that they would all say what you just said. Then there were all those scandals from the 1980s. What was going on with those people? I don't know what to say about any of that kind of thing, but it certainly left me with a suspicion of anyone who acts like they have gotten to the end of the road.

CATHERINE: Yes, self-confidence is quite different than the purification of mind. When people talk about an experience of emptiness or an experience of not-self, they often refer merely to the first stage of enlightenment. I think many meditators have had that experience; it's transformative, so I don't want to diminish its importance, but it is only the first stage. We can't stop there. We must take our initial experiences as the inspiration to continue on the path.

Skillful reflection, not personal affirmation, is important after a spiritual experience occurs. In the wake of what might seem to be a significant experience, meditators can reflect on which defilements have been abandoned and what remains to be dealt with. We can notice over the days, weeks, months, years, and decades if the transformation lasts, if the experience just falls into memory, or if it perpetuates a craving to repeat it and attachment to the conditions that facilitated it. Many people confuse the bliss that comes when they are in the company of a pure-hearted guru with their own spiritual accomplishment. Many meditators confuse the temporary perceptual changes that accompany concentration with liberating insights. The concentrated mind is utterly still, happy, quiet, expansive, and bright. Students who confuse rapture, bliss, and radiant light, which are natural features of concentration, with spiritual experiences may claim: "I am free" or "I have realized enlightenment." It may, however, be nothing more than a minor stage in the development of concentration, the effect of an expansive object such as consciousness or space, or the temporary intensification of wholesome mental factors. Many people have known only coarse sensual pleasures in their lives, so when a nonsensual pleasure develops during meditation or due to faith in a guru, it can be construed as much more important than it actually is. Experiences associated with concentration, concepts, feelings, or sensations are not equivalent to the nonattachment to all mental and material processes that characterizes the liberating realization of *nibbāna*.

I appreciate the systematic structure of insight meditation: 1) insights into the impermanent, unsatisfactory, and not-self characteristics of mental and material processes produce dispassion and detachment; 2) this detachment may facilitate a realization of *nibbāna*; 3) the meditator can reflect on the experience of *nibbāna* to analyze the mental factors that were present and absent; 4) the meditator may later return to that realization and master access to it; 5) then the meditator continues to observe the mind day after day and year after year to see what defilements arise when stressed, tired, pressured, hungry, or in pain. Is there greed, anger, or selfishness? This review checks how we are living, and can help us determine if indeed a real transformation occurred. We see the change not in the memory of an event, but through a pure response to difficult life situations.

The daily life review is a vital part of realization. The Buddha even asked Venerable Sariputta, his chief disciple, to reflect on the quality of his mind when he walked to the village for alms. How was his mind disposed? Were there any hindrances? Were faith, energy, mindfulness, concentration, and wisdom strong? We must continually check our minds to determine if hindrances are still present, and then further strengthen wholesome states. This sort of review and continuous observation of the mind is an essential part of any spiritual experience.

We don't really integrate an experience into our daily life. Instead, an experience occurs, and we observe the effect of it on our daily lives. It is not useful to think, *Oh, that was a great experience, and now I am going to try to make that happen in all my meditations.* That's just grasping the pleasure associated with certain experiences. Instead, we should recognize the event, and then see what effect it has on our lives. We must learn to relate to spiritual experiences with wisdom. Most will just come and go; we might learn something or gain inspiration. Some might provide a pleasant abiding in which the mind may periodically rest. But any experience that affirms the meditator's self-existence or halts the aspiration for the higher attainments that further purify the mind might not be worthy of the label "spiritual experience."

BOYLE: That's what you were saying.

CATHERINE: It may be interesting to talk about how we feel during a spiritual experience, but the meditator should know what it was an experience of. What is the object of consciousness that is experienced?

BOYLE: Well, let me ask this. When you are talking about the object of consciousness, I'm not exactly sure what you mean. At this moment I am aware of talking, but I'm not thinking, there are no extra thoughts going on, no verbal dialogue going on in my mind. Words are just emerging from my mouth. I don't know what the object of consciousness is.

CATHERINE: You are aware of sound, you are conscious of sounds, thoughts, hearing, or perhaps the impulse to speak.

BOYLE: That's true. I can be conscious of all that I feel.

CATHERINE: Every momentary perception is flavored by a feeling tone—pleasant, unpleasant, or neither-pleasant-nor-unpleasant. Sitting here is a body that is composed of various material elements, and there is consciousness of sound, sensations associated with gestures and posture, and thoughts about the topic of our conversation. All this is influenced by your intentions, understanding, and purpose. We are not just blabbering and making random sounds without causes, reasons, or effects; this conversation involves many mental and material processes. So when we say we are just aware of being here, we're actually aware of thousands upon thousands of different momentary occurrences.

BOYLE: There are so many things I'm not paying attention to.

CATHERINE: Right, when consciousness is occupied with one object, it is not concerned with something else. On a conventional level, we'll say that we are having a conversation while sitting in a room on a lovely winter day in California. Then we look at the refined facets of this event and see that we are actually having an experience of sound, pressure, and various mental states such as tiredness, joy, delight, or interest. Many of these distinct mental or material components of experience could be an object of attention. When we are mindful of our experience, we might be capable of discerning what is valuable or distinct about a "spiritual experience." Clarity regarding our object helps sort out liberating experiences from states of temporary happiness, expressions of concentration, or perceptions of space or consciousness that people so often misperceive as spiritual experiences. With clarity about what the experience is *of*, then even if it's a pleasant, mind-blowing experience, we won't delude ourselves into thinking it is more significant than it actually is.

7

Interview with Gil Fronsdal

Gil Fronsdal has written Unhindered: A Mindful Path Through the Five Hindrances *and* The Monastery Within: Tales from the Buddhist Path. *The interview was held in his office at the Insight Meditation Center of Redwood City, California, on November 10, 2009.*

BOYLE: Path stories begin somewhere, so could you start with how you got interested in Buddhism?

FRONSDAL: I was first introduced to Buddhism and Eastern religions at the age of eleven when I traveled with my parents to India, Thailand, and Japan. The accommodating, ecumenical spirit of Hinduism inspired me. The large statues of the reclining Buddha made a deep impression, as I decided that sleeping on my right side was the ideal way to sleep! And reading Hermann Hesse's *Siddhartha* at fourteen inspired me with ideals of peace and simplicity.

But it was in college that I turned to Buddhism as a practice. It was a time of ferment, activism, and tension on many campuses, including the University of California at Santa Barbara, where I went for two years. Just before I started there, a big oil spill occurred in the Santa Barbara Channel, and the beaches still had oil washing ashore. I was very affected by reading *Limits to Growth,* an influential book for the environmental movement. I became an ardent environmentalist and decided to major in environmental studies.

As my friends and I explored issues of environmental degradation and what to do about it, we first concluded that the solutions had to be political, and we began taking political science classes. But as our late-night conversations continued, we began to think that a deeper shift in "consciousness" and worldview was needed. This led to an exploration of Eastern religions, especially Daoism and Buddhism.

At the same time, my male friends and I were contending with the possibility of being drafted to fight in the Vietnam War, which we opposed. In our long debates on the war, as the extreme pacifist in my dorm, I was often arguing my position. Because it was a form of pacifism that advocated nonviolent civil disobedience, I realized that if I was going to act on my beliefs, I might have to participate in protests where my life was in danger. But I knew that college students had been killed in such protests, and my fear of dying seemed to stand as an obstacle to following through on my beliefs. This bothered me greatly, and so I looked around to see what I could do to overcome this fear.

I settled on Buddhist practice as a possible solution, but environmentalism and pacifism weren't enough to get me to actually start practicing. At twenty I dropped out of college and traveled across the United States. I landed in an eight hundred-person hippie commune in Tennessee called The Farm, where *Zen Mind, Beginner's Mind* was so popular it almost seemed to be the Bible of the community. When I read it, I was surprised that the teachings in the book made complete sense to me—it was as if the book expressed what I believed but didn't yet know. After four months on The Farm I hitchhiked to the San Francisco Zen Center, the temple of Suzuki Roshi, the author of *Zen Mind, Beginner's Mind*. I stayed at Zen Center for two weeks and was introduced to Zen meditation. I felt as if I had come home. Practicing Zen was what I wanted to do.

Even so, I didn't stay at Zen Center. I decided that before I could dedicate myself to Zen practice, I had to take care of some loose ends. One of them was to go back to Norway, where I was born, so I could figure out my relationship to my home country. So at the age of twenty-one I spent a year in Norway. A good part of that year I lived and worked on a small dairy farm. I loved the farm life enough that I felt drawn to both Zen practice and becoming a farmer. In order to pursue both, I then spent two years at UC Davis to get a degree in agronomy as well as to be close enough to the San Francisco Zen Center that I could visit regularly.

It was at Davis that I began meditating consistently twice a day, except Sundays. I was motivated by a wish to overcome the unhappiness I felt. At the time I knew almost nothing about the inner, mental aspects of meditation practice, including any concept of meditation states. I didn't know anything was supposed to happen when you meditated. I had no idea that thinking was a problem or was to be stilled. I just knew Zen sitting was the right thing for me to do. The way I meditated was to practice unconditional acceptance of the present moment. I just sat there and accepted whatever was there, in the present. I feel fortunate that I was ignorant of the many theories and teachings about meditation. The ignorance served me well. Within two or three months, the original reasons I had wanted to meditate fell away as the obvious emotional suffering I had disappeared. It just wasn't there anymore.

Even though my original reasons for sitting ceased, I kept meditating twice a day, forty minutes each time, without any conscious rationale for it. Maybe because I am rationally inclined, I thought it was bizarre that I would do something without a reason. I therefore spent a few months exploring the question, Why do I spend so much time meditating every day, without a reason? Eventually the answer that came to me was that I sat to express myself. In the same way an artist might express herself on canvas, through dance, or some other medium, meditation was the deepest, most complete form of self-expression that I knew.

As I continued to meditate in this way, my subjective experience of myself in meditation changed. The most significant change was an increased sense of personal integrity. Eventually, the contrast between the integrity I felt in meditation and the integrity I felt outside of meditation became an issue for me. Noticing this, I became interested in bringing this meditative integrity into my daily life. I continued to sit every day, without any idea that something was supposed to happen in meditation. In addition, however, I became interested in finding out how to have this inner sense of integrity or purity in the rest of my life.

To do this, I realized that I needed help. I wanted to be in a community of other people trying to do the same thing. That's why, when I graduated from college in 1978, I went to the San Francisco Zen Center. In the times I had visited, people there functioned as mirrors in which I could see myself better. This helped me to avoid succumbing to personality habits that seemed to lack the integrity I valued. The reason I went to Zen Center was not so much to do more meditation, but rather to better integrate what was happening in meditation with my daily life. However, one result of going there was that I meditated more, and as I meditated more, the desire to do that integration work became even stronger. So I decided to go to Tassajara, Zen Center's remote mountain monastery, because I thought the monastic life would further help with bringing my *zazen* experience into daily life and into my relationships with others.

BOYLE: What was it like to be meditating at Zen Center?

FRONSDAL: In the nine months before going to Tassajara I lived at Green Gulch, Zen Center's farm in Marin County. While there I worked in the fields, doing physical work that I enjoyed a lot. Green Gulch was a very simple place then. I would get up in the morning, meditate, have breakfast, go work in the fields, have lunch, work in the fields, take a shower, have dinner and meditate, go to sleep. That was the routine. And it was great. The physical work in the fields and the meditation complemented each other really well. What happened was that when I sat down to meditate, things would just fall away. My mind became very still and peaceful. It was there at Green Gulch that I began to have the experience of my breathing stopping during meditation. I remember the first time this happened. I was so surprised I gasped, because I was afraid I was going to die. Once I got used to it, the meditative stilling where breathing stopped became quite nice and nourishing. As I didn't know much about Buddhism, I didn't know that anything like this could happen. The practice was a somewhat intuitive following of a path. It just felt so right, and I was going along that path.

During a *sesshin*, a seven-day retreat, I did have one meditation experience at Green Gulch that got my attention more than any other. The retreat was not easy for me due to all the physical and emotional pain I experienced. It never occurred to me that I could move to alleviate the physical pain or to do anything about the emotional pain. I continued, the best I could, practicing unconditional acceptance of what is, finding a way to be with the pain without resisting it or succumbing to it. The effort to do this increased my focus and concentration. Then during one period of meditation I decided, for reasons I don't recall, to have an intense concentration on my breath, to not let one breath go by without knowing it. So for one sitting I gave everything I could to not missing a single breath. And I pretty much succeeded. At the end of the sitting I thought, *Well, that was interesting, but nothing really happened.* The next thing in the schedule was that we had afternoon tea served to us in the meditation hall. We would remain in our meditation posture while servers brought us tea and a cookie. I received the tea and held the cup in my hands. As I lifted the cup to my lips and the tea went into my mouth, the world stopped! This stopping was a remarkable experience for me that I have never been able to adequately convey in words. Part of the experience was my mind having the unusual thought *As the tea touches my tongue, I stop the sip.* I was quite surprised that in the words and in the experience, there was no self. Without any of my usual self-referencing, it was as if everything stood still. I had no context or understanding for this experience. It didn't occur to me to tell my teacher about it, even though for me it was remarkable and inspiring. Over time I got sidetracked by the spontaneous words my mind spoke during the experience and began studying words and language rather than the nature of the stopping.

BOYLE: But you remember the experience.

FRONSDAL: Yes. The experience was phenomenal.

BOYLE: Do you think it occurred because of the practice that you had been maintaining, like this special *zazen* session where you were paying strict attention, as much as you could, to each breath? Sometimes experiences happen *after* something like that.

FRONSDAL: Yes, I agree. Since then I have learned of others who have had similar experiences. In fact, the ancient Zen records have stories of people who practiced a lot of meditation, and then when their mind was somehow prepared, some significant experience was catalyzed by a very ordinary occurrence in daily life.

BOYLE: What happened to you after this experience?

FRONSDAL: During that summer at Green Gulch, I was planning to start graduate school in soil science in August at the University of California at Berkeley. I had been interested in working in soil conservation. On a Sunday morning at the beginning of August I realized that classes would start in a few weeks, and that I needed to at least go over to Berkeley to find an apartment. I began questioning whether I should or shouldn't start graduate school. I wondered whether I should continue practicing at Zen Center, perhaps even going to Tassajara. I went to the noon service at Green Gulch, where we were chanting the *Heart Sutra*. While I was chanting, a deep knowing welled up inside of me. Without knowing why, with a knowing that involved a physical shift inside, I knew what I had to do. I knew I was going to Tassajara. I had no doubts about this.

I went to Tassajara in January of 1980, and much of importance happened for me there. One of the things I learned is how much of spiritual transformation happens slowly, drop by drop, through the ongoing practice and the daily lifestyle in the monastery. The most valuable parts of my Zen training were not the result of particular experiences or insights but rather the slow, day-in-and-day-out process of doing the practice, living a life of practice.

During my early years of Zen practice, my sense of compassion grew slowly. I wasn't interested in becoming compassionate, and the change was so gradual I didn't recognize it as it was happening. Much of this change I attributed to becoming familiar with my own suffering. During the long hours of meditation, the presence of my inner pain opened something within. Rather than becoming enlightened, I was becoming "compassioned." "Compassionment" instead of enlightenment. This became important because with time, compassion became an important motivating principle for my life. I hoped to live in a way that would help others.

I loved being at Tassajara. Though it sounds strange to say so, I felt it was the perfect lifestyle. Getting up at four in the morning and meditating and working and being with other practitioners made me quite happy. Mostly. The main exception was on the days off, which occurred every five days. With time off from meditation and work, I was left with myself and my many mental preoccupations. It was during these long hours of free time that I had to face my demons. One of the big challenges had to do with what I was going to do with my life. While I was happy at Tassajara, I wondered what was next. Perhaps go back to graduate school? Perhaps become a Zen monk? I had a strong wish that my life be about service to others. However, I didn't trust my motivation to be helpful. I believed too many people want to be of service for reasons that are selfish. I therefore spent a year reflecting, especially on those days off, on the purity of my motivation to help others. After a year I decided it was pure enough and that it was, therefore, okay for me to have this motivation.

Around the same time, I saw a *Newsweek* article with photographs of the Israeli bombing of the refugee camps in Beirut. This had a big impact on me. I think this was a kind of turning point for me, toward wanting to help alleviate suffering for others. I felt I had benefited so much from practice that I wanted to now focus more on supporting other people.

Then one day during the summer the abbot came to the monastery, which was unusual as he usually didn't visit during the summer. As this meant I could have an interview with him, I went and sat on the porch of the building I lived in, looking down at Tassajara Creek, and intensely reflected on what to do with my life. Graduate school or monastic ordination? In one moment the same, sudden inner knowing I'd had at Green Gulch happened again. Suddenly I knew as clearly as I could know anything that I was going to become a Zen monk. The knowing occurred without any reason for the decision. Later I came up with explanations for it, though these rationales seemed minor compared to the deep inner conviction.

I then had an interview with the abbot and asked to be ordained. He agreed, and seven months later we had the ceremony. A month or two after I was ordained, the abbot declared he was changing the title for those who were ordained from "monks" to "priests." I was taken aback by this because

I had signed up to be a monk. I associated priests with clerics who did Sunday services at local churches. I was interested in monastic life, not being a priest. But since my motivation was to serve others, with time I accepted the title Zen priest instead of Zen monk.

BOYLE: What were some of the challenges you had living at Tassajara?

FRONSDAL: Community life was difficult. There were times of conflict and tension in which I had to confront difficult aspects of myself. One of the things I saw dramatically was how much I wanted people to like me. I saw what a burden it was to try constantly to arrange for this. I engaged in all kinds of social gymnastics to try to make people like me. It was so clear that it was not healthy. I practiced hard to overcome this, and discovered I felt much lighter when I wasn't as concerned with whether people liked me or not.

At Tassajara my meditation continued to deepen. One of the things that kept happening was that my mind would get very empty, very still. It felt like the mind was not caught by anything, concerned with anything, or involved with anything. At times when it was most empty I would experience a dropping away of consciousness. It was like the bottom falling out of a bucket.

BOYLE: Could you say something more about what that kind of "dropping" was like?

FRONSDAL: There are a variety of ways consciousness can drop. At Tassajara it had a particular pattern in the way it occurred. Usually the mind would drop away and then the body would drop or suddenly fall forward. Then my body would reflexively jerk up again. It was not falling asleep during meditation, which I had enough experience of to know the difference. It would be a sudden kind of release while the mind was quite clear, still, and empty of thoughts.

BOYLE: What happened after your stay at Tassajara?

FRONSDAL: After I'd been at Tassajara for almost three years, the abbot asked me to move to San Francisco to work at Greens, Zen Center's restaurant. I worked contentedly there for one year. During that time there was a major scandal involving the abbot. Many people who had invested a lot of themselves in working and practicing at Zen Center felt deeply betrayed and hurt. For me, I hadn't been at Zen Center long enough to have sacrificed a lot of myself to support the abbot or support Zen Center. The many benefits I had received while there were happily independent of the abbot's conduct. I didn't feel I had wasted my time or that something terrible had happened directly to me. While I valued the abbot as my teacher, I didn't have a deep personal or heartfelt connection to him. In fact, the first time I ever saw him, I saw something about him that made me think, *Oh, I don't think I can approve of this person's lifestyle, but I think I can learn about Zen from him.* While now I don't think it is wise to separate one's lifestyle from one's Buddhist practice and understanding, at the time it saved me from the deep sense of betrayal others felt with the scandal.

For me, the important result of the scandal was that it freed me from any sense of obligation I had to my teacher. He had ordained me, and I had committed myself to many years of training under him. With his departure, my commitment ended. This didn't disappoint me. Rather, I was relieved, because Zen Center was beginning to feel a bit claustrophobic. I felt a need for a fresh perspective on life and practice, and I couldn't get it if I stayed immersed in the Zen Center world. So my first thought when I heard of the scandal was, *Oh, now I'm free.*

I accepted an invitation to go to Japan and continued to practice Zen there. I visited different Zen teachers and participated in Zen retreats with a few of them. During this period I left Japan and went to Bangkok so I could get a new visa for a longer stay in Japan. A friend of a friend was a Theravada monk at a small, somewhat chaotic monastery outside of Bangkok. Visiting the monastery, I decided, *I'm here, and I'll do whatever the abbot tells me to do, just to find out what he has to teach.* The abbot gave me a little hut at the edge of the monastery and provided daily mindfulness instruction for vipassana meditation.

I practiced under this vipassana teacher while I waited for the visa for Japan. After ten weeks I realized the visa wasn't coming. So my first vipassana retreat was ten weeks long. Basically it was like a ten-week *sesshin*. I'd never sat an intensive retreat for such a long time, and it proved to be an extremely important experience for me. I don't have a particularly good ability to get concentrated, but over those many weeks my concentration built up in a stronger and different way than it ever had before. It was more peaceful than the usual concentration states I had experienced at Zen Center. My mind became very, very still. And in the deepest stillness I touched some sense of self that I had never known before. It was like some core seed of self, deep within. Intuitively this experience seemed really important for me, and I was drawn to touch into it again.

I went back to Japan to do a traditional Soto Zen practice period at one of the better-known monasteries. The time there was a disappointment, partly because after the ten weeks on retreat in Thailand, I wanted to meditate more than we did in the Zen monastery. Also, I had a "dark night of the soul" time because it became very important to touch that core sense of self I had discovered. Nothing else mattered anymore, nothing else was important, nothing else was relevant. It took me about a year before I could get back to Southeast Asia. The longer I waited to return, the more I felt out of sorts. I was determined to go to Burma to the Mahasi Center, a meditation monastery that was the headquarters for the form of vipassana meditation I had learned in Thailand.

I bought a one-way plane ticket; for me, the meditation monasteries of Burma were the end of the road. Nothing else mattered. I didn't know how long I would stay. I did an eight-month vipassana retreat at the Mahasi Center. This was like doing an eight-month Zen *sesshin* where all one does is meditate all day long. I did all the sitting meditation alone in my room and the walking meditation in the hallway in front of my room. Most days there was an interview with a teacher and a Dharma talk, but otherwise there was no talking to anyone.

Those eight months were among the most important times in my life. Most of that time I was extremely happy, experiencing abundant joy and peace. I was engaged in the practice even though I still considered myself a Zen student. It was not so much the vipassana practice that brought me to Burma, but rather the opportunity to do long, silent retreats. I felt I was continuing my practice of Zen meditation, with the vipassana instruction helping me to do so more thoroughly. I had learned how subtle the mind is. I knew that while there might be a general sense of peace and acceptance in my meditation, there could appear, in the cracks of the peace, frequent and quite subtle forms of agitation, desire, and resistance to what I was experiencing. Knowing this, I wanted to get down to the little millisecond movements of the mind. Through vipassana I learned to have a stronger mindfulness and a greater skill in negotiating the subtle movements of the mind. I believed this heightened capacity for attention was a way to sit Zen meditation thoroughly, which for me meant to more fully practice a form of attention that unconditionally accepts the present moment.

BOYLE: They didn't give you specific types of meditation to do?

FRONSDAL: There was a very particular meditation technique taught there.

BOYLE: So you were doing that?

FRONSDAL: Yes. I was very diligent following their instructions. Even though the kind of meta-understanding of what I was doing came from Zen, I was also following their specific practice guidelines. Having the Zen perspective was useful, because the particular teacher I studied with was very demanding and very goal-oriented. Many people found his style of practice too demanding, and, feeling pressured, ended up trying too hard to be able to meditate effectively. For many people the goal orientation he championed tied them up in striving. Fortunately for me, my Zen practice protected me from getting caught up in this goal orientation. At one point my teacher told me that when I sat down to meditate, I should strive for nirvana. I told him I didn't come to his monastery to strive for nirvana. He looked at me like I was from Mars. Then after a little exchange he said, "That's okay, you are not supposed to strive." I thought, *Oh, we're on the same wavelength again.* But then the next day I came back and he said, "Gil, strive for nirvana." I invisibly shrugged my shoulders and from then on ignored this piece of instruction.

The time in Burma was very meaningful and very powerful. I was amazed what the mind is capable of in terms of depth of concentration, stillness, and the deeper stages of vipassana practice. Then early one morning, four months into my retreat, I experienced a stopping or dropping of the mind that was very different than the similar-seeming experiences I'd had during Zen training. It was qualitatively more intense and had a very different flavor to it. At that point in my life the experience was the most meaningful, most beautiful, most profound thing I had ever had happen to me. After that experience, I had a thoroughgoing feeling in my cells that something had been completed.

BOYLE: Did this happen while you were sitting?

FRONSDAL: Yes.

BOYLE: When you got up and walked around in the world, which you alternated with sitting, did that experience continue on through, did you carry that with you out into the walking?

FRONSDAL: Not exactly, it was a relatively brief experience. But the ripples of that experience, the momentum that was set in motion in terms of understanding and feelings lingered. For the first three days they lingered quite strongly—it was as if I were walking on clouds. Although the feelings faded, to this day the experience has remained a touchstone for me. In some way it is ever present, if I focus on it. If you remember, I said earlier that I was motivated to be on a long vipassana retreat because I had to touch the small seed of self I had sensed in deep practice. After this experience, I no longer had the need to touch this place. The issue was resolved, or more likely, dissolved. The intimation of there being some core self no longer existed.

After eight months I left Burma with the idea of continuing to do intensive practice. For a variety of reasons, it took another year and a half before

I did so at a three-month retreat at the Insight Meditation Society in Barre, Massachusetts. There I went through many of the same meditation experiences I'd had in Burma. One morning I again had a significant ceasing of the mind. Though it had a different quality from what had happened in Burma, it came with a greater sense of freedom. In Burma the first thought I had after the experience was, *Wow! This is the most beautiful thing I have ever experienced.* At IMS, the first thought I had was, *Oh my god, there is a lot of work still to do.* It was as if now I truly understood what Buddhist practice is about, and I realized that I had much more work to do in freeing myself from my attachments.

BOYLE: Can you say anything about the relation of the first experience with the second? For example, could you say that the second experience went further and deeper than the first, enough so that you realized the vastness of what you were dropping into?

FRONSDAL: It's hard for me to know what actually happened. I am reluctant to put it in any kind of map, including the Buddhist maps of spiritual experiences. I don't know if it's important to understand what the experiences were. I feel it's more important to understand the function it had for me, the way that I was affected by it, changed by it. Even though during the experience in Burma almost everything dropped away, there was something quite intangible that remained. During the experience at IMS, nothing remained.

BOYLE: The realization that you had a great amount of work to do . . .

FRONSDAL: That was afterward. That came afterward. So both those experiences have been important for me. I think the second was more important. It was a stronger validation of the Buddha's teachings on the Four Noble Truths.

BOYLE: When did you start teaching Buddhism?

FRONSDAL: After this three-month retreat at IMS, people started to want me to teach. I returned to Zen Center, and I was moved along in the teacher-training track there. I was on the cusp of being an apprentice teacher. But I did not feel ready to teach. One reason for this was I did not know much about Buddhism. My ten years of intensive practice had not entailed much study. So in order to prepare myself better to be a teacher, I decided to go to graduate school for a master's degree in religious studies with an emphasis on Buddhism. If I was to become a Buddhist teacher, I had no hopes of making a living doing this. I thought that with a master's degree I could perhaps support myself teaching introductory classes on Buddhism at junior colleges.

So I went to graduate school at the University of Hawai'i and after two years received a master's in Buddhist studies. I was like a kid in a candy store. I just loved it; I loved reading Buddhist texts of all kinds.

At the end of that time Jack Kornfield phoned and invited me to join his next teacher-training group. That was a lovely experience for me when he called and invited me. I had a visceral feeling that all the puzzle pieces in my life suddenly fit together. So in 1989 I started training with Jack to be a vipassana teacher.

BOYLE: You had your M.A. at that point?

FRONSDAL: Just finishing up.

BOYLE: How long did Kornfield's training session run?

FRONSDAL: Four years. Part of the training was to observe the one-on-one discussions between students and teachers on vipassana retreats. I learned a lot through the different styles and approaches of the different teachers I observed. During the four-year training we slowly, step by step, moved into the role of being a teacher. For me it would have been too big of a hurdle to have gone from zero to sixty in one day, to have suddenly gone from being a student to being a full teacher. The four-year training allowed me to grow into the role and to develop some confidence as a Buddhist teacher.

BOYLE: What else were you doing during that four-year period? The training was probably not full time. Had you started the Ph.D. program at Stanford?

FRONSDAL: Yes. I started that in 1990, soon after I started teacher training. When I started at Stanford, I was asked to become the teacher for a small meditation group nearby in Palo Alto. There were twelve to fifteen people who met on a weekly basis. I started teaching and the group slowly grew over time until it became our current center, the Insight Meditation Center. At the same time I was getting my Ph.D. in Buddhist studies at Stanford.

BOYLE: Somewhere in there you studied with Mel Weitsman for several years?

FRONSDAL: Yes, on and off over many years. Mel was the most important Zen teacher I had. He was and remains still the abbot of the Berkeley Zen Center, though for a seven-year period he also served as abbot of the San Francisco Zen Center.

BOYLE: He is someone who studied with Suzuki Roshi.

FRONSDAL: Yes, he was a student of Suzuki Roshi. He was the first Zen teacher I had any regular contact with, while I was a student at Davis. There was a sitting group up there, and he'd come up and do half-day retreats for us. I'd go down to Berkeley to do one-day retreats with him. During the years I was at Zen Center I didn't have much contact with him because I was in the orbit of a different abbot. But then at some point after the scandal I started having more to do with Mel again. When he became the abbot of the San Francisco Zen Center I spent a year working closely with him. Around 1990, soon after I started training with Jack, I was invited by Mel to train for Dharma transmission to become a Zen teacher.

BOYLE: You were at Stanford at that time?

FRONSDAL: I was at Stanford. So it was certainly unusual, I was studying for a triple major all at once: vipassana teacher, Zen teacher, and Ph.D. in Buddhism. Luckily for me, each training could be arranged so I had time for the other two. For example, at Stanford I took advantage of an option to take classes for only two quarters a year. That gave me lots of time to do the other things that I was doing.

BOYLE: So in addition to studying for the Ph.D. and studying with Kornfield, you were training with Weitsman to receive Dharma transmission and leading the sitting group that grew into the Insight Meditation Center?

FRONSDAL: Yes. Mel knew I was teaching for a vipassana group and he knew I was training to be a vipassana teacher. I don't know all of what he felt about this. I always felt he had a small wish I would focus on Zen. However, I also felt he trusted me and the way my life was unfolding. He made it explicit that in giving me Dharma transmission, he was not putting any expectations on me.

BOYLE: So you did three things at once for four years and . . .

FRONSDAL: I also got married during this time!

BOYLE: I was going to ask about that. As a long-term family man, I am aware of the responsibilities and investment of time and energy that takes.

FRONSDAL: Yes, it has had its challenges. I've learned in having family and kids that for me, the kind of person I am, monastic life was easy. Family life is where I discovered many attachments I had but hadn't been aware of. I was pushed, stretched, and challenged in a way that had never happened to me in monasteries. Now for other people, monastic life stretches and pushes them, challenges them, because of who they are. But for me it was the other way.

So I feel it has been really important for me to have a family. I look back at how I taught before I had children. I think I was pretty naïve, not understanding the magnitude of how challenging many people's lives are. From having children I feel I have a better understanding of the challenges people face.

Since you are asking about how practice transforms us, I have been transformed by being a householder, transformed by being a parent. There were times when I thought it was making me a worse teacher, because I wouldn't have time to prepare talks or otherwise get ready to teach. I would be tired. While I had doubts about myself, the feedback I got from my students was that I became a much more accessible teacher. They said my teachings became more relevant to their lives than before.

BOYLE: Do you have more to say about the years since you started Insight Meditation Center?

FRONSDAL: It's been almost twenty years since I started teaching with the original small sitting group. If you want to know how I have been transformed, one of the ways I have been transformed is by this group, by being a teacher for this growing community. It is a co-created phenomenon. I am not a teacher unless there are students. I've matured as a teacher, I hope, over these years, developed as a teacher. But it is really clear to me that this was done in relationship to the students I had. I have been changed by the ongoing contact with a wide range of people and their practice and their sincerity, their dedication, and their struggles. My own practice includes my relationships in our community. I practice together with the IMC community.

I feel very much like I'm a practitioner more than a teacher. I feel very lucky to be a teacher, because sometimes I believe being a teacher is a wonderful way to be a practitioner. It has me reflecting on the Dharma, living aligned with the Dharma, being reminded of the Dharma, and practicing the Dharma most of the time. I feel so blessed that this should be what my life has come to. I feel that also, day in and day out, this has changed me and pushed me to develop, forced me to look at myself. This is a great place for self-honesty, to look at what my relationship is to people, to listen, to examine my motivation in teaching, what I want, what I don't want, my concerns, my fears and desires. There has been plenty of material.

BOYLE: Is there anything else you would like to say?

FRONSDAL: It has been odd for me to talk about my personal history during this interview. It feels a bit like talking about someone else. I don't feel such a strong identification with the person I have been talking about, through all these years, but it's what you wanted.

BOYLE: In describing your experience at IMS, you said that what happened wasn't just a dropping but a realization there was so much work to do, there is so much there. It was more like an opening into something that would be very challenging. Do you feel satisfied with your ability to carry this search, this investigation on into this new world?

FRONSDAL: I feel very satisfied and content that I am still practicing. While I am probably not practicing as well as I could if I took more time for retreats and personal meditation practice, I am not so motivated to practice for my own benefit. I am much more interested in supporting other people in their practice. I was ordained as a Zen priest because I wanted to help others. This intention remains what I am most motivated by today.

8
Interview with
Stephen Batchelor

Stephen Batchelor travels and speaks throughout the world. His books include Confession of a Buddhist Atheist; The Awakening of the West: The Encounter of Buddhism and Western Culture; *and* Living with the Devil. *I interviewed him in Albuquerque, New Mexico, on March 8, 2010.*

At the time of that interview, Stephen had just finished writing a quite extensive account of the first part (1972–1985) of his path story, published a few months later in Confession of a Buddhist Atheist. *He suggested that rather than repeating this in the interview, we simply use summary quotes from the book. This seemed like a good idea, but that plan did not work out. Instead, readers are encouraged to go directly to the book, where the relevant material can be found on pages 24–35 and 62–67.*

The in-person interview that follows was conducted March 10, 2010, in Albuquerque. It starts in 1985, when Stephen and Martine left the Zen monastery in Korea where they had been studying, got married, and moved to England. There they settled in Sharpham House, a small alternative community near London.

BOYLE: That was quite a change in your life. How would you describe your Buddhist practice since that time?

STEPHEN BATCHELOR: When I returned from Korea, and I think even while I was in Korea, my practice was far more a process of integrating what I had learned into the context of my life. It was not a matter of seeking some sort of deeper, mystical type of experience. That simply was not, and is not now, of any particular interest to me.

Now to what extent my understanding has deepened, if it has, then it's been done through the context of my life and my work and particularly, I think, my writing. In many ways I feel that having to produce books, either for my own reasons or because in many cases I was commissioned to do so, gave me the framework for reflection, the framework for my meditation. Really, I saw it more as a process of integration. This model, if I think about it now, fits fairly precisely with one of the models that my Theravadan training gave me. Basically it presents the path as one in which, first, there is a period of what they call the phase of accumulation. "Accumulation of merit" is the technical meaning, a period of life in the beginning where you somehow prepare yourself. Then there is the phase of kind of psyching yourself up, which is called preparation. Then there is a phase of seeing, of insight, and that is followed by a period of what they called meditation. It's not really meditation, it is actually more cultivation or development, the period that follows upon the transformative experiences one might have had.

But the real practice during that fourth phase is rather one of familiarizing or tuning one's life to be lived according to the insights and values that have been significant for one as a Buddhist, and have been perhaps at moments highlighted through particular experiences. The emphasis on a particular experience really falls away. So I continue to meditate, I continue to do retreats. But I don't think of my practice as primarily having to do with gaining particular kinds of insights or experiences. It's more a question of refining and deepening the understanding I already have. The second part of the book is a reflection of that process. I think the book breaks quite sharply into these two parts. One is notionally called that of a monk, the next that of the layman. As a kind of psycho-spiritual process, I think it breaks down into the path between the formal training and one's practice after the training, whether it be in Korea or Tibet. But even in Korea, although I did lots and lots of meditation, I began to think of meditation very differently.

BOYLE: How?

S. BATCHELOR: Korean tradition is not like some of the Japanese forms of Zen, where you are put into a sort of pressure-cooker situation where you are expected to resolve certain koans. Resolution of a particular koan is tantamount to another sort of shift in your understanding, or a kind of breakthrough. That is not how it works in Korea. I don't really think it's seen that way in straight Soto Zen either. But we do have this kind of stereotype in the West of Zen Buddhism or even Buddhist practice in general as a progressive deepening of insight, very often characterized by some sort of shattering, revelatory kind of insight or getting into very deep nonordinary states of consciousness. That just doesn't speak to me, period.

Another thing: you mentioned that my presentation of the Buddha's life and his teachings as running in parallel, which I think constitutes the main development of ideas within the second half of the book, is also a reflection of my own process. Definitely. As I get toward the end of the book, it becomes clear that what I now see as the core of the Buddha's awakening is his integration of the Four Noble Truths into his life. And the Four Truths I see really as a continuous positive feedback loop. In other words, I see the Four Truths as four ongoing tasks, each one related to the next. The first, the full knowing and understanding of *dukkha*, or suffering, leads to the second, which is the realization that suffering is caused by attachment, by grasping or craving. This leads to the third truth, which says that the cessation of suffering can be attained through a fading away, a stopping of grasping, of attachment. That is what creates the ground or the foundation for the fourth truth, which says that there is a gradual path to the cessation of suffering called the Eightfold Path, which includes the way we see the world, think about it, speak, act, and work. The Eightfold Path in the model culminates in mindfulness and concentration—in other words, meditation. One has to see that, necessarily, what one is mindful of and what one concentrates on inevitably brings one back to the first Noble Truth, the truth of suffering, which implies impermanence, contingency, and selflessness.

I don't see Buddha's awakening as an awakening to some particular mystical state, but rather an awakening to another way of being in the world. The Buddha is describing an awakening that really cannot be reduced to a particular moment in time, but rather involves the full participation of all of one's human faculties in engaging with the world from another perspective. That, I think, is what is radical about what the Buddha taught. Yet of course, Buddhism as a religion, particularly in many of the ways it is presented in the West, tends to put the emphasis on certain privileged mystical or spiritual experiences, usually gained through becoming proficient in certain meditative disciplines. Now, for some people that may be the case. But it certainly is not the way that I feel my practice has evolved, or the way that my engagement with the Dharma has evolved.

BOYLE: That's clear. And certainly something I can relate to. But you had this intensive period of being a monk, and if you hadn't had some of the experiences that occurred during that time, then you might have been in a different position later on. That is, perhaps the experiences and training you had as a monk helped you understand things and go on from there.

S. BATCHELOR: That is absolutely right. The problem with a human life is you can't rewind it and start again, with a different set of primary conditions, and see if it would have been different. You just can't do that. So, one only has one shot, as it were. I cannot—to be quite frank, I cannot in all honesty say whether if I hadn't done all that meditation, if I hadn't been a monk, my life now would be very different. Maybe, maybe not—it's impossible to say. But certainly, since one has to evaluate and try to articulate one's understanding in terms of what one has done rather than what one didn't do, then the way I see it is that the monastic training gave me a foundation that has become the basis for everything I have done since. I quite clearly see a continuity in what I am doing now, which I honestly do not think would be the same if I had not had both the philosophical, doctrinal training with the Tibetans and the meditative, contemplative training in Korea.

BOYLE: And the training with Goenka?

S. BATCHELOR: Well, the Goenka thing is actually very important. Goenka happens to be the teacher who introduced me to the practice of vipassana. So he stands out. That was, as I say in the book, a very key point. And in some ways my life since I left the monastery has returned more to the tradition of vipassana. Again, that is the form of meditation most explicitly connected to the text of the Pali Canon, so in a sense there is a kind of coming full circle. The Goenka experience, and doing that vipassana retreat, in a sense was always a kind of keynote throughout my Tibetan and through my Korean times, whether I was practicing in the Tibetan tradition or practicing in the Korean tradition. When I would sit in meditation, when I would do formal meditation practice, the ground note would be established by awareness of breathing, awareness of the body as I had been taught in the vipassana school. My Korean teacher did not have much time for vipassana. I think I mentioned this in the book—he said watching the breath is like observing a corpse exhale. He really was very dogmatic in that sense, very sectarian. Irrespective of his comments, that made no difference to my ongoing commitment to that practice as the basis for my Zen practice.

BOYLE: The way you have described your life since returning from Korea, it doesn't have the instability in it that a lot of students, including myself, have experienced over time. You seem to have just moved along on a fairly steady plane.

S. BATCHELOR: It appears to be so. Not that my life has been without its ups and its downs, but I find that my meditation practice is fairly constant. So that's correct, yes.

BOYLE: Maintaining equanimity, being equanimous has not been a problem for you?

S. BATCHELOR: Well, at times yes, but I think that broadly speaking, I do feel that perhaps what my training as a monk has provided me with is a sort of foundation for equanimity. I don't feel like I am so much in search of something, let's put it that way. I don't always feel equanimous, but I am often surprised how other people will comment that I seem to have some equanimity. Perhaps I have always been a bit like this, and that may be one of the reasons I was drawn to Buddhism in the first place. I felt an affinity with that kind of attitude, those cultural values of quiet and stillness. But certainly, like everybody else, I have periods when I am feeling less stable and secure in my life.

BOYLE: In the book you have a quote from the Pali Canon, from the Buddha: "A still calm lay at the heart of this vision, a strange dropping away of familiar habits, the absence, at least momentarily, of anxiety and turmoil" (131). This quote implies that there was a vision or an insight.

S. BATCHELOR: Yes, that's right. That's how I suppose it was. But to be quite honest, since I wrote the book I'm beginning to be a bit skeptical. I must admit to the description I gave of the Buddha's awakening, particularly the idea that he sat beneath this tree and then had this massive sort of transformation. But now I wonder to what extent that might be something that has been rather mythologized, and that in fact his awakening was more something that occurred gradually over a period of time. Buddhism is so keen on this idea of the key moment of the enlightenment. It is very difficult, in a way, to challenge that. In terms of human psychology and development, I feel it's more likely that the Buddha's process was one that evolved over time, perhaps over the six years after he left his home. But again, as I suggested in the book, I find it difficult to imagine that he wasn't pursuing or engaging in similar questions or concerns from a fairly young age. I have a suspicion that the way the canonical account of his enlightenment is recounted is very much from the stance of those more ascetic, meditative members of his community who wanted his life to somehow fit the scheme of the classical Indian ascetic model. And that's how he came to be represented. That's a hunch, not something I can demonstrate or prove, but I am a little skeptical of the idea of him being this very confused person, and suddenly on the night of the enlightenment everything changed.

There is so little material in the canon. The building blocks you have to construct that narrative with are so few and far between. It is very difficult to have any real confidence in canonical material as a sufficient basis for explaining what happened to this man Siddhartha. That's myself. It's almost a caricature, and I think it certainly supports the mythic account, which I think is very valuable, the idea that everyone can relate to. You have a crisis in your life—in the Buddha's case, it was the crisis of feeling trapped in this palace—and then you suddenly have a vision or an experience of the great questions of life and death. That gives sufficient shock to your system to then pursue deliberate religious or spiritual or philosophical inquiry, and then at a certain point that inquiry reaches some kind of conclusion. That conclusion then becomes the basis for what you do.

That's fine. But we don't have adequate data in the actual canon to be able to reconstruct that process regarding Siddhartha Gautama clearly enough. I suppose my own account, or that of anyone who is working as a Buddhist teacher, would somehow mirror the phases of that process. But I think one has to be alert to how much of what comes down to us has a mythic power. The danger is to mistake that for a historical narrative. That, I think, is a big problem. The problem with taking the myth too literally is that when we think of our spiritual practice in life, we are perhaps unconsciously seeking to conform it to the outline of those mythic structures. Perhaps we are even deceiving ourselves slightly in seeking to have a narrative that fits the model we tacitly recognize as the one that is somehow necessary. Perhaps I do that too, I don't know.

BOYLE: This is a good opportunity to get back to your life, because somehow this narrative wasn't all in place at the time you left Korea. Or was it?

S. BATCHELOR: When I came back from Korea, when I ceased to be a monk, clearly my life moved into another gear. I was married. I had to support myself. I had to carve out some kind of career in the world, and so the needs that defined my work were very different than those that I had as a monk. But I do think it fits that narrative scheme. Returning to England from the monastery was really meeting the challenge of applying in the actual world what I had learned. In that sense, it mirrors the period of the Buddha from his leaving home until his enlightenment, followed by that longer period of his life, which we don't pay much attention to in Buddhism, from the enlightenment to his death forty-five years later. There is often the assumption that once the Buddha obtained enlightenment, all he did was walk around India giving brilliant talks, and then one day he dropped down dead. One fails to see that actually in some ways his practice shifted into a different gear, the gear of actually achieving in the concrete world a realization, a manifestation, an embodiment of what he had struggled to achieve through his period of learning and his period of study and his period of meditation as someone who wasn't yet a teacher. What I try to emphasize in the second part of the book is that the Buddha's life after the enlightenment was still a struggle, but of a different order.

BOYLE: Exactly. What I want to do is apply that to you. You've spent your time since Korea actually doing something similar.

S. BATCHELOR: Yes, I suppose so.

BOYLE: That's important to us. Can you say anything about what you have worked with personally since Korea?

S. BATCHELOR: It's very difficult. You see, that is the problem with writing autobiography: the closer you get to the present, the less distance you have to be able to reflect on what you have done and what it has meant to you. I've wanted to write autobiographically for a long time, but I've always been aware that I need some distance in time. I am much more confident in presenting an autobiographical narrative for the earlier years, through Korea. I am far enough away from it to feel far less personal about it. It's almost the story of somebody else. The second part of the book is the phase of my life that I am currently in, and as I think is often the case in anyone's life, there is the formative period and then there is the period when you spend your life doing your work. In some ways the formative period is the more interesting narrative. It's the same with the Buddha. We all know about the Buddha's struggle to become the Buddha. We know very little about the life he then led over the next years. I think that is probably comparable to myself and many of my peers, who can't see the recent process with the kind of clarity with which we can see the earlier process because we can't see the forest for the trees. That is why the tone of the narrative shifts completely in the second part of the book, because I'm still living that part. I'm not old enough, perhaps. If I were eighty or ninety and could look back on my life from that vantage point, I might be able to reconstruct that narrative in perhaps a more telling way. At the moment I can't, because it's what I am doing now. I can only describe the various threads of my interest, of my study, of my research, of my own inquiry, my own philosophical development. I am still involved in that. It's not in any sense complete, not in any sense finished. Maybe it never will be.

BOYLE: In the second part of the book you mention some interesting threads having to do with the nature of the self. Could you elaborate a bit more on how you came to your present understanding of what the self is?

S. BATCHELOR: Well, I think that when I was training as a monk I probably thought of Buddhism in the more traditional way of seeing through the fiction of self. The idea of emptiness was very important to me, things like that. Subsequently when I've looked at passages, somewhat anomalous passages where the Buddha speaks of self in a nonproblematic way, I see that the Buddha describes the self as a project, as something to be realized. It's in that sense that there is not a fixed self. If there were, then there would be little that you could do about it. Your life would not be something that could really evolve or develop, because you already are what you are. That's the problem with some traditions in which there is a belief that there is some true, intrinsic, maybe even quasi-divine nature to your true being. I think Hinduism in particular, and perhaps other theistic traditions, feel that your self is actually already formed.

BOYLE: The soul?

S. BATCHELOR: The soul, or the true mind, or something that is already somehow fulfilled, somehow realized, that we don't notice. Whereas in the Buddhist approach, that whole idea is abandoned in favor of seeing the personal, the self, the soul, as something that evolves. Your practice, whether it be your ethical practice, your meditative practice, or your philosophical practice, is one in which you seek to cultivate that sense of personhood as a farmer cultivates a field or a sculptor fashions a piece of wood. The Buddha uses those images, which I found extraordinarily illuminating because they completely cut against the idea that you evolve by somehow stripping away your sense of self until you arrive at some sort of pure vision of reality, which again is a mystical spin on that idea. What seems to be especially striking when we think of the Buddha engaged with the world and the problems of the world, creating a community, developing and training monks and laypeople, is that he is working with impermanent suffering, with processes of consciousness and feeling and so on and so forth. He wants to find ways we can channel and focus and develop our psycho-physical being into something that embodies the values of wisdom and compassion and care and tolerance and equanimity. It's an ongoing project. It is not something for which there will probably ever be some final state, some final resolution. I suppose the Buddha's story after his awakening, and my own story after my period as a monk, have a kind of parallel. In other words, I find that as a layperson living in the world and trying to understand these things, I find more inspiration in recognizing how the Buddha himself had to struggle with conflicting situations and opposition from other people. That is the phase my own practice is in now. That is perhaps why I am particularly fascinated to discover who this man was, what sort of difficulties he had. There are passages, not many, where the Buddha acknowledges that he is fed up with his community, says he feels hemmed in by it. "Let's get out of this place." I can relate to that. There is something terribly human about that.

BOYLE: You have some stories in *Confession of a Buddhist Atheist* where the Buddha was faced with a situation such that if he didn't please the king, didn't placate the king, then he wouldn't be able to carry on his teaching.

S. BATCHELOR: Yes, exactly.

BOYLE: And he had to make compromises.

S. BATCHELOR: Yes, and that's life. The Buddha in that case is shown *not* to be some sort of radical idealist who would never compromise an inch but would always stick to his guns. The Buddha recognized that if his teaching was to survive in this world and if his community was to be able to mature, then he needed certain material conditions, social conditions, economic conditions that others would have to provide, and some of these others were perhaps not terribly nice people. They had their own agendas, their own ambitions, and he had to work with that. Then he gets caught up in this horrible dilemma because his cousin Mahanama has been deceiving the king. He's in a real catch-22 situation. If he admits it to the king, everything will fall apart. If he doesn't admit it to the king, he is likewise trapped because he will be seen as complicit in the whole deception. He must have known that. It is the fatal flaw. In Greek tragedy it is the worm in the apple, it is the fatal flaw that brings the whole thing crashing down. I find that very, very moving. Yet very few Buddhists are aware of that story.

BOYLE: That is not something I have heard anywhere else.

S. BATCHELOR: It is sometimes mentioned in other books on the Buddha. I don't think anyone else has thought it through in terms of how the Buddha himself would have been caught in basically a trap, a no-exit situation. Again, it's interesting because so often Buddhists will say that everything depends on what you think and on your motives, and that is what determines whether your actions are good or bad. But here you actually have a situation where, irrespective of his motives, the Buddha is caught. He's trapped in a moral dilemma that is not of his own making. Yet it's part of his world. It profoundly affects his ability to realize his project. It has the flavor of the classical tragedies, whether Greek or Shakespearean. It shows that life itself is morally compromised, that you can find yourself in morally compromised situations that are no fault of your own, situations you haven't created.

BOYLE: In the second part of the book you have stories in which someone close to the Buddha was killed or died. When these things happened, he would often say something like, "Well, that's contingent arising," and seem rather unemotional. I can relate to that because I've always thought of myself as less emotional than most people. Then a month ago, the dog that we had for fourteen and a half years died. Now, in my lifetime I haven't had anyone close to me die other than my parents, who were very old and ready to move on. My children are doing fine, my grandchildren are doing great. There has been no personal tragedy. But when our dog died it was like a dagger right to my heart, so painful. I guess I throw that out to see if you have any comments on feeling emotions of sadness or grief.

S. BATCHELOR: Certainly, I think my practice is very much about my relationship to suffering, self-suffering, and this leads to a certain awareness of the poignancy of life, the tragedy of life. It doesn't mean that because you have more equanimity about these things, you don't feel them deeply. I think you do. I feel that the Buddhist teaching is not a recipe for a sort of aloof detachment or a kind of disinterest. What is striking about the Buddha's life is that he's not disinterested in the fate of his world or his family. He's not aloof from these things, he's a participant in these processes. I feel that this practice is not one that makes me less touched by the events of life. If anything, it's the opposite: one's emotional relationship to the world becomes richer. I feel that this practice of the Dharma makes one more sensitive, more sensitized, and again, it's easy to throw out words like "compassion," but surely compassion is only real if it is founded on empathy, on a deepening ability to feel what the other feels. In fact, I end the book by saying:

> Gautama's Dharma calls for a sensibility that infuses and transforms one's relationship with others. . . . To heed the injunction to embrace suffering leads to an empathetic identification with the plight of others. Their pain comes to be felt as one's own. Shantideva, writing more than a thousand years after the First Council of the Buddha's death, expands this further. If the compassionate Buddha regarded others as himself, he argues, then as long as there was pain in the world he suffered too.[1]

That has always struck me as a profound observation, and so in that sense I think it's a mistake to give all this emphasis to the ending of suffering. One of its contemporary manifestations is this presentation of Buddhism as a way to be happy. I think it's basically kowtowing to a kind of Western hedonism. At least the impression is given that if you do this, if you practice Buddhism, somehow you become more happy. I think the word "happiness" in that sense is insipid, almost banal. Yes, of course, we don't seek to be unhappy, we seek in some broad sense to improve the quality of our lives, and we call that well-being or contentment or happiness. Again we are giving too much emphasis to personal affect, whereas the statement of Shantideva we just saw, "If the compassionate Buddha regarded others as himself, then as long as there was pain in the world he suffered too," would seem to qualify it so radically that the use of the word "happiness" in that context would be fairly meaningless. How can you really be happy if you are empathetic, sensitized to the suffering of the world? When you watch on the television news starving kids in Africa, or people who have just had their house and their lives destroyed by an earthquake, how can you look at that and be happy? It seems almost cruel in its detachment.

BOYLE: That's good.

S. BATCHELOR: So, that's where I'm at. I certainly do not practice these things in order to be happy. I seek meaning, I seek purpose, I seek value, and I seek to find a way of being in this world in which its mystery, its tragedy, becomes more and more apparent, more transparent. The challenge of the practice in each moment really is to seek resources in oneself to respond to that. Whether or not it makes you happy is irrelevant.

That's why the training of meditation, etc., comes into play. It constantly returns you to a place within yourself where perhaps you are more able, because you have a certain stillness, a certain equanimity, a certain hope, to respond more truly, more caringly, more honestly, less selfishly. That's what matters. At that point we go beyond Buddhism really. This is really about living the human life.

9
Interview with
Pat Enkyo O'Hara

Pat Enkyo O'Hara is founder and abbot of the Village Zendo in Greenwich Village, and the author of Most Intimate: A Zen Approach to Life's Challenges. *We talked in her office on April 13, 2010.*

BOYLE: Can you talk about how you got started with Buddhism?

ENKYO: There was never a question in my mind about what form of Buddhist practice to follow, because I'm of the generation where Zen was the practice of the moment. It was what was available in our culture. I was in high school in the late 1950s and started reading R. H. Blyth's translations of haiku, the *Faith Mind Sutra*, things like that. His books on poetry were suffused with the Zen values and Zen tradition and the aesthetic of Zen. It was a time when the culture of Zen was introduced through those early translations of haiku, and the writings of D. T. Suzuki.

I was very attracted to it, and yet I was kind of a beatnik and certainly not a joiner. It was already very clear that I was of a different generation than those who immediately joined Zen communities. I didn't join any community for twenty years. I visited a few, but I felt like an outsider. I felt like a rebel. What I saw were the snap decisions I made about what I thought I saw: a kind of conformity that I wasn't attracted to at all. And a kind of holiness that I was not attracted to at all.

I read; I continued to read deeply in the Zen tradition. It's kind of ironic, because in Zen we say that words are not the point. And yet, I would read the words "words are not the point," read that again, and read that again. I would say that my life as it unfolded was suffused with the values that developed from a traditional Zen monastic experience, without ever actually having had that experience. But those values of poverty, of scarcity, of simplicity, of being humble, being ordinary, have been the core values of my life. I have never worked for a profit-making organization in my life. That's karma, of course. I was always working for educational organizations or organizations that worked with the elderly, with the developmentally disabled, with drug treatment centers. So there was something about the whole culture of Zen that I felt was part of me. But I had missed the experience of working with a teacher, the discipline of *zazen*. Because when you sit alone, you tend to sit until something comes up, and then you get up and move. That is haphazard sitting, not like focused, prolonged periods of sitting.

BOYLE: You sat entirely alone from the very beginning?

ENKYO: Yes. I must have been in my late thirties when my son (I was a single parent) was finally old enough to go off to Spain for a summer intensive during high school. I took that summer off and went to Zen Mountain Monastery, which is nearby, a couple of hours from New York City. I went there and practiced and discovered the other side of Zen practice, sitting as part of a group. That was a very disciplined community, a highly disciplined community. In so many Zen centers, when they first started out there was a lot of yelling and shouting, like in the old days of Zen. I don't think that is common anymore in the West. It was good for me, because I learned to toe the line. All these values that I had—"not knowing," "beginner's mind," "being open"—were challenged when I encountered the very hierarchical, very disciplined, and really very militaristic structure of Zen Mountain Monastery.

This was just what I needed at that time in my life, and I was old enough to take it with a grain of salt, to see its value but not feel oppressed anymore. I had finally reached that level of maturity in my life. It was good. It was a great beginning practice for me. I had some experiences during that time because in that particular culture we always sat for two-hour sits, or the samurai students did. We sat through the walking meditation if we were really one of the tough students. And of course I associated myself with that.

BOYLE: Who was running Zen Mountain Monastery?

ENKYO: Daido Roshi (John Daido Loori). I fell for that whole thing. I was going to be the toughest, strongest sitter around, you know. I was not a young woman. And yet I did it, so I had some experiences. But I have never felt that to cling to one's experiences is of any benefit whatsoever. One time recently, last year, I told a group of people about an experience I had while I was eating oatmeal, but the reason I was telling them this was to deconstruct and to avoid the reification of experience. The simplicity of having *satori* when you are eating oatmeal and realizing that the whole world is oatmeal, that you yourself are oatmeal, allows me to pull the curtain back and say, "Listen carefully, this is about you and not about someone else's description of an enlightenment experience." In my view, the experiences that people talk about endlessly are not helpful for beginning students. They are actually like a cloud that goes through the sky. Yes, they are wonderful; you feel high. But I have felt high when I wasn't sitting. So I didn't cling to any of the "experiences" that I had, but I did change, and that's what's interesting for me.

The transformation went like this. I had been a professor of media and a person who worked with marginalized populations, so my interest was in how media can help marginalized populations. You could say that I was something of a do-gooder, living a "doing well by doing good" kind of life. And yet there was always that ability to distance myself. That shifted dramatically, through my practice. There is a kind of intimacy, an ability for intimacy and open-heartedness that arises out of the practice, which I think is the point of practicing Buddhism.

Then, after I had been practicing four or five years, the AIDS epidemic hit. There was a Dharma brother, someone in our community, who received a diagnosis of HIV. We were very close, and somehow I fell into the whole world of what was going on at that time. In the mid-1980s it was a plague, a horrible plague. Here in New York, downtown where I live, you could see it. People were dropping like flies. They were creative, wonderful people, and it was a horror show. I became involved first with Robert, my Dharma brother, who started a meditation group at Gay Men's Health Crisis. I supported him with that, and as he grew weaker I took it over, and came to see the incredible power of practice for people who are in a lot of pain, who are very weak, who are very frightened of dying, who are facing their death, and those around them who are grieving. So it was different. Before this, my practice was about learning to free myself and that kind of thing, being more open, being more aware. Everything shifted, and it became not about me, it became about compassion and about doing and seeing the major effectiveness of practice for healing. Up to that point I had been excited about my Zen practice and about my academic work. I loved teaching, mentoring students, establishing projects that showed how media could help marginalized populations. I was passionate about that. Suddenly I saw that Zen could do that without any media at all, that meditation practice in and of itself was this incredibly empowering tool.

BOYLE: I want to go back to when you began sitting with Daido Roshi, and go into that in more detail. First of all, in terms of mechanics, you had long sittings, two hours at a time. Did you work up to that?

ENKYO: I worked up to that.

BOYLE: Your knees bothered you?

ENKYO: I was in a lot of physical pain at the beginning. I was not a yoga person particularly. I wasn't a particularly athletic or physically oriented person. I have changed. I've become something of a jock now. So sitting was very painful, but working with the pain was terrific in the sense that I learned how to be present to pain, how to observe pain, how, in a way, to manage pain. That experience, which lasted about a year, I would say, was extremely helpful at the bedsides of the men whom I worked with. I would help them simply by doing what I used to do, which is breathe into the area, open the awareness to it. So the very tools I used for sitter's knee or sitter's hip became very useful later on. I remember one time, when I was just wracked with pain, a part of me was saying, *This is ridiculous, this is the most ridiculous thing in the world, and I am doing this to myself. I've got my legs crossed. At any moment I can uncross them, and then I won't feel this.* And then suddenly I had no pain whatsoever. None. Well actually, what had happened is the endorphins had kicked in. It wasn't like some magical mystical tour. It was like the body just said, "Enough." I have always been a realistic person, very grounded in many ways, so I didn't think that was a mystical experience. It was very clear that some brain chemistry had been triggered. You can call that mystical if you want, and certainly a lot of neuroscientists are teaching us that there is little difference.

BOYLE: What form did your first meditation take? Did Zen Mountain Monastery use koans?

ENKYO: This is a good example. I went in with a clear opinion that I did not want to do koans, that I wanted to do *shikantaza*. I was very clear about it. I had read a lot, I thought I knew a lot—I was the classic new student. Immediately Daido said, "No, no, no, you're the kind of person that should be doing koan study." So I was put on the koan Mu very early, just a few months after I started practicing. I continued to be a koan student for the entire time that I studied. I love koans, I think they are wonderful ways of engaging the practice, although they are not for everyone. They are definitely not for everyone. I would say maybe two thirds of the students here at the Village Zendo are koan students and a third are not. We don't say you must be a koan student or anything like that. But I love koans.

Mu is the koan that is talked about the most, the quintessential koan. People have these major breakthroughs with that koan. For me the breakthrough happened when I went on a solitary retreat for a week, after I had been working on Mu for eight or nine months, maybe even a year. Suddenly, like everything else, it was . . . nothing special. *Oh!* I hate to be so deflating, but that was it. It was like, *Oh. Oh, yeah.* When I went back, I completed it and went on to other koans. A lot of the work that I particularly had to do involved getting rid of reification, any kind of reification of these koans or mysteries of the mind. For me the work involved bringing things down to the transformative aspect. How does it change your life? How does it change the way you are with others? This is what is important to me.

BOYLE: Did you have trouble dealing with concentration at the beginning?

ENKYO: When I first started, I was counting the breath. That was difficult; that was a discipline, something that had to be learned. But you know, no more difficult than learning a yoga posture, or learning to do tai chi or something. It was challenging and frustrating, but yet—that's what the mind does.

BOYLE: Right, but then you settled into it.

ENKYO: I did, I settled in.

BOYLE: Would you say you were sitting peacefully with no thoughts in your mind for parts of the time? Or how would you describe it?

ENKYO: Well, what I always tell my own students is that when you are doing it right, you don't know you are doing it right, and then after you have done it right, you don't know you did it right. The bell rings, and suddenly the bell rings again. I've had that experience, but it is not something to cling to. I would say that in order to do koans one has to have a stability of mind, because you don't really work with the koan, you drop the koan into this mind and let it sit there. But you don't do anything to it. You wait until the koan springs forth with its proper response, usually when you are washing dishes or closing the door or something. But that's because the mind is at ease; it's not trying to figure the koan out, strategize or anything, it's just at ease. I found the shift from counting the breath to following Mu to working on other koans and now to *shikantaza* to be seamless. When you say "mindfulness," we are probably talking about the same thing. Just sitting, and just sitting. I found that all these forms of meditation are natural, and not fundamentally different from one another. I mean, the only difference is at the very beginning when you are counting your breaths and you can't get past one or two and you are scared to death, and your mind just won't stop, and you don't even know that you have another mind. That is frustrating, and I think students need to have their hands held during that period of time, until they are able to discover themselves and trust themselves and not be afraid of themselves, of their deeper mind. A lot of people are afraid, and that's why there is such resistance at the beginning. I think a lot of the physical resistance is just the freezing of the body around the fear of opening the mind, the fear of just letting it relax.

BOYLE: That's what I hear in the interviews. But now we are moving up to the time when the AIDS epidemic began to happen and a new thing came in. Could you describe the point when you realized that the sitting that you had been doing had changed you in some way, had had an effect on you?

ENKYO: You know, I would say that the realization is in hindsight, as I look back. One just is living one's life, and one just does what one does. But the quality of the feelings that I had, the depth of understanding, the sudden commitment to work with people who were very ill and to do it a lot . . . I worked myself very hard during that period of time because the need was so great. I had not been that kind of caregiver before. I had done good things, but I had always held back a little, felt a little resentful when overworked. This was a kind of opening of compassion. What it was was the dropping of the distance between me and the other, which one could say is the experience of awakening, when you realize there is no wall between you and the other. The opening of compassion just dissolved that sense of separation, through learning to meet dying and death and physical pain all the time, all around.

So it was a powerful meeting of the circumstances of life and my practice, and it changed me completely. As I said, I loved my academic career and was doing well. But then I was haunted by the need to just do the Dharma, to just be teaching this to people who could benefit from it. I was a full-time professor at the time, and I felt pulled between these different demands. My son was receiving free tuition at the university while I was teaching, so I clearly couldn't leave the university until he had completed his academic career. There were various circumstances that kept me there, but the transformation was clear, and I saw it also in my teaching at the university. There was a softening, in the sense of a greater understanding of what individual students' needs were. Being able to meet people where they were was a very powerful change, rather than having them come up to meet me. I saw that was really important.

Toward the end of that period I ran into some differences of opinion with my teacher, Daido Roshi. I had met Maezumi Roshi, who was his teacher, so I left the Zen Mountain community and began studying with Maezumi. I needed something else, and I could see that that was to move out of the highly disciplined, highly hierarchical system at Zen Mountain Monastery. Daido did a wonderful job; he had many students, and he built an institution that will last for many years. He was wise. So I have nothing ill to say other than it is not my way. I was very fond of him, and I think he of me, and it was difficult leaving. Yet sometimes you just know what you have to do. I began to study with Maezumi Roshi, Daido's teacher. That was difficult for everybody concerned. Maezumi felt a little awkward, but we had a good connection and I had something to learn from him—the value of imperfection.

I come from an alcoholic family. I've had addiction issues myself. I was drawn to a quality that Maezumi Roshi had. He had an incredible courage to keep on, to continue to practice, to continue to teach, to recognize in everyone this intimate quality of buddha nature no matter what delusions and difficulties these people were facing. And first of all, what *he* had to face, the issues in his own life. He had his alcohol issues. He had his womanizing issues. I had done a lot of work with young people with drug abuse problems at drug treatment centers. I had an interest in that. So rather than rejecting Maezumi Roshi, I was drawn to him as someone who had something to teach me. He was so humble and so ordinary and able to be intimate with you immediately. But he had his issues. I never witnessed any of that, interestingly enough. His drinking was done at home, not at the center when I was there, and he had no ongoing relationships with anyone that I could see. I wasn't there spying, I was there practicing. For me, within this quality of, "Yes, it's broken, I'm broken," is the heart of humanity. The men I was working with during the AIDS epidemic were not saints. Actually, we have no saints here at the Village Zendo. That comes out of working with Maezumi Roshi. It is something he didn't talk about but that he embodied. He embodied it in his every gesture, his way of working with you in koans. He was very strict, much stricter that anyone else I ever worked with in terms of koans. Here was a soft man who was so kind and sweet and loving, and boy, like a steel trap with the koans. Amazing.

He died suddenly, and when he died I was kind of devastated, but I had the good fortune of knowing Bernie Glassman. I had done a few projects for him wearing my media hat. I had never studied with him because I thought I knew about social action. I thought that wasn't what I needed to learn. I was wrong, because when Maezumi Roshi died, Bernie kindly offered to complete my studies, which were then almost complete. That was kind—he wasn't really taking on many students then. It was great because I had worked with Daido with his strong discipline, then I had worked with Maezumi Roshi with his intimacy and warmth and ordinariness, and then I worked with Bernie, and he is just completely relaxed. It's as if all those years of discipline had just fallen away. He was a good finishing teacher for me. He was in Yonkers and I was here in the Village, so I was able to see him every week. He was very busy with his projects, so he kind of leaned on me to do a lot of the liturgical teachings. As you know, there is no better way to learn something than to be teaching it. I benefited also from the fact that he is one of the people who know the most about the liturgical aspects of Zen and their background. I studied with him for two years and received Dharma transmission from him.

Once I completed my studies with Bernie Glassman, I continued to work with him. We were founding this new Zen Peacemakers organization, and I worked with him and his late wife, Jishu. His present wife, Eve Marko, was also in the group, and we all worked together. Joan Halifax joined us in that group. Egyoku Nakao and Seisen Saunders were part of the group. We worked on rewording the precepts—the really juicy work you have to do if you want to start a new Zen way of being in this country. We worked on a way of training that combined focusing on peacemaking and at the same time on the old values of Zen. We had to ask, "How would you write that? How would you talk about that? How would you teach that?" So we did that work from 1995 until just a few years ago. We would meet off and on and sit and do this kind of work. It was very intense at the beginning.

BOYLE: In 1997 you received Dharma transmission. Had you started the Village Zendo then?

ENKYO: We started in 1985, and are coming up on our twenty-fifth anniversary now. It started when I first began to practice formally. I realized that I wasn't very disciplined at home. I could do fine at the monastery, but not at home. So I had the idea, *Oh, I'll invite some people in to sit with me.* That's what this place is. It grew from there, one person, then two, then three, then five, then ten. We have a pretty large group now. After I received Dharma transmission I continued to teach at NYU for maybe a year, and then I took two year-long leaves of absence. It was a real struggle for me to let go of a tenured professorship, but I really felt drawn to this work of teaching the Dharma and teaching it in a slightly different way. Although I am conservative in some respects as a Zen teacher, I am not highly hierarchical or a disciplinarian at all. I pay a lot of attention to liturgy. I like liturgy a lot, and although I'll make innovations, our *sesshin*s and our retreats are pretty much sparkling clean and clear, and follow old traditions.

I finally had the courage to retire after twenty years. This enabled me to have a studio apartment nearby, which was necessary in order for this organization to survive. People had not even been paying dues, or putting $5 in the pot, and suddenly we were in a high-rent district. The rent on this place is $10,000 a month. So suddenly this hippie professor has to come up with $10,000 a month and a little stipend for myself to keep me going. I didn't have Social Security at that time, I was too young.

We have mainly well-educated, high-functioning people in our community. A lot of artists, a lot of therapists, teachers, social workers—those are the kind of people who are in our community. All of them feel they are outsiders and rebels and would never join anything, and I keep telling them, "That's okay. We can join this group because we are all outsiders, and so that means no one is an insider." We've done very well. I now have five successors. I am very proud of them. There are three therapists, a chiropractor, and a professor of Latin American studies. One of them is a black man and he may be (we're not sure) the first black male *sensei*.

BOYLE: While this was going on, what was happening with you?

ENKYO: It's like the story of the Soto person who walks through the mist at night and doesn't realize that her robes have gotten wet, rather than the great thunderstorm of Rinzai *satori*. Very gradually, I have been tamed by this work of teaching. I am very humbled by the task at hand, by the kind of delusions that make it so hard for people to be clear, by the aspects of a person's being that make it hard for them to accept themselves, to be compassionate. When I began, my approach was at a very high level, tinged with too much intellectualism about the Dharma and koans and their saving property. It seems like every year I kind of ratchet down a notch or two and realize it is more about meditation, sitting, good posture, and having supportive people around. So it's like coming out of the clouds. Each year my teaching gets more ordinary and more simple. Simpler and simpler and simpler.

For years we have gone to Sing Sing. A group of us goes to Sing Sing every Sunday and sits with the prisoners there. That's a great project for the people here. Young people come in, and they're all concerned about themselves and their issues. So I say, "Oh, why don't you join the Sing Sing group and go up and sit in a bare and dirty room and see what that's like?" I like to do that. We've started another project that has become a separate nonprofit.

It's a chaplaincy training project. It's becoming very successful. Two priests here were the cofounders of the Zen chaplaincy project, and they run it. It's amazing, we've already had ninety people graduated. They do a year-long foundations program, and we have second- and third-year programs. That's something that has grown up, not intentionally, not something I said we should do. It has grown out of the transformation that occurs when we sit. You know, people's hearts open and they begin to do things.

BOYLE: So in talking about the last ten years of your transformation, your heart has been opening and your mind has been becoming simpler?

ENKYO: Right.

BOYLE: Any other little words you want to throw in to tell people about that?

ENKYO: Well, you know, I think I was a moderately depressed person the first thirty or forty years of my life. Now everything is just actually joyful all the time. Even when I'm with someone who is dying, there is some way to understand that it's all interconnected and that there is a time when we are alive and there is a time when we die. You can feel that at the bedside of someone who is going, or when you are counseling someone who is quite old about life and death.

BOYLE: Especially at that time.

ENKYO: Yes. It's spring here in New York, and it's hard to think about the cold winter we just went through because it is just so beautiful now. I feel kind of joyful all the time. I was kind of an angry young woman, and I don't know where that went. It pops up from time to time, but it's really not there.

BOYLE: You just notice that it's been a long time since . . .

ENKYO: Exactly, exactly.

BOYLE: But you didn't do anything specific to work on it?

ENKYO: No.

BOYLE: Some of the traditions that people I have interviewed represent have these very specific things to do, maybe a specific kind of meditation.

ENKYO: Yes, I admire those forms of working with compassion, *metta* meditation, those kinds of practices. I think they sound wonderful, but they are not for me. My practice is really koan study, which opens up entire worlds. It's uncanny. Every single koan you work on is about your life. When it becomes true, you see something: *Oh, it's about this. It's about my fault-finding or it's about this or that.* But it's not targeted. You don't start out saying, "I'm going to work on my anger here." It's a different form.

BOYLE: Right, but the koans are saying, "Oh, there is a little insight."

ENKYO: Yes.

BOYLE: Now is that an intellectual insight or a spiritual insight? How would you describe it?

ENKYO: I think the insight into the crux of the koan or into the heart of the koan is first like a feeling and then like a thought. It kind of comes out of the body, out of the heart area, and then words come and then it's mental. That's how I understand it. But there is another aspect. After you've had the insight of experiencing the koan, then you are going to have to go and talk to your teacher about it. After the person has presented the koan, has worked through the koans I have them do, my last question always is, "What does this have to do with your life, what is this koan in your life?" You know, it's amazing the tears that come, the laughter, the realizations. Also, when I think back to those early days when I first began to practice, I seem to have had a realization a minute about my prejudices, about the way my mind worked. Not while I was meditating, but when I'd get up and walk out the door. I'd see my habits, I'd see these aspects of my being that I had never seen before, and I would laugh. That's how one lets go of a lot of stuff, a lot of opinion making and so forth. So the Zen style works for me, in the sense that it's not targeted. You don't know where it's going to come from. You are working on a koan, and suddenly you are working with the grief about your father's death. You didn't know that you were thinking about your father, and suddenly it's there. It's kind of like a Rorschach [test]. Koans are old, old stories, involving archetypal kinds of areas where the mind and heart need to work. The heart needs to soften, the mind needs to understand.

I like to be very specific about koans and not misuse them. I encourage people to come in to see me even when they don't have an answer, because as you stand up from your cushion in the *zendo*, as you open the door to the *sanzen* room, as you walk in, as you bow, you don't know at any of those points whether or not something is going to come. Or maybe the teacher will ask you a question that will elicit something.

BOYLE: During these five years when you were studying with Maezumi, is there any particular moment or insight or event that stands out, or comes back to your memory in any way?

ENKYO: I've actually written about this before. It is a short story about when I was in charge of the altars and carrying one of these big ancient wooden cups and dropped it off the side of the banister at Maizumi's Mountain Center in the San Jacinto Mountains. It cracked terribly, it had a big gash in it. I was upset that I had done that; it was a beautiful cup. The Zen center wasn't wealthy, so I said, "Roshi, I'm going to replace that cup,

I'm going to get a new one for you in Japan. I'll order one. I am so sorry that I did that." He took the cup and he said, "Look at the cup, Enkyo, it's more beautiful now than it was before." It was like, here's this man who has been humiliated by many Zen people across the country and abandoned by half his students, and I thought, here he is still teaching, still doing this work, and he is more valuable after all those scandals than he was before. I was this forty-something woman who was changing careers and leaving her academic world in order to follow this crazy man. I just saw the beauty of our humanness through him.

BOYLE: That's the wonderful part.

ENKYO: Yes, and there is a koan about that. It's called the rhinoceros fan, rhinoceros horn fan, and he kept me on that koan for almost an entire summer. Talk about frustrating—I'd go in each time and I was really sure I was right, because it is one of those koans that has seven or eight points. You don't just give one presentation, you have to give seven or eight, because all the great teachers have made comments on this horn fan koan. It was about that, about how each of our own imperfections is our humanity, not something to be rejected but something to be seen and recognized. It's about buddha nature. Like the Mu koan—it's about our buddha nature. Maezumi Roshi was a great teacher for me. He was a heart teacher for me. Of course, I learned so much from all three of my teachers.

BOYLE: But it was in the spirit of gradually getting wet from the soft rain.

ENKYO: Exactly. The big experiences I had, I tried to let go of immediately. I also grew up in the days of psychedelics, so I don't take those kinds of experiences very seriously. What I am talking about are the realizations that come all the time. They don't have to be psychological. They can be moments of inspiration or joy, and then they permeate your behavior. They go into your life. It's great; it's really an underappreciated aspect of life. We who practice this are such a tiny percentage of the population. We are so fortunate. And that's why we are willing to give our lives to sharing it.

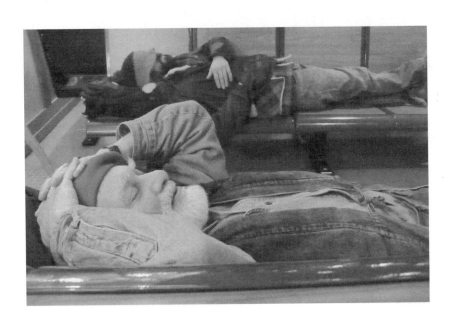

10
Interview with
Bernie Glassman

Bernie Glassman holds retreats not in zendos but on the streets of the Bowery in New York City, and in Auschwitz. His writings include Instructions to the Cook: A Zen Master's Lessons in Living a Life That Matters *and* The Dude and the Zen Master *(with Jeff Bridges). The interview was held April 14, 2010, in Montague, Massachusetts.*

BOYLE: A path story usually starts with how you first heard about Buddhism, or got some feeling that then led you to some contact with Buddhism and beginning some initial training. But for now: you grew up in New York. What started things?

GLASSMAN: I grew up in Brooklyn in a Jewish family, not a religious Jewish family but a cultural Jewish family. My mother died when I was very young, nine years old, but many of the people in my family were in the Communist Party. They were socialists, they were activists. I grew up with that kind of activism, so it's part of who I am. From an early age I was interested in electronics and aeronautics. I got into Brooklyn Technical High School and majored in aeronautical engineering; then in college my undergraduate work was in aeronautical engineering. In my junior year in college, in an English class, we were required to read a book that had just come out by Houston Smith called *The Religions of Man*. Of course he's had to change the title, as it became uncouth to say "man" [it is now *The World's Religions*]. There was one page in it on Zen. I should say that although I did not grow up in a religious family, somehow I had some orientation toward religion, because at the age of twelve I did a personal survey of the question, Is there a God?, collecting pro and con arguments for the existence of God from Dostoevsky, Tolstoy, and Descartes. When I look back, I'm a little surprised at what I did. After reading that book by Houston Smith, and the one page on Zen, it struck me as being my home space. So I started to read everything I could about Zen. There wasn't that much in translation in 1958, but I read all the stuff that there was, Alan Watts, Christmas Humphries, D. T. Suzuki.

Maezumi Roshi was my main teacher. His father was a big figure in a Soto Japanese sect, but Maezumi was somewhat of a rebel and a lay Rinzai teacher. He studied with three different Zen masters, and I had the good fortune to also study directly with those teachers.

I didn't know much about meditation. They didn't stress that, those early writers. I probably started to do some *zazen* around 1960. I had moved to California, and was working in the aerospace industry doing interplanetary work. In 1962 I went to Israel for a year. I was looking to maybe even move there if I could find the right spiritual community. That didn't work out—the country was too chauvinist for me. I came back and was rehired by McDonnell Douglas doing the same work as before, but I also found a Japanese temple, a Zen temple, in downtown Los Angeles, and I started to sit with them.

The main effort of the temple was working with the Japanese community and helping them to acclimate in the society, but there was *zazen* one night a week. So I would sit there, but there was no English, and I decided I could continue on my own. There was a young monk from Japan there whose name was Maezumi. That's how I met Maezumi, in 1962. But I left that temple and continued sitting on my own, even sitting *sesshins* on my own. It wasn't until around 1966 that I heard of a workshop being given by Yasutani Roshi. I had read about him in *Three Pillars of Zen*, so I went to that workshop. The translator was the same Maezumi, whose English was now a lot better. I went up to him and asked if he was still at the Japanese temple where I had met him. He said no, he had started his own sitting place, the Los Angeles Zendo. I joined him, but for a few years it was just the two of us sitting in the morning. Yasutani Roshi would come through and do *sesshins*, and there was always a larger crowd then. There was a fairly large crowd when Maezumi gave talks, but otherwise it was a small sitting group. I became sort of his right-hand person. In 1969 he went back to Japan to finish his studies with Yasutani Roshi. Yasutani had decided not to come to the States anymore, and in 1968 he asked Maezumi to come to Japan. In Japan Yasutani would travel throughout the country doing *sesshins*. Maezumi traveled with him as his assistant and finished his koan study with him. During that year, 1969, Maezumi asked me to lead the L.A. Zendo. I was somewhat of a fierce teacher. I was teaching from 1970 on, and I received Dharma transmission in 1976. In the beginning we were just a group sitting and doing koan study and meditation. We didn't know about the formal titles, the formal processes. Little by little Maezumi introduced all that. Then we moved to another place and were incorporated as the Zen Community of Los Angeles, ZCLA, which is still thriving.

Now, when I first got involved in Zen, it was because I wanted to have the enlightenment experience of all these people I'd read about. I wasn't thinking about serving, when I first got involved in 1958. It was a way of life that I was reading about that had to do with the experience of the oneness of life. My notion was that it was a single experience that you were going to work toward and get and then, *My, now I'm really cool.* I might even have quit smoking cigars, and I did not want to stop smoking cigars, even at that age. In those days my whole focus was on what we tend to call awakening, realizing the way, and I wanted to experience what these people were talking about.

My first major awakening experience was in 1970 with another of Maezumi Roshi's teachers, Koryu Roshi, during a *sesshin*. It was a typical kind of experience, with everything dropping away and being one with everything. I remember seeing trees, feeling wind on me. I *was* the tree. It wasn't my first experience, but it was the first with a teacher there. I had had a similar experience years before on my own, which terrified me and actually made me stop sitting for a year. I thought I was losing my mind. I had nobody to talk to. In fact, it was a year later that I went to see somebody and started the formal practice.

That happened in 1970, when I passed the koan Mu with Koryu Roshi. In the Zen world it was recognized as an enlightenment experience. It was pretty deep, because Koryu Roshi went back to Japan and talked about this amazing thing that had happened. I heard different stories from his students about it. But it was just an experience of being one. Koan study is set up to try to get you to experience this oneness of life first, and then to experience the state of not knowing, the state of complete openness, of being completely open to everything.

I had an experience of not knowing a few years later, in 1976, and it changed my whole direction. It would be called a great enlightenment experience, in which there are no more questions. For the Zen Peacemakers we have three tenets: not knowing, bearing witness, and loving actions. So not knowing is an essential part of Zen training—getting you to experience what we call the sauce from which everything comes. It's a state where there are no attachments to any of your conditionings. Then a major letting go, a deepening of the state of not knowing. I have had a number of experiences along that line. They can and do keep deepening what had previously been experienced. All of them have to do with experiencing that state of not knowing.

This one, in 1976, happened when I was driving to work. I felt the suffering, or the unsatisfaction, of all creations. I call them the hungry ghosts, those seeking for being satisfied. At the same time that I had that experience, I realized that these were all aspects of myself. All this seeking was various aspects of myself. At the same time I made a vow to try to feed, to try to help satisfy those thirsts, those hungers. I say that changed my direction. Before that, my whole goal was to be a monk at the zendo and work with the people coming to the zendo and try to lead them toward these experiences. After that I changed the venue of my work from the zendo to society. I wanted to work with everybody, wanted to figure out what are the ways, *upayas*, of working with people in business and social action and all aspects of life. So I would say that from 1976 to now, that has been my direction.

A little later on I ran into a quote by Kobo Daishi, who lived from 764 to 835. He was the founder of the Shingon sect, the Japanese tantric sect. He is considered in Japan as the number one spiritual leader of Shingon. He said that the way you can tell the depth of a person's enlightenment is how they serve others. That is what I go by. In some ways it's obvious. If you are trying to get enlightenment, or if you're trying to get healthy, or if you're trying to get stable, then everything you are doing is about yourself. That's the depth of your enlightenment. Experience the oneness of life that you see is yourself, and you see yourself as one body. If it's serving your family, that's the depth; if it's your society, if it's the world. Somebody like the Dalai Lama is working for the world, not just his particular Tibetan group. So his enlightenment is that broad.

The experience I had in 1976 led me naturally into working wherever I saw hunger and suffering. People tend to call that social action. I call it the functioning of the realization of the oneness of life. That is, if your realization is on your own body and then something happens to you, you take care of it. You don't say, "Is that me? Should I take care of it? Should somebody else take care of it? Do I have enough skill to take care of it?" You do what you have to do when you run into it. It's the same thing when you run into somebody in the street and they fall. That's you falling, so you pick them up. That's social action. If you run into homeless people, or people at war or whatever, that's you, and you do what you have to do for them. So for me it was just a natural extension. I became very active in that way when I moved to New York, after I left the Zen Center of Los Angeles to start my own community.

Some Zen teachers would say I was moving away from the Dharma, and I would say, "What is the realization of the Dharma? You mean poor people are not part of the oneness of life?" You can do Zen and work on Wall Street, and that's okay. This made me realize that enlightenment experiences can still be limited and bound up in a small circle, and that's the circle in which we work. I began trying to expand my own circle by moving into places where my natural impulse might have been to run away from or avoid them. I would try to work in those arenas. That was my second tenet of bearing witness—to stay within the area in which I wanted to work until I could fully grok[1] what was going on there. The third, the action, was to do something then, not just talk about it, not just preach about it or join conferences about it, but to do actions. That became the basis for what I call the Zen Peacemakers.

We are also family, so not everybody is doing that kind of work. In some sense it doesn't matter if you're doing meditation and you are focused on yourself. That's the place you are at, and that's great. But I feel that naturally, as you deepen those experiences, your work will be going out, just as Kobo Daishi said. I see that. During the last number of years I have also have been spending a lot of energy developing socially engaged Buddhism as a practice. So I am differentiating myself from people who define their practice as including only meditation, maybe visualizations, forms like that, and then say, "Well, you've got to do your practice, and once you get clear enough then you can do your social action or other things and you can do them in a good way." They would say that I'm working on ways of doing social action, while I say that I'm teaching people how to do social action as practice, as a way of realizing the oneness of life.

For me, Buddhism as the religion of awakening is about realizing the oneness of life. Through the years various techniques have been developed. We call them *upayas*. Sometimes those *upayas* then become whole schools. You've got schools that focus on the precepts as a way of realizing the oneness of life and schools that focus on meditation, like Zen. You've got the esoteric schools, which use visualizations and other ways of practicing. You've got psychological schools that work with abhidharma. You've got different schools that focus on different things. I've taken upon myself the task of trying to promote socially engaged Buddhism as a way of realizing the oneness of life. While you are doing that practice you are also helping. But depending on where you are in that awakening, you either realize that you are helping yourself, because it's all yourself, or you think you're helping others. As long as you think you are helping others, you're in a dualistic state and really haven't gotten the oneness of life. I am trying to develop that as an *upaya*.

BOYLE: You talked earlier about the awakening you had in 1976 that led you in this direction. Were there things that happened after that that provided insight, or a realization that went with that transition?

GLASSMAN: Let me give an example. I decided to do a street retreat about twenty-five years ago, to go live in the streets for a week. I invited people to join me. There were about eighteen of us. It was a wide spectrum of people. My first Dharma successor, Peter Matthiessen, was there. He had practiced Zen for quite a while. He was an amazing person, an explorer who had been through so many different experiences. At the same retreat I had a man who was our architect. We were starting to build housing for homeless people, and he had zero experience in meditation, no background in Buddhism. A woman, Anne Waldman, was on that retreat. She's part of the Allen Ginsberg era—she and Allen had actually started the department of poetry at Naropa. She is still involved in that. So she had been through the beat generation and was a close student of Trungpa Rinpoche. A variety of people. I had started that street retreat because I was going to be working with homeless and very poor people and I wanted to experience, to bear witness to their life, to help me as I started designing the work I was going to do. I thought it was just going to be a one-time retreat. What struck me was that our moving into the street to live, with no money, brought us to a place of not knowing much quicker than koan study or years of meditation.

What I realized is that because we were just living in the now, with no idea of what was going on, there was nothing to hang on to. It was totally out of our experience. About 90 percent of that group came to a much deeper place than people who had been practicing 10 years or so. I recognized that this was the first realization of *upaya*. I call it a plunge, plunging into unknown situations, which the brain cannot fathom, cannot rationalize. It's what we try to do with koans, but this was much more real. We were there; we weren't just experiencing and leaving, we were staying in that state. The street retreat turned out to be a very profound experience. There is a liturgy, the liturgy that I favor the most in the Buddhist tradition, that is called Gate of Sweet Nectar, in which we feed the hungry ghosts. We gather the hungry ghosts, and we feed them. It's a very important ritual in Japan.

They have a holiday called Obon that's based on this, in which they bring all the ancestors back and they feed them and they send them back in boats with lanterns and candles. In that first retreat, each day we would gather and share what was going on, and in one of those gatherings somebody said, "I want to offer what we are doing to the buddhas," and somebody said, "We want to offer it to all creation." Things came up in that retreat, from people, that are part of that liturgy. What we were doing was living out that liturgy. The ones who were talking about it didn't know the liturgy. So from then on I actually brought that liturgy into the streets.

BOYLE: Which liturgy is that?

GLASSMAN: In Japanese it's called *kanrunhan*, the Gate of Sweet Nectar. I translated it and changed it. I translated it with my teacher, Maezumi Roshi, and then got his permission to modify it. What we have on the website in English is my translation, to which I have added elements. If you go on my website and look under "Liturgy," you will find it. That practice then became a practice for us, and it's still going on. I have several Dharma successors whose main activity is doing street retreats around the world. It's happening all over. The second time we did this was the Auschwitz retreat, which also was a realization of the depth of the effect that doing those kinds of practices could have. When I went to Auschwitz the first time, it was at an interfaith conference, and I was struck by the vastness. I could just feel the hungry spirits there, and I decided to do a retreat. This has happened to me many times; I will go somewhere and I can feel this crying out and I will go there and do a retreat. I spent about a year and a half organizing the Auschwitz retreat because I wanted to bring as many different voices together as I could. It was very much planned out. I brought children of SS officers, children of survivors, children of the Gypsies who were killed there. We had Gypsies, we had gays, we had maybe twenty different countries and six different religions represented. It was a huge diversity—one group, big diversity.

I planned it so the first day was overwhelming—you could not rely on anything. There was no rational way to figure out what was going on. The place is beyond rationalizing, it is so big. But we made the first day very heavy, so it was a real plunge into this place of not knowing. Being with each other, being with all the different voices—many of the Germans would bring up guilt, and the Jews would bring up anger, and the Poles were bringing up their difference, like, "It wasn't our responsibility." So many different emotions, and people getting upset with each other because they didn't understand the different places they were coming from or what the retreat leaders, their coaches, were trying to do. By the fourth or fifth day we were one family, a family of tremendous diversity. Again, the whole notion of the oneness of life was made so clear by the way this group, which felt so disparate at the beginning, eventually became one family and felt so interconnected. Those kinds of experiences just solidify my feeling that, yes, you can create practice. Then I realized that if you go back, the Tibetans had what they called charnel practices. There is a history of all this, and I am just using modern-day events as ways of helping people go deeper into their practice. These are my feelings—not everybody shares this kind of orientation.

BOYLE: I'm curious, though—do the street or Auschwitz retreats have any of the structure of a conventional retreat? Do you give talks, do you have interviews with students?

GLASSMAN: They all have structures. I am always looking for what is the right structure. On a street retreat we gather at least twice a day. Originally I was trying to gather three times a day, to sit together and to share what was going on. But on the street it's hard to get together three times a day, because we don't go around as a group. I try to keep the number of people on the retreat not too large, so I usually split up the group. The first time there were eighteen, and that's about the largest I would do, but I split it into groups of three, packs of three. I would have a pack leader, and for safety the pack leader was responsible for knowing where the other two people in their pack were. We encouraged people to go on their own, looking for food, looking for places to rest, looking for places to go to the bathroom. There are all kinds of immediate needs that you have, because at night it is hard to sleep, and you are tired during the day. So people were going all over the place, and to get back to meet together three times a day turned out to be very hard. But generally we'd meet twice a day. We would gather as a group to sleep together, again for safety. I wanted all of us to sleep in the same place; we were mixed, men and women. And I wanted everybody to beg; part of the structure was begging, part of the structure was aimlessly meandering. It has a structure, but nothing like zendo structure. It was the same with Auschwitz. Auschwitz had a very strict structure, with a lot of time for individuals to be going around. Same on the streets— there is a detailed structure, but a lot of flexibility within it. So they all have a structure, but they are all different structures. That was part of my quest when I said I wanted to move from the zendo to society. My question was, What do the structures look like in the different aspects of society? I knew the structure of a zendo; I was trained in that very strongly. What is the structure on the production floor of a bakery or in a government agency? Again, they have very different structures. So what I was looking for were the equivalents, different techniques that each worked the same way in their specific structure.

BOYLE: When you described the structure you used for the street retreats, you said that when you got together you did some sitting and people talked to each other?

GLASSMAN: I use what I call the way of council as the structure. People are always talking to each other. Are you familiar with the way of council?

BOYLE: It evokes something in my mind. People gathered together and talking together about some issue.

GLASSMAN: It's a structure I brought into the Zen Peacemakers. It was made popular by the Iroquois Confederacy. There are books on the way of council. Joan Halifax revived it when she set up a place in Ojai, and then Jackson and Gigi Coyle have made that their life, teaching it. I use it a lot. You sit in a circle; there are some basic rules—you speak from the heart, you listen from the heart, and you can't prepare. If somebody is talking, you don't prepare to answer them, you just listen to them, and when it's your turn you speak from the heart. We use that. That was different from zendo structure, where you aren't supposed to talk with each other about what is going on.

BOYLE: This is really important. So you were part of the council but no different from the other people?

GLASSMAN: Exactly, you are all just peers in the council.

BOYLE: Okay, but people were talking with each other?

GLASSMAN: You pass around a talking piece, some special object. While you have the talking piece you can speak, and you speak whatever is coming up from your heart. Everybody else is just deeply listening. The rules of the game are that you can't say anything until your time comes. Yes, you may be affected by what's been said, but you are not putting what you say in terms of responding to somebody else. You are always talking from inside yourself, just saying what's coming out of you, spontaneously. You are not relating it consciously to what others say. It's a little like being in a jazz group.

BOYLE: Yes, I see that part. It's all improvised at the moment it arises.

GLASSMAN: Everybody is affecting everybody else.

BOYLE: In sociology we talk about a contagion effect that is created during social interaction.

GLASSMAN: Yes, sure. That's what happens when a group is going, man. You are doing your thing and you are affected by what everybody else is doing, but you're not trying to do it. It's just happening. So that becomes the sound of the group.

BOYLE: There is such a contrast, such a difference between the hierarchical forms of Buddhism that have been brought over from Asia and this lateral, conversational sharing.

GLASSMAN: I was struck by that, and I actually spent a number of years promoting a new form of Zen group that we call circles. So within the Zen Peacemakers there are circles; there are Zen centers like Enkyo's, and there are also circles around the world that relate to one another as peers. We do train people to be stewards, so there is a steward in the group. The steward is somebody who has been trained in how to facilitate the process. But everybody is a peer, there is no "one teacher" in the group; they are all teachers. It's a very different process than in the Japanese hierarchical structure.

BOYLE: This would be very powerful for all people participating. So what if someone has an awakening of the kind we talked about earlier? You mentioned that you had had an experience way back, and it frightened you so much that you stayed out for a year. When someone has an experience during the retreat, would they go and talk to you about it?

GLASSMAN: When you are a member of the circle your individual experience really becomes an experience for the circle. You don't even have to say anything. It's just like when a musician all of a sudden goes off on some riff because something has hit him. Everybody is feeling it, and everybody changes. For me it's a wonderful transition. Say we're talking about the interconnectedness of life, and all of a sudden things like individual experiences become not as meaningful as circle experiences, group experiences. My understanding is that when anybody has an experience, the whole world is having an experience. That's what Dogen calls "cosmic resonance." By moving from individual practice to circle practice, you are moving into that realm of cosmic resonance and into a different kind of experience. That doesn't mean that you individually don't have an experience, but the whole group has it, and there is group support for it. The members of the group can talk to each other.

BOYLE: So if you have an experience, you can say something about it or not . . .

GLASSMAN: But either way, the group is having it. If it does come up in the conversation, the group will grok it. That's happened on the street and also in Auschwitz. The people who go to Auschwitz and the people who go on the street are transformed. If they meet somebody who was on the street retreat in a completely different place, they both understand what they are talking about. They both felt the experience, in very similar ways. They have a harder time talking about it with people who haven't done a street retreat, who haven't experienced it. So the street retreats, as well as Auschwitz, become group experiences. We are going to Auschwitz in June, and there will be 160 people. They'll be very close afterward, and they will be close to other people who went to Auschwitz previously. They will have a harder time talking to other people about what they have experienced because those people haven't experienced it. Of course, the individual experiences will be different, one from another, but there will be a point of connection. They will be able to talk about it. It's fascinating.

BOYLE: Yes, it is.

GLASSMAN: That has been my experience. I've been doing this for a while now. This will be our fifteenth year at Auschwitz. I stopped going to them for a while, and then I went back after the tenth anniversary and it affected me so much that I went again for the eleventh year. Then I stopped. I wasn't going to go to anymore, but Peter Matthiessen asked if I would do one more. He went on my first Auschwitz retreat, and he's generally been with me every time I've started something new. He came on that first retreat. He's a writer, and he was affected so deeply that he started writing about the various things that arose there. He is still writing, and now he has a pretty big manuscript. He called me about a year ago and said he needs to go back once more because there is still some stuff unresolved. He asked if I would do one more, and that's why I am doing the one in June. It's been going on for fifteen years now, and he is still dealing with stuff from it.[2]

BOYLE: Very powerful.

GLASSMAN: Of course most people who visit Auschwitz, they go and they get a hit, whether it's revulsion or whatever, and they leave right away. So this becomes very different, and we are bringing together so many different groups, so many different voices.

BOYLE: In the remaining time I am interested in hearing about the Zen Houses. I can really relate to those. The sociologist in me finds it easy to relate to community organizing, and how Zen Houses could nourish a neighborhood, raise the level of social capital, that sort of thing.

GLASSMAN: After my first street retreat, which was twenty-five years ago, I realized there were no Buddhist groups helping us on the street. In fact, there were no Dharma groups out there, and when I say "Dharma" I am including Hindu. The main people who were helping us were Christians. There was one Islamic group, but they would only help Muslims. There was nobody but the Christians who were just there to help people.

One of the things I said then was that one day I may start doing the same thing. Of course, I got involved in the Greyston Mandala project in Yonkers, which was doing social service, but on a huge scale. Then a few years ago, I said, "It's time to start creating Dharma centers where the main focus is not just on individual enlightenment and the individual, but on serving the community, serving the people. Not neglecting the individual, but expanding the focus from the individual to the community." That was the start of the notion of Zen Houses. What I want is to do it in such a way that those three Buddhist tenets are there. My feeling is if you are coming from a place of not knowing, bearing witness, and loving actions, then you bring dignity. For me it is service with dignity, service with love. Love isn't enough—you can love your dog and you can love your children, but you don't necessarily give them dignity. You look at them as different from yourself. They are not a peer. I want to stress that.

We just had our first offering as a soup kitchen here at Montague Farm this Saturday, this past Saturday. You wouldn't know it was a soup kitchen. This is a very poor area—it's called the Appalachia of Massachusetts. So we've created a meal. From Friday to Sunday there are no meals being offered in this area, no soup kitchens. Families are nervous about bringing their kids to a soup kitchen. Most of these are single-parent families, but there's always a partner somewhere. My aim was to create a meal that was not only not threatening to the families but also inviting. So we called it the Montague Farm Café: fine food, music, games, and puppetry. We are going to add to it a wellness component with physical checkups, massage, different things like that. The first meal was offered this Saturday. We had about eighty people. We picked people up from shelters in different areas. We arranged transportation. But nobody in the room knew who was poor and who was wealthy. There were tons of games for the kids and all kinds of stuff. That is kind of a model.

BOYLE: People came from all around?

GLASSMAN: It was a different feeling from any soup kitchen I've ever been in. We had a menu, and on the back of the menu we had a dollar pasted. People could either keep it or donate it, so all the kids could either keep it or make donations. We probably had about forty kids there.

Each Zen House will be different. Part of their task will be feeding people, part of it will be creating jobs in the community or stuff like that. That's what we plan to do.

11
Interview with
Joseph Goldstein

Joseph Goldstein, with Sharon Salzberg and Jack Kornfield, founded the Insight Meditation Society in 1974. His writings include One Dharma: The Emerging Western Buddhism *and* Mindfulness: A Practical Guide to Awakening. *We talked on April 14, 2010.*

BOYLE: The way I have been doing these path interviews is to start with the first little glimmerings that led you to study and practice Buddhism.

GOLDSTEIN: When I was a child I was prone to having temper tantrums. These made me and everyone around me quite miserable. But I didn't know what to do about it. Then when I was about ten, I had my first insight into the working of my mind, in a childlike but somewhat profound way. Just after one of these big outbursts of anger, I looked into my mind and I realized that there was the possibility of a space between the impulse of the temper outburst and the action. I saw that in that space there was a choice, and in a kind of young and naïve way I realized what we are often told—count to ten before you say anything. That's what I started doing, and it worked—the impulse for the outburst would pass. It was amazing. It was a real transformation, in that particular context.

Then when I was twelve, my father died suddenly, of leukemia. It took me quite a while to process this emotionally, because in my family background death wasn't really a topic of conversation. It wasn't talked about. So I, being a twelve-year-old, was holding these emotions without really understanding them. Even though it took me a long time to process emotionally, it gave me a very immediate understanding of death—now someone is here, and now they're not here—of what that experience is like, and the realization that it could happen at any time, it's not just sometime in the future.

I finished high school, went on to college, and started studying philosophy. I was interested in trying to understand life. Studying philosophy with that end in mind was frustrating, because at the university at least, the professors were not particularly interested in applying philosophy to living life wisely. But in one class we were reading the *Bhagavad Gita*, and one line jumped out at me, even though I didn't really understand it. The line was, "Act without attachment to the fruit of the action." This was my introduction to the notion of nonattachment. I didn't really have any understanding of it or quite know what it meant, but nevertheless it was something that registered very deeply as something I wanted to explore. Years later I heard the Dalai Lama express this same teaching, "Act without attachment to the fruit of the action." But he expressed it in another way. He said that it's the motivation behind the action that is the real measure of it, and not whether the action leads to success or failure. Everything rests on the tip of motivation, beginning to see the motivation and to work with it. We can't control the outcome, because it's dependent on so many other things. But what we can do is purify our motivations. That's within our power.

Then in my junior year, in 1964, I met some people who were training for one of the very first Peace Corps groups. They inspired an interest in the Peace Corps, and I applied to go to East Africa. Some karma intervened, though, and I was sent to Thailand instead. It was in Thailand that I had my first introduction to Buddhism. I went to a temple where they had courses for Westerners, but I was so much still in my philosophy mode that I went with a copy of Spinoza in my hand. I went to many groups and asked so many questions that people actually stopped coming because of my persistent questioning. Finally one of the monks, probably out of desperation, asked me why I didn't start meditating. I was young, twenty-one years old, and it was all very exotic to me. So I got a cushion and mat together and then set the alarm clock for five minutes. I didn't want to sit too long. But even in those first five minutes, something really important happened. It wasn't a great enlightenment experience, but I did see very clearly that there is a way to look into our minds as well as a way to look out through them. This was revelatory, really. When you think of how we grow up in our culture, there's very little guidance about looking inward. It's all about looking out. So to see that there was a way, a systematic way, for looking in, that was really powerful.

While I was teaching English during my second year in the Peace Corps, I decided to undertake a project I had been wanting to do since college, which was to read Proust's *Remembrance of Things Past*. He had a kind of mystical but transforming experience as he passed a pastry shop and smelled some madeleines fresh from the oven. It called back all his memories of childhood. In the last fifty pages there's quite an interesting exploration about the nature of time, and his understanding of how the past is contained in the present. This is what his experience was: the aroma brought back the past, into the present moment. I had a sudden insight of how everything that I called the past was really just a thought in the mind. That's how we experience the past. It's always now, it's always present. And then my mind made the leap to the future. It was like, *If the past is really the present, then the future is the same. Thoughts of planning, of anticipating, of imagining, are all actually happening right now.* It was such an important and freeing insight, to realize that these huge burdens of past and future that we carry around are just thoughts. Think how much of your thought activity is of past and future—probably a huge amount. Depending on your level of insight at the moment, these thoughts are either very light, if we see them just as thought, or very burdensome, if we give a reality to the past and the future as really existing out there. This was a very freeing understanding to come to.

Then at the very end of my time in the Peace Corps I was sitting in a friend's garden. He was reading from a text then called *The Tibetan Book of the Great Liberation,* and now, in a new and better translation, titled *Self-Liberation Through Seeing with Naked Awareness.* The refrain in the text, over and over again, was, "Look into your mind, look into your own mind. Look at the nature of your own mind." I was sitting, quite concentrated at the time, and I was listening to the text, "Look into the nature of your own mind." Then it said, among other things, "The nature of the mind is unformed, unborn." My mind opened, in some way, to that experience of what the unborn is, what the unborn means. It can mean different things. We can understand "unborn" from different sides. Sometimes, some traditions talk of unborn awareness, which means that there is no beginning. It is unborn, and in that sense outside of time. It can also mean unarisen. What's unborn is unarisen, unoriginated, nonoccurrence. Just look into your own mind. When we look into our own mind, the nature of the mind is unformed, unborn. What is the reality that is before occurrence, before arising?

Something really opened at that point. In the moment of recognition after that happened, the phrase kept coming into my mind, *There's no me, there's no me,* when seen from the perspective of nonarising, nonoccurrence. This was extremely disorienting. I was just sitting in my friend's garden, listening to this text, and all of a sudden there was this huge seismic shift. I was about to leave Thailand after having been there for two years. It was unsettling; I didn't have any context for understanding the experience or what had happened, but I knew that in some fundamental way something had shifted. Then for a while, maybe a week before I was actually leaving, I started getting seduced by the thought, *Maybe I'm enlightened. Maybe I'm all done, and there's no self, there's no me, there's no one there.* But then I'd be walking down some dark Bangkok street at night and fear would arise. I thought, *Hmm, something's still here,* and that kind of illuminated the issue. I slowly started to realize that this experience was not the end of the spiritual path, it was actually just the beginning. People have different kinds and different levels of intensity and different levels of transformation, but all kinds of openings, like this, are really intimations of possibilities. They are the transforming experience of what's possible, not some final accomplishment. This is such an important point on our spiritual journeys, because at different times in our practice we may have real transforming moments of understanding, where something radically shifts. It's important to see it in the correct way.

The great twelfth-century Korean Zen master Chinul had a framework of teaching called sudden awakening/gradual cultivation. I very much appreciate that framework, because it acknowledges the power of those moments of sudden awakening, and also reminds us that it needs a gradual cultivation. It's not the end of the path. Here's what he says:

> Although coming into this life we may suddenly awaken to the fact that our self nature is originally void, and calm, and no different from that of the Buddha, old habits are difficult to eliminate completely. Consequently, when we come into contact with either favorable or adverse objects, anger and happiness blaze forth. Adventitious defilements are no different from before. Nevertheless, although you must cultivate further, you have already awakened suddenly to the fact that deluded thoughts are originally void and the mind nature is originally pure.

I find that a very good framework for understanding. We can have a transforming experience of the empty nature of phenomena and still appreciate the fact that there is a lot more work to do.

BOYLE: So because the cultivation is gradual, it's not so easy to pick milestones to talk about, as it is for sudden awakening?

GOLDSTEIN: Exactly. The particular moment of an experience is a big milestone, but then there is the gradual process of integrating that experience into our daily life. That takes years of practice for most people. One's life experience and meditative experience continually reveal those places where we're still attached and where we get caught in some identification or other.

BOYLE: You would catch yourself getting caught?

GOLDSTEIN: Yes, but of course, when we are caught, we are usually lost. If we were really awake, we wouldn't be caught. But in the moment when we begin to be mindful of being caught, the fruit of that initial experience is that even the "caughtness" is seen as not self. We see long-established habit patterns still playing themselves out, but they no longer have the same power because underneath we understand that this habit itself is selfless. So the habit has loosened up a lot. This really helps; an understanding of selflessness has helped me a lot over the years, even in times of being caught in various things, by freeing my mind from a lot of self-judgment about my failings. Because as I said, I now understand that caughtness itself is selfless. That's really quite a benefit, because self-judgment is a very prevalent pattern in people's minds.

BOYLE: Now when you are caught, you just notice it and proceed?

GOLDSTEIN: Yes, just investigate it and ask, How did I get caught here? without all those undertones of self-judgment. I'll give you an example. At one point I was on retreat and a strong feeling of guilt came up about something I had done. It was just an unskillful act, but it came up in my mind and I was seeing it and not feeling very good about it. I was really caught by it, caught by the guilt. At a certain point I started wondering, *What's going on here, why am I getting so caught in the guilt?* So I looked more carefully, more mindfully, and I saw basically that guilt was an ego trip. It was just a lot of "I," a lot of self-ing in a negative way. "I'm so bad," but with an emphasis on the "I." As soon as I saw that guilt was just a trick of the ego, then I used a kind of expression that sometimes you find in texts, where Mara will appear to the Buddha and the Buddha will say, "Mara, I see you." So that's what I did with the guilt: *Mara, I see you. This is just a trick of the ego,* and in that moment the guilt really dissolved. I then began to see the difference between guilt and remorse. There can be a wise remorse about unskillful actions, but guilt is an unskillful, unwholesome mindset because it's just reinforcing the sense of self. It's not that the mind never gets caught in things anymore, but it can see things from the perspective of selflessness. And that is very freeing.

BOYLE: Then shortly after this experience you came home?

GOLDSTEIN: Yes. I came back from the Peace Corps to the States profoundly moved by what had happened. And then, of course, I tried to repeat the experience. I would ask people to read the text to me again, but clearly that was not the right approach. So I decided I needed a teacher, that I should go back to Asia to find a meditation practice that both expressed and deepened this understanding. I went to India, and ended up in Bodh Gaya, the place of Buddha's enlightenment. It's a very special place, and in 1967 there were only a few Westerners there, studying with a teacher named Munindra. They took me to meet him, and I began practicing with him. When I first met him, and even as I got to know him well over many years, he did not fit my image of a guru at all. He didn't have what I thought was the gravitas of an enlightened being. Of course, this was a great teaching in itself. It forced me to cut through attachments I had to concepts about how wisdom should manifest.

One time he was in a bazaar in Bodh Gaya, and he was haggling, bargaining, for a little bag of peanuts, which of course is customary in India. But I was there studying, he was my teacher, and I said, "Munindra-ji, what are you doing, why are you bargaining over these peanuts?" He said, "The path of the Dharma is to be simple, not to be a simpleton," and he went right on bargaining. He was so engaged with the world, he was so interested in everything, he was so open-minded. Over those years, as more Westerners came and wanted to study with him, he would always encourage them to explore whatever they wanted to explore. One of the lines I remember him saying was, "Go. Explore. The Dharma doesn't suffer in comparison to anything." His faith in the Dharma, his appreciation of it, was so complete. That was a beautiful teaching, because it inculcated a sense of openness. We don't have to hold on to our practice with fear, or try to be protective of it. Our practice can be a very openhearted sense of exploration of the world, of our lives. It's simply to be aware of what's arising and not cling to it. What could be simpler? Be aware of what's arising and don't cling to it. One of the things I most appreciated about that introduction with Munindra was that there was no form, no structure to join. All he said when I came was, "If you want to know your mind, sit down and observe it." It seemed so simple, and such common sense. How else can we know our mind, except by looking in, by observing it?

I spent a good part of the next seven years at the Burmese *vihar* in Bodh Gaya. The *Visuddhimagga*, "The Path of Purification," which is a classical Buddhist commentary, lists all the attributes of a conducive place to meditate. The Burmese *vihar* had none of them. It was right on the main road, so buses and trucks would be going by all the time. Directly across from it was a public water tap, so people would be coming there to wash, to do their laundry, to talk. It was surrounded by small Indian villages, which often were playing music over loudspeakers. All of this was going on. In India they have rope beds, which are quite comfortable except that the bed was about five feet long. That was a little problematic for me since I'm 6'3". And there were a lot of mosquitoes. So I'm sleeping on this five-foot-long rope bed, with no mosquito netting (until I wised up), wrapped up in whatever clothes I had around. The food was really poor. With all of these conditions, however, I felt such immense gratitude for having a place to practice, a place that honored practice. In the midst of the craziness of the world, here was a place where people were honoring the journey of looking inward, of just sitting and walking.

When I first started practicing, concentration did not come easily at all. I'm not one of those people who just sit down and their minds settle into deep meditation. My mind basically wandered the whole time. I would be sitting and thinking. It was kind of fun. I was enjoying my thoughts, and the hour went pretty quickly. It took a long time for the mind to begin to quiet down. I couldn't sit cross-legged for more than five minutes, the pain was so intense, so I sat in a chair. But because I'm tall, the chair wasn't that comfortable. So I put the chair on bricks. I put cushions on the chair, and then a mosquito net. It was like sitting on a great throne. It was a little embarrassing when Munindra would come in, but it worked. That reinforced my pragmatic approach. The posture doesn't really matter, if we find one where we can sit pretty still, observe, look, and do this with commitment.

When I left Bodh Gaya for the first time, Munindra said something whose depth of meaning I have so come to appreciate over the years: "The Dharma protects those who protect the Dharma." That has such powerful implications for how we live our lives. What it means is that as we protect the Dharma it protects us, from excessive greed, excessive hatred, excessive fear. Then we know to some extent what renunciation means, what letting go means. "The Dharma protects those who protect the Dharma."

So I spent most of those seven years in India, with some trips back and forth to the States, mostly to work to make some money to go back. The first few times of coming back to the United States were difficult. For me, not only was it a transition from intensive practice to more engagement in the world, it was also a transition from the simplicity of India to being in America. That, in some way, was even harder. So basically what I did that first time or two was just sit around listening to Bob Dylan, doing those things one did in the '60s, feeling depressed. But then I would go back to India and get all energized by my practice again. What was interesting is that after doing that back-and-forth a few times, I found the transitions much easier. I began to see and understand those times of change as being as much [part] of the practice as being in intensive retreat. It's just another form. Other things are happening, but the retreat never ends. The Dharma is our life. It doesn't make sense to be committed to awakening on retreat and somehow to let that go when you leave the retreat. All the forms of transition and activity are as fruitful for Dharma practice as being in retreat, even if the first few times of transition are difficult, as they might well be.

BOYLE: Another theme I wanted to cover involves *metta*, loving-kindness. This has been a big part of your teaching. When did your interest in *metta* begin?

GOLDSTEIN: On one trip back I saw the movie *Charley*, which showed some people being cruel to someone who was mentally challenged. The cruelty of it somehow touched my heart, as well as seeing my own potential for doing unkind things. When I went back to India I told Munindra that I wanted to do some *metta* practice, because seeing that cruelty was so painful. This was my first intensive period of *metta* practice. After about a month of doing *metta* intensively, along with my mind getting quite concentrated, there were tremendous feelings of happiness. It was just wonderful happiness. Of course my first reaction was, *Oh great, this is how it's going to be for the rest of my life.* I was quickly disabused of that idea, but it did point to the possibilities of a kind of happiness I hadn't found before.

There are a couple of things to note about that. One of the first things I saw when I did *metta* meditation for the first time was that it has two aspects. First, it is a concentration practice rather than an insight practice, because when you are doing *metta* it's not for the purpose of seeing the impermanence of things, as in insight practice. It was while doing *metta* that first time that my mind got really concentrated. Second, it's also not for the purpose of experiencing selflessness, because you are actually dealing with the concept of self: *metta* toward oneself, *metta* toward others. So *metta* meditation is operating on a different level from insight meditation. It's operating as a concentration practice.

But sometimes when I was doing *metta* meditation it would call up its opposite. Once I was sitting in an inside room in the Burmese *vihar*, getting very concentrated and blissful. There was a window out into a corridor, and sometimes I would leave pieces of fruit on the windowsill. I'm sitting there feeling expansive, feeling quite a lot of bliss—*May all beings be happy, may all beings be blissful*—when I hear this little rustling outside the window. A Nepali man had come to practice, and he had a servant boy with him, so the thought comes into my mind, *That little Nepali kid is stealing my fruit.* The contrast was so amazingly blatant. Very often in the midst of all our *metta* it touches the other side, and the contrast helps illuminate those times when we're feeling its opposite.

BOYLE: I know about that instability pretty well, because sustaining *metta* practice has always been difficult for me. How did your work with *metta* practice develop from there?

GOLDSTEIN: Well, there are a couple of things. One is, as I said, that doing the *metta* practice and the happiness that came from it really helped in the development of concentration. Happiness is a foundation for concentration. When I'd go back and do the insight practice, the concentration helped deepen the insight practice, so the two kept feeding on each other in that way. Then as the insight practice develops and matures, one begins to see that one's awareness itself is imbued with a certain quality of *metta*. Because there is less defensiveness, there is more openness, so it's not limited to feelings toward other people but becomes expressed in awareness of whatever is arising, as an openness of the heart and mind. When I was doing insight practice, when thoughts of people came up in the mind, even people I might have had difficulties with, the mind was holding them in a place of greater care, greater love, greater forgiveness. The two practices in some way began to merge.

Many years later I was studying with Tibetan teachers. One, in particular, was Nyoshul Khen Rinpoche. He was talking about *bodhichitta*. In the Tibetan framework, relative *bodhichitta* is compassion, ultimate *bodhichitta* is emptiness. Something happened in me where I really understood that compassion is the expression of emptiness, that compassion is the activity of emptiness. Before that, in some way I had kept the wisdom aspect and the compassion aspect separate. I knew that they both needed to be developed, but I hadn't seen them as being the same thing. That was a big change for me, because it affected my whole understanding of what the bodhisattva vows meant. Years later I came across this teaching by Dilgo Khyentse Rinpoche that expressed the very same understanding. He said that when you recognize the empty nature of phenomena, the wish to bring about the good of others dawns, uncontrived and effortless.

One last story about the Bodh Gaya years. Munindra had the habit of bringing any Western traveler who came to Bodh Gaya to meet me, just to chitchat. Munindra would meet them in the bazaar while he was haggling for peanuts. I would be sitting in the *vihar* doing my meditation practice, and he would bring all these people he had met in the bazaar in to see me. I got to where I dreaded his footsteps. I would have the thought, *Please, let it not be Munindra*—not a good thought to have about one's teacher. I would have to get up from these deep states of stillness and chat. At first I was terribly annoyed and irritated, and then of course my practice would be annoyed and irritated. But he kept doing it, he didn't stop. So at some point I just had to give up, and I realized that it didn't matter at all. If I stopped resisting it, I could be sitting in a really quiet space, somebody comes, I get up and talk with them. Not a problem. If I'm not making it a problem, they leave and I go back to sitting. So that was a great lesson in how we can hold on so tightly to protecting our space. That can become its own hindrance. Be open to what comes.

BOYLE: Do you still get caught in this?

GOLDSTEIN: Yes, although caught in it less and less. I learned something. In some ways a feeling of impatience is good feedback that we haven't let go of attachment to whatever state or situation we are in. We get impatient because we think we would rather be doing something else rather than what is right in front of us. Two common experiences can be useful because they provide feedback by showing us that we are out of the present moment in some way, or resisting the present moment. The feeling of impatience is one, so when we are feeling impatient, that could be a good signal to just settle back and relax into what's happening now. The other feeling that I found really helpful as a signal in that regard is a feeling of rushing. Very often during the day we find ourselves rushing. Well, what's also interesting is that rushing is not really a function of speed. People can be rushing when they are moving pretty slowly. It's when our mind is ahead of ourself, our mind is already at some later step and not settled back into the body, not taking the present step. So we can be moving really quickly and either rushing or not rushing—it's our choice.

BOYLE: Yes, when my mind is spinning around like crazy, I may not be making much progress on the physical plane.

GOLDSTEIN: So it's helpful to find these ordinary states in our lives but to see them in a different light, to see that they are actually telling us something in terms of our practice.

BOYLE: You returned to the United States in 1974, when you were thirty years old. A year later, you, Sharon Salzberg, and Jack Kornfield decided that, given the growing interest in vipassana meditation, you should create a center. This led to founding the Insight Meditation Society in Barre, Massachusetts, on a shoestring, and for the next ten years you worked hard at IMS while traveling and teaching around the world. Then came the 1984 Winter Olympics.

GOLDSTEIN: Yes. I was feeling that something was missing, although I didn't know what. I realized that I had this unfulfilled aspiration to really do more practice. I had been so busy teaching. I had been sitting every year, usually for a month, but didn't feel it was enough. Then watching the Olympics and the ice-skating team of Torvill and Dean win the gold medal with a perfect score inspired me with thoughts of what is needed to bring something to that level of mastery. This was the background to my meeting with Sayadaw U Pandita.

We had invited Sayadaw to come to the Insight Meditation Society in the spring and summer of 1984 to teach a three-month course. It was really intense. He's a very demanding teacher, and at one point I told him that going to interviews with him was like going to a dentist. He challenged us to practice with a new level of ardency. Over the next eight or nine years I did a lot of retreats with Sayadaw, and the relationship became a lot easier. I remember going into one interview and he was in a bit of a fierce mode. I reported what was going on, and he proceeded to point out all the defilements in my mind that were contained in my report. I started to laugh, and that laugh was an important moment, because until then I would have taken it as a judgment and judged myself. But somehow, I had practiced long enough with him so at that point I just gave a laugh of acknowledgment. It was so interesting. As soon as I got lighter with what was in my mind, Sayadaw also seemed to get much lighter in our relationship. It was like he was just waiting for me to lighten up. So it's really useful to see how we are the ones who are holding the self-judgment.

BOYLE: Was that laugh part of an experience that was almost a milestone?

GOLDSTEIN: Yes. In some styles of teaching the teacher will continually be looking to press your buttons, until you stop reacting. That was an example. It made things much easier. Sitting with Sayadaw taught me a lot about finding the right balance, between not coasting on past experience and also not getting caught up in expectations, not getting caught in that striving mind. I came to understand that learning the art of right effort is really a lifetime endeavor.

Sayadaw also suggested at this point that we practice more intensively the *brahma viharas*—what in Buddhism are called the "divine abodes." These are the practices of loving-kindness, compassion, sympathetic joy, and equanimity. That's when we immersed ourselves in *metta* and the other *brahma viharas*. For me it took quite a while to feel connected with them. At first I would be doing *metta* meditation without really feeling much. Then as the feeling of loving-kindness started coming, I would fall into another trap. I would be looking to see how I was doing—*Oh, the* metta *feeling is getting stronger*—being more concerned with how I was doing than with the well-being of the other person. All of this was an interesting time of learning. I also began to see the interconnectedness among vipassana, mindfulness practice, and the *brahma viharas*. I saw how they really supported and fed and nurtured one another.

This took me to the early 1990s. Then I began to feel again that there was something missing, that there was some piece that didn't yet feel fulfilled. These cycles are so interesting to me. They point to the vastness of the Dharma, and how we're always just at the edge of what's unknown. It's always [about] finding new aspects to practice and understand.

At this time there was a really wonderful moment in my practice. I was on a two-month dzogchen retreat in a Zen center in upstate New York, and in the course of a talk by Nyoshul Khen Rinpoche, something clicked in my mind. I understood that compassion and emptiness (of self) are not two different things, that compassion is the activity of emptiness. As I mentioned earlier, this was a big realization for me, because I somehow had been keeping them separate. This brought things together in the most beautiful way, and led me to a whole new understanding of the bodhisattva vows. I had been reading them for many years: "Beings are numberless, I vow to save them; Delusions are inexhaustible, I vow to end them," etc. I had been reading and reflecting on these vows for a long time. They seemed beautiful, but also impossible to actualize, so I just put them aside. But with this understanding of the interrelatedness of compassion and emptiness, suddenly the vows made more sense to me. If we have these aspirations, and they are resting on the shoulders of the self, they're too big. How could a self ever fulfill them? But if we see that compassionate activity is the working of selflessness, or emptiness, then it's not resting on a notion of self, it's the activity of Dharma, it's the activity of empty phenomena, it's the activity of wisdom. Then it becomes a way of life, unfolding. It's not self-centered.

This was really a big turning point, but at the same time a big spiritual crisis was looming on the horizon. I realized that my Burmese teachers and my Tibetan teachers were saying quite different things about the nature of reality, the nature of freedom, the nature of awakening. In the Burmese teachings, ultimate freedom transcends even awareness. Awareness itself is seen as a conditioned phenomenon, and *nibbana*, ultimate truth, transcends even awareness. In the Tibetan dzogchen teachings, and also in the Thai Forest tradition, pure awareness *is* freedom. Freedom transcends awareness, freedom is awareness. Great teachers, people I had tremendous respect for, people who I felt were realized persons, people who I felt had really experienced the truth, were saying opposite things about what I felt to be most important in my life. This was a crisis—what to do? I became plagued by the question, Who's right? Somehow I felt that if I could just think it through, then I would know. I was on a two-month retreat, and the first month my mind was completely engaged with this dilemma. I felt like my whole spiritual path depended on a resolution of this. The resolution finally came when I realized that I was asking the wrong question. I reframed the question so that instead of asking who was right, I asked, Is there one Dharma of liberation that includes them both, that embraces them both?

This led me to two understandings. The first was that with respect to the fully awakened mind, I didn't know. And that not knowing was tremendously freeing. It was a mantra for me: "Who knows?" I just settled back, did the practice, let it go. The second enabled me to settle back into a variety of practices. That was the realization that all of the teachings, from all the different sides and all the different traditions, really are skillful means for liberating the mind and not statements of ultimate truth. I had been taking both of the teachings as stating the ultimate truth, so obviously if they were opposites, there was going to be a problem. But if we take all teachings as skillful means for liberating the mind, then we have to ask the pragmatic question: Do they work? Each of several quite opposing teachings can serve to liberate the mind. So I framed my understanding in the little phrase, "metaphysics as skillful means." All the metaphysical systems can be seen as skillful means.

All these systems converge in the understanding that the heart is liberated in nonclinging, that that is the nature of the free mind. Buddha said very clearly that nothing whatsoever is to be clung to, as "I" or "mine." So now when people ask me what I practice—vipassana, Tibetan, etc.—I answer, I practice nonclinging. Everything else is simply a skillful means to support us in that practice.

A few years ago I was on sabbatical and did a long retreat, and in the middle of the retreat all these teachings fell into a beautiful whole. It all began with the Buddha's enlightenment song:

House builder of self, you have now been seen.
You will build no house again.
The rafters are broken, the ridge beam shattered.
My mind has attained the unconditioned.
Achieved is the end of craving.

I saw that this was really a practice in the moment. Moment to moment, we can be noticing: is the mind craving, is it reaching out, is it grasping, or not? So the mind can begin to experience at least a taste of the freedom that the Buddha was talking about. In the moment we can really have that taste. I think the reason I like that framework of Chinul's, sudden awakening/gradual cultivation, is because it acknowledges that there can be radically transforming insights but still more work to do. It can happen, but it is very rare that somebody gets fully and completely enlightened all at once. The danger is that people can have a real awakening experience and, because it's so powerful, think that it's all done. For me, it's been a matter of continual deepening.

BOYLE: This covers your path story pretty well. Is there anything else you can think of that you would want to add?

GOLDSTEIN: Well, I will just say this. There is one teaching of the Buddha's that I think sums up in many ways the whole path, when he says, "Nothing whatsoever is to be clung to as 'I' or 'mine.' Whoever hears this has heard all of the teachings. Whoever practices this practices all of the teachings; whoever realizes this has realized all of the teachings." I think this points to the real heart of what practice is all about. "Nothing is to be clung to as 'I' or 'mine.'" To me that's a very clear expression to refer to when people want to know, What I am doing? What is the practice about?. This kind of re-clarifies what it is we are actually doing. I like it as a very simple expression of the core.

12
Developing Capacities
Necessary for Awakening

In their interviews, the teachers told about the paths they followed during their Buddhist training, the practices they engaged in, and the teachings they studied. In this chapter I try to sort out patterns that run through many or all of the interviews. These are eleven examples of successful paths, so the challenge is to identify the ingredients of success.

We first need to recognize that the eleven teachers are a distinctive group of people who share some unusual personal qualities. All of them except Enkyo O'Hara began serious Buddhist study and training at a very young age—in their teens or early twenties. They were highly motivated, and clearly drawn to Buddhist study as a calling, not a secondary activity. It is also striking, given the dominance of self-help narratives in American Buddhist publications, that there were relatively few mentions of emotional issues that impelled them to explore the Buddhist path. Furthermore, they were gifted with high levels of intelligence—four earned Ph.D.s and five had at least bachelor's degrees, while two followed a pattern popular at that time and dropped out of the education system without entering university.

Because each of the eleven teachers began training in one of the three traditions of Asian Buddhism that are especially well represented in the West (Tibetan, Zen, and Theravada), there was obviously great variation in the teaching methods, doctrines, and practices they encountered. It seems safe to say, on the basis of this admittedly small sample, that no one approach is superior. During their training, most of the interviewees at one time or another studied in traditions other than the one they had started in, so by the time of the interview they were familiar with most of the ideas, pedagogies, and practices that have been brought to the Western world from Asia. My conclusion is simply that while different people are drawn to different traditions, according to these interviews, teaching tradition does not seem to be a major factor in success along the path. Some of the teachers said the same thing, and none of them makes claims for the superiority of one approach over another.

MARTINE BATCHELOR: I don't think it matters too much what you do, if you do Zen practice, or Tibetan practice, or vipassana practice.

JOSEPH GOLDSTEIN: So now when people ask me what I practice—vipassana, Tibetan, etc.—I answer, I practice nonclinging. Everything else is simply a skillful means to support us in that practice.

Another way to look for the characteristics of a successful path is to focus on what the teachers said was important for them on their journey. Here again, specific differences between practices don't seem to be as important as the contribution those practices made toward progress, the *function* they performed in carrying development forward. Meditation provides a good example here, because as noted, each teacher spent a great amount of time engaged in one or more forms of meditation.

There are many variations in the details of meditation practices (especially if one goes beyond sitting meditation to include all activities that require or encourage attentional control). But in functional terms, the teachers reported in their interviews that meditation helped them develop three main qualities or abilities: a) *quieting the mind* so that it can be free of internal conversations; b) *letting go*, or arriving at a state of nonattachment with respect to desires, fears, beliefs, or ideas—in fact, all the conditionings we have taken for granted as part of the experience of living in the world; c) cultivating *compassion*, or feelings of empathy and kindness.[1]

While the teachers interviewed here used meditative practices to help develop all of these capacities, they reported using other "skillful means" as well. So I take up each quality and look at what the teachers had to say about its development.

Controlling Attention and Quieting the Mind

Meditators quickly learn that they must find a way to control attention in order to direct it away from the internal chatter that tends to take over when the mind has nothing else to do. This might involve concentrating on the breath as it goes in and out, or practicing a visualization, a koan, or a mantra that is recited silently. All of these ultimately focus attention on some aspect of immediate sensory experience. Lately, neuroscience research has shown that meditation improves attention[2] (this is not exactly a surprise to meditators, but empirical evidence is always nice to have). Some studies have also indicated that areas of the brain associated with discursive thinking show reduced activation during meditation.[3] However, if no one form of meditation is better than others for quieting the mind, then what does make a difference? Not surprisingly, success in developing control of attention seems to correlate with the amount of time one puts in doing it and how hard one works at it. Eventually, the payoff comes when the mind can be quietly attentive to perceptual experience in the moment without requiring any special effort. Consider this quote from Ajahn Amaro's interview:

My mind had always been very chattery, but after six or seven years of meditation it was getting quieter, and during the winters there [at a small monastery in Northumberland, UK] I noticed that it was getting much easier for my mind to be still. Whereas before I'd always experienced meditation as a wrestling match, where you're trying to get your mind to quiet down, to be reasonably steady and stable, it became easier to just stop thinking. I would decide, *Okay, let's just stop thinking*, and my thoughts would stop.

But effort is also important. Shinzen Young was forced into proving the extreme case here, during a hundred-day winter retreat in Japan. In addition to the usual stresses of Japanese retreats, such as sitting cross-legged for long hours and sleeping very little, he had to pour ice water over his naked body three times a day and dry off with a frozen towel. But he learned from it:

I had noticed during this ordeal that if I stayed in *samadhi*, in a concentrated state [of sensory attention], it was not exactly pleasant, but manageable. But if my attention was scattered, if I was in a lot of thought, it was hellacious. On the third day of this hundred-day commitment, looking at ninety-seven more days, I had an epiphany: *Okay, there are three forks in this road. I'm either going to spend ninety-seven days in abject misery, or I'm going to give up and go back to the States in black disgrace, or I'm going to stay in some sort of samadhi state for the next ninety-seven days.* I didn't like the first two alternatives, so the third is what I tried to do. . . . By the time the hundred days were over, the *samadhi* at some level or other was permanent. I was always aware of being in that state, all the time, 24/7.

In sum, across all the interviews, developing an ability to dwell for at least some periods of time with a mind that is quiet, peaceful, and attentive seems to be taken for granted by the teachers as a necessary condition for progressing along the path. Then other things may begin to happen. One of the most common experiences here is an increase in the clarity and brightness of perception, as Stephen Batchelor notes in his book, *Confession of a Buddhist Atheist*:

The mindfulness sharpened my attention to everything that was going on within and around me. My body became a tingling, pulsing mass of sensations. At times when I sat outside I felt as though the breeze was blowing through me. The sheen of grass was more brilliant; the rustling leaves were like a chorus in an endlessly unfolding symphony. At the same time there was a deep stillness and poise at the core of this vital awareness.[4]

Ajahn Amaro says much the same thing:

On one of those nights I remember, I sat up all through the night and was sitting there as the dawn came. What happened was the recognition that the mind was free of any kind of obstruction. . . . The mind was just clear and bright. There was mindfulness, there was energy; it was tranquil and peaceful and bright. There was a clear sense of how beautiful the mind is, and how utterly simple, how completely ordinary, how beautiful it is when not cluttered with obstructions. . . . In a sense it was a profound experience of normality, but in that it was incredibly sweet and delightful.

Also evident in these descriptions is an increasing experience of quiet peacefulness and equanimity, as the language-based mind loses some of its grip. Shaila Catherine notes that she began to feel "a stillness so deep that nothing other than a profound sense of peace would pervade my perception of things . . . along with a decrease in the tendency to become irritated and distracted."

With this quote from Shaila we move beyond simply quieting the mind to other kinds of subjective phenomena that also come with meditation. Because meditation has multiple effects, a number of secular programs for teaching have been developed and are prospering, most notably Mindfulness-Based

Stress Reduction and spinoffs from it.[5] And of course, meditation practices are found in all the major religious traditions and in the religious rites and shamanic practices of many Fourth World cultures.

Letting Go

I use the term "letting go" to emphasize that we are talking about a process of letting go rather than achieving a state of detachment. Practices to nourish letting go include gradually learning to live without conditioned desires and habits and to question beliefs and ideas. The teachers used many equivalent terms for this process: "de-grasping," "nonclinging," "doubting," "ceasing to crave," or simply "relaxing completely." Joseph Goldstein emphasizes their function, to assist in achieving "nonattachment," and traces its importance back to Buddhism's origins: "There is one teaching of the Buddha's that I think sums up in many ways the whole path, when he says, 'Nothing whatsoever is to be clung to as "I" or "mine." Whoever hears this has heard all of the teachings. Whoever practices this practices all of the teachings; whoever realizes this has realized all of the teachings.'"

The practical problem is that a true state of nonattachment is extremely difficult to achieve. You can work at letting go, but you can't just will yourself to be nonattached. You have to work your way toward it patiently and wait for it to happen—and that is where meditation comes in. In the Japanese tradition, koans are used to facilitate the letting go of ideas. But they may take a while. As Enkyo O'Hara remarked: "You drop the koan into this mind and let it sit there. But you don't do anything to it . . . because the mind is at ease; it's not trying to figure the koan out, strategize or anything, it's just at ease." With that kind of preparation, degrees of nonattachment may begin to be reached. Ajahn Amaro described how he learned his first lesson in letting go during his first days in a Thai monastery:

There's no supper in Theravadan monasteries, just one meal a day, in the morning, then nothing until the next day. There we are, sitting meditating in the evening, and I start to get hungry, and I think, *Hmm. I'd really like some pineapple. Now, this is a desire. What was it that [my teacher] was talking about?* "When a desire arises you can just watch it." But I really want some pineapple. But he said, "If you just wait, and watch that desire, then you'll see that it passes away." So I stayed there for a while, and then I tried to go back to my breath and was following my breathing, and then my mind got caught up with something else. Then I suddenly realized, *Oh, I've forgotten about the pineapple.* What hit me was that, *Ah, I didn't get the pineapple, and* nothing is missing. That was a huge "Aha!" experience. That was it. Something clicked. *I didn't get the pineapple and nothing is missing. He was right.* Somehow the implications of that all clicked, almost audibly, saying, *That's it! All you've got to do is stay with this and it will be the way out.*

John Tarrant provided another excellent example, from further along on his path of preparation: "I was in a very, very deep place in a retreat once and my mind got incredibly busy. In previous retreats I had found that to be a problem, but this time I just found it funny. That's when everything stopped . . . I started just laughing. Then everything seemed filled with light, and all the people seemed wonderful. That went on—the laughter went on for six months or so."

Based on her own experience, Shaila Catherine gave this description of how meditation can give rise to nonattachment: "The mind was thoroughly disenchanted, and yet utterly free from aversion. This strange combination of equanimity, concentration, and clarity facilitates a breakthrough that releases attachment."

Notice the word "breakthrough." When nonattachment occurs during meditation, it tends to come in a moment, as release or insight, like John Tarrant's opening into laughter quoted earlier. But in addition to or accompanying meditation, other strategies for letting go were reported. Some of the most well known, like Zen koans, are intended to provoke questioning, ambiguity, or skeptical inquiry. Martine Batchelor talked about her experience after meditating on the koan "What is this?" for some while: "Then I understood what to me is the most important thing about meditation— the de-grasping effect. Cultivating concentration and inquiry dissolves the grasping. But it is a subtle effect . . . just doing meditation, something is released. So then when you are again in contact with a certain situation, you don't grasp at it anymore."

Ajahn Amaro told about a time many years after the pineapple episode when his meditation began to feel stale, like he was stuck in a little gray box. This went on long enough that he started thinking of it as a problem, and wondering what he should do:

Maybe there's something here that's getting in the way. There was a plugged-up feeling. I thought, *What's here that could be getting in the way?* I went through the usual list: there was no aversion, no greed, no fear or lust. So what could be here that could be clogging everything up? Then I suddenly realized: I *am.* . . . I remembered a practice Ajahn Sumedho had taught, years before, using the question, Who am I? . . . What happened was that . . . there was an immediate transformation.

Amaro's story is important not only because it illustrates how meditating on a koanlike question can facilitate nonattachment but also because it involves a particularly important kind of letting go—letting go of the self. Here is another version of that kind of detaching, in which one suddenly sees aspects of the self that had been hidden and that one might prefer not to know. Martine Batchelor again: "I was asking my koan, What is this? and suddenly I saw that I was totally self-centered. That was the first time I saw that, ever. Up to that moment I thought I was the greatest, most compassionate person in the world. And then I saw very clearly that all my thoughts, feelings, and sensations were about me. That was really important to me."

As noted earlier, koans are specific questions used to sharpen the letting go edge of meditation, but the questioning needn't be done only while in formal meditation. The habit of questioning what one has always taken for granted was also reported as a detaching practice, as in John Tarrant's interview: "I think having a lot of questions . . . allows you to embody what you've discovered." Specifically, questioning undermines beliefs, which is necessary because attachment to beliefs creates obstacles on the path to awakening. Tarrant says, "One way to explain what being in prison is like is believing things."

Now, letting go of a belief seems clearly different from letting go of a desire or a fear, but actually they both involve breaking out of (or simply escaping from, dissolving) what we have always taken to be reality. Questioning reality is one way to encourage nonattachment, but sometimes everyday life has lessons to teach about letting go. An unusual situation may shake up a reality that was taken for granted, loosening old ties and making possible fresh insights. A former sociology colleague of mine, the late Harold Garfinkel,[6] used this as a research strategy and called it "disrupting normal reality in order to reveal its underlying features." One year he told his students that when they returned to their residence later that day, they were to pretend that they were total strangers who didn't know anyone there—roommates, parents, whomever—and then maintain this act as long as they could. Some of his students were also in my classes, and they described the experience as "mind blowing." Bernie Glassman had a similar idea in mind when he designed his "street retreats," in which participants lived like homeless people on the streets of New York's Bowery, with no money, no meals, no bathrooms, and no protected place to sleep:

> What I realized is that because we were just living in the now, with no idea of what was going on, there was nothing to hang on to. It was totally out of our experience. About 90 percent of that group came to a much deeper place than people who had been practicing 10 years or so. I recognized that this was the first realization of *upaya* [skillful means or pedagogy]. I call it a plunge, plunging into unknown situations, which the brain cannot fathom, cannot rationalize. It's what we try to do with koans, but this was much more real.

All together, the teachers described a comprehensive toolkit of "skillful means" that help facilitate the process of detecting, weakening, and dissolving attachments. Sometimes this is painful, sometimes it is great fun. Freeing oneself from attachments that one very possibly was not even aware existed can allow a shift to a new perspective. When this happens, what might once have provoked anxiety becomes pleasant, freeing, and satisfying. Stephen Batchelor described his experience this way:

> One evening at dusk . . . I was abruptly brought to a halt by the upsurge of an overpowering sense of the sheer strangeness of everything. It was as though I had been lifted onto the crest of a great wave that rose from the ocean of life itself, allowing me for the first time to be struck by how mysterious it was that anything existed at all rather than nothing. "How," I asked myself, "can a person be unaware of *this*? How can one pass their life without responding to *this*? Why have I not noticed *this* until now?" I remember standing still, trembling and dumb, with tears in my eyes.[7]

Compassion and Empathy

Compassion plays a deep and complicated role in the awakening process, according to the interviewees. Because compassion has many shades, it is well to clarify things by turning again to some words from Stephen Batchelor's interview: "One's emotional relationship to the world becomes richer. I feel that this practice of the Dharma makes one more sensitive, more sensitized. . . . It's easy to throw out words like 'compassion,' but surely compassion is only real if it is founded on empathy, on a deepening ability to feel what the other feels."

I like this because the word "compassion" has always been a little rich for my cool scientific mind to feel comfortable with. Grounding compassion on "empathy" makes it more solid. Other words are also used, such as "love," "kindness," "sympathy," "caring." Those are all just words, however, and it is the feelings that go with them that are important. So I will assume that whatever the words, it is the quality of feeling that the interviewees were talking about as they described aspects of their own experience with compassion.

First, how did they go about developing compassion? Certain kinds of meditation are specifically designed for this. Usually the meditator is instructed to focus on or visualize themes involving love or feelings of loving-kindness (*metta*), such as picturing a mother holding her baby. Such meditation practices are often discussed and prescribed in the vipassana literature. I know of no equivalent training in the Zen tradition, although it may exist. Joseph Goldstein said this about his experience with *metta* meditation:

> After about a month of doing *metta* intensively, along with my mind getting quite concentrated, there were tremendous feelings of happiness. It was just wonderful happiness. . . . The *metta* practice and the happiness that came from it really helped in the development of concentration. Happiness is a foundation for concentration. When I'd go back and do the insight practice, the concentration helped deepen the insight practice, so the two kept feeding on each other in that way. Then as the insight practice develops and matures, one begins to see that one's awareness itself is imbued with a certain quality of *metta*. Because there is less defensiveness, there is more openness, so it's not limited to feelings toward other people but becomes expressed in awareness of whatever is arising, as an openness of the heart and mind.

Goldstein found that *metta* practice brought a more open, less defensive attitude, which suggests less need to protect oneself from what is happening in the moment. That would allow for developing feelings of trust, closeness, and hence empathy with the people present in that moment.

Meditation practices with no special compassion-nurturing component (for example, mindfulness meditation) sometimes had similar results. For example, Shaila Catherine said, "I usually noticed the benefits of meditation in how I engaged with my activities at school, at work, and with family. There was a distinct increase in equanimity, generosity, kindness, and patience."

Gil Fronsdal described the unfolding of compassion as an almost unconscious process:

> I wasn't interested in becoming compassionate, and the change was so gradual I didn't recognize it as it was happening. Much of this change I attributed to becoming familiar with my own suffering. During the long hours of meditation, the presence of my inner pain opened something within. Rather than becoming enlightened, I was becoming "compassioned." "Compassionment" instead of enlightenment.

John Tarrant also talked about compassion as an unexpected side benefit that emerged during the koan practice he had been following for some years:

> The big thing . . . that I should say, is I actually wanted clarity, but I found there was a warmth and a heart quality in the koan tradition. . . . The thing I found was just the warmth and the loving quality of my experience of the universe. We're not here for very long, and it's beautiful. And maybe we can look after each other. . . . There's a fundamental vastness and eternity about that experience of the kindness of the universe. It's not just a personal feeling.

From the interviews, therefore, it seems that compassion may be both a contributor to and a consequence of progress toward awakening. For Bernie Glassman, the opening of compassion was not something he had been working on directly. After sixteen years of meditation and koan study, he had a profound awakening experience, and the feelings of compassion that came with this were so strong that they changed the direction of his life:

> I felt the suffering, or the unsatisfaction, of all creations. I call them the hungry ghosts, those seeking for being satisfied. At the same time that I had that experience, I realized that these were all aspects of myself. All this seeking was various aspects of myself. At the same time I made a vow to try to feed, to try to help satisfy those thirsts, those hungers. I say that changed my direction. Before that, my whole goal was to be a monk at the zendo and work with the people coming to the zendo and try to lead them toward these experiences. After that I changed the venue of my work from the zendo to society. I wanted to work with everybody, wanted to figure out what are the ways, *upayas*, of working with people in business and social action and all aspects of life.

Two conclusions are suggested. First, compassion can be nurtured intentionally, through special practices, but it can also just appear along the path, unintentionally, as a by-product of other practices. Second, as Joseph Goldstein noted, the practices used to develop compassion can themselves have beneficial by-products like improved concentration, greater openness, and feelings of happiness. I think the last is especially important, because it shows that feeling compassion is more than a moral obligation—it is also a huge, perhaps supreme, positive reward in itself.

The final topic for discussion concerns the relation of compassion to awakening. I use Fronsdal's term "becoming compassioned" to emphasize that, like "becoming awakened," it is a process rather than a state. There are four possible relationships:

1. Becoming compassioned is a necessary condition for becoming awakened.
2. Awakening can be experienced without any special prior development of compassion, but becoming compassioned then occurs as a necessary part of becoming awakened.
3. Becoming compassioned can take place without becoming awakened.
4. Awakening can occur without becoming compassioned.

The interviews provide examples of the first two possibilities. That does not rule out the third and fourth, but we will have to go outside of the present group of teachers to explore them.

Enkyo O'Hara exemplifies the first case, where becoming compassioned precedes awakening. Her process began with many years of traditional Zen study and meditation in the Japanese tradition, which did not explicitly include components designed to cultivate compassion. Then the AIDS epidemic hit Greenwich Village, where she lived and taught, and without thinking of this as any kind of special Buddhist practice, she plunged into working with the victims:

> The quality of the feelings that I had, the depth of understanding, the sudden commitment to work with people who were very ill and to do it a lot . . . I worked myself very hard during that period of time because the need was so great. I had not been that kind of caregiver before. I had done good things, but I had always held back a little, felt a little resentful when overworked. This was a kind of opening of compassion.

The opening of compassion that Enkyo experienced from this work had a huge impact on her life, deepened her Buddhist practice, and was very much a part of her awakening.

Second, the interviews also showed that the experience of awakening is usually accompanied by a strong opening of compassion. The quote from Bernie Glassman's interview cited above provides an example of how awakening can occur without any prior attention to compassion, but with compassion emerging as an integral part of the experience. Joseph Goldstein makes this a bit more complicated when he says that based on his own experience and on classic Buddhist texts, the relation between awakening and compassion depends on how far one has advanced in terms of an aspect of the path known as *bodhichitta*:

> In the Tibetan framework, relative *bodhichitta* is compassion, ultimate *bodhichitta* is emptiness [awakened consciousness]. Something happened in me where I really understood that compassion is the expression of emptiness, that compassion is the activity of emptiness. Before that, in some way, I had kept the wisdom aspect and the compassion aspect separate.

Goldstein is saying that compassion is the activity of emptiness (which is what one experiences during awakening). This is a profound statement, and it will be explored more fully in chapter 15. If human beings cannot experience awakening without also experiencing compassion, then this has interesting implications for an ongoing controversy about the origins of morality. Some contend that humans can't be expected to behave virtuously unless they adhere to a religious belief system that defines good behavior and requires it of members. Others argue that a predisposition toward what most humans agree is good behavior has, in effect, been built into our DNA through millennia of evolution. In Goldstein's Buddhist version, the potentials for both awakening and compassion are present genetically, and each must be nurtured. But when fully experienced they are two aspects of the same thing—you can't have one without the other.

The problem, though, is that "awakening" and "compassion" have only vague meaning. The next chapter will try to fill this out somewhat, but for now the conclusion is simply that meditation practices designed to strengthen feelings of compassion work. There is some scientific support for this: meditators perform better on psychological instruments measuring emotional awareness and sensitivity,[8] and brain scans of these people show increased activity in brain areas linked with empathy and ability to infer what other people are thinking.[9] Meditation is not the only way to develop compassion, of course. Life presents many opportunities, as with Enkyo's plunge into helping AIDS victims, or anyone doing things that naturally bring out feelings of loving-kindness. So there is abundant evidence both that developing compassion can help bring about awakening and that awakening can bring with it a strong opening of compassion. The unresolved remaining question is whether or not these two relationships have exceptions. In particular, is it possible to experience awakening without developing compassion, either prior to or as part of the experience? Is compassion a necessary condition for awakening? That question will be examined carefully in the next chapter.

Whatever Buddhist tradition they started in, when relating their path stories all eleven teachers recalled progressing along three lines of development: quieting the mind, letting go of conditionings, and opening up to compassion and empathy. Many different practices were employed, but the specific techniques didn't seem to be particularly important, so long as the practitioner becomes able to control attention and make progress toward detaching. Overall, two of the qualities Buddhist practice seeks to develop—quieting the mind and letting go of conditionings—seem to be necessary conditions in order for awakening to occur.

The third quality, compassion, seems to have a more complex relationship with awakening. Although it is probably true that the ability to quiet the mind improves with the amount of time spent meditating and the effort given to it, "feeling increased compassion" did not follow a prescribed path. Furthermore, while for some of the teachers interviewed here, developing compassion preceded awakening, all of them reported that by the time awakening occurred, compassion was also present. However, possible exceptions to this optimistic rule have popped up elsewhere and will be examined in the next chapter.

A final note: there is a kind of mythic Buddhist model that if one works hard for a long time, then one will experience sudden total enlightenment. The interviews show more a pattern of small or medium-size insight experiences that occur along the path, sometimes almost unnoticed. These experiences then inform practice, whether or not one is aware of it at the time. One insight experience often leads to another, and at some point we might begin to call them awakening experiences. The point is that rather than a period of training and practice leading directly to awakening, what we actually find in the interviews is continued interaction between practice and experience, with practice improving along the path as one gains a little more insight into what is going on. These moments of insight often serve as signs along the way—the teachers refer to them as milestones, or watersheds—to which one can return if one strays from the path. But eventually, as Stephen Batchelor especially pointed out, one becomes concerned not so much with learning about awakening but with understanding life from the perspective of awakening and finding ways to live that life authentically, while being faithful to what one has learned.

13
Properties of Awakening Experiences

Buddhist literature often points out that the practices discussed in chapter 12 should be done for their own sake and not with the thought of attaining anything. Practicing without thought of gain definitely is the way to meditate, but practicing in this way will nevertheless lead somewhere. Where it led these eleven teachers is the subject of this chapter.

In their interviews the teachers described their insights into awakening in the best words they could find, a much appreciated effort. However, in trying to find the right vocabulary for describing an ineffable experience, the problem is not so much a lack of words as an overabundance. Here is a good example. In his interview, Shinzen Young said, "Then suddenly there was no boundary to me at all. I was so shocked I actually got up. And there was still no boundary to me. I was walking around, looking at things, and there was no border between me and anything else."

When Shinzen first told me this story, I couldn't relate to it at all. Did he mean that his senses had gotten so fuzzy that he couldn't tell where his skin ended and the surface of objects began? After transcribing and editing the interview, I sent it to him, along with some questions, one of which asked him to say more about "no boundaries." Here is his e-mailed reply:

> I've found that over the years I go through different personal conceptual fads as to my favorite way of describing what I experience. First it was "no boundary," then it was "no self," then it was "no self and no world." For the last few years, it's been "expansion and contraction as a form of nondual awareness linking form and emptiness during daily life."

That kind of flexibility in word choice can make textual analysis a bit tricky. When two teachers use quite different terminology, a lot of judgment is required to decide whether or not they were talking about the same thing. This is the core problem of ineffability: if both person A and person B have had the same experience, they probably can find words that evoke a shared meaning. Otherwise there is a problem, as Bernie Glassman noted when talking about his street retreats: "The people who go on the street are transformed. If they meet somebody who was on the street retreat in a completely different place, they both understand what they are talking about. They both felt the experience, in very similar ways. They have a harder time talking about it with people who haven't done a street retreat, who haven't experienced it."

The absence of shared experience has never kept people from trying to communicate, however. Through the centuries Buddhists have used a number of strategies to convey at least an approximation of what awakening is like. One favorite approach is basically an operational definition—tantalize people with words that deliberately avoid a specific definition, like "impermanence," "emptiness," or "nirvana," then tell them that in order to learn the meanings, they must go through the operations (practices) necessary to produce the experience in themselves. A second approach, used by Gautama himself, is to define awakening as the negation of more familiar words. In the *Heart Sutra*, for example, we learn many things that awakening is *not*.

> There is no form, no sensation, no perception, no memory and no consciousness; no eye, no ear, no nose, no tongue, no body and no mind; no shape, no sound, no smell, no taste, no feeling and no thought; no element of perception, from eye to conceptual consciousness; no causal link, from ignorance to old age and death; no suffering, no source, no relief, no path: no knowledge, no attainment and no non-attainment.[1]

An apophatic definition like this asserts a relationship (negation) between the new term and an existing shared semantic system. However, "awakened consciousness" can also be defined in terms of its relationship with contemporary systems for understanding "ordinary consciousness." In chapter 17 I take a stab at modifying existing conceptual theories of consciousness in a way that allows both ordinary and awakened consciousness to be included. Then both forms of consciousness can be defined relative to each other, so that at least a conceptual relationship between the two is established. Here, however, I work from the bottom up, examining what the teachers said in their interviews about insights into awakening and then sorting their statements into categories that describe the properties of awakened consciousness.[2]

Although the properties identified all involve positive features, it has become increasingly clear in recent years that awakening has its limitations. The final section confronts the accumulating evidence that awakening cannot be equated with saintliness because awakening without compassion sometimes occurs. Only by looking at both its positive and negative features can we really move toward an adequate understanding of awakened consciousness.

The Process of Awakening: Sudden or Gradual, Total or Incremental, Temporary or Permanent?

The legend is that Gautama had one huge awakening experience, which gave him perfect understanding and changed him completely and permanently for the rest of his life. No one knows if that legend is true, but it has had a strong, perhaps oppressive impact on the way people have thought about enlightenment for 2,500 years.[3] In the interviews, none of the teachers reported an epic breakthrough of the kind the Buddha is said to have experienced. We do not find in their accounts anything resembling what Martine Batchelor referred to as "big bang" and Ajahn Amaro called "*Shazam!*" experiences. These may happen to some people sometimes, but future research will have to find them. For the teachers interviewed here, awakening unfolded in a series of experiences, usually over some period of time. I conclude that, at least in the Western world today, awakening usually occurs in incremental steps.

Given that an experience has occurred, do its effects on consciousness (and hence behavior) last and become permanent, or is there backsliding that then requires long periods of hard work to overcome if one is to master what one has learned? Joseph Goldstein said, on the basis of his experience and the words of his teachers, that a moment of sudden awakening typically is followed by a period of gradual cultivation. This fits a theme mentioned in other interviews. Gil Fronsdal, for example, said that during the earlier part of his training he would react to an experience with something on the order of "*Wow! This is the most beautiful thing I have ever experienced*," but later on, after a particularly profound experience, his first thought was, "*Oh my god, there is a lot of work still to do*. It was as if now I truly understood what Buddhist practice is about, and I realized that I had much more work to do." On the other hand, Shinzen Young said that his first experience of "no boundaries" never went away—it has always been with him. Therefore, I conclude that for some people, important experiences of awakening can have permanent effects. That does not mean that "full" and "perfect" awakening has been achieved. Rather, it means that one has climbed a step up and does not slip back. Shinzen continued his studies and training, on his own and then with a new teacher, Joshu Sasaki, even though his realization of "no boundaries" had remained permanent.

The final question to ask about awakening as a process is, Does awakening occur through sudden experiences or as a continuous, gradual transition? Are awakening experiences like climbing stair steps or like a walking up a ramp? The answer seems clear, both from the interviews and from reports by other people: awakening experiences are sudden. They happen in an instant, whether the change is subtle or profound. In that sense, awakening experiences are like other insights—they come in flashes and are usually preceded by a lot of work. So the key aspect to appreciate is that something, no matter how tiny, has changed qualitatively. What is it like when awareness feels qualitatively different even though nothing physical in the sensory field has changed? This quote from John Tarrant gets at the heart of the issue: "You get the figure-ground reversal: what you thought was foreground is not so important and what seemed like background comes forward. You and the trees and the people are not different."

A good example of figure-ground reversal is the experience of looking at an Escher print—one's perceptual awareness switches back and forth between two quite different views. A sudden change in perspective just happens, probably with all of the noise and fireworks of a soap bubble popping. This change can be extremely subtle and easy to overlook. In their interviews the teachers over and over again talked about how the new perspective provided by an awakening experience seems simple and ordinary, not complicated or esoteric in any way. So in examining the descriptions of awakening experiences, we need to be sensitive to sudden but subtle and ordinary-seeming changes in the perspective through which awareness is presented. Suddenness is a defining property—any sudden insight deserves careful attention, even if it seems minuscule on the surface.

Inferring the Properties of Awakened Consciousness

It is time to return to the interviews and review what the teachers had to say about awakening and its aftermath. The analytic method used for this is the same as in chapter 12. I selected from the interviews those passages that pertained to either an awakening experience or something about the teacher's life after awakening, then looked for similarities in the reports of other teachers. These were qualitative judgments; I try to make the interpretive process explicit so that others can reach their own conclusions. Several of the teachers started out by denying that they had attained anything or experienced anything worth talking about, but in what they said later on there are nuggets scattered all along the way. With this as a warning that the task is not straightforward and the conclusions are not obvious, let us look more closely at what they said and try to trace some common themes.

The segments chosen from the interviews are numbered for ease in referring to them later. I begin with the full version of the Shinzen Young quote cited earlier to illustrate problems of ineffability:

1. I put down the *zafu* and sat down, and the instant I sat down, the koan was there: "Who am I?" Then suddenly there was no boundary to me at all. I was so shocked I actually got up. And there was still no boundary to me. I was walking around, looking at things, and there was no border between me and anything else. . . . There was a kind of intimacy between inside and outside. . . . [I thought,] *There is just no boundary separating me and what is around me.*

Ordinary consciousness is organized from the perspective of the self as central actor. That self is assumed to operate in the world autonomously and appears to be separate from people and objects in the environment. When Shinzen awakened to the fact that this construction is artificial (that is, when he perceived the world around him from a new perspective), he saw that he was actually just a part of what was going on, not separate from it. This realization came as a sudden shock. Everything felt different.

A similar experience was reported by Enkyo O'Hara:

2. This was a kind of opening of compassion. What it was was the dropping of the distance between me and the other, which one could say is the experience of awakening, when you realize there is no wall between you and the other. The opening of compassion just dissolved that sense of separation.

When we stop seeing things from the perspective of a self separated from other people, we instantly feel closer to them. Realizing the illusory nature of the separated self, we no longer need to protect it, which opens up a greater sense of empathy and compassion for others.

When I asked John Tarrant, "What is life like for you now compared with before you left Australia?" his answer also had to do with being free of walls:

3. Well, I had so much going on in my mind then. The simplest way to put it is, I was caught. I would have moments of freedom, and huge amounts of non-freedom. One easy way to describe "being present" is in terms of the interior decoration model. It's like you're in prison when you're trying to just paint the walls, rather kick them down. Even if you're trying to kick down the walls, you're still in prison. When you're free, you can't find any walls.

Tarrant expresses the same idea without specifically referring to the self: ordinary consciousness brings with it barriers that not only separate us from what is going on around us but also prevent us from living life freely, as it can be lived.

Ajahn Amaro also used the metaphor of eliminating walls or boundaries. He related this experience to a specific aspect of self that cares about performing well and competing successfully with others. After many years of practice, he started to feel dull and constrained, as if trapped in a little gray box. Then he tried meditating on the classic question Buddhism uses for investigating the self: "Who am I?"

4. What happened with me was that the walls of the little gray box just fell open. It was like suddenly being in a field of flowers, and warm sunlight. *Oh, this is different. It's a whole different atmosphere.* I'd had that experience early on, about how the inflated sense of self and ambition and competition can take over, but I'd never realized how insidious, pervasive an effect this more subtle kind of self, this "me, the doer" can have. . . . Its influence had been invisible, like gravity—I didn't even notice it was there.

Amaro's experience requires much less interpretation. When the sense of self as "me, the doer," in charge of and responsible for his life and actions, disappeared, awakening could take place.

These four teachers all mention a disappearance of barriers, boundaries, or walls that had previously closed them in and created a sense of separation. They all point to the same cause—the sense of self and relation to others that, from the perspective of awakened consciousness, is artificial. Quotes 1–4 can therefore be summarized conceptually as one way awakened consciousness does not *add* anything but simply *deletes* a key feature of ordinary perception.

Property 1. No separation from one's environment. Awakened consciousness arises from seeing the environment as a whole system, with the self as one more or less equal part of it. It is distinctly different from the perspective of a self that stands apart from the rest of the system. We experience ourselves as part of what is going on around us—not as the director or principal actor in that system, and not separate from it. As a consequence, we feel more intimately involved in our environment, freer, more connected with what is going on and more sensitive to the existence and feelings of those around us.

An awakening experience is described by James Austin, a neurologist and longtime Zen student, in the appendix. He had this particular experience while standing on the surface platform of a London subway station. I include his account because, as I have emphasized, different people describe what may be quite similar experiences in very different ways. Austin's description is that of a scientist, and it has a distinctly clinical and objective quality. It centers on a sudden shift in perspective in which he is no longer the central actor, but simply one part of what is happening overall. Austin calls the perspective of ordinary consciousness the egocentric mode of processing, and the awakened mode the allocentric (other-centered) mode for organizing perception. His research on the neurological basis for these two modes is discussed more fully in the next chapter, but here his description of Property 1 clarifies the difference between a system-centered and a self-centered perspective.

There is a relationship between no separation and the feeling of more intimate involvement with people and other elements of our environment that was first noted in the discussion of compassion and empathy in chapter 12. It is clear now how development of empathy and compassion through meditation or through other events can make it easier for an awakening insight of no separation to break through in the mind. At the same time, when someone experiences no separation without having had any special experience with compassion, empathy and compassion may nevertheless appear. That is exactly what Joseph Goldstein said in his interview. Paraphrasing him slightly, "Compassion is the expression of awakening; compassion is the activity that accompanies awakening."

The next few quotes report a rather different quality. Here is a story Gil Fronsdal told, from fairly early in his path, when he was sitting a Zen *sesshin*:

5. We would remain in our meditation posture while servers brought us tea and a cookie. I received the tea and held the cup in my hands. As I lifted the cup to my lips and the tea went into my mouth, the world stopped! This stopping was a remarkable experience for me that I have never been able to adequately convey in words. Part of the experience was my mind having the unusual thought, *As the tea touches my tongue, I stop the sip.* I was quite surprised that in the words and in the experience, there was no self. Without any of my usual self-referencing, it was as if everything stood still.

What was involved in Fronsdal's sensation that the world stopped? My interpretation expands on what he said about self-referencing. It starts with the idea that ordinary awareness is generated, moment by moment, as sensory inputs are interpreted according to what is already in the mind. If all we have known previously is a somewhat distorted awareness that nevertheless flows along like a movie, then even a small change in perspective will feel like the movie has stopped—the frame[4] used to process the sensory information has instantly changed too much for the awareness to feel continuous. When Fronsdal had his instant of awakening, ordinary consciousness was suspended, and during the moments that followed, nothing seemed to happen. But the movie projected by ordinary consciousness stopped. Without that storyline and drama, the world just is, quietly.

John Tarrant's experience of that stopping, quoted in chapter 12, also took place during a *sesshin*: "That's when everything stopped . . . I started just laughing. Then everything seemed filled with light, and all the people seemed wonderful." Here is another quote from Tarrant's interview that can be juxtaposed with Fronsdal's, although it gets into some other issues as well:

6. Then I thought, *Oh, that's in a way how I've always experienced reality, as sort of a flash that shifts.* So in some fundamental way, that's why I like the systems that show you things changing in jumps, rather than a slow progression.

Shaila Catherine gave a rather lengthy description of an awakening. Because it includes several important details, I will take portions of that description in turn and add my comments in italics after each:

7. The experience . . . is beyond the relation of self and other, beyond the concept that "I am having an experience" or "I had an experience." *Awareness has ceased being organized from the perspective of the self.*

Everything appeared as just concepts representing dynamic processes or changing things. I knew what my social responsibilities, commitments, and duties included, and I performed family and work tasks effectively. I could function well, because the concepts were clear. *The scripts and role responsibilities of everyday life were still understood clearly, but as impersonal concepts without emotional attachments.*

But each moment of seeing, hearing, feeling, and tasting was known right in the moment of contact, as ephemeral and completely devoid of any reference to me. *Awareness expressed the action of each moment, without the background sense of past and future that awareness-as-a-movie provides, and without emotional loadings.*

It was a surprisingly different way of being in the world. I felt light, buoyant, and unperturbed by any event. *She no longer cared about how events in the world affected the self.*

Feeling light and buoyant is a theme that often came up when the interviewees described an awakening. Metaphors of walking on air were used in two interviews, as when Gil Fronsdal described something that happened in India several years after the tea-sipping episode (5) related earlier:

8. The ripples of that experience, the momentum that was set in motion in terms of understanding and feelings lingered. . . . It was as if I were walking on clouds. Although the feelings faded, to this day the experience has remained a touchstone for me. In some way it is ever present, if I focus on it.

Here is another reference to walking on air. Ken McLeod reported having this conversation with an old friend, during which the friend asked him:

9. "Ken, what's life like for you these days?" [I replied,] "Well, imagine that you're walking over the Grand Canyon." He said, "Walking into the Grand Canyon?" "No, *over* the Grand Canyon." Now, it's not the Wile E. Coyote thing, where if you look down you start to fall. You're not sure what's up, what's down, what's forward, what's back. That's what life is for me today.

That seems to fit with "light, buoyant, and unperturbed," although there is more going on here that will be taken up shortly. For now, quotes 5–9 can be summarized like this:

> *Property 2. No emotional attachments to the self.* We can observe what is going on in the world and act appropriately, but emotional connections with the scripts that normally govern this activity have come unplugged and the flow of awareness that was organized around the self, playing the central role in the drama, "stops." Because we no longer feel any responsibility for managing events or for protecting or advancing the interests of the self, we feel a sense of freedom and lightness, peace and equanimity.

However, McLeod's story in quote 9 goes beyond this. He talked about proceeding through life without any conscious expectation about what was going to happen at each moment. That has some serious implications. Consider what Bernie Glassman said about "not knowing," based on what he'd learned through a series of deepening realizations:

> 10. Koan study is set up to try to get you to experience . . . the state of not knowing, the state of complete openness, of being completely open to everything. . . . "Not knowing" is an essential part of Zen training—getting you to experience what we call the sauce from which everything comes. It's a state where there are no attachments to any of your conditionings.

The requirement of having "no attachments to any of your conditionings" is not specific to "not knowing"; properties 1 and 2 also require detaching from conditionings. But quotes 9 and 10 together suggest an additional feature, emphasizing a more dynamic quality. Now, although the storyline of ordinary consciousness has stopped, a new kind of experience has begun. This is described vividly by Stephen Batchelor:

> 11. All of a sudden I found myself plunged into the intense, unraveling cascade of life itself. That opaque and sluggish sense of myself, which invariably greeted me each time I closed my eyes to meditate, had given way to something extraordinarily rich and fluid. It was as though someone had released a brake that had been preventing a motor from turning and suddenly the whole vehicle sprang into throbbing life. Yet it was utterly silent and still. I was collapsing and disintegrating, yet simultaneously emerging and reconstituting.

There was an unmistakable sense of proceeding along a trajectory, but without any actual movement at all.[5]

"Collapsing and disintegrating, yet simultaneously emerging and reconstituting"—these qualities of Stephen's experience echo Glassman's "the sauce from which everything comes." So the by-products of this ineffable experience include a new way of being alive, underscored by a fascination with how fluid and dynamic this feels.

Stephen went on to talk about obstacles that prevent experiencing life in this way, like our erroneous conviction that the permanent and autonomous self that we think we are truly exists. So long as we believe in that self, we are separating ourselves from the world around us. In different words, Shinzen Young referred to the same idea when he compared two states of awareness that he experiences alternately "hundreds, probably thousands of times during the day":

12. [In the first, awakened state, at each moment] "my experience is the flow of expansion/contraction and zero. . . . [In the second, more ordinary state,] my experience is that of a fixated self encapsulated in rigid time and space. . . . And each time, I'm aware that myself and the surrounding scene are born from and return to [zero, nothingness].

The terms "expansion/contraction" and "zero" are a bit obscure outside of the special teaching system Shinzen uses, but the quote as a whole conveys the feeling of the idea that awareness, and action, burst forth in each moment and then disappear instantly as the awareness and action of the next moment appear. This contrasts with the way ordinary awareness feels, "encapsulated in rigid time and space." Compare this with what Bernie Glassman called "the sauce from which everything comes" in note 10 above.

Taking quotes 9–12 all together, the best way to summarize is to observe that they point toward two conclusions. First, the sense that we are autonomous actors guided by our thoughts is replaced by a realization that our actions emerge in the moment, without our being aware of what we are going to do before we do it. Second, in order to understand how this way of being unfolds, we must start by understanding how awareness and action are generated, together, as different aspects of one process.

Property 3. Not knowing: Awareness co-arises with action, freely, at each moment. What we become aware of and what we find ourselves doing in each moment emerge together, as unconscious processing in our brains and bodies interacts with our environment. This way of living feels deliciously fluid and dynamic.

With each of these experiences of detaching from the self and from the stories in which it is implanted, we escape from ordinary consciousness to some extent. What happens during this process is discussed conceptually in chapter 17, but a homely illustration can be offered here. We know that when we feel self-conscious, we are very much out of touch with the moment. Property 3 points in the other direction—when we are free of self-consciousness, we know what it feels like to act spontaneously. As Ken McLeod remarked: "You're not sure what's up, what's down, what's forward, what's back." The difficult part, of course, is arriving at a place where that is always the way life is.

Summary Remarks on Awakening Experiences

Although the analysis and interpretations carried out in this chapter are necessarily tentative, I am grateful that the material the teachers provided in their interviews has allowed me to proceed this far. The goal was to take "awakening" out of the obscure and somewhat opaque world of Buddhist teaching and cast it in a form that could be communicated to anyone (given the limits of working in strictly conceptual terms).

That goal was accomplished in several ways. First, the interviews spoke for themselves in showing what can happen if people work at their practice intelligently and diligently. Second, statements from the interviews that seemed to refer to similar qualities were grouped together into three clusters, and the similarities within and differences between these clusters added qualitative meaning to the analysis. Third, the properties implicit in each cluster were given explicit conceptual definitions.

Finally—if all of this analysis and conceptualizing has made awakening sound complicated and esoteric, that is misleading. Here are two quotes as reminders that when it actually happens, awakening feels perfectly simple, obvious, and ordinary, as well as wonderful. After all, it is simply a matter of being free of attachments.

JOHN TARRANT: What do you call an awakening? It's just a matter of, can you step into reality?"

ENKYO O'HARA: Now everything is just actually joyful all the time. Even when I'm with someone who is dying, there is some way to understand that it's all interconnected and that there is a time when we are alive and there is a time when we die.... It is just so beautiful now. I feel kind of joyful all the time.

Comments by the Teachers on My Interpretations of Their Interviews

When chapter 12 and the preceding sections of the present chapter were ready, digital files were sent to each of the teachers, along with a note warning them that excerpts from their interviews had been used, sometimes with considerable interpretation, as the "data" from which the conclusions reached in these chapters were derived. I asked them to let me know, first, if they had any problems with the way I had interpreted the material from their interview, and second, if they wanted to make any additional comments.

Eight of the eleven responded, and no one complained about my interpretations. Hopefully this means that my qualitative analysis did not bias or distort the conclusions significantly. No one suggested any refinements or additions to the properties induced, which may only mean that they had better things to do than fuss with conceptual abstractions. Aside from some friendly exchanges, therefore, only a few comments were substantive enough to be included here.

Referring to what he had said about using different terms at different times to describe his experience of no separation, Shinzen Young said that recently he has been toying with calling the experience "True Love," which resonates with what Enkyo O'Hara reported. Ajahn Amaro commented on my gratitude to the teachers for the awakening insight I experienced during the interview process: "I am delighted that the process of writing the book is proving so illuminating to you—it's rare that the act of verbal creation can have such a liberating effect, although one of the Buddha's disciples (Ven. Khemaka) became enlightened by listening to his own Dhamma talk."

But the most extensive comments came from Ken McLeod, with whom I'd had several long and illuminating discussions when he passed through Albuquerque. My wife, who sat in on one, calls them arguments. But we think they are just good examples of how debates between a lumper (me) and a splitter (him) can be both animated and productive. As you might guess from that introduction, McLeod does not particularly like the fact that in chapter 12 I lumped quotes from eleven different interviews into three capacities that Buddhist training seeks to develop, and in chapter 13, into three properties of awakened awareness. He worries especially about

the human tendency to regard similar descriptions of experiences as indicating that the experiences are the same. From my perspective, I think this is not only impossible to determine but also probably unlikely in fact. [My] point . . . is to raise the question or possibility that each person's experience is unique and has been arrived at by a unique path.

This is more than a warning of the need to be very careful when making the kinds of inductive leaps I engage in here. McLeod is concerned that people may not remember to look critically at the process and skeptically at the conclusions. Particularly with an exploratory effort like the present project, both scientific and Buddhist detachment are required: "The danger, as I see it, is that when a path is described or defined, whether through observation, measurement, or patient reflection, everyone else's experience is then appraised by the criteria that were developed, a rather Procrustian approach, perhaps."

I said I would include a warning to readers about this, to which he added: "The warning won't always be heeded, but it should be there, all the same. Maps such as these can be helpful, but then, just as some people go to the 'or' with distinctions, others try to fit their experience into other people's classifications and maps."

Two final comments by McLeod: first, "the relation between awakening and compassion is, I think, quite complex," and we should not reduce it to one or the other. Second, he thought it was important, at some point, to consider another question: "how people of considerable awakening can visit great suffering on others (I'm talking about sexual, power, or financial abuse). This question is, of course, outside the scope of your current research, but perhaps it lurks in the background." That remark pushed me to add the next section.

What Is Awakening Not?

There has been a tendency, at least in contemporary Western Buddhism, to conflate awakening with saintliness. The evidence on that is now conclusive—neither meditating, nor being on the path to awakening, nor having an awakening experience or two, nor being officially accredited as having attained enlightenment guarantees moral perfection. History tells us that

Gautama, and the many others who have awakened since him, lived inspiring and morally impeccable lives, but the recent record of Buddhism, both in the West and in Asia, contains many blatant exceptions. The well-publicized scandals reported both for Buddhist teachers who came to the West from Asia and for Westerners who became Buddhist teachers themselves leave most Buddhists scratching our heads and wondering what is going on. If they were awakened, and if awakening produces wise, caring, and morally elevated people, then why did they do those things? So at this point we need to answer the question pursued through the last two chapters. Is compassion a necessary part of awakening or simply a correlate, something that usually, but not always, accompanies awakening?

Proving that something is not a necessary condition requires only finding one solid case as an exception. However, determining the truth of that exception beyond the shadow of a doubt sets high standards for investigation. The scandals I am familiar with have usually have involved sex, drugs, or alcohol (mostly sex).[6] (In the background is the strong support by the Japanese Zen establishment for the Japanese military effort during World War II, which was blatantly counter to the teachings of Gautama.[7]) The sex scandals make for sensational reading and have been documented in books, reported in many newspapers and magazines, and covered at length on the Internet (see especially sweepingzen.com). This makes for a lot of material to sort through, first to find cases in which a presumably awakened person is reported to have deliberately and consciously behaved in a way that is hurtful to others, and second to make sure that that person was truly awakened, that some other person was truly caused to suffer, and that no extenuating circumstances were involved.

Of the many well-documented cases in which certified Buddhist masters used their authority and the trust placed in them to impose sexual activity on their students, I feel most comfortable examining that of my first teacher, Joshu Sasaki Roshi.[8] Besides having personal experience with him, I have been able to talk with some of the women involved and to communicate about this with another of his students, Shinzen Young.

Sasaki's history of alleged abuse extends back at least seventy years.[9] His story can be read in detail in the special file Sweeping Zen has maintained on the website sasakiarchive.com. Here is an excerpt from the original posting on that site, by a former monk:

[Sasaki] has engaged in many forms of inappropriate sexual relationship with those who have come to him as students since his arrival here more than 50 years ago. His career of misconduct has run the gamut from frequent and repeated non-consensual groping of female students during interviews, to sexually coercive after hours "tea" meetings, to affairs and sexual interference in the marriages and relationships of his students.[10]

So there are four key questions. First, was Joshu Sasaki truly awakened? Second, did the women truly suffer? Third, was Sasaki aware that he was inflicting pain? And fourth, were there extenuating circumstances that might excuse his behavior? With respect to the first question, Sasaki was granted *inka* as a Zen master in the Rinzai lineage in 1947, so he had the credentials. Looking back over the ten years I studied with him, I have no reason to doubt that he had fully experienced awakened consciousness as defined by the properties discussed in this chapter. His speech always seemed to convey, implicitly but confidently, that he was a fully enlightened being. My remaining question, which I would ask of all people who have had deep experiences of awakening, is whether he was operating within awakened consciousness all of the time, 24/7. I suspect that a good part of the time he was pretending, acting out superbly his role of the modern Japanese Zen master.

Shinzen Young says in his interview, and added in recent e-mail correspondence, that although he is "hugely, hugely upset" by the Sweeping Zen revelations, he still considers Sasaki a paradigm for spiritual creativity and profound realization. And as far as I know, all of his other students, including those who resigned and rejected him for his sexual abuse, currently express only the deepest conviction that he was an awakened person.

The second question is whether the women involved truly suffered. Apparently there were hundreds of cases, mostly involving breast fondling. However, only a smaller number say they experienced suffering. Two of the three women I talked with found the touching curious and questionable, but benign. Shinzen Young commented,

> When I started to check with my students to find out what their experiences were, the result I got back from most of my women students was just, "Yes, I was touched, but I just considered it part of the practice, and I got so much out of the practice that I kept going back."

On the other hand, most of these women were only attending retreats. Those who lived full-time in Sasaki's centers and monasteries had more intense stories, particularly those who served as his *inji* (personal attendant). While there are a number to choose from in the personal accounts at hand, this poem by someone I knew, Chizuko Karen Tasaka, gets to the heart of the issue most directly and poignantly. Karen wrote this in 1988 and tried to get it to Sasaki (whether she succeeded or not is uncertain—his staff was very protective). She died in 2010 after a long illness; here are portions of the poem.[11]

Roshi, you are a sexual abuser
"Come" you say as you pull me from a handshake onto your lap
"Open" you say as you push your hands between my knees, up my thighs
fondle my breasts
rub my genitals
french kiss me

you put my hand on your genitals
stroke your penis
jack you off?
this is sanzen?

my friend—she was inji
sex with roshi

she tried to say no
you demanded, demanded, demanded
demon demand the force of a tornado

sex with roshi
for whose best interest?

I told you I don't like it.
I asked you why you do this?
You said, "nonattachment, nonattachment, you nonattachment"

I told you as shoji, "women very angry, very upset"
I asked you why you do this.
You said: "Be good daughter to roshi, and good wife to G. [her husband].
Roshi, that is incest. So many women trying to shake the shame from their voices of
Sex with roshi

We came to you with the trust of a student
You were our teacher
You betrayed us
You violated our bodies
You rape our souls

You betrayed our previous student-teacher relationship
You abuse us as women
You emasculate our husbands and boyfriends

Roshi, you are a sexual abuser
Your nuns you make your sexual servants
Your monks and oshos are crippled with denial
Roshi, Sexual Abuser.

So I conclude that the case of Joshu Sasaki shows that it is possible to achieve awakened consciousness (full- or part-time) and yet consciously inflict suffering on other people. This leaves the fourth question: Were there extenuating circumstances that might excuse his behavior? The usual answer given by his monks and nuns about the breast fondling (the only form of sexual abuse we lay students knew about during the time I was involved) was that he felt this helped loosen attachments caused by sexual hang-ups. Since it was hard for me to imagine the women I knew who reported breast fondling having any sexual hang-ups, this seems a rather flimsy excuse. Sasaki may have believed it, however. For male students he sometimes recommended pornography because he felt it had helped him with his hang-ups (see the posting by Bob O'Hearn on sasakiarchive.com).

Shinzen Young suggests a more nuanced rationale, sort of a "tough love" approach to compassion: "In Sasaki's way of thinking, the most compassionate thing to do for any human being is to utterly destroy them while *truly* coming from a place of emptiness and unconditional acceptance of them just as they are. This represents an extreme case of a certain style of Zen that is adopted by certain Zen teachers."

Shinzen added that this strategy might occasionally work, but "if you combine it with an authoritarian social structure and a personality style that discourages ordinary communication and feedback, you've got a prescription for disaster."

The compassion Shinzen suggests might have been guiding Sasaki is conceptual, in that it can be put into words that describe a pedagogical

PROPERTIES OF AWAKENING EXPERIENCES   223

technique. In that sense it is similar to conceptual models for behavior, such as the Buddha's teachings about moral behavior. Although such conceptual systems are important, when we think of compassion in relation to awakening, we are really focusing on feelings. Shinzen concluded in his e-mail that the important thing Sasaki lacked was empathy. Now empathy, in turn, is a somewhat complex word. It requires sensitivity to the feelings of others, which has been shown to vary considerably over human populations. According to author and activist Temple Grandin, total lack of this sensitivity is the defining characteristic of autism. Empathy also assumes caring, as in "I feel your pain" rather than "I sense that you are experiencing pain." Lack of empathic caring is the defining characteristic of psychopathy; psychopaths show almost no sense of caring, and the rest of the population is spread out along a continuum from low to high.[12] At the same time, psychopaths score well above average on sensitivity to what others are feeling (a skill that, according to Kevin Dutton in his study *The Wisdom of Psychopaths*, they then use to manipulate).

Therefore, if we require a compassion that includes both aspects of empathy, Shinzen and I agree that Joshu Sasaki did not have it. The conclusion therefore must be that it is possible for awakening to exist without compassion. That may make a lot of Buddhists unhappy, but I think its implications are healthy and long overdue. If "awakened consciousness" does not guarantee compassion, then we are better off thinking of it as merely a radical change in perspective, one whose potential exists, albeit in a dormant state, in all humans. Several of the teachers made a similar distinction. Gil Fronsdal, for example, talked about becoming awakened and becoming compassioned as separate processes. The theoretical relationship between them is clear: awakening is a rearranging of the mind to provide a completely different perspective for awareness; compassion is an opening of the heart, a primordial feeling that opens up a new dimension of experience.[13] Awakening provides a new platform for mental operations, while compassion provides feeling that brings it to life. Buddhists, or anyone else seeking to realize all the potentials that being born as a human being provides, need to work on developing both.

However, if awakening is possible without compassion in the sense of empathy, then we still have to account for why that combination is not particularly rare. As a sociologist, I have to ask, What are the social conditions that have produced so many Buddhist teachers who apparently lack true empathy? One clue provided by the rich record of recent Buddhist scandals is that most of these men come from Japanese Zen traditions and almost none from the South Asian Theravada or vipassana traditions. So the next question, therefore, is, Are there differences between these two Buddhist traditions that could be responsible for the glaring disparity in cases of sexual abuse?

To begin answering this, we have to look at differences in the training and teaching offered by each tradition. Traditional Japanese Zen has long been known for revering the samurai tradition, and Japanese Zen teachers strongly supported the Japanese war effort during World War II.[14] Some sixty years after Pearl Harbor, the head temple of the Rinzai Zen tradition, Myoshin-ji, finally issued an apology for supporting a war that destroyed twenty million lives (the support went beyond words—for example, Zen temples had conducted fund-raising drives to purchase military aircraft).[15] Sasaki was in his thirties during World War II, and he apparently absorbed the samurai attitude—I remember him making derogatory remarks about the anti-Vietnam War peace movement back in the early 1970s.

As for compassion, some years ago I did a careful study of the Zen, Sufi, and Christian mystical literature, collecting quotes as I read the books and putting the quotes into categories (just as I have done here). I was very surprised that the category I had labeled "Love/compassion" was full of things Sufi or Christian mystics had said, but absolutely empty of anything from Zen. A similar comparison of Zen and vipassana teachings today would almost certainly reach the same conclusion. Traditions like vipassana that emphasize compassion in their training may succeed in two ways: by increasing levels of compassion in students who stay with the program and by discouraging and selecting out students who don't know what compassion is and don't want to waste time with it. In traditions like Japanese Zen, however, students without compassion might feel quite at home. Here I am talking about special cases—the contemporary Zen priest Ittetsu Nemoto is one inspiring example of dedicated compassion.[16] Most Zen students who become awakened probably have and value compassion whatever their training, and the American Zen teachers interviewed for this book have all found ways to build an emphasis on compassion into their own teaching programs.

But the issue is not whether most Zen masters have compassion, but how it is that a small but substantial number show no evidence of caring about the suffering their behavior inflicts on students. The clinical definition of psychopathic personality disorder (which fits roughly 4 percent of the contemporary American population) offers some clues. While they show an almost total lack of caring about the suffering of others, psychopaths rank well above average on personality characteristics associated with awakening (e.g., mindfulness, ability to focus, and control of attention). In *The Wisdom of Psychopaths*, Dutton argues that a large proportion are nonviolent, stay out of prison, and are highly successful in their chosen careers—he cites Steve Jobs as a good example. So a psychopath would make a good Zen student, would probably enjoy doing things he is good at, and might be motivated to develop these skills further. As such a student rose in the Zen hierarchy and became a teacher, other traits characteristic of psychopaths would help: charm, charisma, and ability to manipulate. And as a Zen master, another set of psychopathic characteristics—fearlessness, mental toughness, and ruthlessness—would allow him to use his status, personal power, and lack of compassion to pursue and get away with (for a while) the abusive behaviors in question here.[17] If one doubts that psychopaths would pursue a "spiritual" calling, it is relevant that in his study of successful men in Great Britain, Dutton found that members of the clergy ranked seventh from the top on psychopathic traits.[18]

The argument, in other words, is that there is an almost perfect fit between psychopathic tendencies and the requirements of traditional Japanese Zen, and almost nothing to prevent psychopaths from becoming Zen masters. So what has been happening in the United States over the past thirty or forty years should come as no surprise—it is the kind of outcome that would be expected. That is where conceptual morality enters to reinforce experiential development. In the Buddhist tradition, *sila* are the precepts setting forth Gautama's teachings about morality.[19] Vipassana groups, but not the Zen tradition I knew, study and meditate on the precepts, discussing them among themselves and holding them in mind as they meditate. This seems to provide an important and realistic safeguard against awakening without compassion. As Ajahn Amaro has said, "Life without *sila* is like a car without brakes."[20]

Some American Zen teachers know this too. Bernie Glassman's whole teaching is built around the theme of "socially engaged Buddhism." Members of the sangha vow to live a life that manifests the Three Tenets (listed on www.zenpeacemakers.org):

Not-Knowing, by giving up fixed ideas about ourselves and the universe
Bearing Witness to the joy and suffering of the world
Taking Action that arises from Not-Knowing and Bearing Witness

Only the first reflects the properties of awakening derived in this chapter. The second and third show the importance that Glassman assigns to compassion. And he is not alone—I cite him only as one example of the growing emphasis in Western Zen on becoming compassioned as well as becoming awakened.

May all people who are interested in awakening remember the parallel importance of compassion, and may all people who are attracted to a teacher they feel is awakened remember that awakening does not necessarily guarantee compassion.

14
Evolution of Ordinary and Awakened Consciousness

At this point we have defined "awakened consciousness" by deriving from the interviews three properties that distinguish it from "ordinary consciousness." But while we know ordinary consciousness very well because we have lived with it every day since early childhood, in many ways it is too familiar, too taken for granted, too much an intrinsic part of us to allow us to really appreciate how special are the properties of awakened consciousness. The present chapter goes back to the roots of consciousness in animals and follows the evolution to the ordinary consciousness of humans. Our brains got bigger and more differentiated. We invented language and began to talk. As we talked with each other, we began constructing symbolically represented models of the world to go along with and extend the perceptually represented awareness of the world with which all animals before hominids had lived. Life in social reality has many wonderful advantages, but also a fatal weakness. It is very hard for humans to remember that we built social reality ourselves, as a synthetic construction. Instead we almost always think it is actual reality. Because of this, our awareness is limited to the way perceptions are filtered through social reality and reflected, to paraphrase Plato, as images on the walls we have built around us. That, in outline, is the story of evolution I will present here.

Origins of Consciousness

"Consciousness" is usually defined as a subjective experience in which we are aware that we are experiencing awareness.[1] Neuroscientists and philosophers have been diligently studying this by asking how activity in the brain translates into that experience. They call this "the hard problem," and I'm sure it is. Fortunately, they have made some progress on portions of it. I start with the work of neurologist Antonio Damasio[2] because his evolutionary approach identifies critical early ways ordinary consciousness began to split off from what became awakened consciousness.

Simple one-celled organisms show awareness in that they respond to environmental stimuli with fairly complex patterns, for example by moving away from negative stimuli. Even these very simple organisms show a motivation to continue existing, "a stubborn insistence to remain, endure, and prevail"[3]—an ability to respond differentially to stimuli that feel good or bad is critical for survival. So with the very beginnings of life was a primitive ability to experience positive or negative feelings.

A little further along the evolutionary path, multicellular animals began to develop specialized nervous systems with enough neurons to map a stimulus by forming a preliminary network of neurons representing the properties of the sensory input. Neuronal maps "represent things and events located outside the brain, either in the body or in the external world."[4] The entire body is represented in the nervous system by neuronal maps, providing a kind of virtual double. According to Damasio, these interoceptive maps "provide a direct experience of one's own living body, wordless, unadorned, and connected to nothing but sheer existence."[5] Signals produced by these body maps are "*felt*, spontaneously and naturally . . . prior to any other operation involved in the building of consciousness. They are *felt* images of the body, primordial bodily feelings, [which are] the primitives of all other feelings, including feelings of emotions."[6] So at this second level of awareness, more complex and subtle internal conditions of the organism are mapped and linked with a diverse palette of what Damasio calls primordial feelings.

Damasio emphasizes the evolutionary fact that as nervous systems became more and more differentiated, interoceptive mapping continued to take place in the oldest part of the brain, the lower brain stem. No structures developed in the cerebral cortex to duplicate this function, so in humans the brain stem is still the sole provider of awareness about how the body feels, of "the information necessary for the organism to regulate its life."[7] As Craig points out, interoception continues to be the basis for emotional awareness.[8] As a result, in order to "be in touch with one's body," as Western Buddhists might say, relevant areas of cerebral cortex must be in good communication with the lower brain stem, which is some distance away and can be reached only when signals are relayed through other structures.[9] Damasio comments further:

The brain stem-cortex mismatch is likely to have imposed limitation [on] the development of cognitive abilities in general and on our consciousness in particular. . . . Increased cognitive demands have made the interplay between the cortex and brain stem a bit rough and brutal, or, to put it in kinder words, they have made access to the wellspring of feeling more difficult. Something may yet have to give.[10]

So neuroscience research indicates that somewhere in the evolution of human consciousness, interoceptive awareness may have become vulnerable to interruption and weakening. This marks a point where further evolution of ordinary consciousness may have come at some cost, making inputs from the brain stem about one's body and primordial feelings problematic. However, there is also preliminary evidence that interoception can be reinvigorated through practices such as meditation.[11] This, of course, suggests one way what people do in their day-to-day lives affects awareness.

Damasio's third level, which he calls core consciousness,[12] extends the process of developing neuronal maps to proprioception (how the body feels during motion and action) and exteroception (perception of objects and events located outside of the body). At this stage the brain constructs maps that allow the organism to match up sensory stimuli with previous experience of objects and actions to produce images. It also forms maps of these maps, which represent what psychologists call event-schema or scripts. But the organism itself is a central part of the maps, indeed the protagonist, so the self as an identifiable mental object appears in awareness "in the form of images, relentlessly telling a story of such engagements."[13] This mapping of perceptual information, and the ability to learn from it by constructing higher-level maps, allows the organism to live in a rich and detailed perceptual world and to flow swiftly and instinctively with what is happening at the moment. As Damasio notes, while this form of consciousness draws on memory, its essence is "a sense of the here and now, unencumbered by much past and by little or no future."[14]

In their pure states, therefore, awareness and cognition at this third level operate entirely on the basis of perceptual representations that are activated by the sensory contents of immediate experience. Note that there is no provision here for conscious awareness. I will therefore refer to level three as awareness rather than consciousness. It is tempting to simply call this "animal awareness" because it clearly is the dominant mode among animals. That would set up very nicely a fourth level reserved for humans only, based on our ability to include in our awareness and in our thinking (both

230 EVOLUTION OF ORDINARY AND AWAKENED CONSCIOUSNESS

conscious and unconscious) representations of sensory images not present in immediate experience—i.e., images based on percepts available only in memory. However, contrasting animals and humans doesn't quite work here because some animals seem capable of mental operations that verge on level four, while humans are certainly capable of level three processing. It is instructive to look carefully, first at humans doing level three processing and then at animals doing level four processing.

A good example of humans operating solely on the basis of level three processing is the special condition called blindsight, which occurs with people whose visual nerve pathways have been disrupted in a certain way. These people are not consciously aware of seeing anything—their visual field is blank. However, when they are told to walk through a long room full of furniture and other obstacles, they do it in full stride without stumbling or bumping into things. Perceptual information from their eyes is processed normally, to the point where directions are sent to their muscles and their bodies move appropriately. But specific brain injuries prevent the information from reaching the areas of their prefrontal cortex that are responsible for conscious awareness. Although they walk fluidly and effectively, all they are consciously aware of seeing is blackness.[15] Damasio notes that at level three there is "no need at all for a single screen to display the images,"[16] and the evolutionary psychologist Nicholas Humphrey concluded that even animals with clever brains may lack conscious awareness.[17] The lesson, therefore, is that humans don't need conscious awareness nearly as much as we think we do. We can process ongoing perception at an unconscious level in ways that involve complex analysis and expert motor skills, just as animals do.[18]

Blindsight, of course, immediately suggests the property of awakening discussed in chapter 13 as "not knowing." During the experience of not knowing, action does not follow conscious awareness but is allowed to precede it without interference. This also seems to be true for the "in the zone" experiences people report in sports.[19] However, both the experience of not knowing and expertise in a sport require preparation and training, because humans have a problem that animals don't: sophisticated use of level three processing requires unlearning the conditioning we acquired in the process of mastering ordinary consciousness.

Although level three processing may come more naturally for animals, they also need a certain amount of practice and training to master the considerable potentials they are born with. Animals can learn fairly complex new behaviors. They can solve problems through trial and error and perhaps through insight.[20] Animals can't tell us what they are taking into account mentally, so we have to decide on the basis of their behavior whether they are engaging in level four processing. This means finding things they can do that require processing information not present in immediate experience.

In general, animals have difficulty with tasks that require taking account of objects that are not immediately present. In Köhler's famous experiments, for example, chimpanzees were able to figure out how to stack boxes and then climb up on them to get a banana that had been placed high on a wall—so long as the bananas and all the boxes were present at the same time. If one of the boxes was out of direct sight, however, the problem was much more difficult. The chimps had walked right past the box while entering the lab, but once inside the room they had to rely on short-term memory. Köhler's "genius" chimp, Sultan, eventually solved the problem, but only after he had been taken back through the entry a second time to refresh his memory—and then he had to reenter the room and see the bananas and the other boxes again before he would go back to retrieve the crucial third box.[21]

Other studies also suggest that animal cognition runs into limitations when the task requires going beyond immediate experience.[22] One example comes from research on what Piaget called "object permanence."[23] In these experiments, animals (or human infants) have to track the position of objects they can't see. One of the tasks used at advanced levels is basically the classic shell game: a tasty treat is placed under one of three inverted cups, which are then moved around several times before the animal is invited to choose the cup it wants. Resnikova says that only great apes, parrots, "and possibly dogs" succeed at this stage.[24] Human infants accomplish it at about age two, which is when "words involving movement and disappearance are acquired."[25] The task doesn't seem very difficult, but it does require continuing to hold in mind an object that ceases to be present perceptually—and seems to indicate a capacity that only a few species of animals possess.

A second exception comes from research with mirrors. Chimpanzees, orangutans, elephants, magpies, dolphins, and orcas respond to their images in mirrors with behavior that implies awareness of an equivalence relation between the image (which they can see) and something representing "them" (which they can't see).[26] For example, when a stripe is painted on a chimpanzee's face and a mirror is held up, the chimp usually touches its face to explore what it sees. This is interpreted as a form of self-awareness that allows the chimpanzee to "take itself as an object" and associate that object with the image seen in the mirror. As Povinelli has pointed out, this task requires only perceptual representations,[27] but the self that is constructed from perceptual information must be represented in mental processing as something that is independent of immediate perception. The fact that so few species can extend their cognitive processing to include mental objects not present in immediate experience underscores the evolutionary gap that had to be crossed in the transition to level four processing.[28]

Linguists (see Fitch[29] and Bickerton[30]) point out that animals that have been taught a protolanguage by humans perform better than other members of their species in laboratory experiments—that is, they seem to show improved cognitive capacity (or at least improved capacity for solving problems posed to them by humans) when they have learned to associate arbitrary symbols with perceptual representations. So in order to understand how humans acquired their considerable superiority over animals in level four processing, we need to move to research on how some creatures in the genus *Homo* began inventing language.

Evolution of Language

The brains of australopithecines—early hominids, possible ancestors of modern humans—were about the same size as those of modern chimpanzees, and their capacities to think about things not present in immediate experience were also probably similar (although superior to almost all other animals). While all other animals have some kind of communication system, none of the systems use that cognitive advantage to allow what linguists call "displacement," the ability to communicate about things not immediately present in space and time.[31] Animal communication systems use a small, closed set of signs (sounds, gestures, or smells) for conveying "biologically critical meanings" such as warnings, alerts, intentions, and context-specific information.[32] The simplified protolanguages that humans teach to animals go beyond this with words or symbols that can be used whether the objects are present or not—that is, they allow displacement. The communication systems of bees and ants allow displacement, but their mechanism for signaling the location of a food source they have discovered does not rely on cognitive ability. For mammals and birds, cognitive capacity improved with evolution, but their communication systems did not take advantage of the improvement. In the words of Tecumseh Fitch: "animals have surprisingly rich mental lives, and surprisingly limited abilities to express them."[33]

Somewhere along the hominid line, our early ancestors began finding ways to communicate with each other about things they could probably visualize but that were not perceptually present. So the big question is, how did this kind of communication get started?[34] What led some early hominins to invent language? Linguists, not to be one-upped by neuroscientists, call this "the hardest problem." The difficulty, of course, is that language leaves no physical evidence until it is somehow written down, so we don't know what was really going on with, say, *Homo erectus* a million years ago. However, there are some fragments of solid research evidence and some interesting ideas based on that evidence.

Since no one was there to teach early hominids a protolanguage capable of handling displacement, they had to invent one on their own. There is considerable controversy about how they accomplished this; most linguists are open to the idea of a gradual, long-term process, starting with a basic protolanguage that chimpanzee-size brains could handle that gradually evolved (but the evolution would have occurred in the brain, as it became able to learn and use more sophisticated languages). The alternative argument by Chomsky and his colleagues is that one minor genetic mutation was all that was necessary to make possible brains like ours, with full capacity for Universal Grammar built into them at birth.[35]

Those who consider Chomsky's position "magical thinking" are left with the fact that if protolanguages existed, we know absolutely nothing about them. Botha, for example, compares the concept of protolanguage with the Higgs boson, which was called the "God particle" for many years because although physicists knew it must exist in order for their theories to be true, they had absolutely no evidence one way or the other. Eventually they found the Higgs, and it is at least possible that geneticists will someday understand the way DNA determines the linguistic capabilities of brains,[36] and that samples of hominin DNA going back two or three million years will become available for analysis. Until then, all we know is that we have language and chimpanzees don't, and that many of us believe evolution through protolanguage is the most plausible place to look for explanations.

The key word is "plausible." A leading candidate for a plausible protolanguage theory is offered by Derek Bickerton in his book *Adam's Tongue*,[37] and although a plausible scenario should not be confused for fact, his theory illustrates the problems early humans had to overcome. He notes, from the archeological evidence, that an important part of the diet of early hominids like *Homo habilis* must have consisted of the bones of large mammals, gathered after they died and cracked open with stones to yield the nutritious marrow. Bipedalism and the ability to use their hands to grasp and pound would have given hominids an advantage over other scavengers. Although this strategy was successful, the technology did not change until early *Homo erectus*, almost two million years ago. Associated with *erectus* bones from that time, we have found bones of large mammals, such as elephants and woolly mammoths, with cut marks on them of the sort that would be made by using sharp pieces of flint to slice off the flesh. But underneath the cut marks lie the tooth marks of lions or other large carnivores—early *erectus* apparently had to wait until those predators had eaten their fill. Then, from a bit later in time, paleontologists suddenly found bones with the cut marks first and then tooth marks on top of them. Somehow, *Homo erectus* had found a way to keep the lions at bay until *they* were finished cutting off flesh.

How did they do this, since their only weapon, a simple stone axe, did not change throughout their time on this planet? Here we enter the realm of plausible conjecture. Bickerton suggests that the only way they could keep a pride of lions away from a dead mammoth was to gather together in large numbers. Since their living units were small, he concludes that they must have found a way to recruit neighboring groups. Enter displacement—they had to improve their communication system sufficiently to be able to go to their neighbors and tell them a mammoth was dying somewhere off in the distance (just as bees and ants bring news of food). Then several small groups could band together temporarily. This indicates how fortunate it may have been, in evolutionary terms, that three conditions occurred at the same time: the technology for exploiting an existing food source (flint knives to slice through the thick hides of large animals), a way of actually putting the technology to use (through social cooperation), and a way of tapping an existing cognitive capacity in order to communicate, through language, about things that were not perceptually present.

The change in the layering of teeth marks and knife (flint) marks on bones is "hard evidence" that needs to be explained. Evolution theory says that events like the beginning of language do not occur unless driven by conditions that select for it. To simply say, "They grew bigger brains for no particular reason, and because they got so smart they invented language, but that is unrelated to the bone marks" doesn't work. Bickerton's theory shows what an explanation for the origins of a protolanguage that allows displacement should look like, and this underlines some key points.

First, the early stages of language development had to cross the divide between immediate experience and all the other things that we can talk with each other about today. Second, the processes pushing this development forward almost certainly involved communication that both enabled and required social cooperation.[38] Social cooperation apparently began before *Homo erectus*—there is evidence that australopithecines were already cooperating at levels significantly greater than occur today among chimpanzees or other higher apes.[39] So the first step that Bickerton talks about was quite momentous. By learning to transcend immediate perceptual awareness through language, our evolutionary ancestors found a way to make practical use of their improving capacities for both cognition and cooperation.

The evolution of language still had a long way to go, and the advantages of improved communication would continue to be an evolutionary force leading toward what linguists call "true language."[40] We have no definitive record of how protolanguage developed into true language; this probably took another million and a half years. According to the archeological record, there was little or no change in the technology or ceremonial artifacts of *Homo erectus* during this time. Brain size increased from 700 to as much as 1,000 cubic centimeters, however, which suggests that improved cognitive abilities were being selected for. Given that neither technology nor art nor anything else that leaves a durable record changed, brain size may have increased primarily because it allowed more complex and sophisticated language use. We have no indication of what communication was like among Neandertals or other recent but now extinct *Homo* species. Bickerton therefore ends by giving as his guess that true human languages came into existence at, or perhaps slightly prior to, the time modern humans appeared. That was less than 200,000 years ago.

Constructing Social Reality

The invention of language created, in the minds and brains of the humans inventing it, a system of symbolic representations parallel to and intimately linked with the system of perceptual representations already in existence. These symbols replicated the perceptual system and helped extend it beyond the limits of immediate experience, but that is not all. By making possible the creation of words and phrases not linked with percepts, and rules to govern syntax, semantics, and logic, the system allowed abstraction and imagination and the invention of worlds expressible in language that are only indirectly linked with anything experienced through the senses. But most important of all for understanding the nature of ordinary consciousness, the invention of language must have been accompanied, inexorably, by the construction of social reality.[41]

In the classic formulation of Peter Berger and Thomas Luckmann, social realities are constructed during "symbolic interaction,"[42] that is, during conversation and other communications of words or symbols.[43] Whenever we talk with each other about the world, we are operating within a social reality that was constructed by our ancestors but is continually being reinforced, modified, and added to with each new conversation.[44] The basic idea is intuitively convincing, but the philosopher John Searle has carried it further by showing carefully and systematically how social reality is constructed from linguistic declarations.[45] In order for an element of social reality to come into existence, two or more people must declare that it exists. A statement like "You should come with us to [the dying elephant]" declares, among other things, a norm of cooperation, so the question then becomes, how simple can a protolanguage be and still make possible the declarations that construct social reality? I would think the answer is, fairly simple, in which case social reality began to exist long before *Homo sapiens.*

The statements that make up social reality can be combined and interwoven in many ways, but particularly in stories. We hear and construct stories that explain and direct our lives, tell us what to do and how to feel, and allow us to interpret and make sense of what is going on around us. We typically play the role of central protagonist, and this adds drama and emotional content to what might otherwise be an objective, dispassionate account. Social realities contain vast stores of useful as well as emotional (and sometimes distorted or deluded) information. The sharing of this information unites people in a culture and worldview, and provides the basis for social organization.

From the perspective of awakened consciousness, however, the problem occurs when social realities become reified into something much more absolute. As Berger and Luckmann emphasize, during infancy we learn to accept social reality as real, something not to be questioned, "given," "unalterable," and "self-evident," not just one alternative among many possible ways of representing the world but the one true version of reality. Social reality gradually takes over the way we view the world, to the point where it becomes difficult to see the world in any other way.[46] Research over and over again shows that what we think shapes what we perceive, and what we think is in turn largely shaped by the social reality we grew up in and have lived in since. But because social reality is so much a part of us, glimpsing it for what it is is almost as difficult as getting outside of our skin. The first trap of ordinary consciousness, therefore, is being unable to see social reality for what it is, and therefore unaware that we go through life experiencing a limited and somewhat distorted representation of what we take to be the real world.

Social reality not only conditions but also provides explanations for what we experience. The stories that make up social reality give meaning to our lives; they apply beliefs and cultural patterns to specific situations in a way that makes life feel more plausible and worthwhile for the individual: "Proverbs, moral maxims, wise sayings, mythology, religions and other theological thought, metaphysical traditions and other value systems are part of the symbolic universe."[47] As a result, our lives feel more satisfying and comfortable. It is no surprise, therefore, that the members of a group cling to their social reality—without it life would be uncertain, unstructured, and perhaps unbearable.

Finally, social reality is the home of the social self, which only roughly resembles the self we perceive, feel, and remember through our senses. The social self represents us within social reality as who we think we are, our "self-construct" or "self-image." We learn the characteristics of our social self (i.e., build the mental representations that we take as being who we are) from infancy on through interaction with other people. As John Tarrant pointed out in his interview, a very important insight on the Buddhist path comes when we realize that we are not the idea we have of who we are: "At first I realized that the thoughts were just there, even if they were stopping me from experiencing things, because my mind was too full. And then later on I realized, *Oh, it's the identification with the thoughts, not just the thought that's there.* We think we are our thoughts. We define our consciousness by what we are thinking, and think it's us."

The social self is defined by how it fits into the stories that social reality generates, as either an actor, an observer, or an experiencing agent.[48] We are not merely observing the stories as they unfold, we are a completely involved part of them. The social self positions us in roles that we then try to act out within the ongoing story that social reality is continuously generating. These stories might center around physical events that are actually taking place, imaginary events that might take place in the future, or events from the past that we are still processing. The crucial point is that we *care* enormously about how our social self is doing in each story.[49] Is it performing competently or messing things up again? Is it well thought of and praised by others, or criticized and scorned? Our actions are shaped by this context—as Erving Goffman pointed out, presentation of self is an ongoing and emotionally sensitive preoccupation.[50] Because it is so much at center stage during most moments of our lives, the social self is the gorilla glue that attaches us to social reality.

Because social reality is constructed from language, its hold on each of us is dependent on our using language as the "primary operating system" with which our minds operate. Consider the case of the neuroscientist Jill Bolte Taylor, who suffered a massive stroke that temporarily incapacitated the language regions of her left hemisphere. In *My Stroke of Insight: A Brain Scientist's Personal Journey*, she recounted what the total absence of language did to her awareness:

> Without a language center telling me: "I am Dr. Jill Bolte Taylor. I am a neuro-anatomist," . . . I felt no obligation to being her anymore. It was a truly bizarre shift in perception, but without her emotional circuitry reminding me about her patterns of critical judgment, I didn't think like her anymore. . . . [She] had grown up with lots of anger and a lifetime of emotional baggage that must have required a lot of energy to sustain . . . and with this obliteration of memories I felt both relief and joy. . . . On this special day, I learned the meaning of simply "being."[51]

That is, the total elimination of language disabled most of the mental representations that had previously structured Taylor's social self and embedded it in social reality, leaving her with feelings of joy and a sense of "simply being."[52] Of course, since language and therefore all the rest of her social reality were also temporarily disabled, leaving her with only perceptual reality, she could not function at all normally until her brain gradually repaired itself. Note that with awakened consciousness there is no loss of knowledge about social reality, only loss of emotional attachment to it. Shaila Catherine's interview (chapter 6) describes this perfectly.

As with the first trap of ordinary consciousness (blindness to the fact that social reality distorts our awareness of perceptual reality), humans have difficulty believing that the social self they think they are exists only as an idea. The evolutionary psychologist Nicholas Humphrey concluded, after studying primates, hunter-gatherers, and a variety of modern societies, "There is a remarkable convergence in the accounts which people of all cultures and all races give" of the nature of their selves:

In association with my body there exists a spirit, conscious of its existence and continuity over time. This is the spirit, mind, soul, which I call "I." Among the chief attributes which I possess are these: I can act, I can perceive, I can feel. Thus it is I, who, by exertion of my will, bring about almost all my significant bodily actions. . . . Functioning as "I" do as a unitary being, I work like this: by planning my actions in relation to what my perceptions tell me about their probable effects, I try to satisfy whatever wants or aspirations my states of feeling have aroused.[53]

Careful investigation of any kind has always concluded that this version of "self" is just a construct, and recent work drives the point home even more forcefully. Research stemming from Benjamin Libet, for example, shows that when someone is told to press a button the moment a light appears, they actually press the button slightly *before* they are aware of perceiving the signal.[54] Even when shown the data, furthermore, subjects remain intuitively convinced that they first saw the light appear in awareness and then directed their fingers to push the button. That is, it *feels* right for humans to believe they have a self that responds to conscious awareness and exercises free will, even though this construct does not fit the facts. Torey comments on this: "While humans are ignorant about their brain's inner workings, they want to be soothed by comforting projections. . . . The brain is ill motivated to penetrate and solve the riddle of its own function. It risks having to abandon long-standing and comforting projections."[55] So accepting without question that the social self is really what we are is the second trap of ordinary consciousness.

Social reality and the social self are two of the most important concepts in contemporary social science. Literally thousands of laboratory experiments show that the way people perceive the world, the way they feel about it, and their beliefs, opinions, and actions are strongly refracted by their social realities and the ways their perception has been framed or primed. Eyewitness reports of accidents or crimes notoriously show that people see and react to the same event in amazingly different ways. Undergraduates learn about social reality and the social self in introductory courses, and those of us who have been around for a long time still return to those ideas for new insight. My postdoctoral mentor in mathematical sociology, Harrison White, after years of pondering and analyzing social life, concluded that we need to pay more attention to language and to work harder at penetrating "the common-sense that conceals the inner mechanics of social reality," the "mysterious carapace" that encapsulates people and alters the way they experience the world.[56] We will also see powerful use of these concepts in Anthony Giddens' analysis of modern society in chapter 16, including his use of the same word, "carapace," to describe the shell of social reality in which we live our lives.

Ordinary Consciousness Involves the Brain as Well as the Mind

The purpose of this chapter was to investigate ordinary consciousness by following its evolution from animals to modern humans, from unconscious processing of immediate perception to the invention of language and construction of social reality. The story is not over, however. Social reality is a necessary concept for understanding ordinary consciousness, but it is not sufficient. Social reality is constructed in the mind, using language as the building material and social interaction as the dynamic process. To adequately account for ordinary consciousness, however, we need to include not only operations of the mind but also operations of the brain and interactions between mind and brain.

To understand how brain operations got involved, we begin with the research on how specialized systems in the brain became differentiated, over time, to handle the complex processing required for language. Anatomical differentiation started long ago, before the first words of the first protolanguage were uttered; in species much more primitive than hominids, the hemispheric differentiation that led to language specialization was already under way.[57] In humans, left (and to a lesser degree, right) hemispheric specialization for language functions is beautifully intricate and fairly well understood.[58] However, understanding how the brain handles social reality is just beginning. Indeed, studying the neural complexities involved in navigating as a social self through a world interpreted and modeled by social reality will probably keep neuroscientists occupied for some time to come.

It is difficult to explain the always sudden (if subtle) transition between ordinary and awakened consciousness without positing the existence of two specialized brain systems. Science often advances when existing theory cannot account for a newly discovered or previously ignored fact. The recent positive identification of the Higgs boson, after years of searching for it, was necessary because existing theory was unable to account for some anomalous evidence. The revised theory that worked best postulated the existence of a previously unknown particle, and physicists went looking for it. In the same way, I am saying that in order to account for the facts of awakening, an alternative brain system must be there to take over when the dominance of the system responsible for ordinary consciousness is sufficiently weakened.

The facts of awakening were described in chapters 12 and 13. People committing to the Buddhist path undergo a long period of training to quiet the mind and to free themselves from attachments to desires and beliefs. The core of these beliefs, and the ones most difficult to detach from, are beliefs that social reality and the social self are real. It is not easy to quiet the mind of words or to examine the ontological basis of social reality and one's social self so deeply that they no longer seem real, but both can be done. Unfortunately, as many have discovered, arriving finally at a state where the mind is quiet, free of desires, and no longer attached to social reality and the social self does not automatically produce awakening. Often something extra has to be there,[59] some sort of catalyst that can spark the sudden flashing into existence of awakened consciousness. And even after some familiarity with awakened consciousness, returning to it from a long spell in ordinary consciousness is not a gradual transition but a discrete change of state, like flipping a switch. I therefore conclude that each form of consciousness is produced by a distinct brain system, but that one and only one system is dominant at any given moment. I cannot think of any way the mind alone, without some sort of switching taking place in the brain, can make the sudden and total transitions.[60]

During the interview with Ajahn Amaro, there was a little episode where he looked at me and raised his right eyebrow, high on his forehead. I interrupted the interview at that point to say that my father could raise his right eyebrow in the same way and that I had always tried to imitate him. But no matter how much effort I put into it, I could never get in touch with the nerves that control the muscles that move that eyebrow. Learning how to raise one's right eyebrow seems to me something like switching to awakened consciousness. It can be very difficult to connect with capacities that are present in our bodies but that we have never used before (or at least, to begin using capacities that have never been freed from domination by ordinary consciousness). Similarly, the mind can be in a state ready for awakened consciousness, but the brain can still be using the system that produces ordinary consciousness.

Fortunately, a theory that identifies specific brain structures and links them with ordinary and awakened consciousness already exists, in the work of the neurologist James Austin. Austin is one of the few scientists to have personally experienced awakening, so like everyone else with this experience, he had no real choice but to devote himself to doing what he could to share the information with the rest of the world.[61] This meant looking for a neurological way to account for the remarkable facts he had learned. He began going through the huge literature of neuroscience for research findings that could provide an explanation, and he succeeded in identifying two neural systems. One he calls the "egocentric" processing system. This system produces conscious awareness as interpreted by social reality and is responsible for ordinary consciousness. The other system he calls "allocentric"; it is responsible for the processing that produces awakened consciousness. So, even if one has learned to go for fairly long periods of time with no words entering one's awareness, with desires thoroughly tamed and beliefs properly questioned, as long as the egocentric system remains dominant, one is still aware of the world as presented by ordinary consciousness. That world is experienced more clearly and peacefully, and with fewer illusions, but still without the change in perspective and special energy provided by awakened consciousness.

Now systems for producing ordinary and awakened consciousness, perhaps Austin's egocentric and allocentric systems, are assumed to be available in the human brain. We are born with these systems, but the way we put them to use is not determined at birth, and the way they are used as we grow up then determines how strong and effective each will be, and which will be dominant. Studies of neural plasticity, for example, show that the thickness of the cortex in a specific area varies with the amount and kind of activity that area has been engaged in.[62] Plasticity has been shown most clearly in areas of the cortex that control attention, but the hypothesis extends more broadly. Not only the "strength" but also the contents of our brain change with both perceptual and conceptual learning. Coming to a new understanding about what is really important in life, for example, must rearrange our neuronal maps and in this way modify the momentum and direction of ordinary consciousness. So the claim here is that what we do, what we experience, and what we think about shapes and tunes the relative dominance and compatibility of the egocentric and allocentric systems, and hence ordinary and awakened consciousness.

The thesis of this chapter has been that the evolution of ordinary consciousness in humans can be seen as involving three big steps. The first was the ability to somehow hold in mind during cognitive processing, as "working memory," mental representations that do not refer to immediate experience. The second step was the invention of language. The development of language built on and further encouraged the predisposition of humans toward social cooperation and cohesive social groups, as mutually reinforcing processes. Third, at some point during the long process of inventing language we began constructing social reality. Social realities made it possible for groups to function flexibly and efficiently, and to pass on acquired knowledge and skills to succeeding generations. Although any social reality is a synthetic construction, humans evolved with the ability to take strong group consensus as the evidentiary basis for believing that their particular synthetic construction is real. As brain systems specializing in social reality became dominant, humans began identifying who they were with the social self they had constructed, mostly during childhood, through interaction with others. This process was further reinforced as the members of a group came to identify with the symbolically constructed social self that represented them in social reality. Without social support for believing in that reality , life in ordinary consciousness lacks an authentic feeling of meaningfulness.

What the evolution of human consciousness accomplished, therefore, was the creation of a whole new cognitive system, using symbolic rather than perceptual representations. As a result, humans live in the world our ordinary awareness tells us we are living in. Symbol systems are very useful, and the social realities constructed from them make possible human life as we know it. But these evolutionary processes came at some cost. When the world as seen through the structures of social reality is believed to be the real world, and the social self that connects us to that world is also seen as unquestionably real, there are three not-so-desirable side effects. First, as Damasio warns, communication problems between brain stem and cortex impose limitations on our awareness of what is going on in our body and on the "primordial feelings" provided through interoception. Second, greater attention to symbolically represented reality reduces attention to perceptually represented inputs in general, which sets up the third dysfunction: our conscious awareness becomes dominated by whatever is produced by or filtered through social reality. That is the ordinary consciousness with which we are still struggling to live.

The next chapter explores the processes through which human babies acquire ordinary consciousness and become adult members of society.

15
The Awakened Baby?

Chapter 14 followed the evolution of ordinary consciousness from animals to humans. Without making any claims about ontogeny recapitulating phylogeny, it is interesting to look at research on how consciousness develops as human babies grow up. I rely primarily on University of California, Berkeley psychologist Alison Gopnik's *The Philosophical Baby*[1] because it incorporates in a comprehensive way recent as well as earlier work in developmental psychology, and because it focuses on babies' minds and awareness as they grow to later childhood.

According to Gopnik, babies up to about one year old have these characteristics:

1. Language acquisition is minimal.
2. Attention is diffuse rather than concentrated.
3. They are beginning to develop causal models of the world ("Even young babies who can't talk yet have some ability to anticipate and imagine the future").
4. They have empathy: "Literally, from the time they're born children are empathic. They identify with other people and recognize that their own feelings are shared by others. In fact, they literally take on the feelings of others."

As one-year-olds grow into early childhood, language development accelerates and attention becomes more concentrated, focusing on smaller areas within a frame rather than taking in the whole frame. Meanwhile, models of the world and abilities to manipulate and imagine these models become more sophisticated, while empathy may diminish to levels more commonly seen in adults. These developments are often intertwined, so they need to be followed closely. I pay special attention to language acquisition, which increases exponentially from age one to age five, and to cognitive functioning over the same period.

Here is what seems to happen. First, babies quickly develop their ability not only to represent but also to imagine events that might happen in the future as well as events that could have happened in the past, but didn't. This is a gradual process from birth to age five. "Children's brains create causal theories of the world, maps of how the world works," Gopnik writes. "These theories allow children to envisage new possibilities, and to imagine and to pretend that the world is different."[2] That is, they learn to call up and manipulate mental representations and project them into the (imaginary) past and possible (or impossible) future. They use this knowledge to "construct alternate universes—different ways the world might be."

Second, although these abilities can be seen emerging even in babies who can't talk yet, they accelerate with language acquisition. "The development of language almost certainly plays a role. . . . [It] provides us with a medium for telling ourselves, as well as others, what happened and what to do." "Learning language gives children a whole powerful new way to imagine. . . . Babies start talking about unreal possibilities at the same time that they start to use tools in an insightful way. Being able to talk about possibilities helps you to imagine them."[3] Therefore, language acquisition extends and strengthens a child's ability to construct and manipulate mental models, and shows up behaviorally in both problem solving and the use of tools.

Third, while language acquisition proceeds quickly, in parallel with the development and use of mental models, to describe and manipulate external events, use of language to talk about inner events and the self does not really become prominent until the child is six years of age or older. That is, children readily use words to talk about events that are going on around them, including those that they are a part of, but it takes longer for them to begin using words to represent the self. "Once they can talk, one- and two-year-olds can report specific events that occurred to them in the past. . . . But children start to weave those memories into a continuous narrative—a narrative in which they are the hero, or at least the protagonist—only when they are older."[4]

Using words to represent the self goes along with being able to look at that self from the perspective of another person (the "looking-glass self"), which is more complicated than merely being aware that one is interacting with that person. "Even very young babies have some sense of self," says Gopnik. "They can recognize themselves in a mirror and distinguish themselves from other people. . . . But they don't seem to have the experience of the inner observer."

Observing oneself from the perspective of others seems to require inner speech, and children develop that only later. For example, Gopnik says that preschoolers (ages three to five):

> "don't understand that your thoughts can be internally generated. They don't understand that thoughts can simply follow the logic of your internal experience instead of being triggered from the outside."[5]

> "[They] deny experiencing visual imagery or inner speech, although they understand perfectly what a picture or a sentence is like."[6]

> "They also say you can't talk to yourself in your head. [The researchers] asked them to think about how their teacher's name sounded. They denied that there was any voice in their head doing the naming, and if you explicitly asked them they were as likely to say that there was a picture in their head as a voice."[7]

Babies and young children have not yet acquired autobiographical memory and executive control. "They don't experience their lives as a single timeline stretching back into the past and forward into the future. They don't send themselves backward and forward along this timeline as adults do, recapturing for a moment that past self who was the miserable loser or the happy lover, or anticipating the despairs and joys of the future." Babies and young children have not yet learned to project their thoughts into either the past or the future, and they do not appear to have formed a self-construct that can represent them in thoughts about the future. For one thing, "while they can formulate plans for the immediate future, this does not include thoughts or feelings about what that future state will feel like."

If Buddhist practice works to quiet inner conversation in order to weaken attachments to the social self, Gopnik is in effect describing the reverse process: children first learn to use language, then several years later begin using inner speech, and as part of this process they develop what we recognize as the social self.

Fourth, as language use develops more and more powerfully, attention changes. Babies' attention is diffuse, in fact rather similar to the experience of mindfulness in adults: "Rather than determining what to look at in the world, babies seem to let the world determine what they look at. And rather than deciding where to focus attention and where to inhibit distractions, babies seem to be conscious of much more of the world at once."[8] Along with this, "younger children concentrate less well but remember more and learn from the full visual field," whereas "older children concentrate on one thing at a time."

Diffuse, receptive attention continues through preschool age. Children this age think that whatever is in the immediate visual field is in awareness, but nothing else. In one study, preschool children were shown a video in which a woman is looking at a framed photograph of children and pointing to some of them. When the children watching the video were asked, "Was the woman thinking about the kids in the picture?" they all said yes. But when they were asked if she was thinking about the frame of the picture, they said, "Yes, she was thinking about that too." They said she wasn't thinking about things not in the visual field, for example a chair in the next room. "But they do believe she will be thinking about everything she sees."[9]

Fifth, empathy: just as children from ages one to six are slow to develop a separated self, they begin as babies with a great capacity for empathy, which tends eventually to decline unless nurtured. In addition to experiencing the pure feeling, or sensing, that lies at the heart of empathy, infants very quickly begin to make distinctions and generalize: "One-year-olds understand the difference between intentional and unintentional actions, and behave in genuinely altruistic ways. Three-year olds have already developed a basic ethic of care and compassion."[10]

It was suggested in chapter 13 that empathy and the first property of awakened consciousness, no separation, usually go together, so an increase in one brings about an increase in the other. Gopnik notes this same tendency in children, pointing out that as children age, empathy and a sense of no separation both *diminish* at the same rate: "Moral thinkers from Buddha to David Hume to Martin Buber have suggested that erasing the boundaries between yourself and others . . . can underpin morality. We know that children's conception of a continuous separate self develops slowly in the first five years."[11]

There is, therefore, an intriguing inverse symmetry between the processes through which a baby turns into an older child or adult and the processes through which an adult moves along the path toward awakening. The baby must learn to represent the world around it and to manipulate those representations mentally, and then learn names (words) for the representations and rules of language for manipulating the words. As this is happening, the baby's attention becomes more focused and event oriented, less diffuse and receptive. Empathy, which is in full bloom in babies, gradually diminishes. Especially from age six on, inner speech grows more prominent, and with it the "continuous separate self" of adults emerges.

If that same baby, now grown to adulthood, decides to undertake a Buddhist path toward awakening, then she begins with the extremely difficult task of quieting inner speech. As one "skillful means" for doing this, she will probably engage in forms of meditation involving mindfulness. This will help rebuild her capacity for diffuse, receptive attention while improving her ability to turn off inner speech. Along with this, she must work to detach from all conditionings, particularly from social reality, the symbolically represented models of the self and the world to which she has become firmly attached. So the hypothesis is that finally, with her mind quiet and attentive and her emotional attachments to social reality weakened, she is prepared to experience a form of awareness that is similar to what she knew as a baby, but with all the information and skills she has learned since then still active and available.

In sum, as babies grow up, they gradually weaken or lose the three abilities that Buddhist practice seeks to strengthen (mindfulness, nonattachment, and empathy). Along with this, Gopnik describes how children develop a "continuous separate self" at the same time that they are learning to use language in more complex ways, particularly as inner speech. Recent neuroscience research finds that until age twelve, children are not nearly as good as older children and adults at either thinking about what they might do in imagined events or anticipating mentally how others will then view them.[12] Doing these things requires being able to project the self into event sequences and imagine the social consequences, to take the role of the other and understand their viewpoint (Theory of Mind). These skills continue to develop, in parallel with improved ability for introspection, well into adolescence.[13]

And at this point, the baby turned child, then adolescent, then adult is prepared to live in modern society with fully developed ordinary consciousness.

16
The Human Condition and How We Got Into It

Chapter 14 concluded that all humans have capacities for both ordinary consciousness and awakened consciousness, but that we have considerable choice, as individuals and as groups, about how we use, develop, and maintain those capacities. The present chapter looks at the specific forms ordinary and awakened consciousness have taken in different societies. Two themes are prominent: for all of its other powers, ordinary consciousness operating on its own is, in the long run, uncomfortable and relatively inflexible; and humans are aware, consciously or unconsciously, of the weaknesses and discomforts of ordinary consciousness, and over time have developed some interesting responses to cope with this problem, often referred to as "the human condition."

Pirahã Exceptionalism

The linguist Daniel Everett originally went to the Amazon as a young missionary to translate the Bible into the language of the Pirahã, a hunter-gather-fisher tribe.[1] Famously, rather than Everett converting the Pirahã to Christianity, the Pirahã gradually converted him to atheism, but in the process he mastered their language and spent many years living with them. His work with the Pirahã has generated two articles in *The New Yorker* magazine (something that most social scientists can only dream of). It also produced quite a bit of controversy, mostly concerning technical linguistic issues not really relevant here.[2] However, it is their language and how it fits with the rest of their culture that makes the Pirahã so interesting.[3]

The Pirahã speak a particularly ancient form of preliterate language. According to the cognitive anthropologist Brett Berlin, "The plausible scenarios . . . suggest that early language looked something like the kind of thing that Pirahã looks like now."[4] Pirahã language suggests a compromise between the advantages of prelinguistic, perceptually represented consciousness and what we pride ourselves on today as the full conceptual development of symbolically represented consciousness.

In *Don't Sleep, There Are Snakes*, Everett describes the dominant, guiding principle of the Pirahã: "The Pirahã language and culture are connected by a cultural constraint on talking about anything beyond immediate experience . . . the Pirahãs only make statements that are anchored to the moment when they are speaking." In application, this rule says that in order to be meaningful, a statement cannot stray more than two degrees of separation from immediate experience. If someone describes something they personally experienced at an earlier time (one degree of separation) or heard about from someone else who was alive during the lifetime of the speaker (two degrees), then it will be accepted as meaningful. A major reason Everett failed as a missionary was that when the Pirahã asked how he knew that Jesus had said the things reported in the Bible and found that neither Everett nor anyone he had ever known personally had actually seen or heard Jesus, they discarded the whole subject as meaningless. Even a second degree of separation is unusual: "Occasionally [the Pirahã] will talk to me about things that they have heard that were witnessed by someone now dead, but this is rare, and generally only the most experienced language teachers[5] will do this, those who have developed an ability to abstract from the subjective use of their language and who are able to comment on it from an objective perspective."[6] Even the ability to include in one's conscious awareness items that involve two degrees of separation from immediate experience, although available in the Pirahã language, is a skill that has to be nurtured.

In many ways, Pirahã life is quite similar to the training that Buddhism recommends for students undertaking a path to awakening. The most efficient way to show this similarity is to systematically compare Pirahã culture and lifestyle with the three preparations on the Buddhist path to awakening that were described in chapter 12. On the basis of this comparison, I will conclude that the guidance and behavior patterns that Pirahã culture provides very closely resemble life in a Buddhist monastery, in spite of obvious differences on the surface. Buddhist monasteries attempt to create an environment and a set of practices that develop the qualities necessary for awakening. My thesis is that Pirahã language, culture, and everyday life nurture the same qualities, with the result that the Pirahã live naturally with something fairly close to awakened consciousness.

Mindfulness

The first preparation on the Buddhist path involves learning to control the attention and quiet the mind, with these two qualities then coming together in the cognitive mode called mindfulness. So the first question is, Does Pirahã life include anything equivalent to formal meditation? Unless Everett left something out, the answer is no. In *Don't Sleep, There Are Snakes*, for example, when the Pirahã are sitting down they mostly seem to be talking with each other. My argument is that the Pirahã don't need special practices like sitting meditation. From birth on, their culture and way of life guide them (more or less force them) to live in a mindful state, and their language restricts their talk to the here and now. Let's look at this more closely.

The Pirahã language contains no abstractions, such as categories, principles, or even words for colors. It lacks words for numbers and hence for counting, including quantifiers such as "most" or "all"; the absence of numbers in Pirahã appears to be unique among the world's languages (although now-extinct languages and earlier stages of existing languages apparently also lacked numbers).[7] There are no words for subjective states like motives, will, or urges, nor for causal thinking or purposive problem solving in general. Pirahã also appears to be unique in not allowing recursion, whereby one phrase or thought can be embedded within another.[8] And the emphasis on immediate perceptual presence applies to space as well as time: when someone walks away and is no longer in sight, for example, the Pirahã use a word that Everett translates as "gone out of experience." As a result, when Pirahã talk they are forced to pay attention to the here and now by the simple absence of any linguistic alternative.

The Pirahã emphasis on living in the moment is reinforced by their lack of concern about the future. Just as Pirahã language cannot express intention, planning, or causal analysis, their cultural orientation is not to be concerned about what will happen tomorrow. Everett noted, for example, that the Pirahã do nothing to preserve the food they catch or gather each day and do not take care of any tools they have made or been given. He concluded that "planning for the future is less important for the Pirahãs than enjoying each day as it comes,"[9] but he also noted that this "certainly wasn't laziness, because the Pirahã work very hard."[10] The Pirahã live in a rather hospitable environment that makes available all that they need, year round. If they do their work of fishing, hunting, and gathering every day, their food needs are met. So their environment supports equanimity, which is also a quality Buddhist practice works to attain.

By not giving attention to things that happened in the past or might happen in the future, and by focusing on perceptual reality rather than hypothetical situations or abstractions, Pirahãs keep their minds relatively free of the wandering-mind conversations that Buddhists seek to quiet. So what is going on in Pirahã minds that might detract from mindfulness? It would certainly be interesting to ask them, but pending that research, here is a list of topics that Everett says they *don't* occupy themselves with:

1. Worrying. If you're not concerned with controlling what the future might hold or whether good or bad things will happen to you, what is there to worry about? Everett notes, "I have never heard a Pirahã say that he or she is worried. In fact, so far as I can tell, the Pirahãs have no word for worry in their language."[11]

2. Blaming or seeking retribution. A Pirahã named Kaapasi got drunk and shot his brother Kaaboogi's dog, killing it. While Kaaboogi was holding the dog and crying, Everett asked him if he was going to do anything to Kaapasi. Kaaboogi looked at Everett with a puzzled expression and said, "I will do nothing. I won't hurt my brother. He acted like a child. He did a bad thing. But he is drunk and his head is not working well. He should not have hurt my dog. It is like my child."[12]

3. Anger: "anger is the cardinal sin among the Pirahãs" (although it occurs sometimes, especially after drinking). Rather than expressing anger, other forms of sanction are used for social control, e.g., "giggling, smirking, and laughter."[13]

Nonattachment

The second capacity that Buddhist practice seeks to develop involves loosening the emotional bonds or expectations of gratification that we experience as desires, aversions, fears, or felt needs. Pirahã culture does a good job of eliminating attachments to material objects, food, and the outcomes of events beyond human control: "Pirahã laugh at everything. They laugh at their own misfortune: when someone's hut blows over in a rainstorm, the occupants laugh more loudly than anyone. They laugh when they catch a lot of fish. They laugh when they catch no fish. They laugh when they're full and they laugh when they're hungry."[14]

And as in Buddhist monasteries, this nonattachment begins with self-discipline, a kind of mental toughness that the Pirahã call "hardness." The development of this inner strength begins in infancy, when Pirahã children are taught to accept what comes along without complaining:

Any baby who cuts, burns, or otherwise hurts itself gets scolded (and cared for too). And a mother will often answer a baby's cry of pain in such circumstances with a growl of disgust. . . . She might pick it up by an arm and angrily (but not violently) set it down abruptly away from the danger. But parents do not hug the child or say things like "Poor baby, I'm so sorry, let Mommy kiss it and make the boo-boo better." The Pirahãs stare with surprise when they see non-Pirahã mothers do this. They even think it is funny. "Don't they want their children to learn to take care of themselves?" the Pirahãs ask me. . . . This style of parenting has the result of producing very tough and resilient adults who do not believe that anyone owes them anything. Citizens of the Pirahã nation know that each day's survival depends on their individual skills and hardiness.[15]

Another kind of nonattachment concerns attraction of the social self to status, power, and ego enhancement. Like almost all hunter-gatherer societies, Pirahã social structure is egalitarian. This is carefully enforced by social norms and practices—activities that involve any kind of competition are discouraged.[16] At the same time, Pirahã are more individualistic than some other hunter-gatherers in that there appears to be less communal sharing—in normal times, each family is expected to take care of its own food, shelter, and other needs.

Compassion, Empathy, and Kindness

As one might guess from their emphasis on self-reliance and mental toughness, the Pirahã are not demonstrative or overt when it comes to compassion. In chapter 12 I commented that for me "feelings of kindness" seemed better than "compassion" for describing this cluster, and "kindness" is the word Everett uses for the Pirahã: "[They] are patient with me. They are stoic with themselves. They are caring for the elderly and the handicapped."[17] They like to touch to show affection. They live in a tightly knit community of trust, "trust that each member of the community will understand each other member of the community and share the same values."[18] However, the Pirahã manifest their kindness and empathy in distinctly muted ways. Everett tells the story of a young woman who died in a breech childbirth. The Pirahã custom is for women to deliver by themselves, in the river, with help only from their parents. Her parents lived in another village, however, and her husband was away on a fishing trip, so the woman was alone and crying out in agony during the long ordeal. The rest of the village gathered on a hillside above the river and watched her die, but did nothing to help. Everett notes that there was nothing they could have done—the Pirahã have no doctors and no way of dealing with emergencies like breech deliveries. They accept death stoically, in line with their belief that people must be strong and get through difficulties on their own.[19] Everett felt that from the Pirahã perspective, they did what was right, and were not being cruel or thoughtless.

Positive Features of Pirahã Consciousness

If the Pirahã live their lives in accord with practices that Buddhist teachings recommend, then to what degree are they experiencing awakened consciousness as their dominant mode? The three properties of awakening that were derived from the interviews in chapter 13 (no separation, no attachments to the social self, and not knowing) were phrased as negations of ordinary consciousness, the same device Gautama used. That apophatic approach may not work with the Pirahã; they don't seem to experience qualities like separation or attachment to self in the first place, so they may have nothing to awaken from. We have to look instead for statements or qualities that describe their typical form of consciousness in positive terms, words that stand by themselves rather than deriving meaning from contrast with an opposite term.

Everett discusses one feature of Pirahã culture that may qualify on a technical level. It applies to the aspect of no separation that involves spatial orientation.

[Researchers have] discovered two broad divisions in the ways culture and languages view local directions. Many cultures are like American and European culture and orient themselves in relative terms, dependent on body orientation, such as left and right. This is called endocentric orientation. Others, like the Pirahãs, orient themselves to objects external to their body, what some refer to as exocentric orientation.[20]

In James Austin's terms, these would be called egocentric and allocentric orientations, respectively, and growing up with an allocentric perspective on one's relation to others could help prevent the feeling of being a private person separate from others that is characteristic of Western ordinary consciousness.

Another indicator of awakening might be the ubiquitous happiness of the Pirahã. "Since my first night among them I have been impressed with their patience, their happiness, and their kindness. This pervasive happiness is hard to explain."[21] When a group of psychologists from MIT visited, one of them commented that the Pirahã appeared to be the happiest people he and his colleagues had ever seen.[22] Everett adds that of the more than twenty isolated Amazonian societies with which he has had contact over a thirty-year period, only the Pirahã manifest this unusual happiness. Now, happiness was not mentioned much in chapter 13 as a feature of awakening, because it is considered slightly bad form among Buddhists to talk about how happy one is. References to happiness don't show up very often in the interviews—the teachers seemed to want to emphasize that one does not pursue Buddhist training with the goal of achieving it. Nevertheless, good feelings come along with the other properties of awakening, whether they are called "happiness," "peace," or maybe "grace." So given that interpretation, the happiness of the Pirahã can be taken as indicating that they are doing something right.

Finally, from the original teachings of Gautama onward, awakening has been recommended as the ultimate relief from emotional suffering. Much carefully controlled research today has concluded that meditation has positive effects on mental distress and the various personality disorders.[23] So when Everett notes that the Pirahã "show no evidence of depression, chronic fatigue, extreme anxiety, panic attacks, or other psychological ailments common in many industrialized societies," this can be taken as further indication that, whether or not the Pirahã can be called "awakened," their consciousness is at least somewhere in that vicinity.

Negative Features of Pirahã Consciousness

Not only do the Pirahã appear to manifest some positive aspects of awakening, they also show some of its limitations. First, while the Pirahã are monogamous, they have distinctly permissive attitudes about sex. Unmarried Pirahãs have sex as they wish, but extramarital sex also occurs. It is frowned upon "and can be risky," but it happens, and the Pirahã are usually casual and unemotional about it. So they resemble many Western Buddhists in this respect (although because there are no men with higher status than others, they cannot behave like Buddhist teachers who use their prestige and power for sexual purposes).

Also like some Buddhists, and like all too many other Fourth World societies, the Pirahã have a fondness for alcohol. From the stories Everett tells, they apparently drink to excess whenever alcohol is available. They do "bad things" when they get drunk, and they continue to drink whenever the opportunity arises, even though they know what will happen as a result. For example, one afternoon during Everett's second visit a trader came up the river in his boat, got all the Pirahã drunk, and told them that Everett was taking advantage of them and cheating them. The Pirahã got angry about this, and later that evening Everett could hear voices in the dark talking about killing him. Suddenly his trusted language teacher, Kohoi, appeared from the bush and said he was going to shoot him. Fortunately, Kohoi didn't actually have his shotgun with him, and Everett had learned enough Pirahã to calm him down. The next day Kohoi came to his house and spoke for the village: "We're sorry. Our heads get really bad when we drink and we do things that are bad."[24] While aggression in general is not condoned, getting drunk seems to be accepted even though the Pirahã know it can easily lead to violence.

Social Reality

The Pirahã have a fully developed culture, which by definition is a social reality shared by all. Attachment to social reality is a defining feature of ordinary consciousness, yet the Pirahã seem to live a life that incorporates many of the features of awakened consciousness. The question therefore is: How psychologically and emotionally attached are the Pirahã to their social reality? Do they accept it subjectively as ruling their lives, or do they see it more objectively, as someone with awakened consciousness might? Everett tells a story that suggests the former. The Pirahã rely on fishing for a major part of their sustenance, and they use canoes for doing this. They know how to make canoes out of bark, but they prefer using the more durable dugout canoes that local Brazilians make. They can only get dugout canoes by stealing or trading for them, so there is a chronic shortage. One day several Pirahã approached Everett and asked him to buy them a canoe, to which he replied, "Why don't you make a canoe?" "Pirahãs don't make canoes. We don't know how." So Everett decided to help them learn, and brought in a master canoe builder from a village several hours away. When he arrived, Everett instructed him to let the Pirahã do all the work, that he should supervise and instruct rather than work on the canoe himself. "After about five days of intense effort, they made a beautiful dugout canoe and showed it off proudly to me. I bought the tools for them to make more. Then [a few days later] the Pirahãs asked me for another canoe. I told them that they could make their own now. They said, 'Pirahãs don't make canoes' and walked away."[25]

End of story, and they never built another canoe. Everett's conclusion was that "Pirahãs don't import foreign knowledge or adopt foreign work habits easily, no matter how useful one might think that the knowledge is to them." To do so would involve questioning social reality. This is rare in all societies, including preliterate ones.

A second aspect of social reality, to which modern humans are especially attached, is the social self. In a small, relatively undifferentiated, and egalitarian society like that of the Pirahã, the strongest defining characteristic of the social self is simply "I am Pirahã." There is no concern about being better than others (indeed, a cultural value discourages it), but there is an emotional motivation to conform to Pirahã rules and standards. This also seems, from my limited reading of the ethnographic literature, to be true of most hunter-gatherer tribes.[26] Without attachment to the social self, methods of social control like shaming, which are favored by hunter-gatherers, will not work (see the discussion of psychopathy in chapter 13). My conclusion, therefore, is that in this respect the Pirahã have a social self with which they identify. But the social self coexists with a self based on interoceptive and proprioceptive inputs much more harmoniously for the Pirahã than for most contemporary Americans.

Lessons to Be Learned from the Pirahã

My conclusion, therefore, is that the Pirahã keep immediate perceptual awareness alive and vigorous by tying language fairly closely to immediate experience and by emphasizing immediate experience in their culture and lifestyle. Taken together, Pirahã language, culture, and lifestyle essentially *impose* mindfulness and nonattachment as everyday practices. In terms of the theory developed in this book, following this way of life makes it possible for the Pirahã to enjoy the happiness, psychological freedom, and positive personality traits associated with following the Buddhist path toward awakening. At the same time, Pirahãs show typically human attachment to social reality. That ordinary and awakened consciousness may coexist in some sort of balance is perhaps the most important lesson to be learned from the Pirahã.

Even preliterate peoples sometimes have a sense that living within ordinary consciousness is limiting, that it serves as a kind of shell separating them from a more real reality. Many hunter-gatherer cultures include institutional patterns with which they attempt to reach beyond ordinary reality for answers or for help in living with the problems and strains of the world. The Pirahã have no concept of god, or gods (which is important in its own right), but they believe they encounter spirits regularly, both while awake and in dreams. Listening to spirits that appear in dreams does not (from the Pirahã point of view) contradict the principle of immediate experience because so long as it is happening right now, both dreaming and listening to spirits while awake count as immediate experience. Spirits sometimes tell the whole village what they should or should not do: "Pirahãs listen carefully and often follow the exhortations of the [spirits]."[27]

What Pirahã culture does not seem to provide are special practices individuals can use to transcend ordinary consciousness. These seem to be fairly common in other hunter-gatherer cultures—for example, the !Kung of the Kalihari use a practice called !Kia, which makes it possible for the practitioner to "transcend himself and develop extraordinary powers during certain periods. It reaffirms his relationship with the supernatural and leaves him with a feeling of well-being. For a few of the most powerful healers, !Kia also seems to raise their general level of being; their ordinary lives take on a special, spiritual quality."[28]

It is interesting that the Pirahã do not have such practices and expressed no interest in the subject to Everett. Maybe they don't feel a need for it, or perhaps for other reasons the notion that something lies beyond the form of consciousness they normally experience never occurs to them. This whole subject—preliterate approaches to transcending ordinary reality—is a rich field with a wealth of published material available that might be productively re-explored from the perspective of awakened consciousness.

Postliterate Societies

The Pirahã are offered as an example of how language (along with other cultural patterns) can shape ordinary consciousness, in their case by being restricted to immediate experience. Languages that emphasize the concrete as strongly as Pirahã does may have been typical of all early human groups; we only know about the present. What seems fairly certain, however, is that the invention of writing not only made it possible to record language but also almost certainly changed language in the process. Rather than one person talking to another face to face one person makes marks on a physical material in such a way that another, unknown person, perhaps in a different place at a later time, can decode the marks and then put into spoken words a reasonably accurate version of the meaning the author was trying to express. Writing had to make up for the absence of facial expressions, gestures, and shared understanding of context. The hypothesis is that as language changed to accommodate writing by filling in these information gaps, and as subsequent generations grew up using that language, their ordinary consciousness was changed in subtle ways.

Because we don't know what a language was like before it was put into written form, we have to investigate indirectly. One strategy is to study the very first texts to appear in written form and compare them with later texts. This approach assumes that the earliest written records available today fairly closely reflect the language spoken in that society before writing appeared. This is a reasonable assumption because it probably took several centuries for the effects of writing to manifest themselves at all widely in spoken language, and hence for children to grow up with their consciousness shaped by that new language. Julian Jaynes used this method in comparing the language of the *Iliad*, and the form of consciousness implied in that text, with the language and consciousness evident in the *Odyssey*, which was written down several centuries later. He chose the *Iliad* because he felt that it was the first written text translated with sufficient accuracy to allow reasonable inferences about the consciousness of its author(s). Given the events described, the *Iliad* was probably composed orally in the twelfth century B.C.E., about the same time that written Greek appeared,[29] and the *Odyssey* came along maybe four hundred years later. Jaynes' book, *The Origins of Consciousness in the Breakdown of the Bicameral Mind*,[30] not only is controversial but also has been called preposterous, largely because in addition to the linguistic analysis, he builds an imaginative theory that eventually includes auditory hallucinations and hemispheric differentiation of the brain. My interest is primarily in the linguistic analysis, which seems to have escaped controversy.[31]

Jaynes concluded that the language of the *Iliad* lacks several important features found in the *Odyssey* (and in written languages generally). First, there are no words for subjective states. For Jaynes this meant no consciousness, literally, no conscious awareness, because for him consciousness is only possible when one can examine one's awareness through introspection.

This requires holding one's feelings and self in conscious awareness. Jaynes' conclusion was that without a language capable of describing feelings and self, we cannot hold them in conscious focus, and hence we cannot be aware of ourselves.

Second, the *Iliad* contains no words for static abstractions. Words that in the *Odyssey* refer to states and abstractions have to do, in the *Iliad*, with motion or agitation, maybe vibration or flow. Again, the language of the *Iliad* seems more in line with the Pirahã emphasis on perceptual experience. Abstractions have no direct perceptual base; they exist only in represented reality.

Third, the *Iliad* does not use concepts that refer to will or agency. "The beginnings of action are not in conscious plans, reasons, and motives; they are in the actions and speeches of gods"—which are heard as auditory hallucinations. Furthermore, "The individual obeyed these hallucinated voices because he could not 'see' what to do by himself." Jaynes assumes here that if a language does not include words for causal analysis and agency, its speakers lack the linguistic tools necessary for solving problems. Jaynes thought that because preliterate minds were so poorly prepared for rational problem solving, at crucial times they relied on auditory hallucinations (voices of the gods speaking to them with advice). Of course, this seems very similar to the way Pirahãs listen to spirits for advice on problems.[32]

Overall, therefore, what Jaynes concluded from the *Iliad* seems very similar to what we found with the Pirahã. Both languages stay close to immediate experience, and thus allow less opportunity for thinking about things that don't exist. Comparing the *Iliad* to the *Odyssey*, or Pirahã to modern English, the latter cases contain more abstractions, more static concepts, and much greater capacity for talking about and manipulating mental representations that are not present at the moment and may never have been present in perceptual experience. The effect of written language on consciousness was therefore to shift attention from immediate perceptual experience to the processing of words and symbols. As part of this transition, egocentric processing and hence ordinary consciousness became more dominant.

All together, the invention of writing made possible important social, technical, and artistic developments, but there was a price to pay—people began to experience the constraints of ordinary consciousness more poignantly. They were also, however, now able to think and talk about what they were experiencing, which introduced a radically new variable into the equation.

Gautama's Insight

Gautama lived from approximately 480 to 400 B.C.E., and although the linguistic record for the area where he grew up is sketchy, there is evidence of written language existing in the Indus Valley much earlier.[33] Therefore, it is reasonable to assume that the language(s) he used and thought with had undergone the postliterate transition just discussed. At any rate, Gautama came to realize, from his own personal experience, that ordinary consciousness necessarily and unavoidably involves *dukkha*, a term that has been variously translated as suffering, discomfort, anxiety, or dissatisfaction. This realization had doubtless occurred to other people, but the use Gautama made of it in his teaching has influenced history ever since. Now, along with the advantages stemming from further development of ordinary consciousness, we have increasing levels of *dukkha*, with which we are still struggling. The rest of this chapter will look at how people and cultures have tried to deal with the tension between ordinary consciousness and *dukkha*, so we should start by being clear about what Gautama meant by this term. His words have been analyzed in some complex and elaborate ways, but for present purposes a simple three-category scheme works quite well:

1. Physical *dukkha* includes the suffering and pain associated with giving birth, growing old, being sick or injured, and dying.
2. The *dukkha* of change involves the anxiety or stress of living in times of change, especially change that is uncontrollable and continuous.
3. Existential *dukkha* refers to a basic sense that life, by its very nature, is flawed, imperfect, and meaningless.

The second and third categories are of special interest here.

Following the invention of writing, two responses to the problems of *dukkha* developed that continue to be important forces in the world today. Gautama, of course, perfected the tradition of penetrating ordinary consciousness by awakening from it. His teachings spread across Eurasia, not only in Buddhism but also as influences on Sufism[34] and in turn Christian mystics like Meister Eckhart, Teresa of Avila, and John of the Cross. Even today in Islam, Christianity, and other modern religions we can find (if we look hard enough) hints of the message that awakened consciousness is available to everyone as a natural part of being human, and that there are certain practices and teachings, centered around meditation, that can be used to experience it within oneself.

At about the same time that Gautama was spreading his teaching throughout northern India, the Golden Age of Greece was in bloom, and Socrates was wandering around Athens asking people questions, using rational inquiry to probe deeper and deeper below the surface of what had always been taken for granted. He was certainly not the only Greek philosopher to use language and rational inquiry as a mechanism for penetrating social reality. But while other Greeks were questioning traditional explanations for why things are the way they are in the physical world, Socrates turned his inquiry to the very heart of existential *dukkha*, the nature of the social self. As Paul Johnson emphasizes in his recent biography, Socrates concentrated especially on "the internal world of man," that is, the nature of the self, saying, for example, "I know you won't believe me, but the highest form of Human Excellence is to question oneself and others."[35] Questioning of this sort can, of course, disturb people as well as enlighten them, and eventually got Socrates sentenced to die by drinking poison hemlock (which illustrates how sacred and psychologically essential social reality has always been). But killing people seldom prevents the questions they are asking from spreading.

Rational inquiry into the nature of the self was not confined to Greece. Even before Socrates was making trouble in Athens, Gautama could draw on thriving traditions of rational inquiry into the self in South Asia. This shows strongly in some of the practices taught by Gautama for achieving nonattachment, for example meditating on the question, "Who am I?" But Greek philosophers probably had more direct influence on intellectual developments in Europe and their fruition in the Age of Reason and Kant's celebration of enlightenment. These developments have changed the world drastically in the past few centuries.

The growing use of language not only to construct social reality but also to question it led in two directions. By questioning what we know about the physical world, the scientific revolution in particular gave rise to the tremendous explosion of innovation that has raised our standard of living so dramatically. This has prolonged life expectancies (the average Pirahã lives forty-five years; the average American lives about seventy-eight years). It has probably also reduced the amount of physical *dukkha* the average person suffers. But the dramatic and accelerating transformation of social life instigated by technology and science has not been good for those who suffer from the *dukkha* of change. Furthermore, the kind of questioning of the self that Socrates encouraged has made it almost fashionable today to suffer from existential *dukkha*. Because of these changes, the world we live in is fundamentally unlike anything that existed previously. At its core is a kind of crisis of consciousness, in which social realities are proliferating but at the same time fragmenting and being torn apart. Understanding ordinary consciousness as it exists in all these forms has become a very challenging task.

Ordinary Consciousness in Modern Society

When I was a young professor in the sociology department at UCLA, another young professor in that department was Anthony Giddens. We talked; had dinner together once or twice, with our first wives; but never got too close, perhaps because he was working in the classical tradition of social theory and I was trying to do something with mathematical sociology. And then we went our ways. As I was preparing this chapter, however, and looking for relevant material, I finally read his *Modernity and Self-Identity: Self and Society in the Late Modern Age*.[36] I had read and benefited from several of his other books through the years, but Tony has been as prolific as I have not, and although *Modernity* was published in 1991, I took it up fresh twenty years later. The reason I go into all this is that although he and I came to the problems of modern consciousness from very different directions, in a rather amazing way we ended up with the same conclusions. After working through all the steps described earlier in this book and following the evolutionary sequence presented in chapter 14, it was as though when I finally arrived at modern society I found him already sitting there, saying much the same thing. This was so wonderful! Two people working on the same problem from different starting points but coming up with very similar answers. Not exactly the same, but definitely mutually validating. In this section I examine the convergence.

Giddens begins with the "extreme dynamism" of the modern world. "The modern world is a 'runaway world': not only is the *pace* of social change much faster than in any prior system, so also its *scope*, and the *profoundness* with which it affects pre-existing social practices and modes of behavior." If radical and accelerating social change is the central force in modern society, then Gautama's insight predicts it will be accompanied by increases in *dukkha*. Giddens uses other words, of course, but his logic is the same. *Dukkha* occurs when social reality is threatened, in this case because it no longer fits well enough with the changes that are taking place to provide people with satisfactory explanations and meaning. In Giddens' terms, shared trust in social reality is crucial because it provides "the main emotional support of a defensive carapace or protective cocoon which all normal individuals carry around with them as the means whereby they are able to get on with the affairs of day-to-day life."³⁷ Having that way of life threatened opens the door to *dukkha*: "On the other side of what might appear to be quite trivial aspects of day-to-day action and discourse, chaos lurks. And this chaos is not just disorganization, but the loss of a sense of the very reality of things and of other persons."³⁸

Society today is changing faster and at deeper levels than efforts to patch up social reality can keep pace with. Social reality gets updated over generations, while society is now being transformed radically within individual lifetimes. This is why, in today's world, the social reality of each new generation tends to be so different from the social reality of their parents (or for that matter, the social reality of their children, who have grown up taking for granted the extension of full human rights to racial minorities, women, and homosexuals; sexual permissiveness; and widespread questioning of religious beliefs and the effectiveness of drug laws).

As social change disturbs, twists around, and rips up the fabric of social reality, shared trust that we know what is really real is weakened. People become more and more vulnerable not only to the *dukkha* of change but also to existential *dukkha*, in which all aspects of life begin to seem inauthentic. When the taken-for-granted nature of social reality is itself called into question, the foundation that makes it possible to feel in touch with something real can disappear very quickly. Giddens calls this "ontological insecurity," which is the perfect phrase. So the dynamism of modern society unavoidably, as an unintended by-product of both material and intellectual progress, threatens our sense that life is real and has purpose by introducing doubt about social reality.

If the runaway pace of social and cultural change causes increased *dukkha*, then we must move back a causal link and ask what is responsible for the accelerating dynamism of modern society. I have already pointed toward Socrates and his friends, but Giddens has a more subtle analysis. He develops the concept of "institutionalized reflexivity," by which he means that questioning existing ideas has moved from being something the occasional philosophically inclined individual does to an accepted and encouraged social value. The questioning could involve looking for more cost-effective ways to increase widget production, or it could open a debate on the validity of religious beliefs. The important point is that when it becomes institutionalized, questioning social reality becomes an integral part of social reality itself. Today, Socrates' "methodological principle of doubt" and the tradition of rational inquiry following from it are more likely to earn people status and prestige than to get them executed.

To summarize Giddens' thinking in my terminology, the tradition of penetrating ordinary consciousness by questioning social reality has, in the modern world, greatly accelerated social change. This threatens and disrupts social realities, which in turn increases the incidence and severity of *dukkha*. In particular, by eroding the foundations of ontological security, the institutionalization of questioning has caused widespread increases in existential *dukkha*. So the next question becomes, How are people in modern societies responding to the increases in *dukkha* they are experiencing? What happens in a world that, directly or indirectly, encourages radical doubt about social reality? What do people do when the solidity of what they experience as reality develops fissures? How do they try to protect themselves from what Giddens calls "the looming threat of personal meaninglessness"?[39]

The first line of defense is to block out doubt. This can be attempted with drugs, alcohol, or other addictions and compulsions. For other people, the threat of personal meaninglessness seems to be held at bay by the demanding pressures of day-to-day activities—trying to keep up with work and routine tasks, planning for and worrying about day-to-day events. Giddens notes that concentration on the details of everyday activities can substitute for meaningful explanations why we are doing them.

A second strategy involves learning to tolerate the ambiguity that threatens ontological security.[40] One may undergo psychotherapy and work on personal problems like depression, anxiety, or anger. One might take lessons from the wisdom of the ages or from current research on happiness[41] and work to deepen and expand relations with family and friends, to emphasize helping others rather than paying so much attention to oneself, and to limit one's desires to modest and attainable gratifications. These are all good things, encouraged by all world religions and certainly in line with Buddhist training. However they do it, more and more people seem to have learned to tolerate ambiguity, to accept mystery and randomness and find pleasure in actively questioning reality.

Third, if the first two strategies don't work, one can try to deal with *dukkha* in the same way that one can react to a shoe that doesn't fit: try to find another that fits better, a social reality that replaces ambiguity and meaninglessness with explanations that feel solid and authentic. Given the diversity of modern society, one can look for a social group that offers both a more congenial version of reality and emotional support from its members. Giddens notes as a prominent feature of modernity "a burgeoning preoccupation with the reconstruction of tradition to cope with the changing demands of modern and social conditions"[42] (and he wrote this before the Tea Party appeared on the American scene). Looking back to a mythical past may add legitimacy to a social reality that tries to copy it. Today an amazing variety of social realities are available, and people can shop around for one they like.[43] As a very important example of this, Giddens discusses religious belief systems:

> Religious symbols and practices are not only residues from the past; a revival of religious or, more broadly, spiritual, concerns seems fairly widespread in modern societies. Why should this be? . . . The reasons concern quite fundamental features of late modernity. What was [expected] to become a social and physical universe subject to increasingly certain knowledge and control instead creates a system in which areas of relative security interlace with radical doubt and with disquieting scenarios of risk. Religion in some part generates the conviction which adherence to the tenets of modernity must necessarily suspend: in this regard it is easy to see why religious fundamentalism has a special appeal. But this is not all. New forms of religion and spirituality represent in a most basic sense a return of the repressed, since they directly address issues of the moral meaning of existence which modern institutions so thoroughly tend to dissolve.[44]

Changes in Religious Affiliation as Attempts to Reduce *Dukkha*

Religious belief systems can provide a version of social reality that allows people to make sense of their lives and feel that their lives are worthwhile. Religious groups also provide social support for holding those beliefs. There are many religious belief systems and groups today, and quite a lot of movement among them. Best of all, for a sociologist, there are data on what has been happening in the religious marketplace. In 2007 the Pew Research Center surveyed more than 35,000 adult Americans, asking them about both their current religious affiliation and the religion in which they were raised.[45] At the time of the survey the respondents' average age was 52, so the data show changes in religious choice over at least a full generation. A rather substantial 42 percent had moved to a different religious category from the one in which they were raised. The guiding hypothesis is that because of rapid social change, the social reality offered by the religion these people grew up in no longer fit the lives they were experiencing as adults. This produced *dukkha*, which they then tried to resolve by moving to a new religious category.

TABLE 16.1

Changes in religious affiliation from childhood to middle age

(percent of total sample identifying as affiliated with each religious category)

	Current religious category	Childhood religious category	Change from childhood to current
Evangelical Protestant	34.2	31.0	3.2
Mainline Protestant	22.6	27.3	−4.7
Catholic	25.1	32.3	−7.2
Jewish	2.1	2.4	−0.3
Liberal religion	34.2	31.0	3.2
Atheist or agnostic	22.6	27.3	−4.7
"Nothing in particular"	25.1	32.3	−7.2
Buddhist	2.1	2.4	−0.3
Total	100.0	100.0	

Source: Pew Research Center survey of 32,004 Americans, 2007

Table 16.1 summarizes patterns of change in religious affiliation by starting with the present distribution of American adults across nine religious categories and comparing their current category with the one they were brought up in as children. Children are typically raised in the religious category of their parents, so the table says that a generation ago, when they were children, 31 percent of the population attended evangelical Protestant churches while 60 percent attended either mainline Protestant or Roman Catholic churches. I want to focus for now on the latter group, because these are the religious categories that people left when they grew up—combined, the percentage of Americans attending these churches dropped from 60 to 48 percent. In one generation, something on the order of 42 million people who had been brought up in mainline Protestant or Roman Catholic churches moved to other religious categories.[46] I interpret this exodus to mean that for many of the people who were born into them, the social reality proclaimed by these traditional religions no longer supported their life experience and no longer provided security against *dukkha*.

Where did these people go? There are three patterns. First, there was a net increase of 3.2 percent in the evangelical Protestant category. Evangelical churches usually emphasize traditional beliefs and collective expression of spiritual experience, and in line with this, 60 percent of evangelical respondents said they believed that the Bible is the word of God and should be taken literally, word for word. This compares with 27 percent of mainline Protestants and 21 percent of Roman Catholics, who shared the fundamentalist belief in biblical literalism. So this pattern fits the prediction that one way to resolve the *dukkha* of modern society is to move to a religion that provides both a traditional belief system and strong group support.[47]

Second, some people dealt with a social reality that no longer felt real by moving in the opposite direction, either choosing a religion that put less emphasis on traditional beliefs or withdrawing from organized religion entirely. Overall, 10.2 percent of the Pew sample moved in this direction. This included 1.3 percent moving to a more liberal religion and 3.5 percent becoming atheists or agnostics. The largest increase, 5.4 percent, was among people who withdrew from organized religion without declaring their present orientation—the people Pew lumped together as saying, "Nothing in particular."

Third, the only category in the survey that represents the tradition of transcending social reality by moving toward awakened consciousness is Buddhism. The number of respondents who identified as Buddhists was small (1.3 percent) but it had more than doubled in size. Furthermore, the great majority of Buddhists today (76 percent) were raised in another religious category, which is a dramatic inflow. So while the numbers are small, they suggest an increased interest in the possibility that Buddhism holds out for relieving *dukkha* by transcending it. Furthermore, Buddhists are not the only people who engage in practices like meditation. In a large and well-designed survey by NIH in 2007, 9.4 percent of American adults said they had engaged in some form of meditation in the past 12 months, up from 7.6 percent in 2002.[48] It appears that reasonably large and growing numbers of people are pursuing approaches to *dukkha* reduction that involve alternatives to religious belief systems.

Overall, then, the Pew data support Giddens' theory and also my version, *dukkha* reduction theory. When their social reality is threatened, people seek to change by reasserting (and if necessary reinventing) a more traditional social reality; minimizing their present social reality by questioning it and learning to tolerate ambiguity; or seeking to transcend it by pursuing a path like that offered by Buddhism.

What Lies Ahead for Awakened Consciousness?

To answer this question, we must start by looking more broadly at the responses to ordinary consciousness that dominate American society today and extrapolate from them to predict the future. As table 16.1 indicates, dynamism rules in America, with multiple versions of social reality being asserted and questioned and competing responses to *dukkha* prominently visible in patterns of changing religious affiliation. The next step is to look at patterns of change in areas other than religion that also suggest responses to *dukkha* reduction, and then consider how these broader patterns might affect the future of awakened consciousness.

In a democratic society elections really can make a difference, and the way Americans vote is fairly strongly associated with their response to *dukkha*. In the 2012 presidential election, 79 percent of white evangelical Christians voted for the conservative candidate, Mitt Romney. White non-evangelical Christians also voted for Romney, but by a smaller margin (57 percent). Meanwhile, 70 percent of the religiously unaffiliated and 73 percent of those affiliated with non-Christian religions (including Buddhists) voted for Barack Obama. None of these percentages changed much over the past four presidential elections—the political preferences of people in these four religious groups seem to have been fairly stable. What has changed, as the table indicates, is the number of voters in each group. The largest group, white nonevangelical Christians, diminished substantially as members moved to other religious categories. Some became evangelical Christians, but more moved into the unaffiliated or non-Christian categories, and the increased numbers of unaffiliated and non-Christian voters provided enough votes for Obama in 2012 to more than offset the white evangelical vote for Romney.[49] When these votes were combined with the strong pro-Obama vote of Hispanics, blacks, and other minority groups, the presidential election was decided for the Democratic candidate. The important lesson is that the growing numbers of people who left traditional American religion had a significant impact on whether their government would move in a conservative or progressive direction. So responses to *dukkha* may have become a significant factor in American politics.

This can be carried a little further. Quite a large body of research has been studying the personality traits of political conservatives, with the consistent finding that conservatives are somewhat more fearful and anxious than liberals, significantly less tolerant of ambiguity,[50] less open and curious,[51] and likely to prefer quick answers to thinking issues through carefully.[52] All of which says that political conservatives experience more *dukkha* than other voters in times of change, and that they like the clear-cut answers to life's important questions that a traditional (and unquestioned) social reality can provide. In this way political conservatism both correlates with and resembles the thought processes of religious fundamentalism—both seem to offer a safe haven from the anxieties and ambiguities of social change.

However, there is a twist. Conservative political ideology, certainly in America today, also opposes government programs that seek to help the poor—in fact, there has been a marked increase in inequality over recent decades as intense efforts by conservatives have stalled or turned back progressive political action. In the long run, this will directly affect the growth of Buddhism and similar programs, because so far in the West people attracted to Buddhism have come almost entirely from the economically secure and well-educated portions of society. Given the demands of the Buddhist path as described in this book, it is almost certain that even marginally poor people will be much more concerned about food and shelter than about ontological security. While taking Buddhism to the poor should certainly be encouraged, it would also be helpful to reduce inequality and thus produce a larger pool of potential recruits. I doubt that Buddhism or similar approaches to awakened consciousness are even on the radar of conservative leaders right now; it is nevertheless true that political conservatism de facto puts limits on the potential spread of awakened consciousness by trying to keep poor people poor and working-class people threatened by declining numbers of steady, decently paying jobs. So the relation between *dukkha* and politics may translate into whether the kind of society we live in is compassionate, and along with this, whether it encourages interest in awakened consciousness.

Another important feature of conservatism today is science denial[53]—Republicans are much more likely to deny evolution, climate change, scientific economics, and even scientifically designed opinion polling than are Democrats or other liberals.[54] Science denial is doubtless derived from the centuries-old American tradition of anti-intellectualism,[55] but it has reached such a strong force that Republican politicians know they cannot be supported by their base unless they oppose science. If political conservatism is a reaction to the *dukkha* produced by change, science denial is a reaction to the *dukkha* produced by questioning traditional beliefs. When science says that a religious belief is not true, denying the validity of the science is one way to protect traditional beliefs. But children are taught in public schools that science is good, that science is a valued part of modern social reality. So to really get to the core of the *dukkha* produced by questioning, science deniers work also to weaken education, particularly the teaching of science. One leading Republican politician, Senator Marco Rubio, has admitted that the problem with teaching science in school is that it tends to undermine children's faith in what their parents have told them to believe.[56]

While the overall effect of science denial is to weaken the impact of questioning and thus protect traditional social reality, specific types of science denial have their own interesting qualities. Evolution is the mother of all scientific targets for denial because it rejects the origin myth of traditional Christianity. Climate science, which like evolution theory is based on complex analysis that is difficult to test experimentally, threatens both the corporate owners and the employees of traditional extractive industries. Threat brings with it fear, and one way to block out fear is to deny that the threat is true. Furthermore, if the predictions of climate science about global warming were accepted, the conservation measures necessary to control carbon emissions would require people to change some comfortable habits. Finally, denial of scientific economics serves to keep the economy operating below capacity much of the time, which creates more unemployment and more poverty and reinforces the strong trend over recent decades toward increased inequality. Keeping poor people poor means keeping them focused on the *dukkha* of survival and shut off from the luxury of pursuing awakened consciousness.

Denial of scientific economics also illustrates the tendency of people holding on to traditional social realities to avoid issues that require complex thinking. Although the predictions have essentially been proven, the analysis is technical and applies to fairly long time periods. Rather than pay attention to this body of theory and research, people feel more comfortable with folk beliefs about how national economic systems work, especially when these folk beliefs are part of a traditional social reality that is supported by conservative political and religious organizations.

Public opinion sampling provides an interesting contrast, because it can be tested in the short run and almost always makes valid predictions. So denying the science of opinion sampling can be hazardous, as Republicans found in the 2012 election. Most polls consistently forecast victory by Obama, but Republicans apparently felt confident in their ability to dispose of disagreeable predictions by denying the science they were based on.

Right up to the final day of polling they predicted victory for Romney, and when he lost by a substantial margin they were apparently flabbergasted.[57] But four months later, as I wrote this, a news report appeared saying that Republicans were now denying the validity of polls showing that the American public had swung markedly to support of gay marriage.[58] The lesson here is that for some people, clinging to a social reality is so deeply rooted that even facts can no longer affect it.

And that is where we seem to be today. Life in ordinary consciousness always brings with it some *dukkha*—that is the human condition—and as long we remain encapsulated in symbolic reality, there are dimensions of reality that we cannot know. Awakened consciousness, as far as I can see at this point in my investigation, cannot escape the *dukkha* of sickness, injury, and death, to ourselves, to our loved ones, to all people on the planet. The *dukkha* of change, I cannot really comment on—I have always liked change. But for existential *dukkha*, which can be experienced as a persistent itch or an agonizing problem, awakening offers a door to new worlds. *Dukkha* therefore provides an invitation to open the door and walk through. The truly existential question then becomes, When do we recognize our condition for what it is? We answer this question with our lives, on a scale from "very early" to "never."

No one seems to know why people react in different ways to the presence of *dukkha*. In about 1930, a British doctor, working in a traditional village in the Atlas Mountains, got to know the Sufi Master Ahmad Al-Alawi, who stated the situation beautifully but offered no explanation: "Some people are set at rest by very little; others find their satisfaction in religion; some require more. It is not just peace of mind they must have, but the great Peace, which brings with it the plentitude of the Spirit."[59]

The next, and concluding, chapter will summarize a bit more formally what has been said so far about awakened consciousness.

17
Modeling Consciousness, Awakened and Ordinary

The book has looked at awakening from several different perspectives, so there is quite a bit of material out on the table. This chapter reviews that material and tries to organize it more compactly as a working model that can account for both ordinary and awakened consciousness. My intention is to drive home, by expressing it in the contemporary language of cognitive and social science, the fundamental insight of all people who have experienced awakening: that awakened consciousness is a real, natural, and physical possibility for all human beings. The biological and cognitive potentials necessary for realizing it are there right now, built into all of us and waiting to be used. Without the perspective that awakened awareness provides, humans bumble along in a world of distortions and representations—of shadows, as Plato would say. It is my hope that science can help a little bit by making clear that awakened consciousness is just a different way of using the same human potentials that produce ordinary consciousness.

The Basic Model

Human consciousness is sometimes defined as awareness that we are experiencing awareness.[1] All noncomatose humans report having this experience, so it sets up a good goal for neuroscientists who want to understand how the brain produces consciousness. If the goal is to understand how and why the contents of consciousness vary, however, it is not very useful. To understand the similarities and differences between ordinary and awakened consciousness, we need a model that shows how both forms can exist

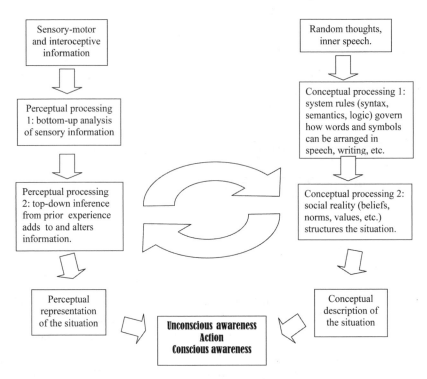

FIGURE 17.1 The processes that produce awareness work to adjust and reconcile perceptual and conceptual representations.

in the same human body, even if only one is active at any given time. Figure 17.1 offers a brief summary of what I take to be general agreement on the basic factors involved in shaping the contents and quality of each moment of consciousness. If some parts of this model look a bit odd, it is because a few things had to be altered in order to include awakened consciousness.[2]

The model begins by assuming that awareness is shaped by both perception and conception, where perception works with external and internal sensory information and conception works with symbols (especially language). In figure 17.1, perceptual processing I follows rules that analyze sensory inputs and shape them into the percepts or perceptual representations that appear in awareness. Conceptual processing I also follows rules, which in this case arrange words (or other symbols) into the sentences that we hear as inner speech. Perceptual and conceptual processing usually go on at the same time, and they interact. As thousands of priming experiments show, while perceptual processing is busy identifying percepts, words that are associated with the percepts are activated and organized. So perception and conception affect each other, even at this early stage.

But bottom-up processing, as this is called, is only the first step toward producing what will appear in awareness. Sensory information is often incomplete, as when one figure in an image is partly obscured by another. Perceptual processing II tries to fill in the missing information by generating completed percepts that are consistent with previous experience (top-down processing). Sometimes this "guessing" can create optical illusions (i.e., errors), but most of the time it is useful.[3] Conceptual processing II works in the same way but even more powerfully, by trying to make both percepts and words consistent with previous experience (especially with the beliefs, norms, customs, and values of social reality). For example, when shown a picture of a multiracial situation on a bus in which a man (who is white) holds a knife in his hand, many respondents later put the knife in the hand of a black man. Eyewitness reports from people who all see the same live incident vary in the same way—awareness is shaped by what we expect to see.

As a result, while we can think hypothetically about perceptual processing producing a "pure" perceptual representation of a situation or conceptual processing producing an "accurate" description of the situation, in fact the two usually interact and are shaped by previous experience all along the way. And as W. I. Thomas pointed out almost a hundred years ago, when we define a situation a certain way, it is real in its consequences.[4] We are perceiving, conceiving, and translating back and forth between the two continuously. Chomsky refers to this as mental activity across two interfaces, the sensory-motor interface and the conceptual-intentional interface.[5]

Before applying the model to ordinary and awakened consciousness specifically, three of its properties should be highlighted. First, the processing it describes is generative, continuously producing fresh versions of awareness from available materials. Second, both perceptual and symbolic processing attempt to maintain consistency among previous experience, incoming sensory information, and conceptual systems like social reality. Third, almost all of the processing shown in figure 17.1 is unconscious. Usually, as the research stemming from Libet's work has shown, unconscious awareness is generated first; it is expressed very quickly in action, and only an instant or so later experienced in conscious awareness. So in the model of consciousness used here, almost everything that goes on is unconscious. That doesn't make conscious awareness unimportant, but relations between the two kinds of awareness deserve a little more discussion.

The prototype example of unconscious awareness is blindsight, in which people who are not consciously aware of seeing anything neverthe-less show by their actions that their brains have carried visual processing to the point where it works perfectly for guiding action but does not enter conscious awareness, due to trauma.[6] I don't know what the experience of blindsight feels like, but I assume that these people are aware that they are aware because their proprioceptive senses tell them that they have success-fully navigated. They are probably also relieved to find out, conceptually, just what causes their condition. This conceptual information would affect their conscious awareness of what they are doing and how they live. The important point is that unconscious perceptual awareness, with or without conscious conceptual awareness, qualifies as a form of consciousness. Ani-mals seem to get by quite well with little or no conceptual awareness, so the argument can be made that animals qualify for consciousness on the basis of unconscious awareness alone. For most of our waking hours we humans could probably also get along just fine in the same way.

Now to apply the model to how ordinary and awakened consciousness operate to carry out important mental functions.

Generating Ordinary and Awakened Awareness

Ordinary conscious awareness is generated when a perceptual representa-tion is modified to be consistent with the conceptual system. In the case of language, the processing also tries to organize representations into a coherent narrative, a story that is consistent with the person's social real-ity, explains what is going on in a situation, and prescribes behavior. Often the story features adventures of the social self in a world defined by social reality. It has a past that the person can enjoy or resent and a future to plan for or worry about. Unconscious processing will try to generate a story that favors the self and is faithful to the person's social reality, even if that requires distorting the immediate situation as represented perceptually.

Carrying out all this symbolic processing requires considerable effort, and that is over and above the processing necessary to generate the initial perceptual representation. In psychology the concept "cognitive load"[7] posits limits on how much processing the brain can engage in at any given time. It seems likely that as the effort devoted to conceptual processing increases, the amount of activity available for perceptual processing will diminish. This would explain the experience, often reported by meditators (see chapter 13), that as their minds become quieter the world around them becomes brighter and more vivid. The implication is that without the burden of symbolic processing (especially the chattering of inner speech that goes on continuously), our conscious awareness of perceptual representations will seem clearer and more vivid.

So far, then, we have two important ways conceptual processing can modify a perceptual representation. First, it can alter the contents and structure of perception to better fit the contents and structure of the symbol system (especially as symbolic information becomes reified into social reality and the self). Second, due to the additional processing demands, it can make the perceptual image available in conscious awareness appear somewhat washed out, less vivid.

There may be a third effect, however, which involves the property of awakening identified in chapter 13 as no separation. As a three-dimensional perceptual image is translated into words to form the linear, one-dimensional sentences of a story, awareness almost necessarily narrows to focus on the actor as protagonist.[8] The remaining dimension, time, is forced to express events from what Austin calls an egocentric perspective,[9] which then becomes the natural way to organize awareness. Through the ages, people have tried to make up for this limitation of egocentric awareness by finding ways to experience action as an organic part of a group rather than as a separated individual. The examples I can think of are nonverbal and involve closely interacting ensembles, such as jazz groups, basketball teams, and improvisational theater groups doing Grotowski exercises.

My argument is that these three features of ordinary awareness occur especially when conceptual processing imposes language on perceptual representations. The task now is to account for why these features do not occur in awakened awareness. A good way to start is to consider some examples identified earlier in which, because the creature in question shows no indication of possessing language, it seems likely that no symbolic processing takes place.

First, animals. Given that all known animal communication systems are severely limited compared with human language, it seems likely that animals operate solely on the basis of perceptual representations[10] (see chapter 14). Of course, we don't really know what their awareness is like because they can't tell us.

Second, babies. As we saw in chapter 15, they show many of the behaviors associated with awakened consciousness. The reasonable assumption is that conceptual processing begins as infants learn to talk; prior to this, babies' awareness must depend on perceptual representations.[11] As the behavior of babies is studied more and more closely, the findings suggest that evidence of awakened consciousness gradually disappears as the child learns language.[12]

Third, the case of Jill Bolte Taylor. A stroke that temporarily eliminated all language processing left her able to function on the basis of perceptual processing. After she regained language capabilities, her descriptions of the awareness she experienced during the stroke were remarkably similar to the descriptions of awakening studied in chapter 13.

In all three cases, since language does not exist, there is the possibility that "pure" perceptual representations, unmodified by symbolic processing, provide the contents for awareness. What about adult humans, for example, those interviewed for this book, who have worked to quiet their minds of inner speaking[13] and let go of attachments to symbolic representations? These people have not lost the ability to speak or comprehend language, and they have intact working memories with extensive stores of symbolically represented information. There is no physical reason their awareness would be restricted to perceptual representations. So what exactly is the role of language and conceptual processing in their awareness?

To explore this question, consider the following comments by Jack Kornfield: he gives a beautiful description of perceptual reality, beginning with its pervasive silence:

> It is not that there are never any thoughts, but for the most part it becomes really silent. It is like going from the windswept, weather-filled atmosphere, getting to the surface of the ocean and then dropping down below the level of the water, like a scuba diver, into a completely silent and different dimension. While there are some reflections that might go by, it is a completely different state of consciousness. . . . Whatever you call it, there is something in the psyche, in the greater consciousness, that knows these states and this terrain. And when the mind is deeply concentrated and open, and resolutions are made, magic happens. And of course, this can lead to the highest magic of all, as the Buddha said, the magic of the wisdom that liberates the heart.[14]

I interpret this quote to say that silencing the mind of inner speaking allows one to settle into a conscious awareness of the moment that is informed only by perceptual representations. When this is achieved, magic happens: awareness changes drastically. However, there can still be some contact with language—Kornfield notes that "some reflections" may go by. I take this to mean that unconscious processing continues during awakening and may involve symbols. The purest instance I know of personally occurred roughly ten seconds into my major awakening experience. A voice in my mind (my voice) said, "So this is what they mean by nothing-ness—no social reality." The voice was not quite accurate—I still knew all about social reality, but the reification and attachment had vanished.[15] In spite of the slight misstatement, however, this was a valuable insight that had never before occurred to me. As the experience went on, additional inner comments arose occasionally, but mostly all was quiet.

Therefore, I conclude that awakened awareness has its base in percep-tual reality. Subjectively, perceptual experience with no conceptual activity going on in conscious awareness feels like the world just the way it is, noth-ing added. Symbolically coded information is available, but social reality and the social self are viewed objectively, almost dispassionately.

Earlier I proposed three ways conceptual processing alters perceptual representations during ordinary awareness. Now we have their opposites, three ways in which, during awakened awareness, perceptual reality is pro-tected from the effects of conceptual processing. First, perceptual represen-tations are not altered to fit social reality, because without reification there is no latent feeling that social reality and the symbolically represented self are "true."[16] Second, the vivid image quality of pure perceptual awareness is no longer diluted by the cognitive load required for conceptual process-ing. Third, because three-dimensional perceptual reality is not translated into one-dimensional language, the allocentric perspective can continue to dominate over an egocentric perspective. The world is organized just the way human perceptual processing presents it, with no dramatic storylines and no self to struggle through them.

If my conclusion is correct, then we have some interesting questions for neuroscience research to investigate. If the brain is switching between neural systems, what are those systems and how do they work? The differ-ences between ordinary and awakened awareness proposed here fit nicely with Austin's distinction between egocentric and allocentric neural sys-tems, so his work provides important suggestions for research. In particu-lar, he identifies a dorsal cortical system as being responsible for egocentric processing and a ventral system for allocentric processing.[17] He points to research on the default network[18] as being heavily implicated with self, and suggests that specific nuclei of the thalamus play a key role in allowing a switch from egocentric to allocentric processing. All that is left is determin-ing exactly what the de-reification network is and how it works. Somehow things happen, probably in the brain, that allow one to sit (stand, walk, live one's life) with an awareness firmly, peacefully, and silently based on pure perceptual reality. Then everything is just deliciously the way it is, and one feels no more important than any other thing or person.

Emotions and Feelings

There are hundreds, probably thousands, of words available to denote the various emotions experienced in ordinary consciousness. But what about awakened consciousness? Did the Buddha experience emotional states other than equanimity and compassion? In the most serious effort I know of to uncover Gautama as a flesh-and-blood person, Stephen Batchelor concludes that he certainly knew about, and had to deal with in himself, a wide range of familiar emotions.[19] Being familiar with them doesn't mean being at their mercy, of course, so the project now is to understand the role of emotions and feelings in ordinary and awakened consciousness.

First, some definitions. Damasio and Carvalho identify emotions with action sequences that our bodies engage in and our minds think about.[20] Emotions are thus cued by our perceived relationship with the external environment, while feelings are interoceptive experiences that tell us what is going on in our bodies.[21] Extending this definition to ordinary consciousness, emotions are usually triggered by stories or scripts activated by the conceptual system to frame our awareness of the moment. Socially appropriate emotions are coded into the story. We learn both the basic storyline and the emotional reactions that are expected to accompany it during childhood, so most of the time we react the way we have been programmed to react when we encounter (or think about) a situation that fits the operative storyline. Social reality therefore plays a large role in emotion, and to a considerable extent, during ordinary consciousness we experience emotionally what the drama generated by our conceptual system tells us we should experience.

Then what about awakened consciousness? If the contents of social reality are viewed objectively, not from the perspective of the social self as a subject in that reality, the experience might be compared with playing a role in a play but knowing that it is just pretend. Without reification, we have removed the linchpin that connects situations and action sequences with emotional responses. Without a social self struggling along in the storyline provided by social reality, whatever happens in a situation happens, and that is just the way the world is. But this takes us back to the previous question. If letting go of the perspective of the self living in social reality is the essence of awakening and emotions are no longer triggered by the script being followed, what can be said about feelings?

One way to answer is to return to the discussion of animals in chapter 14. Whether animals experience what we call emotions is controversial, but there seems to be general agreement that even quite primitive species possess a basic core of feelings. These certainly survive in humans, so we can use them to narrow the question: Do people react emotionally during awakened consciousness in the same way they do during ordinary consciousness to situations associated with fleeing, fighting, feeding, or sex? Maybe there is not so much difference. If danger threatens, why not flee? If someone attacks a child, why not try to fight the attacker off? If awakened people go without eating for some time, they presumably experience hunger just as ordinary people do. And as for sex, the lesson of chapter 13 was that awakened people can certainly experience arousal.[22] Whether these immediate reactions should be called emotions or feelings is of course an open question. But it seems that awakened consciousness does not react with the full repertoire of emotions to the scripts that add drama to a situation.

Thinking

Chapter 14 argued that what eventually separated humans from other animals during the course of evolution was an improved capacity to make available during unconscious processing percepts and symbols that refer to phenomena not present in the immediate situation. Early *Homo* species used this capacity to invent language and to include both percepts and symbols in the processing leading to unconscious awareness—that is, to do what we call thinking. So the question to be addressed now is, What is thinking like in ordinary and in awakened consciousness?

Holding the contents of conscious awareness steady for even a moment ("paying attention" to the contents of awareness) introduces feedback in which the contents of consciousness become sensory and conceptual input for a new cycle of processing and awareness. The brain examines the contents of conscious awareness and, following its normal course of activity, generates new awareness and action (see figure 17.1). The contents of conscious awareness thus become part of the information that unconscious processing processes, rather like looking in a mirror. This ability to respond to conscious awareness as new input allows the unconscious part of the brain to talk to itself. It also allows us to meditate, by keeping our attention focused on perceptual rather than conceptual awareness. And especially, it makes possible the achievement of which our species is most proud—reflective thinking.

In order to use conscious awareness effectively, we therefore need to draw on and develop further our capacity for attention, which allows us to control the contents of conscious awareness. For example, we can direct the focus of our attention by zooming in or out on current perceptual inputs, by emphasizing verbal thoughts rather than percepts (or vice versa), by letting memories or new thoughts be inserted into the display or blocking them out. We can allow free association in response to the display or require a tight focus on following familiar logical steps to solve a problem. These dynamics show up very clearly in Daniel Kahneman's masterful *Thinking Fast and Slow.*

Kahneman uses the term "fast thinking" to refer to cases in which unconscious processing responds to a situation by acting on it immediately and conscious awareness simply shows the resulting thought or action.[23] The decision may involve language, as when we say something spontaneously without pausing for a moment to reflect on it (to "think before we speak"). What we say may be brilliant and perfectly appropriate, or embarrassingly stupid—fast thinking can go either way. Fast thinking works better when attention is focused on the moment and our minds are free of distractions, as when Olympic athletes visualize their routine before beginning their actual event. When attention is focused and distracting thoughts are no longer present, optimal action is possible. At this level, fast thinking can approximate the third property of awakened consciousness, "not knowing," as discussed in chapter 13.[24]

Kahneman's "slow thinking" takes place when unconscious processing responds to a situation but attention delays action until the recommended action is displayed, examined, and perhaps resubmitted for further processing and new suggestions. Slow thinking imposes a time-out to look for better information or try different procedures, perhaps using rules of logic or math to do some additional calculations and projections.[25] In that mode we can perform many kinds of mental experiments. The important point is that a feedback loop is under way, as a conversation between unconscious processing and conscious awareness (or better, as the reaction of unconscious processing to the reflection it gets from conscious awareness). If examination of that reflection suggests that it might be a good idea to think about it a bit more carefully, then unconscious processing can respond with new contributions, which can in turn be examined. So slow thinking uses unconscious processing to propose solutions and decisions, awareness monitors the thought process and provides reflection, and attention shuts out distractions and maintains the integrity of the display.

From this a major question emerges: Is slow thinking possible while in a state of awakened consciousness? I propose, as hypothesis, that it is not, that awakened consciousness is restricted to fast thinking. The interviews did not go far enough to say much about this, so I am relying on my own experience here. When I am in a mental state that approximates awakened consciousness and I try to think about something carefully, using slow thinking, I quickly find myself switched back into ordinary consciousness. That happens every time I sit down to work on this book. The slow thinking goes well, but returning to awakened consciousness requires concentration and may take a while, depending on how long and how deeply I have been doing the slow thinking. Someone more advanced than I who is firmly rooted in awakened consciousness may be able to do slow thinking without losing his or her grounding in perceptual reality. I hope to pursue this matter further in future research.

By way of summary, I can state the obvious: both fast and slow thinking work better when a high level of attention is maintained,[26] and both are driven by unconscious processing, which never rests. But unless it is controlled by attention, unconscious processing may use its reflection in conscious awareness to carry on more or less random conversations with itself. This is the kind of thing Buddhists call "monkey mind," but to stay within Kahneman's framework I will call it "wandering thinking."[27] Inner conversations can be constructive, and certainly entertaining, but overindulgence in wandering thinking means that conceptual processing strongly dominates perceptual processing. This also means that ordinary awareness is firmly in control.

Meaning

Chapter 16 explored the ancient and modern versions of *dukkha* theory, as exemplified in the thinking of Gautama and Giddens. Life in ordinary consciousness means living within the carapace of symbolic reality, and *dukkha* theory says this experience ranges from dissatisfaction to suffering because ordinary consciousness is inescapably and by definition out of touch with the essence of perceptual reality. First, ordinary awareness must at each moment construct a representation of the world that reconciles social reality with perception. This often requires changing either what our perceptual systems tell us or the definition of the situation that our social reality asserts. If the gap cannot be bridged, the contradictions can be distressing. Second, ordinary consciousness must avoid ambiguity by providing satisfactory explanations why that situation is happening.[28] Both kinds of problems are amplified due to rampant social change and the positive value that social reality now gives to questioning itself.

In both cases, the effect of cracks opening up between perceptual reality and symbolic reality has been to threaten the ability of social reality to provide meaning for life. Efforts to reestablish or rediscover meaning have taken three forms: change social reality so that it better fits what we perceive; cling more strongly to traditional versions of social reality (if necessary, denying the validity of what perceptual experience presents as "facts"); and shore up the social support that makes social reality work. We see all three responses frequently in the world today.

What was only partly discussed in chapter 16, however, is the question of what provides meaning in awakened consciousness. Awakened consciousness is not emotionally concerned about whether the conceptual explanations provided by social reality are satisfying or distressing, because its base is in perceptual reality and scripts generated by social reality are not reified. Instead, meaning is provided by the *feelings* that accompany perceptual experience. Meaning in perceptual reality depends on how the current moment feels, not how its contents are compared with things past, future, or imagined. These feelings (according to Damasio) originate in the brain stem. They come from interoceptive sensory inputs and tell us whether our body is (or is not) all right. I am extending this idea to explain why, in an awakened state, I feel connected in a solid and authentic way with the world around me. Then the world feels good and kind even if bad things are happening at the moment. Those feelings fill life with meaning, so *dukkha* is not a problem. Pat Enkyo O'Hara talks about this as variations on a theme of joy:

> When we think of joy, we think of a buoyant, upward-moving feeling of delight, pleasure, and appreciation. We may associate joy with happy things, with falling in love, or with getting what we want. But actually there is a deeper, more resonant, soulful feeling: the joy of life no matter what the circumstances are. . . . This quality of joy hangs around the edges, allowing you to open yourself to being awake and new with each experience you encounter.[29]

The gulf between meaning provided by the conceptual structures of social reality and meaning provided by this kind of feeling is total, and

TABLE 17.1

Summary of differences between ordinary and awakened consciousness with respect to conscious awareness, emotions and feelings, thinking, and meaning

	Ordinary	*Awakened*
Conscious awareness	The results of perceptual processing are modified to be as consistent as possible with the person's social reality and social (symbolically represented) self. Individuals see the world from an egocentric perspective and experience separation from that world and from other people. Because the amount of symbolic processing required is large, activity devoted to perceptual processing is reduced and the vividness of conscious awareness is diminished.	The results of perceptual processing are not altered by symbolic processing, although the information and expertise encoded in symbolic systems can be accessed objectively (i.e., additively). Individuals see the world from an allo-centric perspective and feel connection with that world and the people around them. Without the intense personal involvement of the social self in the drama and complexity of social reality, more processing time is available for sensory awareness and conscious awareness is more vivid.
Emotions and feelings	Emotions are cued by stories generated by social reality, as learned during childhood. Emotions tend especially to be linked with the self and its adventures in social reality.	Feelings are initiated by interoception, and processed particularly in the brain stem. When there are no attachments to the social self, most of what we usually call emotions do not exist.

(continued on next page)

TABLE 17.1 *(continued)*

	Ordinary	Awakened
Thinking	Kahneman's fast and slow thinking are both available. How well they work depends on attention, which in ordinary consciousness usually requires some effort. Without attention, wandering thinking is the default.	Fast thinking is most developed here and may be the only mode possible. Slow thinking requires holding in conscious awareness symbols (or percepts) that are not present in immediate experience, and wandering thinking allows thoughts to free associate without direction, so both slow and wandering thinking return the thinker to ordinary consciousness.
Meaning, or "ontological security"	In a scientific framework, meaning is supported when the contents of conscious awareness are both logically consistent internally and compatible with perceptual information. One major source of folk meaning comes from shared support within the group for the social reality that shapes conscious awareness. The other source is degree of fit between perception and social reality. To the extent that both degree of fit and social support are low, meaning is threatened or destroyed and the person experiences increased *dukkha*.	Conscious awareness of the perceptual reality of the moment is accompanied by feelings of truth, joy, and authenticity. Perception can be questioned as possible illusion, but that does not throw into doubt feelings that we are a fully connected part of the natural order. Interoception gives rise to primordial feelings based on physical states of our body, some of which (e.g., "happiness," "kindness," "feeling securely grounded") provide meaningfulness of their own.

crossing it can be traumatic for someone on the path to awakening. Several people have told me that at some point they would start feeling rather deep shots of anxiety and find themselves pulling back rather than trying to live mindfully. Letting go of the familiar, ordinary form of meaning and allowing oneself to slide into the other can be a perilous adventure the first time it happens.

Summary of the Model

The question, What is awakening? can now be answered by summarizing each concept as it finds expression in and for ordinary consciousness.

Each row of the table identifies four essential differences between ordinary and awakened consciousness, and for a typical human being living in ordinary consciousness, identifies the changes that must take place in order to move to awakened consciousness. These can be compared with the training practices described by the teachers in their interviews and summarized in chapter 12. For example, to move from ordinary to awakened conscious awareness, one must improve one's capacity for living in perceptual reality by using attention to focus conscious awareness on immediate experience while letting go of conditioned responses to social reality. To move from the emotions of ordinary consciousness to the feelings of awakened consciousness, one must learn to see reactions linked with the social self for what they are (that is, de-reify the self) and focus instead on what the body is feeling. In Kahneman's terms, the cognitive style operative during awakened consciousness is fast thinking. To further develop this capacity, the primary task is to move attention to perceptual reality and away from wandering thinking. Finally, one must learn to accept the source of meaning that is available in perceptual reality while letting go of the emphasis ordinary consciousness places on conceptual or narrative meaning.

Research Implications

The table can also be used to identify promising areas of research. Some are general and some apply to specific topics. Chapter 13 derived from the interviews three properties that describe the way awakened awareness is experienced subjectively. Eleven teachers is a small sample, so one obvious research improvement would be to interview more people. Second, the interviews presented in this book were exploratory because I had no idea where they were going to go. Now that there are some preliminary results to work with, a more structured design would be appropriate. For example, the interviewer could guide the interview to make sure that key topics are addressed and probe to elicit finer-grained details. These extensions of the present research apply at the level of the mind, and I hope to begin working on this approach soon.

General implications at the level of the brain. For neuroscientists, the big challenge has been proposed by James Austin.[30] His theory of egocentric and allocentric processing systems seems (to this non-neuroscientist) to identify in detail various areas of the brain that participate in each system. One problem, of course, is that it is not easy to find people who appear to have experienced awakening and interview them, and it will be even more difficult to get them to spend time in an fMRI machine. Not impossible, however—there have already been several brain scan studies of long-term meditators, and some of them must have experienced awakening.[31] Most research has focused on attention, which is important but leaves other brain activities untouched. It may be possible to find out who these medita- tors are, then ask them to describe their experiences, use this to estimate approximate degree of awakening, and then compare data across catego- ries. So far this does not appear to have been done.[32]

Conscious awareness. Theoretically, conscious awakened awareness is an unaltered[33] version of perceptual reality (with conceptual information avail- able but not reified), while in conscious ordinary awareness the contents of perceptual awareness will have been modified or rearranged to better fit social reality. The key difference is reification, which presently is a mental term. Studying reification (and its opposite, the de-reification that occurs as part of awakening) at the level of the brain may be more accessible than it first appears. Research on distributed association networks suggests that these densely interconnected networks, which widely span discontinuous areas of cortex, are capable of producing sudden shifts in awareness similar to reification-dereification.[34] For example, the "default mode network"[35] appears implicated in shifts from goal-oriented to passively attentive states of aware- ness.[36] This is a different sort of shift, but the findings indicate that major shifts in subjective experience may be linked with measurable brain activity.

Emotions and feelings. The hypothesis is that in ordinary consciousness emotions are cued by symbolic reality, and particularly by the adventures of the social self in situations scripted by social reality. Escaping from this emotional attachment to the social self has been considered, from the teachings of Gautama onward, to be the most important characteristic of awakened consciousness. Research on this topic is therefore both extremely important and very difficult. At the level of mind I see no alternative to simply asking people to describe their subjective experience, although laboratory research might be designed to study emotional responses before and after experiencing awakening. We probably must wait for neuroscience to resolve the hypothesis by identifying the mechanisms that allow selflessness to become operative in the allocentric system.[37]

Thinking. My experience has been that slow thinking is incompatible with awakened consciousness, and my hypothesis therefore is that the brain is organized in such a way that awakened consciousness only allows conscious awareness of percepts or symbols that are immediately present. Slow thinking requires holding in conscious awareness percepts or symbols that do not refer to anything immediate, so of necessity, slow thinking must take place in brain areas that handle ordinary consciousness. What also seems true from my experience is that slow thinking activates other components of ordinary consciousness. As a result, if I do some, I must use conscious attention to switch back once the slow thinking is completed.

I look forward to continuing the research begun here and asking more people to describe their day-to-day experience of living with awakened consciousness. Personally, since writing this book has required a great amount of slow thinking, returning to some semblance of awakened awareness usually requires at least a short period of meditation to quiet my mind. It's easy to imagine that for people more deeply and firmly centered in awakened consciousness the transition back to that state after some serious slow thinking is simple and automatic. Or perhaps people who have developed their capacity for awakened consciousness more fully are able to engage in slow thinking without being pulled back into ordinary consciousness, so that slow thinking is available as a useful tool but does not compete with awakened consciousness.

For now I am sticking with the hypothesis that the brain systems that handle slow thinking are separate from those that generate perceptual awareness. Neuroscience research on this may not be so difficult. It is known that different areas of the brain are active during perceptual processing and language processing. The next step would be to find areas differentiated for fast thinking and slow thinking (brain areas for wandering thinking have already been identified). Once this is done, brain scan research on awakened subjects should be able to determine what is going on in other areas during and after a period of slow thinking. But attention is important, not only in switching from one mode to the other but also in allowing each mode to operate efficiently when it is active.[38]

Meaning. Meaning is something we feel, subjectively, so the question is, What provides or supports this feeling? The answer proposed here is that in ordinary consciousness, meaning is experienced when one's symbolic reality provides coherent explanations for the events of life and is supported by the social group. Meaning in awakened consciousness, in contrast, comes when one's body provides primordial feelings of being whole, connected, and in tune with the world. *Dukkha* theory says that the problem of meaning in ordinary consciousness can never be fully solved. Since ordinary awareness is necessarily a symbolically represented version of awakened awareness, some kind or degree of suffering, dissatisfaction, or feeling out of touch with life always lurks in the shadows.

I'm not sure what neuroscience can do with *dukkha*, but research at the level of the mind can proceed using either self-reports or observed behavior. What people tell you about their state of *dukkha* may not be trustworthy—most would probably respond like the young Ajahn Amaro when a Buddhist monk told him that life is suffering: "No, that's not right; I'm fine, I'm not suffering" (he added, in his interview, that he was big on denial in those days). *Dukkha* is one of those ailments that you may not know you have until you are free of it. But sensitive and carefully designed interviews could provide useful information.

Another methodology for research on *dukkha* theory involves studying responses to social change, as changes in religious affiliation were studied in chapter 16. Many of the problems that have plagued human existence on this planet stem from attempts to find relief from the itch or pain of *dukkha* by developing and clinging to one of the almost infinite versions of social reality our species has come up with over time. Many databases containing useful information on attitudinal and behavioral responses to social change are available for statistical analysis.

Scientists and Buddhist scholars of all kinds will doubtless come up with better research strategies than those suggested here, not to mention improvements in the theory they are designed to address. If the present suggestions help further the scientific study of awakening, then this book will have made its contribution.

Concluding Notes

Through the centuries, awakening has been held out as a beautiful jewel, available for all people to enjoy. Starting with and including Gautama, those who have experienced awakening have wanted to share it, as something that is wonderful and possible. If this book helps make the message relevant to the Western world, that would be personally gratifying. The problem, though, is that helping others experience awakening is not easy, as the past two and a half millennia demonstrate. Nevertheless, if humans are going to stop messing up this planet, we have to find a way to reawaken this potential. In this spirit, I can think of no better way to conclude than by looking carefully and realistically at conditions in the world today that encourage or impede the spread of awakening.

First, in the West at least, Buddhism and other paths to awakening are presently attracting people who come almost entirely from highly educated, relatively well-to-do backgrounds. People who don't know whether they will have a decently paying job next month, or food and shelter for their children, are suffering from physical *dukkha*, not the fancier kind that leads materially comfortable people to become interested in awakening. Working to eliminate the conditions that impose material deprivation on so many people is therefore crucially important if the potential for awakening is to be available to all. Underdeveloped nations need continued economic development, along with improvements in the social and health conditions that support it.[39] But developed nations have their own problems, and in the United States things may be getting worse. There are steadily increasing inequalities of income, wealth, and education; if these trends continue, more and more people will be trapped at levels where material problems overshadow the possibilities of awakening. One important way to help spread the promise of awakening to all people is therefore by working to overcome inequality.

The second set of conditions is positive. Among the large numbers of people who *are* financially comfortable, there appears to be a lot of searching and experimenting going on with respect to values and lifestyle choices. Much of this is certainly encouraged by the institutionalization of questioning discussed in chapter 16, and the accelerating rate of social change that goes with it. There is an interesting coincidence between the values and activities that prepare one for awakening and those that social research has shown encourage happiness (e.g., helping others, spending time in wilderness, meditating). Everyone likes happiness, but as the research makes clear, we are often confused about what will make us happy. There is an important convergence between the research findings on what really contributes to full happiness and the long traditions of spiritual and philosophical wisdom about true happiness. As more people become aware of and influenced by this convergence, the pool of those who might become interested in awakening grows.

One limitation, however, is that most of these lifestyle and value changes involve leisure, not work. People in a wide variety of jobs and professions report experiencing high levels of on-the-job stress, to the point where they have to leave their careers to enjoy happiness or pursue awakening. That should not be necessary. It should be possible to structure the world of work to be at least compatible with awakening, and a large literature of organization theory and practice suggests ways it can be done. I don't want to sound utopian—a corporation whose happy employees are pursuing awakening while they work sounds very nice, but if it is not done right, a company could easily lose money and have to go out of business. The point is that in order for the world to change in a positive direction, we need to balance changes in living patterns that encourage happiness and awakening with the need for efficient production. Someone had to grow the rice that Buddhist monks gather in their bowls during their rounds of begging.

Being a numbers person, I was impressed by the announcement of the King of Bhutan in 1972 that his country would begin paying attention to both Gross National Product and Gross National Happiness. If we had measures of GNH as well as GNP visible in the news, we could see how we are doing relative to other nations and be reminded to pay attention to both happiness and production. That would be a step in the right direction, but like many steps in a new direction, it immediately opens up another problem. Chapter 13 concluded, after careful consideration, that awakening does not have to include compassion (conversely, we know from the many examples of compassion in the world that compassion does not require awakening). Compassion, it appears, must be cultivated for its own sake. A nation without the qualities of compassion would be a sad place to live, so perhaps we also need a measure of Gross National Kindness. A world whose nations are trying to rank high on all three measures, while not necessarily perfect, would be an amazing improvement.

APPENDIX
Interview with James Austin, Neuroscientist

Conducted July 27, 2010, at Boyle's home in Albuquerque, New Mexico. This interview is included because while Austin has experienced awakening, he is a scientist rather than a Buddhist teacher—so his more clinical style of description makes an interesting contrast. It seems clear, however, that he and the eleven teachers are talking about the same thing.

BOYLE: What led you to begin Buddhist study?

AUSTIN: Back in high school, I got an early glimpse of the kinds of existential issues involved in Buddhism. During a severe case of pneumonia, I confronted the prospect of leaving the hospital feet first. Luckily, this illness responded to sulfadiazine, but that experience left me more sober than the average teenager. It contributed to an ongoing interest in the larger questions: Why are we here? What *is* all this? Going on into academic neurology was a way to further explore these questions and to become awed by neurobiology. But for decades, Buddhism held no particular interest for me. Unitarianism seemed quite adequate for my purposes. Then I chose to spend a neuropharmacology research sabbatical in Kyoto.

When some good friends heard that I was going to Japan, they gave me Eugen Herrigel's book, *Zen and the Art of Archery*, to read on the flight over. I really didn't understand what archery had to do with Zen. But after arriving in Kyoto in 1974 and settling into that wonderful atmosphere, my lingering curiosity encouraged me to discover what was really involved in Zen. So my interest in Zen Buddhism came about by chance, evolved from curiosity, and was superimposed on a long-standing deep question: What's the *big* picture?

Dr. Yoshi Osumi was a faculty member in this same department of pharmacology at Kyoto University. He had trained at Yale, and his earlier visitors from America had found an English-speaking Zen master at Daitoku-ji, a nearby Zen monastery. I was curious to meet a Zen master, so I asked Dr. Osumi if he could arrange for an interview. That meeting with Nanrei Kobori-Roshi at the monastery introduced me to Zen Buddhism. I began formal *zazen* practice with him in July 1974. On Tuesdays, Thursdays, and Saturdays, I practiced meditation and learned how to work outdoors, improving the landscape at Daitoku-ji with a dozen or so other trainees, most of whom were Westerners from different countries. On Mondays, Wednesdays, and Fridays, I was totally occupied day and night with research on the norepinephrine pathways that lead from the brain stem up into the cerebral cortex.

I was lucky to be introduced to Zen by an English-speaking Zen master. Kobori-Roshi had studied at Claremont College in California for a year after the war, and this experience helped him communicate with his students. He guided my early training in ways decisive for who I am today. My sense of gratitude to him is profound.

In December, I participated in an intensive seven-day retreat. Although leg and back pains were difficult, by the evening of the second day of this *sesshin*, I was feeling one-pointed, poised, alert, mentally calm, and physically stable. Few word-thoughts remained in my consciousness. We happened to be sitting in a small, unfamiliar zendo. During the final sitting, I looked up at the single electric light bulb that dangled from the ceiling, and then lowered my eyelids slightly to reduce the brightness. Then my consciousness went blank.

This blank interval lasted an indeterminate period of time. All during this, my posture seemed to have remained erect. As this condition of no awareness waned, consciousness then moved smoothly and seamlessly into a state of hyperawareness. A small red maple leaf suddenly materialized way up high in the extreme left corner of what was now a black visual field. Its colors glowed vividly. Along the leaf's edges and veins, sharp contrasts and surface markings were intensified in exquisite fine-grain detail. Meanwhile, no one was doing this perceiving, because no sense of a personal *physical* self remained. When the leaf vanished, only a glistening blackness—blacker than black—was present throughout an absolutely silent, vast, 360-degree enveloping space.

Next to enter this enchanting scene was a deep, serene comfort, a profound sense of satisfaction, the way one feels on a cold, snowy holiday while sitting snug indoors by a warm fire. A blend of mental clarity and physical lightness developed as this feeling subtly waned. Finally, when I stood up at the end of sitting, my body felt so unusually light that all its movements seemed to perform themselves.

At my next interview with Kobori-Roshi, I started to tell him about the leaf. His face darkened, and he shook his head and said, "NO! When you concentrate too hard, you may see things." This was disappointing, but the experience lingered in memory. Five years later, I returned to Kyoto again and paid Kobori-Roshi an informal visit. Without mentioning the leaf, I then described the rest of the experience. This time, his response was totally accepting, and he said, "Yes, when I had that, it was like being in a vacuum." I gathered that such an experience might be welcome, but more as a matter of fact than as anything special.

Two words describe this experience best: "internal absorption." Direct experience had informed me that my physical sense of self could completely drop out of my awareness. Nothing I had ever learned as a neurologist had prepared me for a state during which the sense of my physical body would disappear. I realized that something powerful was going on during meditation. Several other phenomena were also part of that experience. First, the hallucination of the Japanese red maple leaf taught me that I had hidden compartments in my brain. Some of them could not only register a maple leaf (for I had repeatedly focused my camera on this very leaf several weeks previously) but also later recall its image out of memory, and then project it up to a spot so high that it could easily be seen by my "mind's eye" but not be seen with my eyes, because my forehead was in the way.

Second was the huge, jet black, completely silent space. This space had opened up to envelop the "no person" awareness back in its center. Being in such a vacuum was another demonstration of the power of meditation. For a neurologist, internal absorption was a real eye-opener. How could consciousness be "turned on" inside such a 360-degree space when all sense of one's physical body was also being turned off?

Fortunately, research developments worldwide were making it possible to propose an explanation for such a jet blackness (a total lack of vision), for its absolute silence (a total lack of hearing), and for the complete dropping out of the physical (somatic sensory) sense of self. Interpreted neurologically, these negative phenomena could represent "a *dearth* of self." Such a preliminary event could be referable to a small region down in the back and lower part of the thalamus. Moreover, the thalamic nuclei down there could be blocked by a very thin normal inhibitory layer called the reticular nucleus. This reticular nucleus encloses the thalamus like a tight cap. In a sense, its drawstrings can operate selectively.

I continued formal Zen training and daily life practice during the interval between 1975 and my next sabbatical. Most of this sabbatical, during 1981–1982, was spent in London. There, I kept sifting through the rapidly expanding neuroscience literature, trying to discern how the brain changed during meditation and during alternate states of consciousness. The setting at the London Zen Centre was also propitious because it was led by Irmgard Schloegl (Myokyo-ni), another excellent teacher, whose previous Zen training had also been in Kyoto.

On the second morning of a two-day retreat in March, I woke up early and got on a London subway train bound for the Zen Centre. It was a peaceful, balmy Sunday morning. Absentmindedly, I wound up at a station I had never seen before. I surrendered to the reality of having been so stupid that I would miss the start of the first sitting. Because I exited the train on a surface platform and was now above ground, I could look around and off into the distance. The view in the foreground revealed only the dingy interior of the station. Some grimy buildings occupied the middle ground. Fortunately, while idly surveying this ordinary scene—unfocused, no thought in mind—I happened to look up and out into a bit of open sky above and beyond.

Instantly, with no transition, the entire view acquired three qualities: absolute reality, intrinsic rightness, and ultimate perfection. Every detail of the entire scene was registered, integrated, and found wholly satisfying. The new scene was set gently, not fixed on hold. It conveyed a slightly enhanced sense of immediacy. Yet the scene's purely optical aspects were no different from the way I had perceived them a split second before. This pale gray sky was no bluer; the light was no brighter; the detail, no finer-grained.

But the scene was transformed in other ways. There was no viewer. Every familiar psychic sense that "I" was viewing this scene had vanished. A fresh new awareness perceived the whole scene impersonally with the cool, clinical detachment of an anonymous mirror, not pausing to register the paradox that no "I-Me-Mine" was doing the viewing.

This new awareness further transfigured the scene with a profound, implicit, totally perfect sense of absolute reality. After what was perhaps only a few seconds, a series of deep realizations began to blend into this enhanced sense of reality. One of the unspoken messages was that this is the *eternal* state of affairs—things have always been this way and continue just so indefinitely. A second insight conveyed the message that there is nothing more to do: this train station and the whole rest of this world were so totally complete and intrinsically valid that no further intervention was required. The third insight plumbed a deeper visceral level: there is absolutely nothing whatsoever to fear.

Then another wave of insight interpretations welled up. By this time, some kind of diminutive subjective sense—equivalent to a lowercase "i"—was emerging, because something vaguely conscious was stirring with faint discriminations. The insights were that:

This totally new view of things was too extraordinary to be communicated. No conceptual framework, no words existed to describe the depths and the quality of these insights. Only a person who had undergone the same experience could understand.

"i" couldn't take myself so seriously any longer.

A wide buffer zone relieved this diminutive sense of "i" of any tendency to get involved in doing anything. The zone seemed almost to occupy space, because mingled with the feeling of literally being distanced from outside events was a disinclination to approach and to act in any way.

BOYLE: I remember experiencing that, a lack of motivation to do anything, a complete absence of even the slightest kind of desire or concern.

AUSTIN: Yes. This "unmotivation" is a singular quality. It seems to represent the ultimate dissolution of all approach behavior. In your case, how much time elapsed between the very first event that entered your experience and when your mind began later to interpret and comment on the experience?

BOYLE: The time interval must have been short, because almost immediately a voice in my mind said, "So this is what they mean by nothingness—no social reality."

AUSTIN: In London, many seconds elapsed during which there wasn't any "I" around that was doing any commenting. Everything was registering, but no "I" was in there personally enjoying it or appreciating it. It was just there anonymously. Just this.

As my physical and mental sense of self began to return, the combination conveyed an unparalleled feeling of total release. Clear, simplified, free of every limitation, feeling especially *good* inside. Revived and enormously grateful! Yet this expansion of capacities remained silent and internal. It was quiet and profoundly peaceful, rather than exciting. In my case, because this awareness had just been directly experienced as no subject inside, "objective vision" was the short phrase that leaped easily to mind. As minimal degrees of self-reference began to grow within awareness, they gradually rediscovered a physical center within the body of a vaguely familiar person standing on the platform. A thoughtful I boarded the next subway train to the Zen Centre, feeling awed, deepened, and calmed within a profound, ongoing intellectual illumination.

This direct experience was a "*death* of self." This person's former intrusive psychic sense of self had dropped completely out of consciousness, taking with it all references to his physical, somatic sense of self. After that taste of *kensho* in London, my studies of the neuroscience literature intensified.

BOYLE: What do you mean by the "psychic sense of self"?

AUSTIN: I mean all those intangible mental attributes that you and I usually engage in, the ones we might choose to describe using operational terms that represent aspects of our "I," or "Me," or "Mine." All these abstract mental operations are self-centered. Some are affirmative and adaptive; others can invoke fear or anger and prove counterproductive. Our word descriptions allow us usefully to conceptualize our sense of self—pro and con—using psychological terms. Notice how these intangible mental attributes differ from the tangible, concrete aspects of our physical bodies. In arriving at these mental/physical conceptual distinctions, I found the old Greek word, *psyche*, was helpful. I could use it to include the more complicated cognitive functions, emotional feelings, and instinctual drives implicit within our psychic sense of self. This allowed another Greek term, *soma*, to be used when referring to one's physical sense of self.

There's a neuroanatomical basis for this distinction between the soma and the psyche. For example, some regions in our cortex represent the somatic sensory functions of our body—our limbs, lips, tongue, etc. These are reasonably well defined higher up in the parietal lobe over the back of the brain. Networks up here in the *dorsal* parietal and frontal regions are ready to help us answer such practical physiological questions as: Where is this fruit on the table in relation to Me? Their functions combine to enable "Me" to reach out and grasp it. Our primary and secondary somato-sensory association cortex are each represented along this more dorsal, "northern," self-centered route. Of course, our psyche is more complex, and its layers are represented among levels elsewhere in the brain.

In the decades after London, I continued to join and sit with various Zen groups, both Rinzai and Soto, and with Buddhists in the Theravada tradition. Important early during this period was the way the research literature started to refer to the self/other boundary. Issues related to the egocentric

and allocentric processing systems of the brain seemed especially important. So, in *Zen and the Brain* (1998), I began to introduce these two key
prefixes: ego- (meaning self-centered) and allo- (meaning other-centered).
Don't be daunted by either one. The terms refer to the two different ways
our brain represents the "reality" of items in space in terms of their three-
dimensional coordinates. The brain defines egocentric coordinates with
respect to our personal lines of sight. These point the location of some fruit
on a table back to the axis of our own body and to our internal, subjective
frame of reference.

   In contrast, the brain defines its allocentric coordinates with respect to
an external frame of reference. In doing so, it uses pattern recognition systems that chiefly reside in the temporal lobe. Having asked "What is it?"
questions, they then identify the fruit and specify that it is an apple, an
impersonal object residing "out there" in space. During the next decade,
functional MRI research became increasingly sophisticated. This enabled
many of the links between the concepts of attention, and self and other, to
be assembled into a plausible model hypothesis for *kensho*. I do appreciate
that these attempts at reductionism carry the dual risks of seeming not only
premature scientifically but also irrelevant within some traditions of Buddhism that I also value highly.

   However, while writing the chapters for *Zen–Brain Reflections* (2006),
I thought it reasonable to expand on the earlier model role of the reticular nucleus. How could its normal functions and the inhibitory roles they
appeared to play in internal absorption be extended to *kensho*? A working
hypothesis suggested itself: the "cap" of its inhibitory functions could be
tightened over other thalamic nuclei farther forward in the thalamus. Now
the blockade could include the so-called "limbic" nuclei. These are crucial
to the functions of our psyche. If the reticular nucleus inhibited the limbic nuclei for a brief interval, this could create a novel wakeful state during
which the person's overconditioned psychic sense of self could vanish.

   Day and night, our usual states of consciousness depend on the discrete
physiological selectivity of this reticular nucleus. We rely on its fine-tun-
ings to open up and enhance, or to close down and block, the co-arising
oscillations that link our individual thalamic nuclei with their critical tar-
get regions up in the cortex. Still, an important question remained: Where
do the signals come from that normally activate, or deactivate, the pivotal
gatelike functions of this inhibitory nucleus? Might some answers begin
in the ways meditation trains our brain's array of attentional responses? If
so, then what about those old Zen stories that describe monks and nuns

having been triggered into states of *kensho-satori* when their attention was suddenly captured by an unexpected sensory stimulus?

At this juncture, it helps to recall three points that have received major emphasis in Zen Buddhist traditions. First, the key issue: our becoming liberated from the maladaptive, overly reactive influences of our overconditioned personal self. Second: the long necessary prelude—our training awareness to attend to each present moment. Third: the fact that words and concepts mislead us. With regard to the self, studies by Marcus Raichle and colleagues at Washington University emphasized that several "hot spots" exist in the normal brain. These special regions stay active in normal subjects even when their minds and bodies might seem to be resting under passive conditions. The two largest of these normal highly metabolically active areas are located deep along the midline of the brain. One is in our medial prefrontal cortex. The other is in the medial posterior parietal cortex. As research in this new century progressed, a consensus emerged that would correlate many of our basic self-referential, autobiographical functions with the activities linking these two hot spots (and including that of the third spot, out in the lateral parietal cortex of the angular gyrus).

We further activate these three regions each time we need to access a broad spectrum of our self-centered processes. We access the short-term, working memory end of this spectrum in order to accomplish our daily tasks. We can access other personalized memories only by including those specific links to the particular details of our outside environment that anchor each such incident in one brief instant of our long life story.

The research team at Washington University also went on to study three other conditions. The crucial point here is that during each occasion, the three self-centered regions became deactivated. Notice when these self-referent "hot spots" became "cooler": first, when the researchers assigned any goal-oriented task that, overtly or covertly, caused their subjects to focus their executive attention on this task from the "top down." Second, when any fresh, unexpected sensate event occurred, one that could also capture their subjects' attention, but this time from the "bottom up." Third, during slow, intrinsic brain rhythms. These arose normally, only two to four times a minute, on an almost independent, endogenous cycle.

In short, this new evidence pointed to a vital, inverse, reciprocal relationship. You might think of it as resembling a seesaw. On one side of this seesaw relationship are our top-down and bottom-up forms of attentiveness. These dorsal and ventral attention systems, respectively, are each represented over the outside surface of the brain. On the other end of the relationship are those mostly medial frontal and parietal regions, the ones just described that are so essential to the operations of our psychic, auto-biographical sense of self. They reside chiefly inside our brain.

This seesaw metaphor is of particular interest to meditators for two rea-sons. First, it reemphasizes that attention plays a crucial vanguard role in all of their meditative training. In fact, only when attention plays this role, directing our brain into particular processing channels, can we normally accomplish any task. Our conjoined attentive processing functions ensure that we respond to an explicit task, or to an implicit task when unexpected circumstances call for a brisk, reflexive subconscious reaction.

Second, the seesaw metaphor helps clarify what happens when a sudden triggering stimulus captures the attention of a sensitized brain, as the sharp call of a crow once did for Master Ikkyu. The neuroimaging results clarify how in these first milliseconds the loss of self-centeredness so distinctive of *kensho* could be precipitated when such an unexpected event commands a shift in attention.

In general, the research findings also suggest that when meditators adhere to a long-term, balanced program of training, their attentiveness, the blended assets of such a top-down/bottom-up approach, will become both complementary and more effective than any single concentrative or receptive practice of training per se.

The evidence that our self-centered functions decrease at the same instant that attention increases is relevant to *kensho*'s brief state of awaken-ing, not only because it helps clarify how the person's old, intrusive ego-centric "I-Me-Mine" could drop its overconditioned limbic fears. This same inverse relationship also provides room to envision what happens— simul-taneously—when the "other" innate functions of the brain's allocentric processing networks are finally released. During these same crucial milli-seconds, the person's bottom-up systems of reflexive attention can take the lead in directing their adjacent other-centered modes of insightful process-ing. To what end?

In this model, what opens up during this allocentric release is a one-phase, unified field of nondual consciousness. The model envisions that these "southern" pathways of the brain are now liberated to draw on their inherent semantic resources of meaning. Normally, we've seen that these same lower pathways are asking "What?" types of questions of the pattern recognition functions in the lower cortical and subcortical processing net-works, and are receiving meaningful answers. Now, during *kensho*, their trajectories along the ventral occipital → temporal → inferior frontal regions can provide a fresh glimpse of ONE world. This one-phase, enhanced mode of allocentric perception is transfigured by an enhanced sense of all things as they really are. This novel perspective arrives only when those old, intrusive veils of our dominant egocentric self are no longer interposed.

Can large compartments of our normal brain really register "their" independent perspective on the world "out there" in such a highly objective manner? Can such a state be liberated from every grasping attachment and rejection that issues from the subjective core of our own self-centeredness? Don't expect that our conventional sovereign egocentric logic will easily welcome such far-out notions. These normal covert allo-mental functions arise so subconsciously and anonymously that such notions seem counterintuitive. Even so, these same "southern" pathways are normally interpreting implicit meanings every second into what they see, identify, and reify "out there."

In a 2008 article in the *New York Times*, David Brooks coined the term "neural Buddhism." The story I've been narrating is of a wandering "neural" Buddhist path. I don't know how its meanderings might parallel or depart from the path stories of the more accomplished full-time teachers you've also been hearing from. Decades after a severe case of pneumonia first made me really aware of impermanence, this neurologist was a relative latecomer to Zen. Ever since, for thirty-six years, I've been trying to repair my ignorance, aided by language and concepts drawn from a field of biomedical research that has been exploding exponentially. My writings can best be viewed as one meditator's attempt to clarify this very complex field at the dynamic interface between the Zen Buddhist path and the neurosciences.

The glimpse today from this biased perspective suggests that four key issues are involved on the Buddhist path. The crucial distinctions are between top-down and bottom-up attention—between ego- and allo-processing—between self and other—between the focused concentrative and openly receptive styles of meditation. Will these major distinctions and all their implications sink in before another three and a half decades have elapsed? Let's hope so, for future generations will need to clarify how their ongoing awareness becomes more enlightened—not just for the brief formative moments we've discussed so far, but awakened throughout each minute and hour of their ongoing daily life practice.

Notes

Introduction

1. Berger and Luckmann 1966.
2. Everett 2009.
3. Giddens 1991, 40.
4. Giddens 1991, 36.
5. See the Pew Forum on Religion and Public Life, *U.S. Religious Landscape Survey*, Pew Research Center (2008).
6. W. I. Thomas and D. Thomas 1928.

5. Interview with Martine Batchelor

1. M. Batchelor 2006, 41.

8. Interview with Stephen Batchelor

1. S. Batchelor 2010, 238.

10. Interview with Bernie Glassman

1. See Robert Heinlein, *Stranger in a Strange Land* (New York: Putnam, 1961). Grok: to understand so thoroughly that the observer becomes a part of the observed— to merge, blend, intermarry, lose identity in group experience.
2. Matthiessen finished the novel based his experiences at the Auschwitz retreats, including the one referred to here, shortly before he died. *In Paradise: A Novel* was published in April 2014.

12. Developing Capacities Necessary for Awakening

1. These categories, in one form or another, go back throughout the history of Buddhism to the early teachings of Gautama. See Shankman 2008.
2. Farb, Segal, and Anderson 2012; Lutz, Slagter, Rawlings, Francis, Greishar, and Davidson 2009; Wallace and Hodel 2009.
3. Brefczynski-Lewis, Lutz, Schaefer, Levinson, and Davidson 2007.
4. S. Batchelor 2010, 25–26.
5. Fishman and Young 2002; Young 2011.
6. Garfinkel 1999.
7. S. Batchelor 2010, 30.
8. Ekman, Davidson, Ricard, and Wallace 2005; Condon, Desbordes, Miller, and DeSteno 2013.
9. Lutz, Brefczynski-Lewis, Johnstone, and Davidson 2008; Lutz, Greishar, Perlman, and Davidson 2009.

13. Properties of Awakening Experiences

1. Red Pine 2004, 2–4.
2. A similar approach was used by Full, Walach, and Trautwein in analyzing the interviews they had conducted with expert meditators in Burma, with compatible results. See Full, Walach, and Trautwein 2013, 55–63.
3. Which is another reason for using the word "awakening" rather than "enlightenment."
4. Goffman and Berger 1974; Lakoff 1996.
5. S. Batchelor 2010, 29–30.
6. There is an extensive literature on these issues, and several websites are devoted to current events. See Edelstein 2011; Bell 2002; Downing 2002; O'Brien 2011.
7. See Victoria 2006 and 2003.
8. There was nothing dramatic about my leaving. My practice was evolving at that time toward being more and more quiet, doing *shikantaza* (mindfulness meditation) rather than working on koans. I tried to communicate something about this to Sasaki in *sanzen*, but he would have nothing of it. He insisted that I stick with koans. So I decided that he was not a good teacher for me and ceased going to see him. But I remain deeply grateful to him for getting me off to a good start and pointing me in the right direction.
9. I first heard about Sasaki's behavior from two women in the 1970s, who told me he would sometimes reach out and fondle their breasts during *sanzen*. They didn't seem terribly upset about it, and I didn't hear anything else for about fifteen years, when a traumatic scandal broke out at Bodhi Manda Zen Center in Jemez Springs, New Mexico. By that time I was no longer a student, but I heard indirectly that Sasaki had promised not to behave that way anymore. Another twenty-three years went by, and the cover-ups worked well enough that

only insiders really knew what was going on, until the story finally erupted on the website sweepingzen.com. One of his top-level monks broke the silence that Sasaki's organization had maintained around him, and a flood of additional postings poured in.

10. Martin 2012. According to other postings on sasakiarchive.com (a website maintained by Sweeping Zen), Sasaki (who died in 2014) had been confronted with the problems caused by his abusive sexual behavior many times. He never explained or gave excuses, and he never changed his behavior. He also threatened, lied, and coerced to get students and monks to keep quiet and do what he wanted.

11. For the full poem, go to http://sasakiarchive.com/PDFs/20130221_Chizuko_Tasaka.pdf.

12. Dutton 2012.

13. Many people are very attached to a conception of enlightenment that includes compassionment. That's still another reason for calling it awakening.

14. Victoria, 2003, 2006.

15. See Jalon 2003.

16. McFarquhar 2013.

17. All of which means that one should not be surprised to find Zen masters who are also clinical psychopaths. If someone is considering studying with a teacher in the Japanese Zen tradition, they might first want to use the PCL-R (http://www.psychforums.com/antisocial-personality/topic62959.html) to rate that teacher themselves.

18. Interview with Dutton on *To the Best of Our Knowedge* (ttbook.org), January 3, 2013. CEOs ranked first.

19. Stephen Pinker has argued that the incidence of violence in societies has declined as "modern civilization" developed new forms of morality (Pinker 2012). For example, the moral principle of behaving toward others in the way you would want them to behave toward you requires either great empathy or the intellectual apparatus for a sophisticated "theory of mind" that allows you to "take the role of the other" in social situations and act accordingly. If you are able to put yourself in the role of the other person intellectually and predict her feelings and you have been trained by your culture to care about how other people feel, then even without intuitive emotional feelings of empathy, many potentially negative behaviors will be controlled.

20. Amaro 2009.

14. Evolution of Ordinary and Awakened Consciousness

1. Where "awareness" means we take account in our behavior of at least some perceptual information about the here-and-now. Conscious awareness means we can talk about this.

2. Damasio 2012.

3. Damasio 2012, 35.
4. Damasio 2012, 18.
5. Damasio 2012, 21.
6. Damasio, chap. 3; see also Francesca Frassinetti, Maini, Benassi, and Gallese 2011.
7. Damasio 2012, 250.
8. 2003 and 2004.
9. Recent neurological research gives some support for this: see Farb, Segal, and Anderson 2012.
10. Damasio 2012, 251.
11. Jocelyn Sze showed that that "people who meditate have greater interoceptive awareness than dancers who, although they also have trained awareness of their bodies' movements, are perhaps less in tune with their emotional states." Quote from Emma Seppala, *Scientific American*, April 3, 2012, http://www.scientificamerican.com/article/decoding-body-watcher/. On the other hand, Khalsa, Rudrauf, Damasio, Davidson, Lutz, and Tranel (2008) found no evidence that experienced meditators were able to perform a laboratory heartbeat detection test any better than nonmeditators. However, this does not seem to have involved "primordial feelings" either.
12. Damasio has been criticized for some looseness and circularity in the way he defines "core consciousness." For example, John Searle complains that Damasio has "smuggled consciousness into his conception of [self] without explaining how it got there" (2011, 52). See also Block 2010. My view is that you can define "self" in several ways, so long as you are clear about which definition you are using.
13. Damasio 2012, 203.
14. Damasio 2012, 16.
15. de Gelder 2010, 61–65. See also Koch 2012, 20–21.
16. Damasio 2012, 206.
17. That is, all cognitive processing could take place at an unconscious level. Quoted in Gallup 1998, 70.
18. Several studies summarized by Koch 2011, 22–23, show that unconscious processing is capable of rather complicated feats. See also Hassain, Uleman, and Baugh 2004.
19. My favorite "in the zone" sports story, and very close to property 1 of awakened consciousness, described in chapter 13, is Bill Russell's. See Nelson 2005.
20. Insight has been studied among animals as mental trial-and-error learning, but though the animals are clever and their behavior hints at being able to work with nonpresent mental representations in the way humans do, the results are more tantalizing than convincing.
21. Köhler 1926.
22. Suddendorf (2013) and Shuttleworth (2010) provide extensive overviews of this.
23. Piaget 1937.
24. Reznikova 2007, 186.

25. M. Tomasello and J. Farrar, cited in Reznikova 2007, 186. These findings could also be explained by higher levels of unconscious awareness, so, as with much animal research, the results remain ambiguous.

26. Gallup 1998; Reiss 2011.

27. Daniel Povinelli, cited in Gallup 1998.

28. See for example Premack 2007.

29. Fitch 2010.

30. Bickerton 2009.

31. Hockett 1960; Hockett and Ascher 1964.

32. Fitch 2010, 175.

33. Fitch 2010, 148.

34. For an excellent coverage of the transition from animals to humans-with-language, see Hurford 2007.

35. Berwick et al. 2013; Chomsky 2011.

36. M. Somel et al. 2013.

37. Bickerton 2009. Bickerton is a respected linguist with a long career of important research, but some reviews have taken issue with his work on the basis of traditional linguistic principles. One ends by saying that while *Adam's Tongue* "doesn't actually explain how language evolved," it might account for how "some kind of protolanguage with displacement" evolved, which is a huge contribution. See Balari and Lorenzo 2010.

38. The evolution of cooperation is, of course, at least as deep and complex as, and certainly intertwined with, the evolution of language. Martin Nowak (2012) analyzed "several thousand papers scientists have published on how cooperators could prevail in evolution" and identified five mechanisms or scenarios which are most often mentioned as responsible.

39. Michael Tomasello, cited in Natalie Angier, "Thirst for Fairness May Have Helped Us Survive," *New York Times*, July 4, 2011.

40. A language that allows a spoken message to be decoded by another person with no loss of meaning or information.

41. Social reality is as much a part of us as the lexicon and grammar of the language that expresses it, so in one sense a social reality is the set of all verbal descriptions that a group of people can both utter and agree to be true. But just as a specific sentence is generated within the syntactic constraints of a grammar, the way social reality is applied to interpret and represent a specific situation must be generated within the constraints of some underlying, perhaps inchoate, set of themes.

42. Berger and Luckmann 1966.

43. This, of course, is a deep subject—see, for example, Kempson 1988.

44. One component or aspect of social reality is what is now called Theory of Mind, all the stored information that makes it possible for one person to infer what is going on in another person's mind. For thorough coverage of the way children learn language and theory of mind at the same time, see the collection of research

articles in Astington and Baird 2005. I do not know of similar developmental studies of the co-learning of language and other aspects of social reality, although they probably exist.

45. Searle 2010. Strictly speaking, Searle is concerned with the kind of speech act called a "status function declaration."

46. We can approximate this by trying to see the world from another perspective, or by being thrust into a very different social world. But this is just changing social realities. From the perspective of awakened consciousness, once a social reality has taken us over, we cannot simply will ourselves to see the world the way it really is.

47. Berger and Luckmann 1966, 60.

48. Wyer 2007.

49. Learning and practicing an extensive repertoire of stories is useful, actually necessary, for living competently in the social world. See the work of Keith Oakley, e.g., Oakley 2011.

50. Goffman 1959.

51. Taylor 2009, 70.

52. This example helps explain why Buddhist practitioners spend so much time working to develop attention and detachment, as discussed in chapter 12.

53. Humphrey 1983, 8–9.

54. Libet and Kosslyn 2005.

55. Zoltan Torey 2009.

56. White 1992, 21.

57. MacNeilage, Rogers, and Vallortigara 2009, 60–67.

58. Gazzaniga 2009.

59. See chapter 13.

60. In his "Dark Night of the Soul," the Christian mystic John of the Cross talked of how, after all the preparations necessary along the path, one must wait for "an inflowing of God into the soul" for secret instruction. See *The Complete Works of St. John of the Cross, Vol. I*, trans. E. A. Peers (London: Burns, Oates & Washburn, 1958), 381.

61. Austin 2009, 2006, 1998.

62. Davidson and Lutz 2007, 172–176; Brefczynski-Lewis, Lutz, Schaefer, Levinson, and Davidson 2007; Holzel, Carmody, Vangel, Congleton, Yerramsetti, Gard, and Lazar 2011.

15. The Awakened Baby?

1. Gopnik 2009.

2. Gopnik 2009, 15–16.

3. Gopnik 2009, 28–29.

4. Gopnik 2009, 138–140.

5. Gopnik 2009, 152.

6. Gopnik 2009, 151.
7. Gopnik 2009, 152.
8. Gopnik 2009, 119.
9. Gopnik 2009, 124.
10. Gopnik 2009, 204.
11. Gopnik 2009, 208.
12. Ferris Jabr, "Blissfully Unaware," *Scientific American Mind* 22 (2011): 14.
13. Remschmidt 1994.

16. The Human Condition and How We Got Into It

1. Everett 2009.
2. Colapinto 2007 and Schuessler 2012.
3. For discussions of how language shapes consciousness, see Whorf 1964; Boroditsky 2011, 63–65; Fausey, Long, Inamon, and Borodistsky 2010.
4. Quoted in Colapinto 2007.
5. Pirahãs who worked for Everett helping him learn their language.
6. Everett 2009a, 132.
7. Frank, Everett, Fedorenko, and Gibson 2008.
8. Everett 2009b.
9. Everett 2009a, 79.
10. Everett 2009a, 78.
11. Everett 2009a, 278.
12. Everett 2009a, 101.
13. Everett 2009a, 104.
14. Everett 2009a, 85.
15. Everett 2009a, 89–90.
16. The classic article is Richard B. Lee, "Eating Christmas in the Kalahari," *Natural History* (December 1969).
17. Everett 2009a, 85.
18. Everett 2009a, 114.
19. Everett 2009a, 91.
20. Everett 2009a, 216. As an example of this, the Pirahã do not indicate direction by pointing.
21. Everett 2009a, 85.
22. Everett 2009a, 278–279. Considering the recent surge of research on happiness and the serious questions that can be raised about basing the findings on self-reports, it is interesting to note the method the MIT psychologists recommended using to study happiness—measure the time people spend smiling or laughing. Complexities involved in studying happiness suggest this is a good idea. For an overview and references, see Pawelski 2011.
23. See among many sources Ivanovski and Malhi 2007.

24.   Everett 2009a, 66.

25.   Everett 2009a, 76.

26.   A slightly more nuanced version of this is reported by the anthropologists Mehl-Madrona and Pennycook from their interviews with elders from twenty-one North American tribes. They had worked with these elders for up to fifteen years, so the informal interviews could explore in depth what these elders understood as "consciousness," "mind," and "self," rather than imposing Western scientific concepts on them. Mind, the elders agreed, exists between people and not within individuals: "Mind consists of the stories told in a relationship that define and de-lineate that relationship," and each relationship "has a mind of its own." Which, of course, is how the social self of other Americans operates, as part of a shared so-cial reality—we simply see it from a more egocentric perspective. Consciousness, on the other hand, was understood by the elders as being "unique to individuals" and is "what remains when all internal dialogue stops." They stressed the impor-tance of "stopping all thought so as to be able to appreciate who we are when the mind is still." Mehl-Madrona and Pennycook 2009. Mehl-Madrona is of Native American descent through both parents, which also facilitated establishing rap-port. The quotes are found on 94.

27.   Everett p. 112. Furthermore, access to spirits is egalitarian: "Seeing spirits is not shamanism, because there was no one man among the Pirahãs who could speak for or to the spirits. Some men did this more frequently than others, but any Pi-rahã man could, and over the years I was with them most did, speak as a spirit in this way." (p. 141).

28.   Katz 1976, 298; Katz 1982. The practice consists of strenuous physical activity, maybe similar to trance dancing, accompanied by intense concentration.

29.   The first clay tablets were found in a cave in Knossos, Crete, in 1400 B.C.E. Note that this is not mainland Greece; the effects on language may have taken longer to diffuse.

30.   1976.

31.   But however preposterous they might seem, Jaynes' notions about hearing the voices of gods have some intriguing parallels, for example among the Pirahã. See also Tuzin 1984.

32.   There is quite a literature on hearing voices in one's mind, both schizophrenic and spiritual. See for example Luhrmann 2012. The framework to be developed in chapter 17 would say that if level four thinking is rudimentary and someone is not used to examining solutions that appear in their conscious display, unconscious processing will still propose solutions, but the person will have difficulty repre-senting the process in conscious awareness. Instead, because the solution seems to pop into their minds mysteriously, they attribute this inner voice to gods or spirits (as do many literate modern people).

33.   These dates for Gautama's life are recent revisions. Dates for written language in the area of Buddha's birth (in what is now Nepal) are unknown, but the existence

of written language in the nearby Indus Valley has been argued by Rao, Yadav, Vahia, Joglekar, Adhikari, and Mahadevan 2009.

34. The mystical tradition within Islam, dominant from about 800 to 1200 C.E. but very much alive today.

35. Johnson 2011, 79.

36. Giddens 1991, 16. See also Giddens 2003.

37. Giddens 1991, 40.

38. Giddens 1991, 36.

39. Giddens has much more to say than I have allowed here. In particular, he discusses two aspects of modern society that also threaten ontological security. First, whereas time and space were once joined together in immediate experience, in modern society they have become separated conceptually as abstract axes that exist independently of each other. What is happening right now, as immediate, locally situated experience, therefore plays a diminished role in consciousness relative to thoughts about the past and future and about events that might be happening outside of the present moment. Second, actual social relations (interaction between two or more people) become "disembedded," "lifted out" from local contexts (18). Rather than interacting with people we know in settings that are familiar, we spend much of our time negotiating roles with people we barely know in situations in which we are not fully comfortable. Rather than the relaxation of a friendly conversation, negotiated interaction imposes a certain amount of stress on the people doing it. We need to keep the complex and sophisticated Theory of Mind we have been constructing since childhood in continuous operation. As Giddens notes, "The consequence of modernity for the individual is an increased cognitive workload and considerable existential anxiety."

40. For a review of the tolerance for ambiguity literature, see Furnham 1995.

41. See for example Gilbert 2006.

42. Giddens 1991, 206.

43. My favorite way of identifying and classifying worldviews was developed by the anthropologist Mary Douglas and extended by the political scientist Aaron Wildavsky. Their starting point is the way a culture (or subculture) thinks people should relate to one another in order for the society to function effectively and harmoniously. Douglas found that cultures around the world could be classified according to which of four models for interpersonal relationships they advocated. In subsequent collaboration with Wildavsky, the models were adapted to subcultures within a society (Douglas and Wildavsky 1983). My slightly tweaked version looks like this: Hierarchical authority: people should be ranked (leaders over followers, men over women, parents over children, and, if extended to the supernatural realm, God over a priestly hierarchy over all others). Directives should pass down through these hierarchies. Individual competition: each person should act according to his or her own interests; the competitive systems that result will produce the best outcomes for that society. Egalitarian cooperation:

people should take account of and respect the needs of others, and work together (each according to his or her own abilities) to ensure a good life for all. Isolation and apathy: people will try to take advantage of me and cannot be trusted, and the world around me is out of my control, so there is no use hoping, much less trying. "Escaping into drugs or alcohol," mentioned earlier, is one possible response here. For more recent work in the Douglas and Wildavsky tradition see Kahan 2012. These worldviews would be only interesting observations about the curious ways people living with ordinary consciousness can construct their social realities, except that they can also cause a lot of trouble in the world. Hierarchical authority is exemplified by Christian and Islamic fundamentalism, which have a long history of inciting religious wars. But even secular people can advocate obedience to leaders and rules as the best way to live. Individualism is exemplified by people who have been inspired by reading Ayn Rand, which in contemporary America brings sympathies for the Libertarian Party, faith in the invisible hand of (unrestricted) free markets, and minimal government. The troubles caused by an Individualist worldview depend on whether you take the perspective of the rich or of the poor. Egalitarianism appeals strongly to many people interested in Buddhism, but has a troubling history of its own: Marx inspired many with his egalitarian message, but the people who put communism into practice turned to hierarchical command as the way to achieve "equality." Efforts to achieve equality as hunter-gatherers typically have done, through consensus and cooperation, have only succeeded in small communities, which leaves a large gap if the Egalitarian worldview is to apply. Apathetic Isolates, sometimes called Fatalists, are a response to existing society, not a model advocated for shaping society.

44. Giddens 1991, 206–207.
45. Pew Forum on Religion and Public Life 2008.
46. Based on the 2010 census estimate for population ages 45–64.
47. It is even more interesting than that, however, because although the evangelical category increased from 31.0 percent of the sample to 34.2 percent, all of this growth took place in nondenominational evangelical churches. This category more than tripled in size, from 1.5 percent of all respondents as children to 4.8 percent as adults. Almost all of the other evangelical churches lost members (Baptists, the largest, lost 4.1 percent). The nondenominational category includes most of the megachurches getting so much attention today. The category is quite diverse and its churches have many interesting features, but in the survey 58 percent were biblical literalists. Part of their growth, therefore, might be attributed to people wanting a faith-based foundation for social reality. But their emphasis on providing strong group support suggests that megachurches may have found the right recipe for replicating the way humans lived with their social realities for thousands of years: no questioning of the prevailing social view combined with cohesive group support.
48. National Center for Complementary and Alternative Medicine 2007.

49. These data come from the Pew Research Center report "How the Faithful Voted: 2012" (November 7, 2012). Unaffiliated and non-Christian Obama voters supplied 19 percent of all votes cast in the election, and black Protestant and Hispanic Catholic voters provided another 14 percent, for a total of 33 percent. White evangelicals made up 23 percent of total votes. Hispanic evangelicals, a group almost as large as Hispanic Catholics, were not included in the publication, but were reported elsewhere to have voted strongly for Obama.

50. Durrheim 1998; Furnham 1995.

51. Mooney 2012.

52. Edelman, Crandall, Goodman, and Blanchar 2012.

53. See Lewandowsky, Oberauer, and Gignac 2013; Shermer 2011.

54. Mooney 2012.

55. Hofstadter 1966.

56. Cited in Krugman, "Grand Old Planet," *New York Times*, November 22, 2012.

57. Joe Hagan, "Blues Cruise," *New York Magazine* (December 23, 2012).

58. Saletan 2013.

59. Lings 1961, 26.

17. Modeling Consciousness, Awakened and Ordinary

1. Definitions of consciousness get very tricky. For a good overall discussion, see Searle 2011.

2. Science assumes that even mysterious phenomena like "awakening" can be explained at a material level, presumably in the body and probably mostly in the brain. B. Alan Wallace makes a carefully considered case for not ruling out nonmaterial explanations—see Wallace 2012. I make the working assumption that material explanations are all that are needed, to get on with the work of trying to construct such an explanation. If that approach ultimately fails, then other directions could be tried.

3. Recent developments in research on perception have featured the concept of "predictive coding." See Seth 2013.

4. Thomas and Thomas 1928.

5. Chomsky 2011.

6. Where awareness is defined being able to take account of information, whether or not that information is part of the experience we call "consciousness."

7. Paas and Sweller 2012.

8. Another example of a radically transformed underlying perspective has to do with mapping the planet Earth onto a two-dimensional Mercator projection rather than a three-dimensional globe.

9. Austin 2013.

10. See also Suddendorf 2013.

11. But see Kouider, Stahlhut, Gelskov, Barbosa, Dutat, Gardelle, Christophe, Dehaene, and Dehaene-Lambertz 2013.

12. For example, Bloom 2013.
13. This is the preferred term of the foremost researchers on inner speech: Hurlburt, Heavey, and Kelsey 2013.
14. Interview with Jack Kornfield in Shankman 2008, 116.
15. See also Shaila Catherine's experience as analyzed in chapter 13.
16. This may not be true—further laboratory experiments will be necessary, and unfortunately they will probably have to be done on awakened subjects.
17. Austin 2013.
18. Raichle 2010, 44–49.
19. S. Batchelor 2010.
20. Damasio and Carvalho 2013.
21. For a similar theoretical system, see Seth 2013.
22. All of these examples were posited as immediate responses in face-to-face situations; it is not clear that fleeing requires fear, that fighting requires anger, that feeding requires craving, that sex requires lust, or that any of the other emotions related to these four (e.g., anxiety, hatred, food obsession, or pornophilia) exist in someone who has let go of the social self.
23. Kahneman 2011.
24. Fast thinking probably also describes animal cognition. For some interesting thoughts on thinking without language, see Terrace 1985.
25. A good research example found that in laboratory tasks that require mental rotation of images (conscious processing), recognition of the object took place first, as an unconscious process, followed by "double-checking" in the form of consciously rotating the object to its usual orientation (DeCaro and Reeves 2002). It also fits in well with the concept of "work space"; see Baars 2006.
26. See Brass and Haggard 2007.
27. The research by Raichle and his associates that identified "default areas" suggests that systems for wandering thinking may have become built into the human brain. See Raichle 2010, 44–49; Christoff, Gordon, Smallwood, Smith, and Schooler 2009; Mason, Norton, Van Horn, Wegner, Grafton, and Macrae 2007. Obviously, acquiring control over wandering thinking is a primary objective of meditation practices.
28. Of course, where and what constitutes a "satisfactory explanation" depends on the criteria used by the person.
29. O'Hara 2014, 37.
30. Austin 2009; Austin 2006; Austin 1998.
31. See especially the work of Davidson and his colleagues (2007).
32. There seems to be some resistance on the part of neuroscientists to combining qualitative or subjective data with their sophisticated brain scan technologies, and that is a sad thing.
33. I.e., homomorphic.
34. Buckner and Krienen 2013.

35. Raichle 2010.
36. Andrews-Hanna 2012.
37. When I asked Austin about this, he suggested some possible mechanisms but left the question open.
38. For example, research has found that performance on the Raven Progressive Matrices test of cognitive ability improves with practice, and that with the proper training, both children and adults can "get smarter"—that is, improve their scores on the test. This was not just a matter of improving specific abilities—the tasks used for training were quite different from the tasks used on the tests. After careful analysis, the researchers concluded that what was being developed was improved ability to concentrate attention on the tasks, not expertise with the tasks themselves. But, one might ask, if improving one's power of attention is the critical skill, then wouldn't meditation also improve performance on the Raven? That is exactly what an experiment directed by cognitive psychologist Michael Posner discovered: subjects who went through a mere five-day training in meditation significantly improved their scores, relative to a randomly assigned control group. See Tang, Ma, Wang, Fan, Feng, Lu, Yu, Sui, Rothbart, Fan, and Posner 2007.
39. Sachs 2006.

Glossary of Buddhist Terms

BARDO A Tibetan word that means "intermediate state," referring to the state of the soul between death and rebirth. It also can be translated as "transitional state" or "in-between state."

BODHGAYA The place of Buddha's enlightenment.

BODHICHITTA Sanskrit term for "mind of enlightenment." *Bodhi* means "enlightenment" and *chitta* means "mind." There are two types of *bodhichitta*—conventional *bodhichitta* and ultimate *bodhichitta*. Generally speaking, the term refers to conventional *bodhichitta*, which is a primary mind motivated by great compassion that spontaneously seeks enlightenment to benefit all living beings.

BODHISATTVA A person who has attained *prajna*, or enlightenment, but who postpones entering nirvana in order to help others attain enlightenment.

BRAHMA VIHARAS The four states of mind—love, compassion, sympathetic joy, and equanimity—to be developed by every Buddhist. Also called the Divine Abodes.

CHARNEL Charnel grounds, in India, are places where unclaimed human corpses are dumped to rot or be eaten by animals. The bodies are not buried or burned; they are just left out.

CHENREZIG, also known as AVALOKITESHVARA The embodiment of the compassion of all the buddhas. Sometimes he appears with one face and four arms, and sometimes with eleven faces and a thousand arms. At the time of Buddha Shakyamuni, he manifested as a bodhisattva disciple.

DAOISM, also known as TAOISM, is a philosophical and religious tradition that emphasizes living in harmony with the Tao. *Tao* means way," "path," or "principle," and can also be found in other Chinese philosophies and religions. In Taoism, however, it denotes something that is both the source of and the driving force behind everything that exists.

DHAMMAPADA "Dharma protector." A manifestation of a buddha or bodhisattva, whose main function is to eliminate obstacles and gather all necessary conditions for pure Dharma practitioners.

DHARMA refers to the Buddha's teachings and the inner realizations that are attained in dependence upon practicing them.

DHARMAKAYA Sanskrit term for the Truth Body of a buddha.

DHARMAVICAYA Applying discernment to things in order to deliver oneself from ignorance and craving. An investigation of the truth, especially about the self.

DOKUSAN is a formal interview with a Zen master during which the student receives instruction. In the Rinzai school, it has the same meaning as *sanzen*, which is specifically a private interview between student and master, often centered around the student's grasp of an assigned koan. If the master rings a bell to dismiss the student, this means that the student's understanding is not right and their work with the koan must continue.

DUKKHA A Buddhist term commonly translated as suffering, anxiety, stress, or unsatisfactoriness.

DZOGCHEN According to Tibetan Buddhism, Dzogchen is the natural, primordial state or condition, and a body of teachings and meditation practices aimed at realizing that condition.

GANHWA SEON is a Southeast Asian tradition of what in Japan is called Zen. It emphasizes directly seeing that one's own nature is originally buddha nature, and that enlightenment is not a matter of emptying out frustrations and revealing the buddha nature. You are originally perfect.

GURU YOGA A tantric devotional process whereby the practitioners unite their mind stream with the mind stream of the guru.

JHANA is a form of Buddhist meditation. It refers to various states of *samadhi*, a state of consciousness in which the observer detaches from several qualities of the mind. The mind has become firm and stable and the ability to concentrate is greatly enhanced.

KAGYU The Kagyu, Kagyupa, or Kagyud school, also known as the "Oral Lineage" or Whispered Transmission school, one of six schools of Himalayan or Tibetan Buddhism (the others are Nyingma, Sakya, Gelug, Jonang, and Bonpo).

KALACHAKRA A high-level tantric yoga deity manifested by Buddha Vajradhara.

KANRUNHAN The Gate of Sweet Nectar, a Japanese Zen text.

KARMA KAGYU or KAMTSANG KAGYU is probably the largest and certainly the most widely practiced lineage within the Kagyu school, one of the four major schools of Tibetan Buddhism (with the Nyingma, Sakya, and Gelug). The lineage has long-standing monasteries in Tibet, China, Russia, Mongolia, India, Nepal, and Bhutan, and current centers in at least sixty-two countries.

KARMAPA A Mahayana Buddhist school founded by the great Indian Buddhist Master Atisha (982–1054).

KEISAKU A flat wooden stick or slat used during periods of meditation to remedy sleepiness or lapses of concentration. This is accomplished through a strike or series of strikes, usually administered on the meditator's back and shoulders in the muscular area between the shoulder blades and the spine. The *keisaku* itself is thin and somewhat flexible; strikes with it may cause momentary stinging if performed vigorously, but are not injurious.

KENSHO is a Japanese term from the Zen tradition. *Ken* means "seeing"; *shō* means "nature" or "essence." *Kensho* is an initial insight or awakening, not full buddhahood. It is to be followed by further training to deepen this insight.

KOAN is a story, dialogue, question, or statement, used in Zen practice to provoke the "great doubt" and test a student's progress. Koans are used in Zen as training devices. Teachers assign them to students, who are expected to "solve" the koan. Koans are distinctive in that the solutions or answers are not produced by intellectual analysis, but by having an insight about some aspect of life or practice.

LAMRIM A Tibetan term, literally meaning "stages of the path," it means graded path, or series of steps on the path. A special arrangement of all the Buddha's teachings that is easy to understand and put into practice. It reveals the stages of the path to enlightenment.

MADHYAMIKA A Sanskrit term, literally meaning "Middle Way." The higher of the two schools of Mahayana Buddhist tenets (the other is Yogacara). The Madhyamika view was taught by Buddha in the Perfection of Wisdom Sutras during the second turning of the Wheel of Dharma and was subsequently elucidated by Nagarjuna and his followers. There are two divisions of this school, Madhyamika-Svatantrika and Madhyamika-Prasangika, of which the latter is Buddha's final view.

MAHASI or *mahasiddha, maha* means "great" and *siddha* means "adept," is a term in Vajrayana Buddhism for someone who embodies and cultivates the *siddhi* of perfection.

MAHAYANA is one of the three main existing branches of Buddhism, and the largest. It refers to the path of the bodhisattva, seeking complete enlightenment for the benefit of all sentient beings. Major traditions of Mahayana Buddhism include Zen and the Vajrayana Buddhist traditions of Shingon, Tendai, and Tibetan Buddhism.

MANDALA Usually the celestial mansion in which a tantric deity abides, or the environment or deities of a buddha's pure land. It is sometimes used to refer to the essence of an element, but can also refer to a schematized representation of the cosmos, chiefly characterized by a concentric configuration of geometric shapes, each containing an image of a deity or an attribute of a deity.

METTA refers to loving-kindness, friendliness, benevolence, amity, friendship, good will, kindness, close mental union, and active interest in others. The cultivation of *metta* is a popular form of Buddhist meditation. In the Theravadin Buddhist tradition, this practice begins with the meditator cultivating *metta* toward themselves, then their loved ones, friends, teachers, strangers, enemies, and finally all sentient beings. In the Tibetan Buddhist tradition, this practice is associated with *tonglen*, whereby one breathes out ("sends") happiness and breathes in ("receives") suffering.

NGÖNDRO The preliminary, preparatory, or foundational "practices" or "disciplines" common to all four main schools of Tibetan Buddhism. The Tibetan term *ngöndro* literally denotes "something that goes before, something that precedes."

NIBBĀNA or NIRVANA *Nibbāna* is the Pali word for nirvana. Classically it refers to freedom from the endless cycle of personal reincarnations, with their consequent suffering, as a result of the extinction of individual passion, hatred, and delusion. In a less metaphysical sense, nirvana means complete freedom from the bondage of delusion.

NYINGMA The Nyingma tradition is the oldest of the four major schools of Tibetan Buddhism (the other three being the Kagyu, Sakya, and Gelug). It literally means "ancient," and is often referred to as the "old school" because it is founded on the first translations of Buddhist scriptures from Sanskrit into Tibetan, done in the eighth century.

PALI CANON The standard collection of scriptures recounting the teachings of the Buddha, as preserved in the Pali language.

PRAJNA is wisdom, understanding, discernment, insight, or cognitive acuity.

RINZAI is one of three sects of Zen in Japanese Buddhism (with Soto and Obaku). It derives from the great Chinese teacher Lin-chi I-hsuan Hui-chao (in Japanese, Rinzai Gigen). Through koans and also various unconventional means, including shouting, beating, paradox, and personally driven reinterpretations of classical Mahayana Buddhist scripture, Lin-chi sought to wake his students from their clumsy slumber.

ROSHI is an honorific title used for a highly venerated senior teacher in Zen Buddhism.

SAMADHI is the highest meditative stage, in which a person experiences oneness with the universe.

SAMSARA The cycle of uncontrolled death and reincarnation.

SANZEN is a formal interview with a Zen master during which the student receives instruction. In the Rinzai school, it has the same meaning as *dokusan*, which is specifically a private interview between student and master, often centered around the student's grasp of an assigned koan. If the master rings a bell to dismiss the student, this means that the student's understanding is not right and their work with the koan must continue.

SATORI is a Japanese Buddhist term for awakening, meaning comprehension, understanding.

SATSANG in Indian philosophy means 1) the company of the "highest truth"; 2) the company of a guru; or 3) company with an assembly of persons who listen to, talk about, and assimilate the truth. This typically involves listening to or reading scriptures; reflecting on, discussing, and assimilating their meaning; meditating on the source of these words; and bringing their meaning into one's daily life.

SESSHIN means literally "touching the heart-mind" and is a period of intensive meditation or *zazen* in a Zen monastery.

SHIKANTAZA is a Japanese translation of a Chinese term for *zazen*, sitting meditation. In Japan, it is a state of diffuse concentration with no focus on objects, anchors, or content, essentially the same thing as mindfulness meditation in Western Buddhism. Insofar as thoughts appear, the meditator simply allows them to arise and pass away without interference.

SHINGON is one of the mainstream major schools of Japanese Buddhism and one of the few direct descendents of the Buddhism that started in the third and fourth century C.E., spread from India to China by traveling monks.

SOTO ZEN is the largest of the three traditional schools of Zen presently found in Japanese Buddhism (the others being Rinzai and Obaku). It usually emphasizes *shikantaza* rather than koan study.

TANTRA Teachings, distinguished from sutra teachings in that they reveal methods for training the mind by bringing the future result, or buddhahood, into the present path. Tantric practitioners overcome ordinary appearances and conceptions by visualizing their body, environment, enjoyments, and deeds as those of a buddha.

TATHAGATA is a Pali and Sanskrit word that the Buddha of the Pali Canon uses when referring to himself. The term is often thought to mean either "one who has thus gone" (*tathā-gata*) or "one who has thus come" (*tathā-āgata*).

TEISHO is a formal oral presentation of Dharma by a Zen master, usually during a *sesshin*. It may appear to be a lecture, but the master is not trying to convey concepts or knowledge. Instead, through the *teisho* the master presents his or her realization.

THERAVADA is the oldest surviving branch of Buddhism. The word is derived from the Sanskrit, and literally means "the Teaching of the Elders." The goal of spiritual practice is for the individual to become enlightened without further reincarnations.

TONGLEN is Tibetan for "giving and taking" (or sending and receiving), and refers to a meditation practice found in Tibetan Buddhism. One visualizes taking into oneself the suffering of others on the in-breath, and on the out-breath giving happiness and success to all sentient beings.

UPAYA In Mahayana Buddhism, refers to a skillful means of instruction (for example, koan study) that leads to some goal, often the goal of enlightenment.

VAJRASATTVA is the aggregate of consciousness of all the buddhas, sometimes appearing in the aspect of a white-colored deity specifically in order to purify sentient beings of negativity. The practice of meditation and recitation of Vajrasattva texts is considered a powerful method for purifying our mind and actions.

VAJRAYANA is also known as Tantric Buddhism, Tantrayana, Mantrayana, Secret

Mantra, Esoteric Buddhism, and the Diamond Way or Thunderbolt Way. The goal of spiritual practice within the Mahayana and Vajrayana traditions is to become a bodhisattva (i.e., attainment of a state in which one will subsequently become a buddha—after some further reincarnation), whereas the goal for Theravada practice is specific to becoming enlightened without further reincarnations. In Vajrayana the practitioner takes his or her innate buddha nature as the means of practice. The premise is that since we innately have an enlightened mind, practicing seeing the world in terms of ultimate truth can help us to attain our full buddha nature.

VIHARA or *VIHAR* The Sanskrit and Pali term for a Buddhist monastery.

VIPASSANA is commonly used as a synonym for vipassana meditation, in which mindfulness of breathing is used to become aware of the impermanence of everything that exists.

VISUDDHIMAGGA is the "great treatise" on Theravadin Buddhist doctrine written by Buddhaghosa in 430 C.E. in Sri Lanka. It is a comprehensive manual condensing and systematizing the theoretical and practical teachings of the Buddha as they were understood by Buddhist elders at that time.

ZAZEN is a generic term for Zen meditation.

ZENDO is a Japanese term translating roughly as "meditation hall." In Zen Buddhism, the *zen-dō* is a center where *zazen* (sitting meditation) is practiced.

References

Amaro, Ajahn. 2009. *Rain on the Nile*. Redwood Valley, CA: Abhayagiri Forest Monastery.

Andersen, Susan M., Inga Reznik, and Noah S. Glassman. 2004. "The Unconscious Relational Self." In *The New Unconscious*, ed. R. Hassin, J. Uleman, J. Bargh, 421–481. Cary, NC: Oxford University Press.

Andrews-Hanna, Jessica R. 2012. "The Brain's Default Network and Its Adaptive Role in Internal Mentation." *Neuroscientist* 18:251–270.

Arbib, Michael. 2012. *How the Brain Got Language: The Mirror System Hypothesis*. Oxford: Oxford University Press.

——. 2013. "Complex Imitation and the Language-Ready Brain." *Language and Cognition* 5:273–312.

Astington, Janet Wilde, and Jodie Baird, eds. 2005. *Why Language Matters for Theory of Mind*. Cary, NC: Oxford University Press.

Austin, James H. 1998. *Zen and the Brain*. Cambridge, MA: MIT Press.

——. 2006. *Zen-Brain Reflections*. Cambridge, MA: MIT Press.

——. 2009. *Selfless Insight: Zen and the Meditative Transformations of Consciousness*. Cambridge, MA: MIT Press.

——. 2013. "Zen and the Brain: Mutually Illuminating Topics." *Frontiers in Psychology*, www.frontiersin.org/Journal/10.3389/fpsyg.2013.00784/.

Baars, Bernard. 2006. "Consciousness Is a Real Working Theatre." In *Conversations on Consciousness: What the Best Minds Think About the Brain, Free Will, and What It Means to Be Human*, ed. S. Blackmore, 11–23. New York: Oxford University Press.

Balari, Sergio, and G. Lorenzo. 2010. "Specters of Marx: A Review of *Adam's Tongue* by Derek Bickerton." *Biolinguistics* 4:116–127.

Baron-Cohen, Simon. 2011. *The Science of Evil: On Empathy and the Origins of Cruelty*. New York: Basic Books.

Batchelor, Martine. 2006. *Women in Korean Zen: Lives and Practices*. Syracuse, NY: Syracuse University Press.

——. 2007. *Let Go: A Buddhist Guide to Breaking Free of Habits*. Somerville, MA: Wisdom.

Batchelor, Stephen. 1998. *Buddhism Without Beliefs: A Contemporary Guide to Awakening*. New York: Riverhead Books.

——. 2010. *Confession of a Buddhist Atheist*. New York: Spiegel & Grau.

——. 2011. *The Awakening of the West: The Encounter of Buddhism and Western Culture*. Brattleboro, VT: Echo Point Books.

Bell, Sandra. 2002. "Scandals in Emerging Western Buddhism." In *Westward Dharma: Buddhism Beyond Asia*, ed. M. Baumann and C. Prebish, 230–242. Berkeley: University of California Press.

Bergen, Benjamin. 2012. *Louder Than Words: The New Science of How the Mind Makes Meaning*. New York: Basic Books.

Berger, Peter, and Thomas Luckmann. 1966. *The Social Construction of Reality: A Treatise in the Sociology of Knowledge*. New York: Doubleday.

Bering, Jesse. 2011. *The Belief Instinct: The Psychology of Souls, Destiny, and the Meaning of Life*. New York: Norton.

Berwick, Robert C., Angela Friederici, Noam Chomsky, and Johan Bolhuis. 2013. "Evolution, Brain, and the Nature of Language." *Trends in Cognitive Sciences* 17:89–98.

Bickerton, Derek. 2009. *Adam's Tongue: How Humans Made Language, How Language Made Humans*. New York: Hill & Wang.

Bless, Herbert, Klaus Fiedler, and Fritz Strack. 2004. *Social Cognition: How Individuals Construct Social Reality*. Florence, KY: Psychology Press.

Block, Ned. 2010. "What Was I Thinking?" *New York Times Book Review*, November 26.

Bloom, Paul. 2013. *Just Babies: The Origins of Good and Evil*. New York: Crown.

Boroditsky, Lera. 2011. "How Language Shapes Thought: The Languages We Speak Affect Our Perceptions of the World." *Scientific American* (February): 63–65.

Botha, Rudolf, and Chris Knight. 2006. *The Prehistory of Language*. New York: Oxford University Press.

——. 2012. "Protolanguage and the 'God Particle.'" *Lingua* 122:1308–1324.

Botha, R., and M. Everaert, eds. 2013. *The Evolutionary Emergence of Language: Evidence and Inference*. Oxford: Oxford University Press.

Botha, Rudolf, and Chris Knight. 2009. *The Cradle of Language*. New York: Oxford University Press.

Buckner, Randy L., and Fenna M. Krienen. 2013. "The Evolution of Distributed Association Networks in the Human Brain." *Trends in Cognitive Sciences* 17:648–665.

Boyle, Richard P. 1985. "The Dark Side of Mead: Neuropsychological Foundations for Immediate Experience and Mystical Consciousness." *Studies in Symbolic Interactionism* 6:59–78.

Brass, Marcel, and Patrick Haggard. 2007. "To Do or Not to Do: The Neural Signature of Self-Control." *Journal of Neuroscience* 27:9141–9145.

Brefczynski-Lewis, J.A., A. Lutz, H. Schaefer, D. Levinson, and R. Davidson. 2007. "Neural Correlates of Attentional Expertise in Long-Term Meditation Practitioners." *Proceedings of the National Academy of Science* 104:11483–11488.

Brewer, Judson A., Patrick D. Worhunsky, Jeremy R. Gray, Yi-Yuan Tang, Jochen Weber, and Hedy Kober. 2013. "Meditation Experience Is Associated with Differences in Default Mode Network Activity and Connectivity." *Proceedings of the National Academy of Science* 108:20254–20259.

Burling, Robbins. 2007. *The Talking Ape: How Language Evolved.* New York: Oxford University Press.

Catherine, Shaila. 2008. *Focused and Fearless: A Meditator's Guide to States of Deep Joy, Calm, and Clarity.* Somerville, MA: Wisdom.

——. 2011. *Wisdom Wide and Deep: A Practical Handbook for Mastering* Jhāna *and* Vipassanā. Somerville, MA: Wisdom.

Chomsky, Noam. 2011. "Language and Other Cognitive Systems: What Is Special About Language?" *Language Learning and Development* 7:263–278.

Christiansen, Morten H., and Simon Kirby. 2003. *Language Evolution.* New York: Oxford University Press.

Christoff, Kalina, A. Gordon, J. Smallwood, R. Smith, and J. Schooler. 2009. "Experience Sampling During fMRI Reveals Default Network and Executive System Contributions to Mind Wandering." *Proceedings of the National Academy of Science* 108:8719–8724.

Churchland, Patricia S. 2013. *Touching a Nerve: The Self as Brain.* New York: Norton.

Clark, Andy. 2013. "Whatever Next? Predictive Brains, Situated Agents, and the Future of Cognitive Science." *Behavioral and Brain Sciences* 36:181–294.

Colapinto, John. 2007. "The Interpreter: Has a Remote Amazonian Tribe Upended Our Understanding of Language?" *The New Yorker,* April 16.

Condon, Paul, Gaëlle Desbordes, Willa B. Miller, and David DeSteno. 2013. "Meditation Increases Compassionate Responses to Suffering." *Psychological Science* 24:2125–2127.

Corballis, Michael C. 2011. *The Recursive Mind: The Origins of Human Language, Thought, and Civilization.* Princeton, NJ: Princeton University Press.

Craig, A. D. (Bud). 2003. "Interoception: The Sense of the Physiological Condition of the Body." *Current Opinion in Neurobiology* 13:500–505.

——. 2004. "Human Feelings: Why Are Some More Aware Than Others?" *Trends in Cognitive Sciences* 8:239–241.

Csikszentmihalyi, Mihaly. 1990. *Flow: The Psychology of Optimal Experience.* New York: Harper & Row.

——. 1998. *Finding Flow: The Psychology of Engagement with Everyday Life.* New York: Basic Books.

Damasio, Antonio. 2012. *Self Comes to Mind: Constructing the Human Brain.* New York: Vintage.

Damasio, Antonio, and Gil B. Carvalho. 2013. "The Nature of Feelings: Evolutionary and Neurobiological Origins." *Nature Reviews: Neuroscience* 14:143–152.

Davidson, Richard, and A. Lutz. 2007. "Buddha's Brain: Neuroplasticity and Meditation." *IEEE Signal Processing Magazine* (September 2007): 172–176.

de Gelder, Beatrice. 2010. "Uncanny Sight in the Blind." *Scientific American* (May 2007).

DeCaro, Stefano, and A. Reeves. 2002. "The Use of Word-Picture Verification to Study Entry-Level Object Recognition: Further Support for View-Invariant Mechanisms." *Memory & Cognition* 30:811–821.

Dessalles, Jean-Louis, and James Grieve. 2007. *The Evolutionary Origins of Language*. New York: Oxford University Press.

DeSteno, David. 2014. *The Truth About Trust: How It Determines Success in Life, Love, Learning, and More*. New York: Hudson Street Press.

Di Sciullo, Anna Maria, and Cedric Boeckx. 2011. *The Biolinguistic Enterprise: New Perspectives on the Evolution and Nature of the Human Language Faculty*. New York: Oxford University Press.

Douglas, Mary, and Aaron Wildavsky. 1983. *Risk and Culture: An Essay on the Selection of Technological and Environmental Dangers*. Berkeley: University of California Press.

Downing, Michael. 2002. *Shoes Outside the Door: Desire, Devotion, and Excess at San Francisco Zen Center*. Berkekey, CA: Counterpoint.

Durrheim, Kevin. 1998. "The Relationship Between Tolerance of Ambiguity and Attitudinal Conservatism: A Multidimensional Analysis." *European Journal of Social Psychology* 28:731–753.

Dutton, Kevin. 2012. *The Wisdom of Psychopaths: What Saints, Spies, and Serial Killers Can Teach Us About Success*. New York: Scientific American/Farrar, Straus and Giroux.

Edelman, Scott, C. Crandall, J. Goodman, and J. Blanchar. 2012. "Low-Effort Thought Promotes Political Conservatism." *Personality and Social Psychology Online Bulletin*, http://psp.sagepub.com/content/early/2012/03/16/0146167212439213.

Edelstein, Scott. 2011. *Sex and the Spiritual Teacher*. Somerville, MA: Wisdom.

Edsall, Thomas B. 2013. "Anger Can Be Power." *New York Times*, October 8.

Ekman, P., R. J. Davidson, M. Ricard, and B. A.Wallace. 2005. "Buddhist and Psychological Perspectives on Emotions and Well-Being." *Current Directions in Psychological Science* 14:59–63.

Everett, Daniel L. 2009a. *Don't Sleep, There Are Snakes: Life and Language in the Amazonian Jungle*. New York: Vintage.

——. 2009b. "Pirahã Culture and Grammar: A Response to Some Criticisms." *Language* 85:405–442.

Farb, Norman, Z. Segal, and A. Anderson. 2012. "Attentional Modulation of Primary Interoceptive and Exteroceptive Cortices." *Cerebral Cortex Advance Access*, January 19.

Fausey, Caitlin, B. Long, A. Inamon, and L. Borodistsky. 2010. "Constructing Agency: The Role of Language." *Frontiers in Psychology* 1:1–11.

Fishman, Barbara Miller, and Shinzen Young. 2002. *Emotional Healing Through Mindfulness Meditation: Stories and Meditations for Women Seeking Wholeness*. Rochester, VT: Inner Traditions.

Fitch, W. Tecumseh. 2010. *The Evolution of Language*. New York: Cambridge University Press.

Flanagan, Owen. 2003. "The Colour of Happiness." *New Scientist* 178:44.

Flickstein, Matthew, Huston Smith, Joseph Goldstein, Ajahn Amaro, Bhante Gunaratana, John Daido Loori, Joan Halifax Roshi, Yongey Mingyur Rinpoche, Gangaji, and Wayne Liquorman. 2011. *Voices of Truth: Enlightened Teachings of Contemporary Eastern Mystics*. Amazon.com (ebook).

Ford, James Ishmael, Melissa Blacker, and John Tarrant. 2011. *The Book of Mu: Essential Writings on Zen's Most Important Koan*. Somerville, MA: Wisdom.

Frank, Michael, D. Everett, E. Fedorenko, and E. Gibson. 2008. "Number as a Cognitive Technology: Evidence from Pirahã Language and Cognition." *Cognition* 108:819–824.

Frassinetti, Francesca, F. Ferri, M. Maini, M. Benassi, and V. Gallese. 2011. "Bodily Self: An Implicit Knowledge of What Is Explicitly Unknown." *Experimental Brain Research* 212:153–160.

Fronsdal, Gil. 2008. *The Issue at Hand: Essays on Buddhist Mindfulness Practice*. N.p.: Bookland.

——. 2010. *A Monastery Within: Tales from the Buddhist Path*. Longwood, FL: Tranquil Moon Books.

Full, Gisela E., Harold Walach, and Mathis Trautwein. 2013. "Meditation-Induced Changes in Perception: An Interview Study with Expert Meditators (*Sotapannas*) in Burma." *Mindfulness* 4:55–63.

Furnham, Adrian. 1995. "Tolerance for Ambiguity: A Review of the Concept, Its Measurement and Applications." *Current Psychology* 14:179–199.

Gallup, Gordon. 1998. "Can Animals Empathize? Yes." *Scientific American Presents*, 66–71.

Garfinkel, Harold. 1999. *Studies in Ethnomethodology*. Cambridge: Polity Press.

Gazzaniga, Michael S. 2009. *Human: The Science Behind What Makes Your Brain Unique*. New York: Harper.

Gergen, Kenneth J. 1997. *Realities and Relationships: Soundings in Social Construction*. Cambridge, MA: Harvard University Press.

Giddens, Anthony. 1991. *Modernity and Self-Identity: Self and Society in the Late Modern Age*. Redwood City, CA: Stanford University Press.

——. 2003. *Runaway World: How Globalization Is Shaping Our Lives*. Oxford: Routledge.

Gilbert, Daniel. 2006. *Stumbling on Happiness*. New York: Knopf.

Giles, Cheryl A., Willa B. Miller, Pat Enkyo O'Hara, and Judith Simmer-Brown. 2012. *The Arts of Contemplative Care: Pioneering Voices in Buddhist Chaplaincy and Pastoral Work*. Boston: Wisdom.

Glass, Jay. 2013. "A Neurobiological Model for the 'Inner Speech' of Conscious Thought." *Journal of Consciousness Studies* 20:7–14.

Glassman, Bernie. 1998. *Bearing Witness: A Zen Master's Lessons in Making Peace*. New York: Harmony.

——. 2003. *Infinite Circle: Teachings in Zen*. Boston: Shambhala.

Glassman, Bernie, and Rick Fields. 2013. *Instructions to the Cook: A Zen Master's Lessons in Living a Life That Matters*. Boston: Shambhala.

Goffman, Erving. 1959. *The Presentation of Self in Everyday Life*. New York: Anchor.

Goffman, Erving, and Bennett Berger. 1974. *Frame Analysis: An Essay on the Organization of Experience*. Boston: Northeastern University Press.

Goldstein, Joseph. 2003. *Insight Meditation: The Practice of Freedom*. Boston: Shambhala.

——. 2013. *Mindfulness: A Practical Guide to Awakening*. Louisville, CO: Sounds True.

Goldstein, Joseph, Jack Kornfield, the Dalai Lama, and Robert K. Hall. 2001. *Seeking the Heart of Wisdom: The Path of Insight Meditation*. Boston: Shambhala.

Gollwitzer, P. M., U. C. Bayer, and K. C. McCulloch. 2004. "The Control of the Unwanted." In *The New Unconscious*, ed. R. Hassin, J. Uleman, and J. Bargh, 485–514. New York: Oxford University Press.

Gofffman, Erving. 1959. *The Presentation of Self in Everyday Life*. New York: Anchor.

Gopnik, Alison. 2009. *The Philosophical Baby: What Children's Minds Tell Us About Truth, Love, and the Meaning of Life*. New York: Farrar, Straus and Giroux.

Gray, John. 2007. *Straw Dogs: Thoughts on Humans and Other Animals*. New York: Farrar, Straus and Giroux.

Graziano, Michael S. A. 2013. *Consciousness and the Social Brain*. Oxford: Oxford University Press.

Haidt, Jonathan. 2006. *The Happiness Hypothesis: Finding Modern Truth in Ancient Wisdom*. New York: Basic Books.

Hassin, Ran, James Uleman, and John Baugh, eds. 2004. *The New Unconscious*. New York: Oxford University Press.

Hockett, Charles. 1960. "The Origin of Speech." *Scientific American* 203:88–93.

Hockett, Charles, and R. Ascher. 1964. "The Human Revolution." *Current Anthropology* 5:135–168.

Hofstadter, Richard. 1966. *Anti-Intellectualism in America*. New York: Vintage.

Holzel, Britta, J. Carmody, M. Vangel, C. Congleton, S. Yerramsetti, T. Gard, and S. Lazar. 2011. "Mindfulness Practice Leads to Increases in Regional Brain Gray Matter Density." *Psychiatry Research: Neuroimaging* 191:36–43.

Hood, Bruce. 2012. *The Self Illusion: How the Social Brain Creates Identity*. New York: Oxford University Press.

Humphrey, Nicholas. 1983. *Consciousness Regained: Chapters in the Development of the Mind*. New York: Oxford University Press.

Hurford, James. 2007. *The Origins of Meaning*. New York: Oxford University Press.

Hurlburt, Russell, C. Heavey, and J Kelsey. 2013. "Toward a Phenomenology of Inner Speaking." *Consciousness and Cognition* 22:1477–1494.

Ivanovski, Belinda, and G. Malhi. 2007. "The Psychological and Neurophysiological Concomitants of Mindfulness Forms of Meditation." *Acta Neuropsychiatrica* 19:76–91.

Jackendoff, Ray. 2002. *Foundations of Language: Brain, Meaning, Grammar, Evolution*. New York: Oxford University Press.

Jalon, Allan. 2003. "Meditating on War and Guilt, Zen Says It's Sorry." *New York Times*, January 7.

Jaynes, Julian. 1976. *The Origin of Consciousness in the Breakdown of the Bicameral Mind*. New York: Houghton Mifflin.

Johnson, Paul. 2011. *Socrates: A Man of Our Times*. New York: Viking.

Johnson-Laird, Philip N. 1983. *Mental Models: Towards a Cognitive Science of Language, Inference, and Consciousness*. Cambridge, MA: Harvard University Press.

Kabat-Zinn, Jon. 1990. *Full Catastrophe Living: Using the Wisdom of Your Body and Mind to Face Stress, Pain, and Illness*. New York: Delta.

Kahan, Dan. 2012. "Cultural Cognition as a Conception of the Culture Theory of Risk." In *Handbook of Risk Theory: Epistemology, Decision Theory, Ethics, and Social Implications of Risk*, ed. R. Hillerbrand, P. Sandin, M. Peterson, and S. Roesser, 725–760. London: Springer.

Kahneman, Daniel. 2011. *Thinking, Fast and Slow*. New York: Farrar, Straus and Giroux.

Katz, Richard. 1976. "Education for transcendence: !Kia healing with the Kalahari !Kung." In *Kalahari Hunter-Gatherers: Studies of the !Kung San and Their Neighbors*, ed. R. Lee and I. DeVore. Cambridge, MA: Harvard University Press.

——. 1982. *Boiling Energy: Community Healing Among the Kalahari Kung*. Cambridge, MA: Harvard University Press.

Keltner, Dacher, Jeremy Adam Smith, and Jason Marsh, eds. 2010. *The Compassionate Instinct: The Science of Human Goodness*. New York: Norton.

Kemeny, Margaret E. Foltz, Carol Cavanagh, James F. Cullen, Margaret Giese-Davis, Janine Jennings, Patricia Rosenberg, Erika L. Gillath, Omri Shaver, R. Phillip, B. Alan Wallace, Paul Ekman. 2012. "Contemplative/Emotion Training Reduces Negative Emotional Behavior and Promotes Prosocial Responses." *Emotion* 12:338–350.

Kempson, Ruth. 1988. *Mental Representations: The Interface Between Language and Reality*. New York: Cambridge University Press.

Khalsa, Sahib, D. Rudrauf, A. Damasio, R. Davidson, A. Lutz, and D. Tranel. 2008. "Interoceptive Awareness in Experienced Meditators." *Psychophysiology* 45:671–677.

Koch, Christof. 2011. "Probing the Unconscious Mind." *Scientific American Mind* 22:22–23.

——. 2012. "Consciousness Does Not Reside Here." *Scientific American Mind* 23:20–21.

——. 2013. "When Does Consciousness Arise in Human Babies?" *Scientific American* 309 (September 1).

Köhler, Wolfgang. 1926. *The Mentality of Apes*. New York: Harcourt Brace.

Kongtrul, Jamgon, and Ken McLeod. 2005. *The Great Path of Awakening: The Classic Guide to Lojong, a Tibetan Buddhist Practice for Cultivating the Heart of Compassion*. Boston and London: Shambhala Classics.

Kornfield, Jack, and Gil Fronsdal. 2008. *The Dhammapada: Teachings of the Buddha*. Boston and London: Shambhala.

Kouider, Sid, C. Stahlhut, S. Gelskov, L. Barbosa, M. Dutat, V. de Gardelle, A. Christophe, S. Dehaene, and G. Dehaene-Lambertz. 2013. "A Neural Marker of Perceptual Consciousness in Infants." *Science* 340:376–380.

Lakoff, George. 1996. *Moral Politics: How Liberals and Conservatives Think*. Chicago: University of Chicago Press.

Larson, Richard K., Viviane Déprez, and Hiroko Yamakido. 2010. *The Evolution of Human Language: Biolinguistic Perspectives*. New York: Cambridge University Press.

Lee, Richard B. 2008. "Eating Christmas in the Kalahari." In *Conformity and Conflict*, ed. J. Spradley and D. McCurdy, chapter 2. New York: Pearson.

Lewandowsky, Stephan, Klaus Oberauer, and Gilles E. Gignac. 2013. "NASA Faked the Moon Landing—Therefore, (Climate) Science Is a Hoax: An Anatomy of the Motivated Rejection of Science." *Psychological Science* 24:622–633.

Libet, Benjamin, and Steven Kosslyn. 2005. *Mind Time: The Temporal Factor in Consciousness*. Cambridge, MA: Harvard University Press.

Lindesmith, Alfred, Anselm Strauss, and Norman Denzin. 1999. *Social Psychology*. Thousand Oaks, CA: Sage.

Lings, Martin. 1961. *A Sufi Saint of the Twentieth Century: Shaikh Ahmad al-Alawi, His Spiritual Heritage and Legacy*. Berkeley: University of California Press.

Lopez, Donald S. 2010. *Buddhism and Science: A Guide for the Perplexed*. Chicago: University of Chicago Press.

Loy, David R. 2003. *The Great Awakening: A Buddhist Social Theory*. Boston: Wisdom.

——. 2008. *Money, Sex, War, Karma: Note for a Buddhist Revolution*. Somerville, MA: Wisdom.

Luhrmann, T. M. 2012. *When God Talks Back: Understanding the American Evangelical Relationship with God*. New York: Knopf.

Luk, Charles. 1972. *Ordinary Enlightenment: A Translation of the Vimalakirti Nirdesa Sutra*. Boston and London: Shamabala.

Lutz, A., J. Brefczynski-Lewis, T. Johnstone, and R. J. Davidson. 2008. "Regulation of the Neural Circuitry of Emotion by Compassion Meditation: Effects of Meditative Expertise." *PLoS One* 3:1–10.

Lutz, A., J. D. Dunne, and R. J. Davidson. 2006. "Meditation and the Neuroscience of Consciousness." In *Cambridge Handbook of Consciousness*, ed. P. Zelazo, M. Moscovitch, and E. Thompson. http://search.credoreference.com.libproxy.unm.edu/content/entry/cupcon/meditation_and_the_neuroscience_of_consciousness_an_introduction/o. Cambridge: Cambridge University Press.

Lutz, A., L. L. Greishar, D. M. Perlman and R. J. Davidson. 2009. "BOLD Signal in Insula is Differentially Related to Cardiac Function During Compassion Meditation in Experts vs. Novices." *Neuroimage* 47:1038–1046.

Lutz, A., H. A. Slagter, N. B. Rawlings, A. D. Francis, L. L. Greishar and R. J. Davidson. 2009. "Mental Training Enhances Attentional Stability: Neural and Behavioral Evidence." *Journal of Neuroscience* 29:13418–13427.

MacNeilage, Peter, L. Rogers, and G. Vallortigara. 2009. "Origins of the Left and Right Brain." *Scientific American* (July).

Macy, Joanna. 1979. "Dependent Co-arising: The Distinctiveness of Buddhist Ethics." *Journal of Religious Ethics* 7:38–52.

Malia, Mason, M. Norton, J. Van Horn, D. Wegner, S. Grafton, and C. Macrae. 2007. "Wandering Minds: The Default Network and Stimulus-Independent Thought." *Science* 315:393–395.

Marr, David. 1982. *Vision*. New York: Norton.

Martin, Eshū. 2012. "Everybody Knows—Kyozan Joshu Sasaki Roshi and Rinzai-Ji." sweepingzen.com.

McFarquhar, Larissa. 2013. "The Last Call." *The New Yorker*, June 24.

McLeod, Ken. 2002. *Wake up to Your Life: Discovering the Buddhist Path of Attention.* New York: HarperOne.

——. 2007. *An Arrow to the Heart: A Commentary on the Heart Sutra.* Bloomington, IN: Trafford Publishing.

Mehl-Madrona, Lewis, and Gordon Pennycock. 2009. "Construction of an Aboriginal Theory of Mind and Mental Health." *Anthropology of Consciousness* 20:85–100.

Mooney, Chris. 2012. *The Republican Brain: The Science of Why They Deny Science—and Reality.* New York: Wiley.

National Center for Complementary and Alternative Medicine. 2007. "The Use of Complementary and Alternative Medicine in the United States." Bethesda, MD: National Center for Complementary and Alternative Medicine.

Nelson, Murry. 2005. *Bill Russell: A Biography.* Westport, CT: Greenwood.

Nisbett, Richard E. 1993. "Violence and U.S. Regional Culture." *American Psychologist* 48:441–449.

Noe, Alva. 2004. *Action in Perception.* Cambridge, MA: MIT Press.

Novak, Martin. 2012. "The evolution of cooperation." *Scientific American* 23 (3) (July/August): 35–39.

Nowak, Martin A., and Roger Highfield. 2012. *SuperCooperators: Altruism, Evolution, and Why We Need Each Other to Succeed by Martin Nowak.* New York: Free Press.

Oakley, Keith. 2011. "In the Minds of Others." *Scientific American Mind* 22:62–67.

O'Brien, Barbara. 2011. "Another Zen Master Scandal." http://buddhism.about.com/b/2011/02/10/another-zen-master-scandal.htm.

O'Brien, Jodi. 2010. *The Production of Reality: Essays and Readings on Social Interaction.* Thousand Oaks, CA: Sage Publications.

O'Hara, Pat Enkyo. 2014. *Most Intimate: A Zen Approach to Life's Challenges.* Somerville, MA: Shambhala.

Olendzki, Andrew. 2011. "The Construction of Mindfulness." *Contemporary Buddhism* 12:55–70.

Oudeyer, Pierre-Yves, and James R. Hurford. 2006. *Self-Organization in the Evolution of Speech.* New York: Oxford University Press.

Oyserman, Dahpna. 2007. "Social Identity and Self-Regulation." In *Handbook of Basic Principles in Social Psychology*, ed. A. Kruglanski and E. Higgins, 432–453. New York: Guilford Press.

Paas, Fred, and John Sweller. 2012. "An Evolutionary Upgrade of Cognitive Load Theory: Using the Human Motor System and Collaboration to Support the Learning of Complex Cognitive Tasks." *Educational Psychology Review* 24:27–45.

Parker, Christopher S., and Matt A. Barreto. 2013. *Change They Can't Believe In: The Tea Party and Reactionary Politics in America.* Princeton, NJ: Princeton University Press.

Pawelski, Suzann. 2011. "The Many Faces of Happiness." *Scientific American Mind* 22:50–55.

Peers, E. A., trans. 1958. *The Complete Works of St. John of the Cross.* Dublin: Burns, Oates & Washburn.

Pepperberg, Irene M. 2008. *Alex and Me: How a Scientist and a Parrot Discovered a Hidden World of Animal Intelligence—and Formed a Deep Bond in the Process.* New York: HarperCollins.

Pew Forum on Religion and Public Life. 2008. *U.S. Religious Landscape Survey.* Washington, DC: Pew Research Center.

——. 2012. "How the Faithful Voted." Washington, DC: Pew Research Center.

Piaget, Jean. 1937. *The Construction of Reality in the Child.* New York: Basic Books.

Pinker, Stephen. 2012. *The Better Angels of Our Nature: Why Violence Has Declined.* New York: Penguin.

Posner, Michael I., and Mary K. Rothbart. 2013. "Development of Attention Networks." In *Cognition and Brain Development: Converging Evidence from Various Methodologies,* ed. B. R. Kar, 61–83. Washington, DC: American Psychological Association.

Potter, Jonathan. 1996. *Representing Reality: Discourse, Rhetoric and Social Construction.* Thousand Oaks, CA: Sage.

Premack, David. 2007. "Human and Animal Cognition: Continuity and Discontinuity." *Proceedings of the National Academy of Science* 104:13861–13867.

Preston, David L. 2012. *The Social Organization of Zen Practice: Constructing Transcultural Reality.* New York: Cambridge University Press.

Raichle, Marcus. E. 2010. "The Brain's Dark Energy." *Scientific American* 302 (3): 44–49.

Rao, Rajesh P. N., N. Yadav, M. Vahia, H. Joglekar, R. Adhikari, and I. Mahadevan. 2009. "Entropic Evidence for Linguistic Structure in the Indus Script." *Science* 324:1165.

Red Pine. 2004. *The Heart Sutra: Translation and Commentary.* Berkeley, CA: Shoemaker & Hoard.

Reiss, Diana. 2011. *The Dolphin in the Mirror: Exploring Dolphin Minds and Saving Dolphin Lives.* New York: Houghton Mifflin Harcourt.

Remschmidt, H. 1994. "Psychosocial Milestones in Normal Puberty and Adolescence." *Hormone Research in Pediatrics* 41, Supplement 2:19–29.

Reznikova, Zhanna. 2007. *Animal Intelligence: From Individual to Social Cognition.* New York: Cambridge University Press.

Ricard, Matthieu. 2007. *Happiness: A Guide to Developing Life's Most Important Skill.* London: Little, Brown.

——. 2009. "The Illusion of the Self." http://www.matthieuricard.org/en/index.php/archives/2009/03/.

Roth, Hal. 2008. "Against Cognitive Imperialism: A Call for a Non-ethnocentric Approach to Cognitive Science and Religious Studies." *Religion East and West* 8:1–28.

Sachs, Jeffrey. 2006. *The End of Poverty: Economic Possibilities for Our Time.* New York: Penguin.

Saletan, William. 2013. "The Gaying of America: Opponents of Same-Sex Marriage Struggle to Explain Why Polls Have Turned Against Them." *Slate* www.slate.com/

bullpen/gay_marriage_polls_bias_and_other_lame_conservative_excuses_for_. html.

Sandstrom, Kent L.., Daniel D. Martin, and Gary Alan Fine. 2009. *Symbols, Selves, and Social Reality: A Symbolic Interactionist Approach to Social Psychology and Sociology.* New York: Oxford University Press.

Saxe, Rebecca, and Simon Baron-Cohen, eds. 2007. *Theory of Mind: A Special Issue of Social Neuroscience.* Florence, KY: Psychology Press.

Schmitt, Frederick F., ed. 2003. *Socializing Metaphysics: The Nature of Social Reality.* Lanham, MD: Rowman & Littlefield.

Schuessler, Jennifer. 2012. "How Do You Say 'Disagreement' in Pirahã?" *The New Yorker,* March 21.

Searle, John. 1997. *The Construction of Social Reality.* New York: Free Press.

———. 2010. *Making the Social World: The Structure of Human Civilization.* New York: Oxford University Press.

———. 2011. "The Mystery of Consciousness Continues." *New York Review of Books,* June 9.

Seth, Anil K. 2013. "Interoceptive Inference, Emotion, and the Embodied Self." *Trends in Cognitive Sciences* 17:565–573.

Shankman, Richard. 2008. *The Experience of Samadhi: An In-depth Exploration of Buddhist Meditation.* Boston and London: Shambhala.

Shermer, Michael. 2011. *The Believing Mind: From Ghosts and Gods to Politics and Conspiracies—How We Construct Beliefs and Reinforce Them as Truths.* New York: Holt.

Shuttleworth, Sara. 2010. "Clever Animals and Killjoy Explanations in Comparative Psychology." *Trends in Cognitive Sciences* 14:477–481.

Somel, Mehmet, Liu Xiling, and Phillipp Khaitovich. 2013. "Human Brain Evolution: Transcripts, Metabolites and Their Regulators." *Nature Reviews: Neuroscience* 14:114–127.

Stanley, Jason. 2011. "Knowing (How)." *Nous* 45:207–238.

———. 2012. "Replies to Dickie, Schoder and Stalnaker." *Philosophy and Phenomenological Research* 85:762–778.

Stanovich, Keith, and R. West. 2000. "Individual Differences in Reasoning: Implications for the Rationality Debate." *Behavior and Brain Sciences* 23:6545–6553.

Suddendorf, Thomas. 2013. *The Gap: The Science of What Separates Us from Other Animals.* New York: Basic Books.

Sumedho, Ajahn, and Ajahn Amaro. 2007. *The Sound of Silence: The Selected Teachings of Ajahn Sumedho.* Somerville, MA: Wisdom.

Tallerman, Maggie. 2005. *Language Origins: Perspectives on Evolution.* New York: Oxford University Press.

Tallerman, Maggie, and Kathleen Gibson. 2011. *The Oxford Handbook of Language Evolution.* New York: Oxford University Press.

Tang, Yi-Yuan, Rongxiang Tang, and Michael I. Posner. 2013. "Brief Meditation Training Induces Smoking Reduction." *Proceedings of the National Academy of Sciences* 110:13791–13975.

Tang, Yi-Yuan Ma, Yinghua Wang, Junhong Fan, Yaxin Feng, Shigang Lu, Qilin Yu, Qingbao Sui, Danni Rothbart, Mary K. Fan, and Michael Posner. 2007. "Short-term Meditation Training Improves Attention and Self-regulation." *Proceedings of the National Academy of Science* 104:17152–17156.

Tarrant, John. 1999. *The Light Inside the Dark: Zen, Soul, and the Spiritual Life.* New York: Harper Perennial.

———. 2008. *Bring Me the Rhinoceros: And Other Zen Koans That Will Save Your Life.* Boston and London: Shambhala.

Taylor, Jill Bolte. 2009. *My Stroke of Insight: A Brain Scientist's Personal Journey.* New York: Plume.

Terrace, H. S. 1985. "Animal Cognition: Thinking Without Language." *Philosophical Transactions of the Royal Society of London* 308:113–128.

Thagard, Paul. 2005. *Mind: Introduction to Cognitive Science.* Cambridge, MA: Bradford Books.

Thomas, W. I., and D. Thomas. 1928. *The Child in America.* New York: Knopf.

Tomasello, Michael. 2010. *Origins of Human Communication.* Cambridge, MA: Bradford Books.

Torey, Zoltan. 1999. *The Crucible of Consciousness: An Integrated Theory of Mind and Brain.* Cambridge, MA: MIT Press.

Tuschman, Avi. 2013. *Our Political Nature: The Evolutionary Origins of What Divides Us.* Amherst, NY: Prometheus Books.

Tuzin, Donald. 1984. "Miraculous Voices: The Auditory Experience of Numinous Objects." *Current Anthropology* 25:579–596.

Tweed, Thomas A. 2000. *American Encounter with Buddhism, 1844–1912.* Chapel Hill: University of North Carolina Press.

Uleman, James S. 2004. "Introduction: Becoming Aware of the New Unconscious." In *The New Unconscious,* ed. R. Hassin, J. Uleman, and J. Baugh, 3–15. New York: Oxford University Press.

Victoria, Brian Daizen. 2003. *Zen War Stories.* New York: RutledgeCurzon.

———. 2006. *Zen at War.* Lanham, MD: Rowman & Littlefield.

Wallace, B. Alan, and Brian Hodel, eds. 2009. *Contemplative Science: Where Buddhism and Neuroscience Converge.* New York: Columbia University Press.

Way, Alison. 2002. *The Transition to Language.* New York: Oxford University Press.

White, Harrison. 1992. *Identity and Control: A Structural Theory of Social Action.* Princeton, NJ: Princeton University Press.

Whorf, Benjamin. 1964. *Language, Thought, and Reality.* Cambridge, MA: MIT Press.

Wood, Michael J., Karen M. Douglas, and Robbie M. Sutton. 2012. "Dead and Alive: Beliefs in Contradictory Conspiracy Theories." *Social Psychology and Personality Science* 3:767–773.

Wyer, Robert S. 2007. "Principles of Mental Representation." In *Social Psychology: Handbook of Basic Principles,* ed. A. Kruglanski and E. Higgins, 285–307. New York: Guilford Press.

Xue, Shaowei, Yi-Yuan Tang, and Michael I. Posner. 2011. "Short-Term Meditation In-creases Network Efficiency of the Anterior Cingulate Cortex." *NeuroReport* 22:570–574.

Young, Shinzen. 2010. *Meditation: A Beginner's Guide to Start Meditating Now.* Louis-ville, CO: Sounds True, Inc.

——. 2011. *Natural Pain Relief: How to Soothe and Dissolve Physical Pain with Mindful-ness.* Louisville, CO: Sounds True.

Yuille, John C., and Lynn Sereda. 1980. "Positive Effects of Meditation: A Limited Gen-eralization?" *Journal of Applied Psychology* 65:333–340.

Index

and activities encouraging happiness, 291; and compassion, 184–85, 199, 201; and concentration, 185; and interoception, 286; and *metta* meditation, 184–85, 199; mistaken emphasis on, 146–47; and Pirahã culture, 255, 257; study of, 309n22; and suffering, 146–47. *See also* joy

Hazel, Peter, 75

Herrigel, Eugen, 293

Hinduism, 144

Homer, 259–60

Hsiang-yen, 42

human condition, 16–19, 249–72; and future of awakened consciousness, 269–72; and Gautama's insights about suffering, 261–63; and invention of writing, 258–60; and Pirahã culture as exception to dominance of ordinary consciousness, 249–58; and politics, 269–72. *See also dukkha*; suffering

Humphrey, Nicholas, 230, 238

idealism, 66, 91

Iliad (Homer), 259–60

impatience, 186

impermanence, 101–2, 113, 117, 139

India, Tibetan Buddhist communities in, 50–52

individualism, 253, 312n43

infants and children: and attention, 244, 246–48; and awakened consciousness, 244–48, 278; and empathy, 244, 247; and lack of self-construct that can be projected into past or future, 244, 246; and language acquisition, 244–46, 248, 277–78; and memory, 245, 246, 247; and perceptual and conceptual processing, 277–78; and social reality, 236, 248

inner speech, 310n26; cognitive load and cessation of inner speech/enhancement of perception during meditation, 276–77; and infants and children, 246, 248; and model of consciousness, *274*; quieting the mind, 192–95 (*see also* awakening, development of capacities for: and

controlling attention and quieting the mind)

insight meditation, 106, 107, 109, 112–13, 117, 184–85; and concentration and *metta* meditation, 184–85. *See also* vipassana tradition

Insight Meditation Center (Redwood City, CA), 8, 132–33

Insight Meditation Society (Barre, MA), 8, 12, 131, 187

Insight Meditation South Bay, 7

International Buddhist Meditation Center (Los Angeles), 27

interoception, 306n11; body maps, 228; and communication problems between brain stem and cortex, 228–29, 243; and emotions, 228; and feelings, 228, 280, 284, 286; and model of consciousness, *274*, 280

Jamgön Kongtrül the Great, 53

Japan: Buddhist communities in, 21–25, 128–29; contrast of Japanese and Korean Zen traditions, 138–39; Obon holiday, 168–69; pedagogy and Japanese culture, 41, 47. *See also* Zen Buddhism

Jaynes, Julian, 259–60

jhāna practice, 7, 106, 108, 112, 318

John of the Cross, 261, 308n60

Johnson, Paul, 262

Joshu Sasaki Roshi, 3, 26–27, 304n8; and flow of expansion/contraction and zero, 27; and samurai tradition, 224; and sex scandals, 219–24, 304–5nn9,10

joy, 99, 129, 158, 217, 284; as one of the four immeasurables in Tibetan Buddhism, 52, 55, 187. *See also* happiness

Kagyu tradition, 53, 318

Kahneman, Daniel, 282–83, 286, 287

Kalu Rinpoche, 5, 49–60, 92

Katz, Michael, 36–37

kensho, 26, 31, 40, 319; neurological basis of, 301–2

koan study, 25, 36–47, 193, 319; and absence of boundaries, 25; and compassion, 46, 200;

nonattachment (*continued*)
166, 197–98; Goldstein and, 178, 182, 186, 189–90, 195; and idealism, 66; and koan study, 95, 96, 153, 195–97; O'Hara and, 153, 195; and Pirahã culture, 252–53, 257; and stages of enlightenment in Theravada Buddhism, 108; Tarrant and, 39, 40, 43, 44, 196; terminology for, 195
"noting" technique, 28
"not knowing," 5, 165–66, 214–16, 230, 282
Nowak, Martin, 307n38
Nyingma tradition, 53, 320
Nyoshul Khen Rinpoche, 185, 188

Obama, Barack, 269, 271, 313n49
object permanence, 231
Obon (Japanese holiday), 168–69
Odyssey (Homer), 259–60
O'Hara, Pat Enkyo, 9–10, 149–60; and absence of boundaries, 154, 209; and awakening experiences/insight experiences, 10, 150–51, 160; biographical sketch, 9–10; and compassion, 10, 151, 154, 158, 201–2, 209; and controlling attention and quieting the mind, 153–54; and death, 158; and depression, 158; and joy, 158, 217, 284; koan study, 152–53, 158–60; and letting go, 153, 154, 195; meditation practices, 152, 153; and monasticism, 10, 149–50; origins of interest in Buddhism, 9–10, 149–51; and pain and physical discomfort, 152; publications, 149; and Sing Sing, 157; as teacher, 156–57; teachers, 10, 150, 152, 154–56, 159–60; and Village Zendo, 10, 155, 156; work with AIDS victims, 10, 151, 154, 201–2
Ondaatje, Michael, 36
ontological insecurity (Giddens's term), 18, 264, 265, 311n39
The Origins of Consciousness in the Breakdown of the Bicarmeral Mind (Jaynes), 259
Osumi, Yoshi, 294

Pa-Auk Sayadaw, 7, 106, 112
Pacific Zen Institute (Santa Rosa, CA), 4

pain and physical discomfort: during meditation, 22–23, 37, 53–57, 124, 152, 183; physical *dukkha*, 261
Pali Canon, 140, 141–42, 320
Pasanno, Ajahn, 87
peacefulness, 108, 109, 129, 194. *See also* equanimity
Pennycook, Gordon, 310n26
perception: and animals, 15, 277; capture of attention by sudden sensory stimuli, 42, 300, 301; clarity and brightness of, 31, 79, 194; and cognitive load, 276–77, 279; feeling tone of momentary perceptions, 118; and impermanence of objects, 113; interoception, proprioception, and exteroception, 229; meaning in perceptual reality, 284, 286; perceptions shaped by conceptual framework and previous experience, 100, 236–37, 275, 276, 283–84; perceptual processing and model of consciousness, 274, 274–79, 285; procrastination driven by five sensory phenomena, 29–30; "pure" perceptual representations and awakened consciousness, 16, 277–79, 284, 287; and silence, 278, 295; and social reality, 243, 286; and unconscious awareness, 275–76
The Philosophical Baby (Gopnik), 244
Piaget, Jean, 231
Pinker, Stephen, 205n19
Pirahã culture, 17, 249–58; and alcohol consumption, 256; and attachment to social reality, 17, 256–57; and compassion, empathy, and kindness, 253–54; and death, 254; and equanimity, 252; and happiness, 255, 257; language and characteristics of awakened consciousness, 249–52; and laughter, 252–53; and mindfulness, 251–52, 257; and nonattachment, 252–53, 257; parenting styles and resilience/self-reliance, 253; positive and negative features of Pirahã consciousness, 254–57; and sexual conduct, 255–56; and spatial orientation, 254; spirit communication, 258, 310n27